Psychology and Climate Change

Psychology and Climate Change

Human Perceptions, Impacts, and Responses

Edited By

Susan Clayton
**The College of Wooster,
Wooster, OH, United States**

Christie Manning
**Macalester College,
Saint Paul, MN, United States**

ACADEMIC PRESS

An imprint of Elsevier

Academic Press is an imprint of Elsevier
125 London Wall, London EC2Y 5AS, United Kingdom
525 B Street, Suite 1800, San Diego, CA 92101-4495, United States
50 Hampshire Street, 5th Floor, Cambridge, MA 02139, United States
The Boulevard, Langford Lane, Kidlington, Oxford OX5 1GB, United Kingdom

Notices
Knowledge and best practice in this field are constantly changing. As new research and experience
broaden our understanding, changes in research methods, professional practices, or medical treatment
may become necessary.

Practitioners and researchers must always rely on their own experience and knowledge in evaluating and
using any information, methods, compounds, or experiments described herein. In using such information
or methods they should be mindful of their own safety and the safety of others, including parties for
whom they have a professional responsibility.

To the fullest extent of the law, neither the Publisher nor the authors, contributors, or editors, assume any
liability for any injury and/or damage to persons or property as a matter of products liability, negligence
or otherwise, or from any use or operation of any methods, products, instructions, or ideas contained in
the material herein.

British Library Cataloguing-in-Publication Data
A catalogue record for this book is available from the British Library

Library of Congress Cataloging-in-Publication Data
A catalog record for this book is available from the Library of Congress

ISBN: 978-0-12-813130-5

For Information on all Academic Press publications
visit our website at https://www.elsevier.com/books-and-journals

Working together
to grow libraries in
developing countries

www.elsevier.com • www.bookaid.org

Publisher: Nikki Levy
Acquisition Editor: Emily Ekle
Editorial Project Manager: Barbara Makinster
Production Project Manager: Priya Kumaraguruparan
Cover Designer: Matthew Limbert

Typeset by MPS Limited, Chennai, India

Contents

List of contributors

Sebastian Bamberg Bielefeld University of Applied Sciences, Bielefeld, Germany

Stuart Capstick Cardiff University, Cardiff, United Kingdom

Daniel A. Chapman University of Massachusetts Amherst, Amherst, MA, United States

Angel Chen University of Victoria, Victoria, BC, Canada

Susan Clayton The College of Wooster, Wooster, OH, United States

Thomas J. Doherty Sustainable Self, LLC, Portland, OR, United States

John Fraser New Knowledge Organization Ltd, New York, NY, United States

Nathaniel Geiger Pennsylvania State University, University Park, PA, United States

Robert Gifford University of Victoria, Victoria, BC, Canada

Meaghan L. Guckian University of Massachusetts Amherst, Amherst, MA, United States

Karine Lacroix University of Victoria, Victoria, BC, Canada

Brian Lickel University of Massachusetts Amherst, Amherst, MA, United States

Christie Manning Macalester College, Saint Paul, MN, United States

Ezra M. Markowitz University of Massachusetts Amherst, Amherst, MA, United States

Adam R. Pearson Pomona College, Claremont, CA, United States

Jonas H. Rees Bielefeld University, Bielefeld, Germany

Jonathon P. Schuldt Cornell University, Ithaca, NY, United States

Maxie Schulte Bielefeld University of Applied Sciences, Bielefeld, Germany

Linda Silka University of Maine, Orono, ME, United States

Paul C. Stern Social and Environmental Research Institute, Northampton, MA, United States; Norwegian University of Science and Technology, Trondheim, Norway

Julie Sweetland FrameWorks Institute, Washington, DC, United States

Janet K. Swim Pennsylvania State University, University Park, PA, United States

Carlie D. Trott Colorado State University, Fort Collins, CO, United States

Lorraine Whitmarsh Cardiff University, Cardiff, United Kingdom

Kimberly S. Wolske University of Chicago, Chicago, IL, United States

Preface

Climate change is one of the most pressing issues facing society. Often described as an environmental problem, it is better understood as a human problem: human behavior is largely responsible, human beings will be affected, and human behavioral change will be required. The role of psychology in understanding and addressing this problem is not widely recognized, however, despite a large and growing body of relevant research. This book is designed to survey recent psychological research on a range of relevant topics. Each chapter presents a review of what is known in the area as well as a new perspective on human perceptions, impacts, and responses to climate change.

Taking a psychological perspective implies an emphasis on people's thoughts, emotions, and behavior; it stresses the scientific method, in which theory is used to guide hypotheses, and data are collected to test the hypotheses; and it is oriented, implicitly or explicitly, toward the promotion of human wellbeing. These papers deliberately reflect on the process of theory-building and/or hypothesis-testing in order to more clearly demonstrate the value of a psychological approach. Underlying all is the goal to promote the involvement of psychologists and psychological research in interdisciplinary collaborations to address climate change.

The first section of the book addresses the psychology behind perceptions of climate change. Chapter 2 discusses factors that influence people's acceptance that climate change is occurring; Chapter 3 describes what we know about climate change communication; Chapter 4 illustrates the importance of social context in climate change communication through a case study of a program designed to promote accurate conversations about climate change; and Chapter 5 explores the role of social identities such as race and class in affecting experiences and perceptions of climate change.

In the second section, we move to human responses. Chapter 6 classifies the human behaviors that contribute to climate change, discussing which might be the most promising targets for interventions on the basis of their potential impact and amenability to change. Chapter 7 presents a taxonomy of the barriers that prevent or inhibit positive behavioral responses, describing how this perspective could help to guide more promising behavioral interventions. Chapter 8 considers collective behaviors in response to climate change, and discusses possible benefits of collective action for individual wellbeing.

The third section of the book presents research on psychological impacts of climate change. Chapter 9 reviews the broad range of impacts that can be expected, from acute impacts on individual mental health to changes in social networks and community wellbeing. Chapter 10 discusses individual factors that might promote risk or resilience to the threat of climate change. Finally, Chapter 11 takes a community-based perspective on risk and resilience.

The challenge of climate change can only be met through the combined efforts of scientists from many disciplines alongside policymakers and other public officials. Our hope is that this volume will help both psychologists and others to recognize the potential contributions from psychology.

Introduction: Psychology and climate change

Susan Clayton[1] and Christie Manning[2]
[1]The College of Wooster, Wooster, OH, United States, [2]Macalester College, Saint Paul, MN, United States

Climate change requires our urgent attention. It is one of the defining issues of our time and a topic of increasing public interest and discussion; it is often described as a "wicked problem," referring to the fact that there is no straightforward solution that will address all of the complex and multidimensional challenges that it presents. As we write, each of the past 3 years has broken previous records for global temperatures, and 2017 is likely to be the second-hottest year ever recorded, just behind 2016 (https://www.ncdc.noaa.gov/sotc/global/2017/06/supplemental/page-1). Unfortunately, this trend is likely to continue. Climate change is transforming our world.

The complexity of the geophysical processes and ecological processes involved, the likelihood of feedback loops, and the possibility of tipping points mean that our best computer models can only provide us with good estimates about the range of effects. Though the effects of climate change for a particular location or precise point in time are uncertain, it is clear that impacts around the globe will be dramatic. Temperature increases are not the only manifestation. There has already been an increase in the number of droughts as well as severe weather events worldwide (e.g., Fischer & Knutti, 2015). Artic sea ice levels are shrinking and glaciers are melting. Because of rising sea levels, coastal flooding has increased in many low-lying areas. The effects on weather and climate have been carefully described, e.g., by the Intergovernmental Panel on Climate Change (IPCC) (2014) and are continually updated with increasing certainty as the scientific evidence accumulates.

Nonhuman species have also been extensively impacted. Changes in their range and relative abundance are most visible, with some species already driven to extinction and many others facing this probability. More subtle effects in physiological and behavioral characteristics have also been documented (Pecl et al., 2017). It is not surprising that animals would change their feeding, predation, and migration habits in response to a changing climate, but the potential for cumulative, downstream impacts of these changes—potentially reconfiguring entire ecosystems—has received relatively little consideration. Species redistribution could have major implications for the many benefits that ecosystems provide to humans, with consequent impacts on the economic sphere (Pecl et al., 2017).

As climate change transforms our world, it will necessarily also transform society. Although many people think first of climate change as something that poses a threat to polar bears, the well-being of human societies is fundamentally tied to

Psychology and Climate Change. DOI: https://doi.org/10.1016/B978-0-12-813130-5.00001-1

ecological well-being in a number of ways. People are already experiencing the effects of changes in the global climate, and these effects are only going to become more pronounced. To prepare for the impacts, we need to have a better understanding of the variety of ways in which climate change is likely to affect people and societies, and the kinds of responses that people and societies will show.

1.1 Direct impacts of climate change on human society

The infrastructure that supports human society was designed under climate conditions that are rapidly disappearing. Roads, bridges, power plants, city sewers, and other parts of the built environment were constructed to withstand a specific range of conditions; however, the "normal" range of conditions has shifted and will continue to shift, as the climate warms. In many communities, these infrastructural systems are already fragile due to age, or stretched beyond capacity because of population growth. With the added burden of extreme weather conditions, many places are experiencing breakdowns in basic services such as water. Infrastructure inadequacy in the face of climate change is becoming obvious as high tides, storm surges, and storm water runoff threaten underground infrastructure in coastal cities such as New York. Climate-change-fueled disruptions to industrial systems will lead to significant economic impacts and likely labor market dislocations as businesses find it too expensive to remain in climate-impacted locations.

Food production will be significantly impacted by climate change. Changing temperatures and precipitation patterns will directly affect the suitability of specific geographic locations for growing specific crops. In addition, crop production is likely to be indirectly affected by climate-change-driven shifts in the distribution of other species, particularly pollinator and pest species. Although some areas may see increased productivity, overall the effect is predicted to be negative (Intergovernmental Panel on Climate Change (IPCC), 2014). Meanwhile, food supplies from nonfarmed sources, including hunting and fishing, will also see dramatic changes. Food insecurity is widely predicted to be a major impact of climate change; malnutrition from the reduced availability of food due to climate change could result in over half a million deaths by 2050 (Springmann et al., 2016).

Occupations will be affected. People working in the agricultural sector are likely to experience major changes and serious difficulties, as described above; many working in tourism or recreation industries will also find their jobs changing or becoming obsolete as conditions in, e.g., coastal areas or ski resorts no longer support formerly popular activities. Human health will be affected. The American Public Health Association has emphasized the threat to health, declaring 2017 as the year of "climate change and health" (https://www.apha.org/topics-and-issues/climate-change). Manning and Clayton, in Chapter 9, Threats to Mental Health and Well-being Associated with Climate Change, provide a brief overview of the many ways human health will be negatively impacted by climate change manifestations such as increased temperatures, changing disease vectors, increased ground-level ozone, and natural disasters.

Climate change also presents serious threats to global security, as it is likely to exacerbate already existing tensions between nations, particularly with respect to access to fresh water. The Pentagon has classified climate change as a threat to national security (e.g., Department of Defense, 2014). Our governance system is not equipped to manage these changes. Old laws and policies will need to be adapted. New laws will need to be written. How will property rights and conservation policies, e.g., reflect the new—and continually changing—geographical realities? We are already seeing challenges related to the opening of the Arctic Ocean to shipping traffic enabled by a decline in sea ice.

1.2 The role for psychology

For most of the previous decades, the preponderance of research and writing on climate change has come from the natural sciences: climate scientists and geologists describing evidence of changes, and ecologists making predictions about their consequences. Because earlier debates were focused primarily on the adequacy of climate models and the evidence for anthropogenic causes, the field of psychology has been underrepresented in both public and academic discourse about climate change. Indeed, for many people, the topic does not seem to have psychological relevance. More recently, however, as natural scientists grow increasingly confident in their predictions, questions concerning humans and their mental and social processes have become more prominent. Why has the behavioral response to such an important threat been so muted? Why has political party become such an important predictor of climate change attitudes? And what types of social consequences can be anticipated?

Human perceptions, behavior, and well-being are clearly implicated as contributors to and/or consequences of climate change. Psychological research on phenomena such as risk perception, denial, threats to mental health, social well-being, and adaptation can and should inform public discussions of the topic. One of the most publically contested aspects of climate change is the extent to which it is a consequence of human behavior (Leiserowitz, Maibach, Roser-Renouf, Rosenthal, & Cutler, 2017); however, the science is clear: the rate and amount of change we are seeing is directly linked to human activity. Psychology, as the science of human behavior, has to be involved in discussions about how human behavior can and should be modified to slow and limit the amount of climate change, and to adjust to new climate realities.

Meaningful and timely action on climate change will require engaging diverse stakeholders, both within and between nations, to develop and implement effective mitigation and adaptation policies; as such, there is an urgent need to better understand the psychological factors that drive differential engagement within pluralistic societies. In response, psychologists are directing more of their research attention to this topic. A search of PsycInfo, the most popular online research database for psychology publications, reveals a dramatically accelerating trend in works with "global warming" or "climate change" as keywords, see Fig. 1.1. The purpose of this book is to organize and summarize recent work in the field of psychology on the issue of climate change.

What does it mean to take a psychological perspective on a problem? Psychology is a broad field, grounded in some fundamental premises. This includes the understanding that individuals matter; that their perceptions, experiences, and reactions are important not only in their own right but also because they are relevant to societal outcomes. Although most of the research on the human side of climate change has emphasized institutional actors like governmental organizations, businesses, and NGOs, individual actions and perceptions matter.

It is widely accepted by scientists that human behavior has played an important role in the changing climate. The IPCC Fifth Assessment report states, "It is extremely likely that more than half of the observed increase in global average surface temperature from 1951 to 2010 was caused by the anthropogenic increase in GHG concentrations and other anthropogenic forcings together" (Intergovernmental Panel on Climate Change (IPCC), 2014, p. 5). Industrial emissions are significant, but individual choices also matter. People make decisions about whether and how far to drive or fly, whether and how much red meat to consume, whether and how many children to have. The aggregate of individual household behavior contributes a significant proportion of carbon emissions (Dietz, Gardner, Gilligan, Stern, & Vandenbergh, 2009); transportation also represents a large amount.

Individual attitudes also influence the policies that are implemented and whether they are upheld. Public attitudes toward "green" technology are significant in determining their adoption, and thus their impact. One of the interesting—and regrettable—aspects of climate change is the extent to which contradictory assertions are made, and denied, by people holding opposing positions about the topic. Scott Pruitt, head of the US Environmental Protection Agency, e.g., has called into question

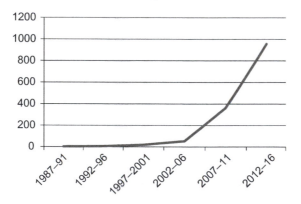

Figure 1.1 Number of entries in PsycInfo with "global warming" or "climate change" as keywords, in 5-year increments.

the link between anthropogenic carbon dioxide emissions and climate change (Chiacu & Volcovici, 2017), despite the consensus among climate scientists. US President Donald Trump, meanwhile, has referred to climate change as a "hoax" (Frisk, 2017). Such statements serve as a reminder that attitudes about climate change are formed by factors other than scientific information.

In addition to an emphasis on individuals, a psychological perspective also implies reliance on research to provide empirical evidence. Some things that may sound obvious turn out not, in fact, to be true when tested by rigorous research. For example, educating people about climate change does not necessarily change their opinions or lead them to greater concern; and paying people for sustainable behavior is generally not the best way to encourage behavior change.

Psychologists study a broad range of nested influences on individuals, from the biochemical to the intrapsychic, interpersonal, and societal, and try to recognize and assess the reciprocal interactions between these layers: the ways in which personal motives are affected by social context, for example. Some of the impacts of climate change will come directly from climate and weather; others are mediated by personal interpretations and social relationships. Psychologists utilize a wide range of methods to assess these influences. Throughout this volume the authors emphasize the source of their information and the research methodologies that were used, as well as the conclusions that were drawn.

Finally, psychology is a value-driven science in the sense that it is always mindful of the goal to promote human well-being. Many psychologists have been drawn to study phenomena related to climate change because they recognize it as a significant threat and they hope to develop interventions that can promote human well-being in the face of environmental change. To be truly effective, these interventions will need to involve researchers and practitioners from outside psychology. Our hope is that, by describing some of what psychologists know about the topic, this volume may help to facilitate such interdisciplinary projects.

1.3   Outline of the volume

Following the introductory chapter, this volume presents three sections focusing on different topics within climate change psychology. In somewhat chronological order, they focus on, first, ways in which people perceive and come to understand climate change; second, human behavioral responses to climate change; and third, impacts of climate change on human health and well-being. It is important to recognize, however, that this separation reflects a useful way of organizing the book rather than a clear distinction among topics. Behavioral responses, e.g., are fundamentally tied to perceptions, and impacts are mitigated by and dependent upon responses. Thus the themes of each section are in fact intertwined.

The first section of the book examines the ways in which the topic of climate change is represented in public understandings. Chapter 2, Perceptions of Climate Change, will review research on perceptions of climate change. Lorraine

Whitmarsh and Stuart Capstick describe what is known about factors that affect public perceptions of climate change as a social and environmental problem, and how these perceptions have changed over time. Their thorough review illuminates some of the most important predictors of climate change perceptions, such as political orientation and personal experiences. More importantly, they draw attention to the complex factors underlying people's perceptions, demonstrating that acceptance, understanding, and prioritization of climate change are not the same thing, and reminding us of the need to consider communication about climate change as a process rather than a single instance of exposure to information.

Building on this in Chapter 3, Climate Change Communication: Challenges, Insights and Opportunities, Ezra Markowitz and Meaghan Guckian discuss research on climate change communication. After describing some characteristics of climate change that make it a particularly difficult issue to communicate about, they describe seven insights with implications for the best practices to maximize the effectiveness of climate change communication. Throughout, they emphasize the importance of testing communicative materials and hypotheses about the best ways to deliver a climate change message.

Chapter 4, Social Construction of Scientifically Grounded Climate Change Discussions, presents a case study of a program designed to improve awareness of, and concern about, climate change. Swim, Geiger, Sweetland, and Fraser discuss the social context for understandings of climate change, particularly the ways in which people get information and the deficit of interpersonal conversations about the topic. They report evidence that training personnel at informal science learning centers (such as zoos) to converse with visitors about climate change can promote conversations and effectively increase knowledge about climate change not only among zoo visitors, but also among the friends and family of the people who were trained. This program provides a model that could be adapted to increase the social exchange of accurate information about climate change in other contexts.

In Chapter 5, A Diversity Science Approach to Climate Change, Adam Pearson and Jonathon Schuldt provide a transition from this section to the next: they use the tools and concepts of social psychology to discuss how social identities such as race, ethnicity, and class affect people's experiences and perceptions of climate change as well as their behavioral and emotional engagement with the issue. Stereotypes associated with these social groups can constitute barriers to effective engagement with the issue but may also be utilized to encourage involvement. The novel diversity science approach to the topic of climate change provided by Pearson and Schuldt illustrates how research at the intersection of psychology, diversity, and climate can advance psychological theory as well as offer practical implications for sparking more productive responses to climate change.

One of the most striking features about climate change is the discrepancy between the magnitude of the problem and the meager size of the response. At both the individual and the societal level, responses to the problem have been insufficient. Even the Paris Climate Accord, widely celebrated when passed as an international commitment to take action, has been described as inadequate to keep global warming at safe levels (LePage, 2015). The second section of the book will focus on how people respond to climate change. This is probably the area that has received the most attention within psychology, and there is a large body of research. Individual behavior changes are an important tool in confronting climate change, in part because such changes can be implemented more quickly than physical infrastructure or policy changes. Wolske and Stern set the stage in Chapter 6, Contributions of Psychology to Limiting Climate Change: Opportunities Through Consumer Behavior, by presenting a classification of individual and collective behaviors that are relevant to climate change and reviewing what is known about the determinants of these behaviors. Taking a rigorous perspective that considers the potential impact of behaviors as well as their potential malleability in response to interventions, they suggest some of the most promising behaviors to target. They also discuss the important role of psychology in interdisciplinary teams designed to affect these behaviors.

In Chapter 7, Understanding Responses to Climate Change: Psychological Barriers to Mitigation and a New Theory of Behavioral Choice, Robert Gifford, Karine Lacroix, and Angel Chen describe a range of barriers that prevent or inhibit more proenvironmental behaviors. Stressing the importance of methodological validity, they describe the evolution of a taxonomy of barriers, and the development of a valid tool of assessing these barriers. They discuss ways in which this tool might be used to guide more effective behavioral interventions that are responsive to the salient barriers in a particular situational context. This chapter not only outlines a new model of environmental behavior that incorporates behavioral barriers, suggesting promising directions for future research, it also illustrates the process by which such a model can be developed and refined.

The second section concludes with a chapter from Sebastian Bamberg, Jonas Rees, and Maxie Schulte that takes a psychological perspective on collective behavior. As Bamberg and his colleagues argue in Chapter 8, Environmental Protection Through Societal Change: What Psychology Knows About Collective Climate Action—and What It Needs to Find Out, an adequate response to climate change necessitates societal transformations that can only be achieved through collective actions. For this reason, psychologists must expand their research focus beyond individual behavioral decisions and think about the group-level motives inspiring group-level actions. Building on a social identity model, Bamberg and colleagues discuss research and present a new model that tries to explain individuals' participation in collective climate action as a function of group identification. Such collective action in turn can provide an experience of collective effectiveness and a source of resilience for the individuals involved.

The third section of the book looks at how people will be affected by climate change, with a specific focus on encouraging resilience. In Chapter 9, Threats to Mental Health and Well-being Associated with Climate Change, Manning and Clayton summarize research on the threats to individual and especially community well-being. They address the impact of both acute events, such as natural disasters, and chronic climate changes, such as rises in average temperatures and in sea levels. They also consider both direct effects of these events and the potential for indirect effects. In particular, their chapter encourages attention to the risk of abstract but wide-ranging impacts on generalized worry and anxiety, identity, social relations, and community cohesion. Research on these more general effects on perceptions is in its infancy, and there is a need for much more investigation into this area.

Thomas Doherty focuses more closely on individual psychology in Chapter 10, Individual Impacts and Resilience, discussing psychological factors associated with concern, with risk of adverse mental health impacts, and with adaptive coping responses. Emphasizing a view of health not just as the absence of disease but as optimal human functioning, he considers the ways in which human flourishing may be negatively impacted by climate change, as well as possibilities for people to thrive by finding meaning in effective responses to the challenge. Throughout the chapter, he also reminds the reader that vulnerability resides in the interaction of individual and societal characteristics, and that creating truly resilient individuals requires addressing societal disparities.

Chapman and colleagues take a community psychology perspective on climate change in Chapter 11, Psychological Perspectives on Community Resilience and Climate Change: Insights, Examples, and Directions for Future Research. They argue for the importance of considering resilience at a community level, as the impacts of climate change, vulnerability to those impacts, and sources of strength will all vary locally. In addition, many of the most significant opportunities for people to respond to climate change will take place at the local level. Reviewing existing literature on resilience both within and outside psychology, they encourage psychologists to do more to address the community level in both research and applications. They make the case not only that psychology can contribute to promoting community resilience, but also that psychology as a discipline can benefit from the interdisciplinary work that is required to help adapt to the impacts of a changing climate.

1.4   Summing up

This volume provides a solid overview of some of the important psychological contributions that can and should inform public discussions of climate change. It is important to acknowledge, however, that it is necessarily incomplete. The work continues to accumulate and we are learning more that is relevant to the psychology of climate change every month. The psychological context for climate change is also evolving; perceptions of, and responses to, climate change will differ according to the sociopolitical context. The unexpected election of Donald Trump to the US presidency in 2016, e.g., and his subsequent withdrawal of the United States from the Paris climate accords have had a vast impact on people's engagement with the issue—witness the People's Climate March of spring 2017—and there has not yet been time for research to explore this trend. In addition, these chapters do not represent all of the important topics that psychology has investigated related to climate change. Some additional work should be acknowledged; e.g., there is more to be said about people's responses to specific policies designed to address climate change, and there is relevant work that focuses on particular settings, such as organizational, marketing, or educational contexts. We hope that psychological researchers are inspired to investigate new areas.

It is also important to note that this book describes the empirical evidence we have *at the present time* of the human implications of climate change. Yet, it is clear from the scientific evidence that what we are experiencing today is just the beginning; a time lag exists between changes in greenhouse gas concentrations and significant shifts in the earth's climate system. These climate shifts will continue accelerating, resulting in increasingly extreme weather-related disruptions. Scientific predictions for the year 2100 suggest dramatically different conditions from today's. Given what we know about the negative impacts at current levels of greenhouse gas concentrations, it is sobering to contemplate humanity's future. For many, this reality is too difficult to face; however, we must overcome paralysis and meet the challenge of lowering emissions.

Humanity still has enormous leeway to determine conditions for the end of this century and beyond, particularly with respect to sea level rise and desertification. The climate disruptions to which our previous emissions have already committed us pale in comparison to what we will face going forward if we do not take remedial action. This book presents lessons that should be harnessed. Psychology alone cannot solve all the problems that are associated with climate change. But psychology can, and must, be part of the multidisciplinary teams that prepare us for the changed environmental conditions we will be facing.

References

Chiacu, D., & Volcovici, V. (2017). EPA chief Pruitt refuses to link CO_2 and global warming. *Scientific American.* Available from https://www.scientificamerican.com/article/epa-chief-pruitt-refuses-to-link-co2-and-global-warming/.

Department of Defense. (2014). *Climate change adaptation roadmap.* 2014. Available at <https://www.acq.osd.mil/eie/downloads/CCARprint_wForward_e.pdf>.

Dietz, T., Gardner, G. T., Gilligan, J., Stern, P. C., & Vandenbergh, M. P. (2009). Household actions can provide a behavioral wedge to rapidly reduce US carbon emissions. *Proceedings of the National Academy of Sciences, 106*(44), 18452–18456.

Fischer, E. M., & Knutti, R. (2015). Anthropogenic contribution to global occurrence of heavy-precipitation and high-temperature extremes. *Nature Climate Change, 5*(6), 560–564.

Frisk, A. (2017). Donald Trump on climate change: A "hoax", "mythical", "man-made". *Global News.* Available from https://globalnews.ca/news/3495239/what-donald-trump-said-global-warming-climate-change/.

Intergovernmental Panel on Climate Change (IPCC). (2014). *Climate change 2014: Impacts, adaptation, and vulnerability.* New York: Cambridge University Press. Available at http://www.ipcc.ch/report/ar5/wg2/.

Leiserowitz, A., Maibach, E., Roser-Renouf, C., Rosenthal, S., & Cutler, M. (2017). *Politics & global warming, May 2017*. New Haven, CT: Yale University and George Mason University, Yale program on climate change communication.

LePage, M. (2015). Paris climate deal is agreed—But is it really good enough? *New Scientist*. Available from https://www.newscientist.com/article/dn28663-paris-climate-deal-is-agreed-but-is-it-really-good-enough/.

Pecl, G. T., Araújo, M. B., Bell, J. D., Blanchard, J., Bonebrake, T. C., Chen, I. C., ... Falconi, L. (2017). Biodiversity redistribution under climate change: Impacts on ecosystems and human well-being. *Science*, *355*(6332), eaai9214.

Springmann, M., Mason-D'Croz, D., Robinson, S., Garnett, T., Godfray, H. C. J., Gollin, D., ... Scarborough, P. (2016). Global and regional health effects of future food production under climate change: A modeling study. *The Lancet*, *387*(10031), 1937−1946.

Part I

Perceptions and Communication

Perceptions of climate change

2

Lorraine Whitmarsh and Stuart Capstick
Cardiff University, Cardiff, United Kingdom

2.1 What are public perceptions and why do they matter?

Understanding public perceptions of climate change is critical in order to build widespread public engagement, and to develop effective communication and educational approaches. Constructing and implementing effective and acceptable policies and socially robust technologies to mitigate and adapt to climate change also requires an understanding of what the public think about climate change and how it should be tackled.

The term "perceptions" has been used to denote a range of psychological constructs, including knowledge, beliefs, attitudes, concern, affect, and perceived risk. We adopt this broad term in order to capture the cognitive (e.g., knowledge), affective (e.g., emotional), and evaluative (e.g., perceived risk) dimensions of individuals' internal representations of the issue, but critically understand these representations to be shaped by social processes and cultural context (Whitmarsh, Seyfang, & O'Neill, 2011). Public perceptions of climate change have received a growing level of research interest since the early 1980s; approaches used to study them encompass in-depth qualitative (e.g., focus group, interview) studies, quantitative (or occasionally mixed quantitative-qualitative) surveys, and—increasingly— experimental-design studies (e.g., framing experiments) as well as parallel methodologies used by other disciplines (e.g., public deliberation, ethnography). Here, we draw primarily on survey and qualitative work to provide an overview of the nature and dynamics of public perceptions of climate change, in order to give a summary of the field.

This chapter reviews the international literature on public perceptions of climate change, thereby providing a foundation for many of the subsequent chapters. The chapter will explore the nature of public understanding of climate change and assess how perceptions have changed over time, and how they vary across and within nations. We consider what is likely to influence public attitudes and understanding; including the experience of weather events, media reporting, political orientation and values, as well as sociodemographic, cultural, and economic factors.

Psychology and Climate Change. DOI: https://doi.org/10.1016/B978-0-12-813130-5.00002-3

2.2   How do people perceive climate change?

2.2.1   Knowledge, skepticism, and concern

Surveys show that awareness and self-reported knowledge about climate change have been rising over the last three decades. In many developed countries, such as the United Kingdom and United States, awareness of "climate change" and "global warming" has become nearly universal (Lee, Markowitz, Howe, Ko, & Leiserowitz, 2015; Nisbet & Myers, 2007; Whitmarsh, 2009). Elsewhere, the degree to which publics have encountered the topic is more variable, with substantial proportions of people in the developing countries still reporting having encountered little or no information about the subject (Brechin, 2010; Lee et al., 2015). Populous regions of the world in which awareness is relatively low include the Indian subcontinent, Indonesia, and parts of sub-Saharan Africa (Lee et al., 2015). Nevertheless, cross-country research carried out in 2014 in three European countries, plus China, the United States, and Canada, concluded that public respondents were, in the main, reasonably well-informed about climate change, with a majority of people correctly answering questions about the causes and consequences of climate change (e.g., concerning the role of carbon dioxide and future increase in extreme weather events; Shi, Visschers, Siegrist, & Arvai, 2016).

On the other hand, the public also appears to have a limited understanding of the relative contribution of different activities to climate change. In particular, there is an underestimation of the role of domestic energy use, meat eating/production, food miles, and food waste (Attari, DeKay, Davidson, & De Bruin, 2010; Bailey, Froggatt, & Wellesley, 2014; Defra, 2007; Whitmarsh et al., 2011). Beyond this, there is also a general tendency to discount one's own contribution to causing climate change and identify causes of climate change primarily with other people or countries (Lorenzoni & Pidgeon, 2006; Whitmarsh, 2009). As we discuss later, this may be explained by individuals not accepting uncomfortable or threatening information (in line with "motivated reasoning").

Although most members of the public do now accept the existence and human drivers of climate change, there remains a substantial minority who deny—or are, to use the popular if inexact term (since skepticism implies being questioning, rather than uncritically rejecting evidence; Lewandowsky, Ballard, Oberauer, & Benestad, 2016), "skeptical" about—climate change (e.g., Smith & Leiserowitz, 2012; Whitmarsh, 2011). The most recent data suggest that in the United States, around one in eight people (13%) think that climate change is not happening and only a little over half of people (55%) see it as mostly human caused (Leiserowitz, Maibach, Roser-Renouf, Rosenthal, & Cutler, 2017). These figures are reflected in European data: Steentjes et al. (2017) find that 16% of Germans and 12% of the UK respondents do not think the world's climate is changing, with less than 50% in each of these countries considering it to be mainly or completely caused by humans. These public perceptions persist despite overwhelming scientific consensus about the reality, human contribution and severity of climate change (IPCC, 2014).

The reasons for this skepticism are complex but include threatened values and ideology (i.e., solutions to tackle climate change tend to challenge free market paradigms and individualism; Campbell & Kay, 2014); media presentation of climate change as controversial and uncertain (Boykoff & Boykoff, 2004), as well as deliberate attempts to undermine and discredit climate science (Oreskes & Conway, 2010); human causes of climate change not being self-evident (Whitmarsh, 2008); and the challenging implications of accepting climate change for lifestyles (e.g., Bain, Hornsey, Bongiorno, & Jeffries, 2012; Whitmarsh, 2011). As we discuss later, there is also considerable temporal variation in climate skepticism among the public.

Beyond people's awareness and knowledge, research has also explored how the public evaluates climate change (i.e., their attitudes), including levels of perceived risk and concern. Overall, most people consider climate change to pose negative consequences (e.g., floods, drought; Lorenzoni, Leiserowitz, de Franca Doria, Poortinga, & Pidgeon, 2006; Poortinga & Pidgeon, 2003) but put in the context of other issues, it is not a priority concern for most people (health, economic, and social issues typically rank higher) and may not even be one of the public's main environmental concerns (Pidgeon, 2012).

The low ranking of climate change as a concern has been argued to reflect a widespread perception among the public that the issue is a psychologically "distant" issue—that is to say, it is seen as something that occurs in remote locations, that will not affect people for some years, and that is uncertain or lacking relevance to one's own social group (Brügger, Dessai, Devine-Wright, Morton, & Pidgeon, 2015; Leviston, Price, & Bishop, 2014; Lorenzoni, Nicholson-Cole, & Whitmarsh, 2007; Spence, Poortinga, Butler, & Pidgeon, 2011). While the public largely accept that climate change is already happening and many believe it will affect their local area (Spence et al., 2011), those in developed countries tend not to feel it poses a prominent personal threat (e.g., Leiserowitz, Maibach, Roser-Renouf, Rosenthal, et al., 2017; O'Neill & Nicholson-Cole, 2009; Whitmarsh et al., 2011). By contrast, communities whose livelihoods are more directly tied to local climatic conditions, such as farmers in developing countries, may perceive climate change in more proximal and immediate terms. For example, Basannagari and Kala (2013) present evidence that apple farmers in the Indian Himalayas are of the view that climate change has led directly to modifications in their land-use practices, delays to harvesting periods, and detrimental effects on fruit quality. In Mexico, Sánchez-Cortés and Chavero (2011) similarly find that as well as perceiving changes to rainfall and temperature, farmers have responded to these shifting conditions by bringing forward their growing season for corn and cultivating new crops.

2.2.2 Perceptions embedded in broader social discourses

Perceptions are formed not only through cognitive processes (e.g., information assimilation), but also through social interaction and within a particular cultural context (Kahan, Jenkins-Smith, & Braman, 2010; Kasperson et al., 1988). Climate change is primarily learnt about through mass media communication, but also through interpersonal communication, formal learning and other channels (Hargreaves et al., 2003). Consequently, communicators such as newspapers and television have played a major role in constructing climate change (Trumbo, 1996), including by emphasizing controversy and debate surrounding the issue (Boykoff & Boykoff, 2004) and linking the issue to relevant social and political developments (e.g., legislation). Critically, they employ emotional narratives to cast the issue in tangible and human terms (Höijer, 2010; Peters & Heinrichs, 2004), using shared social symbols, experiences and values to garner public interest (Hargreaves et al., 2003; McComas & Shanahan, 1999). Although this may enable a public audience to better apprehend the human dimensions and implications of climate change, it has also been suggested that emotionally loaded and fearful representations of risk can prompt a sense of disillusionment or powerlessness, particularly if there is no sense given of a recourse to meaningful action that can address it (O'Neill et al., 2013; Höijer, 2010; O'Neill & Nicholson-Cole, 2009).

Qualitative research indicates that the immediate associations that people hold with climate change are underpinned by recurrent themes; these concern changes in the weather and future climate impacts, the causal role of human activities and natural cycles, and the relationship between climate change and consumer society (Leviston et al., 2014; Smith & Joffe, 2012; Tvinnereim & Fløttum, 2015). Other research has shown, similarly, that the public understands climate change as part of a broader set of social and environmental issues, such as air pollution, industrialization, consumption and over-population rather than as a stand-alone issue (Darier & Schule, 1999; Tvinnereim, Liu, & Jamelske, 2017; Wolf & Moser, 2011). This conceptual linking reflects the media coverage which tends to discuss climate change in the context of local weather-related stories, such as UK flooding (Gavin, Leonard-Milsom, & Montgomery, 2011; Hargreaves et al., 2003) as well as people's underlying understanding of nature and natural systems (e.g., as being cyclical or ever-changing; Connor & Higginbotham, 2013). People's conceptual associations are also likely due to the ways in which climate change, as a new concept, is made sense of in relation to familiar ideas and experiences (Ungar, 2000), a process known in social psychological literature as "anchoring" (Breakwell, 1991; Whitmarsh et al., 2011). The implications of this embedded perspective of climate change are that surveys and interviews will apparently expose "misperceptions" in understanding whereby diverse environmental and social issues are linked to climate change, whereas these erroneous (by scientific standards) statements may rather reflect more complex narratives that are used to make sense of human—nature relationships (Whitmarsh, 2009; Wolf & Moser, 2011). Communicators should use such socially embedded narratives to effectively engage the public with climate change, rather than aiming to impart abstract scientific "facts" that may have little connection to everyday life (Whitmarsh & Corner, 2017).

2.3   How have public perceptions of climate change developed over time and across nations?

Numerous surveys examining public perceptions of climate change are now regularly undertaken across the world. From a review of 33 such studies (Capstick, Whitmarsh, Poortinga, & Pidgeon, 2015), we identified four indicative time periods during which public perceptions appear to shift in a number of ways. We here outline the findings from this review:

- *1980s—Early 1990s: increasing knowledge and awareness*

Data from the 1980s—when public understanding of climate change was beginning to be elicited—are inevitably sparse compared to recent years, but indicate that during this decade public awareness, knowledge and concern rose steadily, soon reaching levels comparable to more recent years. Nisbet and Myers (2007), for example, show that whereas in 1986 less than a half of the US respondents (between 39% and 45%) reported having heard or read anything about climate change, this proportion rose to around three-quarters of respondents by 1990. These authors noted, however, that levels of overall understanding were limited. Various studies also point to a conflation with localized air pollution, Chlorofluorocarbons (CFCs) and ozone depletion in respondents' attribution of causes of climate change (Brechin, 2003). Nevertheless, even at this early point in time, respondents from many parts of the world were already of the view that climate change had begun to happen (Dunlap, 1998).

Despite limited levels of understanding during this early period, polls nevertheless show public concern rose rapidly. For example, only 43% of the US respondents in 1982 saw climate change as either a "very" or "somewhat" serious problem, while this figure had reached 75% by 1989 (Dunlap & Scarce, 1991). Findings from surveys across 24 countries in 1992 also showed just over half of all respondents rated climate change as a "very serious" problem, although there was substantial variability between nations, ranging from 26% of Nigerians to 73% of Germans (Brechin, 2003; Dunlap, 1998). Limited polling data also offers insights into changing perceptions in Europe around this time: a 1988 survey found that more than three-quarters of respondents were already worried about climate change, rising to almost nine in ten by 1992 (Eurobarometer, 1992). Taken together, these studies suggest that by the end of the 1980s when climate change was becoming politically prominent in the United States and Europe, public awareness and concern in several developed countries were already widespread.

- *Mid-1990s—Mid-2000s: Growth and fluctuation in concern*

Whereas the 1980s and early 1990s were marked by a global growth in awareness and concern about climate change, the period that followed entailed a sustained overall growth of public concern with considerable inter- and intranational variation. The overall growth in concern mirrors a rise in media attention to climate change, in turn linked to growing scientific evidence and political attention (Boykoff & Yulsman, 2013). Yet, there was also remarkable volatility in this personal concern about climate change particularly since the late 1990s to the present time, which—as we discuss later—is likely due to various factors, not least changing media coverage

(Capstick, Whitmarsh, et al., 2015a). Despite the temporal variability in this measure, a review of more than 40 US surveys focused on the early 2000s nevertheless concluded that the weight of public opinion in the period 2001–2004 strongly favored US participation in the Kyoto Protocol and decisive action on climate change, in direct contrast to national policy at this time (Brewer, 2005).

By 2007, support for substantial action to mitigate climate change was evident at the international level. Data from several cross-national polls point to growing public concern about climate change worldwide in the 2000s, as well as to strong public support at this time for climate mitigation policies (Brechin, 2010; Globescan, 2006; Kull et al., 2007; Leiserowitz, 2008). For example, a survey of ten European countries carried out in 2005 and 2007 showed a sharp rise from 36% to 55% in respondents' belief that climate change would be "very likely" to personally affect them (Transatlantic Trends, 2007).

- *Mid-2000s–Late-2000s: Increasing skepticism and polarization*

Surveys up to the mid-2000s suggest a broad popular consensus for action on climate change had emerged. By contrast, and despite the growing scientific consensus on the issue, the late 2000s and early 2010s appeared to show the proliferation of public doubts and skepticism about the reality and severity of climate change (see, e.g., Fig. 2.1 for US survey data; Leiserowitz, Maibach, Roser-Renouf, Rosenthal et al., 2017). This unexpected rise in skepticism challenges the simplistic assumption that more scientific information will increase public belief or concern about a risk issue such as climate change (Whitmarsh, 2011). Although trends at this time do appear to indicate growing skepticism about

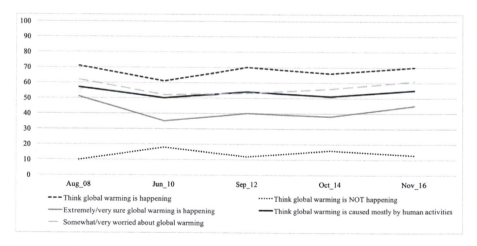

Figure 2.1 US attitudes to climate change between 2008 and 2016, showing a drop in belief and worry about climate change between 2008 and 2010 (%).
Source: Leiserowitz, A., Maibach, E., Roser-Renouf, C., Rosenthal, S., & Cutler, M. (2017). *Climate change in the American mind: November 2016*. Yale Program on Climate Change Communication. New Haven, CT: Yale University and George Mason University. <http://climatechangecommunication.org/wp-content/uploads/2017/01/Climate-Change-American-Mind-November-2016.pdf> Accessed 14.02.17.

climate change, it is nonetheless important to note that clear majorities in many countries still expressed high levels of concern and recognition of the problem throughout this period (Pidgeon, 2012).

US research showed a sharp increase between 2008 and 2010 in the proportion of US citizens who did not accept climate change is happening, that it had an anthropogenic component, or that there was scientific consensus about its human causes (Leiserowitz, Maibach, Roser-Renouf, Feinberg, & Rosenthal, 2014; cf. Schwartz, 2010). During the mid- to late-2000s, related research found that the types of imagery people spontaneously associate with climate change moved in a skeptical direction (Smith & Leiserowitz, 2012). Similar findings have been obtained elsewhere in the developed world (Spence et al., 2011; Whitmarsh, 2011; Ratter, Philipp, & von Storch, 2012). Across Europe, over three surveys conducted during 2008 and 2009, a drop in the perceived seriousness of climate change was observed (Eurobarometer, 2009). In Australia, an increasing tendency to view climate change as exaggerated and/or to denigrate policy designed to address it, was recorded across the 2008−11 time period (Connor & Higginbotham, 2013). Although different survey measures and timings make it difficult to directly compare the magnitude of decline in concern and belief across nations, cross-national surveys indicate declines were mostly concentrated in the developed world (Globescan, 2012).

A process of politicization of climate change was likely to have been a significant contributing factor in these trends (e.g., Whitmarsh, 2011). Following the election of Barack Obama, climate change came to constitute a "litmus test" in the United States, with conservative Republicans aligning with climate skeptic positions as a means of differentiating themselves from Democrats. Other survey-based research empirically bears out the notion of growing polarization, particularly in the latter 2000s. McCright and Dunlap (2011) demonstrate a statistically significant interaction between political affiliation and survey year over the 2000s in the United States. Whereas in 2001 there was an 18% difference between liberals (67%) and conservatives (49%) regarding whether climate change had already begun, this rose to a 45% difference by 2010 (75% of liberals versus 30% of conservatives). Other work similarly affirms polarization in US public views on climate change accelerated in the late 2000s (Brewer, 2012) and suggest that this polarization was stronger than for other social, economic, and foreign policy topics (Guber, 2013). Growing political polarization over climate change is similarly evident, albeit to a less extent than in the United States, in certain other—particularly Anglophone (Painter & Asche, 2012; Whitmarsh, 2011)—countries.

This period also saw considerable international heterogeneity in perceptions of climate change (Gallup, 2014; Pew Center, 2010). In both the United States and Western Europe, sharp declines occurred between 2007/08 and 2010 in the proportion of respondents viewing climate change as either a "somewhat" or "very" serious threat to themselves or their family. By contrast, in Latin America and sub-Saharan Africa growing numbers considered climate change to represent such a threat. Concerning the extent to which respondents saw climate change as being connected to human activities, again, declining proportions were of this view in the United States and Western Europe, whereas in parts of Africa, developing Asia, and Latin America, the human component to climate change was increasingly coming to be acknowledged (Gallup, 2014). Reasons for such international variations and diverging trends in opinion are little understood and complex, though clearly aspects of the surrounding physical and social contexts are important, including levels of risk exposure, cultural values, political context and the nature of media coverage. With respect to the overall surge in concern in Latin America in the late 2000s, this may be related to a growth in climate justice activism linked to left-wing political activism at this time, as well as to the occurrence of extreme weather events (Postigo, Wells, & Cancino, 2013; Smith, 2014). Conversely, other analyses have argued that in the United States and other Anglophone countries, right-wing think tanks and media outlets have been key players in a "conservative counter-movement" that has emerged to challenge climate policy (Dunlap & McCright, 2010; Jacques, Dunlap, & Freeman, 2008; Oreskes & Conway, 2010; Painter & Asche, 2012). This is likely due to what Campbell and Kay (2014) describe as "solution aversion" among right-leaning organizations and individuals, whereby climate policies (e.g., carbon taxes, energy efficiency standards) are seen as threatening cherished ideologies of free markets and unfettered individual choice.

- *Late 2000s to the 2010s: A new phase for public perceptions?*

Cross-national divergences in public opinion trends persist to the present time. Nevertheless, there are signs that in some parts of the world public concern about climate change is stabilizing and in other cases increasing. Surveys undertaken across 28 European countries between 2009 and 2013 suggest that the relative importance of climate change has remained largely consistent over this more recent time period with around a half of respondents consistently considering climate change to be one of the most serious problems facing the world (Eurobarometer, 2014; see Fig. 2.2). Other data suggest that while concern in many developed countries (United Kingdom, United States, Canada, France) has stabilized during the 2010s, the trends for developing countries have been more mixed, with some countries (e.g., China, Mexico, and Kenya) seeing falls in public concern (Globescan, 2012).

British survey data suggest the proportion of people expressing concern and belief about climate change has fluctuated over this period: compared to 82% expressing concern in 2005, only 60% did so by 2013, rebounding somewhat to 68% in 2014. Only 9% doubted the reality of climate change in 2005, rising to 19% by 2013 and declining again to 6% by late 2014 but moving upward again to 12% by 2016 (Capstick, Demski, & Sposato, 2015; Poortinga, Pidgeon, Capstick, & Aoyagi, 2014; Steentjes et al., 2017). Other survey work in 2015 showed only a small majority (59%) of Britons believed climate change is real and human caused and held the view that most or all climate scientists similarly think so (61%; ComRes, 2015); Steentjes et al. (2017) obtain comparable figures 1 year later. Conversely, US data suggests a rise in concern and belief in climate change across the political spectrum; for example, the proportion agreeing that there is "solid evidence" that the Earth is warming has increased steadily from a low point of 57% around 2009 to 67% by October 2013 (Pew Center, 2013). Similarly, there was an increase in the number of people worrying "a great deal" about global warming from 25% in 2011 to 34% in 2014 (Gallup, 2014). Leiserowitz et al.'s (2014) US research suggests increases in

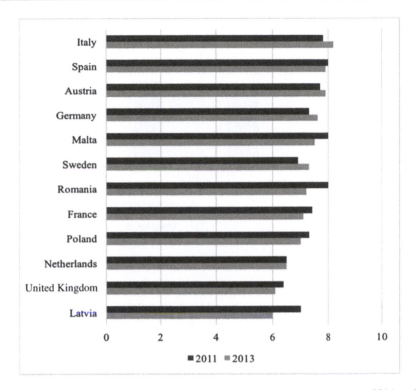

Figure 2.2 European perceptions of the seriousness of climate change, between 2011 and 2013 (1 = not at all serious problem, 10 = extremely serious problem).
Source: Eurobarometer. (2014). Climate change, special Eurobarometer 409. <http://ec.europa.eu/public_opinion/archives/ebs/ebs_409_en.pdf> Accessed April 2014.

acceptance and concern about climate change that are more modest (c. 5%) and only slightly larger than the margins of error of the surveys.

Most recently, in the wake of one of the most contentious US elections in 2016 (and yet one in which climate change was barely mentioned in campaigning or debate), the proportion of Americans who think climate change is happening appears to be remaining steady at 70% in 2016, nearly matching the highest level (71%) measured since November 2008 in equivalent polls (Leiserowitz, Maibach, Roser-Renouf, Rosenthal, et al., 2017). Despite the election of a president who has publically described climate change as a "hoax," Americans largely (69%) still support international action to tackle climate change—and are now also more certain it is happening, with the proportion who are "extremely" or "very" sure climate change is happening (45%) at its highest level since 2008 (Leiserowitz, Maibach, Roser-Renouf, Rosenthal, et al., 2017). Furthermore, it seems the president's position on climate change is not wholly shared by his electorate: more Trump voters (49%) think global warming is happening than do not think so (30%); more support (47%) than oppose (28%) international agreements to limit global warming; and

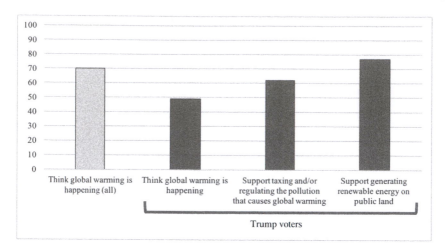

Figure 2.3 Trump voters' attitudes toward global warming (%; data collected November 2016).
Source: Leiserowitz, A., Maibach, E., Roser-Renouf, C., Rosenthal, S., & Cutler, M. (2017). Climate change in the American mind: November 2016. Yale Program on Climate Change Communication. New Haven, CT: Yale University and George Mason University. <http://climatechangecommunication.org/wp-content/uploads/2017/01/Climate-Change-American-Mind-November-2016.pdf> Accessed 14.02.17; Leiserowitz, A., Maibach, E., Roser-Renouf, C., Cutler, M., & Rosenthal, S. (2017). *Trump voters & global warming*. Yale Program on Climate Change Communication. New Haven, CT: Yale University and George Mason University. <http://climatechangecommunication.org/wp-content/uploads/2017/02/Trump-Voters-and-Global-Warming.pdf> Accessed 14.02.17.

most are in favor of renewable energy (see Fig. 2.3; Leiserowitz, Maibach, Roser-Renouf, Cutler, & Rosenthal, 2017). A majority of Americans also opposed Trump's decision to withdraw from the landmark Paris Agreement, by a ratio of 2:1 (Washington Post, 2017).

It is unclear as to the likely direction of future trends in these types of polling data. It may be concluded from the evidence available that the declines in some measures observed in the 2000s appear to have arrested in the United States and Europe as a whole. However, it remains to be seen how the recent unprecedented political changes across several countries (including the United States and United Kingdom) alongside the coming into force in 2016 of the Paris Agreement on climate change (limiting global warming to 2°C above preindustrial levels) will impact on public beliefs and concern about climate change. While the United States has since announced it will withdraw from the Paris Agreement, other countries are reaffirming and strengthening their commitment to tackling climate change. Individuals' belief in and concern about climate change may weather this political turbulence, due to their strong ideological underpinnings (Bain et al., 2012), although—as we now discuss—the multiple factors influencing perceptions make offering firm predictions very difficult.

2.4 What influences public perceptions of climate change?

Much research shows that the public is highly heterogeneous in their attitudes to climate change—both within and between nations. Internationally, there is considerable variation in perceptions, with Latin America and developed nations in Asia showing relatively high levels of concern, compared to other parts of the world (Capstick et al., 2015a). As noted earlier, this is likely due to increased risk exposure, cultural values (e.g., greater concern for the environment), political context (e.g., left-wing politics), and the nature of media coverage. Segmentation studies also point to distinct attitudinal clusters, ranging from the most concerned and active to the disinterested or active deniers, indicating multiple "publics" in respect of climate change engagement (Hine et al., 2014; Maibach, Leiserowitz, Roser-Renouf, & Mertz, 2011; Poortinga & Darnton, 2016; for an overview see Swim & Whitmarsh, 2017). Belief in and concern about climate change varies according to a range of factors, such as gender and age (specifically, men and older people tend to be more skeptical and less concerned; Upham et al., 2009), although studies show values, worldview, and ideology tend to be stronger predictors than demographic, knowledge, or other factors (Kahan et al., 2012; Whitmarsh, 2011).

A person's values, worldview, and ideology are important in large part because they act as filters on how information about climate change is interpreted (Corner, Markowitz, & Pidgeon, 2014). This biased assessment of information, known as "motivated reasoning," involves people seeking out and using information which confirms their existing beliefs, and ignoring or dismissing information which contradicts them—that is, they reach conclusions they *want* to reach (Kunda, 1990). This can mean, for example, that weather events are only seen as evidence of climate change if one already believes in climate change (see below). Several overlapping frameworks have been used to operationalize and explain the ways in which people's more general outlook on life affects their perceptions of climate change. Originating in social psychology, the values framework of Schwartz (1994) has been utilized in several studies showing that the endorsement of "self-transcendent" values—encompassing an emphasis on protecting and caring for other people—is associated with acceptance of the reality of climate change and level of concern about this issue (Poortinga, Spence, Whitmarsh, Capstick, & Pidgeon, 2011), as well as support for policies designed to address climate change (Nilsson, von Borgstede, & Biel, 2004) and willingness to behave in a proenvironmental manner (Evans et al., 2013). Drawing on an alternative conception of the Schwartz framework, others have argued for the importance of egoistic, altruistic, and biospheric value orientations as influences upon recognition of the problem of climate change, policy support, and proenvironmental behavior (negatively so in the case of egoistic values, and in a positive direction for altruistic and biospheric values; Steg, De Groot, Dreijerink, Abrahamse, & Siero, 2011; Steg, Dreijerink, & Abrahamse, 2005; Swim & Becker, 2012). Together, this research on values clearly shows that other-oriented values (e.g., altruism) are correlated with concern about environmental issues (including climate change) and support for climate change policies and proenvironmental action (Corner et al., 2014).

A separate strand of research has highlighted the way in which people's preferences for different types of social relations or "cultural worldviews" influence their risk perceptions about climate change; in particular, those people with a more egalitarian worldview (preferring collective and equal organization of society) tend to be more concerned about climate change than those whose worldview is more individualistic (Capstick & Pidgeon, 2014; Kahan et al., 2010, 2012; Xue, Hine, Marks, Phillips, & Zhao, 2015). These disparities can also be observed on the basis of political affiliation and voting patterns, whereby those with right-of-center political beliefs tend to be more skeptical about climate change, at least within the United Kingdom and United States (Dunlap & McCright, 2008; Eurobarometer, 2009; Poortinga et al., 2011) with this effect appearing to have become more pronounced over time in the United States (McCright & Dunlap, 2011). In sum, there would appear to be a strong and increasingly ideological component to climate change attitudes as the implications of belief in climate change for people's values, lifestyles and societal relations become more apparent and—for many—more threatening. As we discussed earlier, this "solution aversion" is manifesting in an organized denialist movement that is wielding considerable influence in the United States and other Anglophone countries (e.g., Oreskes & Conway, 2010).

Media also plays a key role in shifting public concern away from environmental issues toward other (e.g., economic) ones. Following a peak in public environmental concern in 2007, numerous studies show public concern about climate change then dropped, while doubt and skepticism have risen, in many regions (Capstick et al., 2015a; Leiserowitz, Maibach, Roser-Renouf, Feinberg, & Howe, 2012; Whitmarsh, 2011). While several explanations have been suggested for this widespread rise in doubt and loss of attention (see Pidgeon, 2012), most convincingly, the analysis of US opinion data from 2002 to 2010 by Brulle, Carmichael, and Jenkins (2012) shows the economic recession, along with "elite cues" (i.e., policy developments, politician statements), together shaped media coverage of climate change, which in turn influenced public attitudes toward climate change. Further research by Carmichael and Brulle (2016) also identified a pronounced effect of media coverage on public concern about climate change; this analysis likewise found that media attention to climate change was, in turn, a function of economic and political factors, as well as being influenced by the efforts of social movements and advocacy groups. Since media is the primary source of public information about climate change (Hargreaves et al., 2003), it is unsurprising that it plays such a key role in priming and shaping public attitudes and responses.

There is also a substantial body of evidence exploring the extent to which weather and weather events influence perceptions of climate change (e.g., Reser, Bradley, & Ellul, 2014). Some have suggested that increases in skepticism in the late 2000s may have been due to unusually cold weather in Europe and the United States (Moser & Dilling, 2011; Perkins, 2010). Indeed, there is evidence that people's perceptions of temperature anomalies (e.g., whether they are of the view that recent weather has been "warmer" or "colder" than usual) can affect beliefs

(Capstick & Pidgeon, 2014; Egan & Mullin, 2012; Krosnick, Holbrook, Lowe, & Visser, 2006; Myers, Maibach, Roser-Renouf, Akerlof, & Leiserowitz, 2013; Zaval, Keenan, Johnson, & Weber, 2014), as well as some (albeit mixed) evidence that experience of extreme weather events (e.g., floods, hurricanes) can influence climate change beliefs (Demski et al., 2017; Rudman, McLean, & Bunzl, 2013; Spence et al., 2011). For example, Donner and McDaniels (2013) found that attitudes toward the reality of climate change, and degree of personal concern, were both related to the temperature anomaly over the past 12 months. Other research finds the influence of weather anomalies on climate change beliefs decays rapidly (Hamilton & Stampone, 2013); while several studies note an interaction between political affiliation and weather anomalies on climate change beliefs. For example, Deryugina (2013) found that only Conservative voters' belief in climate change was positively influenced by unusual weather (see also Hamilton & Stampone, 2013). Consistent with this, people who believe climate change is not happening are less likely to remember (accurately) that they had experienced a warmer-than-usual summer during the previous year (Howe & Leiserowitz, 2013). Overall, while the evidence appears to suggest that long-term temperature anomalies have an effect on public perceptions of climate change, there is also a two-way relationship between experience and belief. That is, weather events are interpreted through the filter of extant perceptions of climate change, such that skeptics are less likely to interpret unusual or extreme weather events as being caused by climate change than those who believe climate change is a real and serious risk (Clayton et al., 2015; Whitmarsh, 2008). Furthermore, a meta-analysis of the climate change perceptions literature suggests that experience of unusual and extreme weather plays a minor role in shaping perceptions of climate change relative to other factors, most notably political ideology and values (Hornsey, Harris, Bain, & Fielding, 2016). Similarly, the longitudinal analysis of US public perceptions data by Palm, Lewis, and Feng (2017) shows that—consistent with motivated reasoning—political ideology, party affiliation and environmental values are much stronger influences on perceptions than other factors, including experience of warmer temperatures or extreme weather events.

2.5   Conclusion

Understanding public perceptions of climate change is critical in order to develop effective communication strategies, democratic policies and socially robust technologies. This chapter provided an overview of research on the nature and dynamics of public perceptions of climate change. In sum, awareness about climate change has become widespread over the last few decades, although concern has been more variable across time and space. Skepticism about the reality and severity of climate change grew in the late 2000s, particularly among more right-leaning groups, likely in part due to the increasing politicization of the issue but also reflecting changing economic circumstances and associated media coverage. Factors influencing public perceptions include weather and weather events, media coverage and sociopolitical events, and individual-level factors, particularly ideology.

This chapter has focused on survey and qualitative research on public perceptions of climate change, but there is a growing literature using experimental methods to provide more robust conclusions about how perceptions are and can be shaped. This work highlights how the different elements of the communication process (source, message, audience and context) interact to produce learning, persuasion and behavior change (e.g., Corner et al., 2012; Howell, Capstick, & Whitmarsh, 2016; Morton, Rabinovich, Marshall, & Bretschneider, 2011; cf. Petty & Cacioppo, 1986). Importantly, this work demonstrates that different messages are likely to be received and responded to in different ways by different individuals (e.g., Markowitz, Hodge, & Harp, 2014; Whitmarsh & Corner, 2017); and that communication is often insufficient to lead to behavior change due to the range of barriers to low-carbon, climate-resilient lifestyles (e.g., Lorenzoni et al., 2007). There is much scope to broaden the range of methods used to explore this area, for example to apply more ethnographic or neuroscientific approaches (cf. Kaplan, Gimbel, & Harris, 2016) to understand how individuals perceive and respond to climate change-related stimuli.

References

Attari, S., DeKay, M., Davidson, C., & De Bruin, W. (2010). Public perceptions of energy consumption and savings. *Proceedings of the National Academy of Sciences, 107*(37), 16054−16059.

Bailey, R., Froggatt, A., & Wellesley, L. (2014). *Livestock—climate change's forgotten sector. Global public opinion on meat and dairy consumption.* London: Chatham House.

Bain, P. G., Hornsey, M. J., Bongiorno, R., & Jeffries, C. (2012). Promoting pro-environmental action in climate change deniers. *Nature Climate Change, 2*, 600−603.

Basannagari, B., & Kala, C. P. (2013). Climate change and apple farming in Indian Himalayas: A study of local perceptions and responses. *PLoS ONE, 8*(10), e77976.

Boykoff, M. T., & Boykoff, J. M. (2004). Balance as bias: Global warming and the US prestige press. *Global Environmental Change, 14*, 125−136.

Boykoff, M. T., & Yulsman, T. (2013). Political economy, media, and climate change: Sinews of modern life. *Wiley Interdisciplinary Reviews: Climate Change, 4*, 359−371.

Breakwell, G. M. (1991). Social representations and social identity. *Papers on Social Representations, 2*, 198−217.

Brechin, S. R. (2003). Comparative public opinion and knowledge on global climatic change and the Kyoto Protocol: The U.S. versus the world? *International Journal of Sociology and Social Policy, 23*(10), 106−134.

Brechin, S. R. (2010). Public opinion: A cross-national view. In C. Lever-Tracy (Ed.), *The Routledge handbook of climate change and society.* New York: Routledge Press.

Brewer, P. R. (2012). Polarisation in the USA: Climate change, party politics, and public opinion in the Obama era. *European Political Science, 11*, 7−17.

Brewer, T. L. (2005). US public opinion on climate change issues: Implications for consensus-building and policymaking. *Climate Policy, 4*, 359−376.

Brügger, A., Dessai, S., Devine-Wright, P., Morton, T. A., & Pidgeon, N. (2015). Psychological responses to the proximity of climate change. *Nature Climate Change*, 5, 1031–1037.

Brulle, R. J., Carmichael, J., & Jenkins, J. C. (2012). Shifting public opinion on climate change: An empirical assessment of factors influencing concern over climate change in the U.S., 2002–2010. *Climatic Change*, *114*, 169–188.

Campbell, T. H., & Kay, A. C. (2014). Solution aversion: On the relation between ideology and motivated disbelief. *Journal of Personality and Social Psychology*, *107*(5), 809–824.

Capstick, S. B., Demski, C. C., Sposato, R. G., et al. (2015). *Public perception of climate change in Britain following the winter 2013/2014 flooding.* Cardiff.: Cardiff University.

Capstick, S. B., & Pidgeon, N. F. (2014). Public perception of cold weather events as evidence for and against climate change. *Climatic Change*, *122*(4), 695–708.

Capstick, S.B., Whitmarsh, L., Poortinga, W. & Pidgeon, N. (2015a). International trends in public understanding of climate change over the past quarter century. *Wiley Interdisciplinary Reviews: Climate Change.* doi:10.1002/wcc.321.

Carmichael, J. T., & Brulle, R. J. (2017). Elite cues, media coverage, and public concern: An integrated path analysis of public opinion on climate change, 2001–2013. *Environmental Politics*, *26*, 232–252.

Clayton, S., Devine-Wright, P., Stern, P., Whitmarsh, L., Carrico, A., Steg, L., ... Bonnes, M. (2015). Psychological research and global climate change. *Nature Climate Change*, *5*, 640–646.

ComRes. (2015). *ECIU—Energy and climate change.* <http://www.comresglobal.com/wp-content/uploads/2015/09/ECIU_Energy-and-Climate-Change-Survey_29092015.pdf> Accessed 14.02.17>.

Connor, L. H., & Higginbotham, N. (2013). "Natural cycles" in lay understandings of climate change. *Global Environmental Change*, *23*, 1852–1861.

Corner, A., Markowitz, E., & Pidgeon, N. (2014). Public engagement with climate change: The role of human values. *Wiley Interdisciplinary Reviews: Climate Change*, *5*(3), 411–422.

Corner, A., Whitmarsh, L., & Xenias, D. (2012). Uncertainty, scepticism and attitudes towards climate change: Biased assimilation and attitude polarisation. *Climatic Change*, *114*, 463–478.

Darier, E., & Schule, R. (1999). 'Think Globally, Act Locally'? Climate change and public participation in Manchester and Frankfurt. *Local Environment*, *4*, 317–329.

Defra. (2007). *Survey of public attitudes and behaviours toward the environment: 2007.* London: Department for Environment, Food and Rural Affairs.

Demski, C., Capstick, S., Pidgeon, N., Sposato, R. G., & Spence, A. (2017). Experience of extreme weather affects climate change mitigation and adaptation responses. *Climatic Change*, *140*(2), 149–164.

Deryugina, T. (2013). How do people update? The effects of local weather fluctuations on beliefs about global warming. *Climatic Change*, *118*, 397–416.

Donner, S. D., & McDaniels, J. (2013). The influence of national temperature fluctuations on opinions about climate change in the US since 1990. *Climatic Change*, *118*, 537–550.

Dunlap, R. (1998). Lay perceptions of global risk: Public views of global warming in cross-national context. *International Sociology*, *13*(4), 473–498.

Dunlap, R., & McCright, A. M. (2008). Widening gap: Republican and democratic views on climate change. *Environment*, *50*, 26–35.

Dunlap, R., & McCright, A. M. (2010). Climate change denial: Sources, actors and strategies. In C. Lever-Tracy (Ed.), *The Routledge handbook of climate change and society.* New York: Routledge Press.

Dunlap, R. E., & Scarce, R. (1991). Poll trends: Environmental problems and protection. *Public Opinion Quarterly, 55,* 651–672.

Egan, P. J., & Mullin, M. (2012). Turning personal experience into political attitudes: The effect of local weather on Americans' perceptions about global warming. *The Journal of Politics, 74,* 796–809.

Eurobarometer. (1992). *Europeans and the environment in 1992.* ⟨http://ec.europa.eu/public_opinion/archives/ebs/ebs_066_en.pdf⟩ Accessed February 2014.

Eurobarometer. (2009). *Special Eurobarometer 300. Europeans' attitudes towards climate change.* Brussels: European Commission.

Eurobarometer. (2014). *Climate change, special Eurobarometer 409.* <http://ec.europa.eu/public_opinion/archives/ebs/ebs_409_en.pdf> Accessed April 2014.

Evans, L., Maio, G. R., Corner, A., Hodgetts, C. J., Ahmed, S., & Hahn, U. (2013). Self-interest and pro-environmental behaviour. *Nature Climate Change, 3*(2), 122–125.

Gallup. (2014). *A steady 57% in U.S. blame humans for global warming.* <http://www.gallup.com/poll/167972/steady-blame-humans-global-warming.aspx> Accessed February 2014.

Gavin, N. T., Leonard-Milsom, L., & Montgomery, J. (2011). Climate change, flooding and the media in Britain. *Public Understanding of Science, 20,* 422–438.

GlobeScan. (2006). *Poll: Global views on climate change.* <http://www.worldpublicopinion.org/pipa/pdf/apr06/ClimateChange_Apr06_quaire.pdf> Accessed February 2014.

Globescan. (2012). *As Doha conference gets underway, climate concern falling sharply.* <http://www.globescan.com/news-and-analysis/blog/entry/as-doha-conference-gets-underway-climate-concern-falling-sharply.html> Accessed February 2014.

Guber, D. L. (2013). A cooling climate for change? Party polarization and the politics of global warming. *American Behavioral Scientist, 57,* 93–115.

Hamilton, L. C., & Stampone, M. D. (2013). Blowin' in the wind: Short-term weather and belief in anthropogenic climate change. *Weather, Climate, and Society, 5,* 112–119.

Hargreaves, I., Lewis, J., et al. (2003). *Towards a better map: Science, the public and the media.* London: Economic and Social Research Council.

Hine, D. W., Reser, J. P., Morrison, M., Phillips, W. J., Nunn, P., & Cooksey, R. (2014). Audience segmentation and climate change communication: Conceptual and methodological considerations. *WIREs Climate Change, 5,* 441–459. Available from https://doi.org/10.1002/wcc.279.

Höijer, B. (2010). Emotional anchoring and objectification in the media reporting on climate change. *Public Understanding of Science, 19*(6), 717–731.

Hornsey, M. J., Harris, E. A., Bain, P. G., & Fielding, K. S. (2016). Meta-analyses of the determinants and outcomes of belief in climate change. *Nature Climate Change, 6,* 622.

Howe, P., & Leiserowitz, A. (2013). Who remembers a hot summer or cold winter? The asymmetric effect of beliefs about global warming on perceptions of local climate conditions in the U.S. *Global Environmental Change, 23,* 1488–1500.

Howell, R., Capstick, S., & Whitmarsh, L. (2016). Impacts of adaptation and responsibility framings on attitudes towards climate change mitigation. *Climatic Change, 136*(3), 445–461.

IPCC. (2014). Core Writing Team. In R. K. Pachauri, & L. A. Meyer (Eds.), *Climate Change 2014: Synthesis Report. Contribution of Working Groups I, II and III to the Fifth*

Assessment Report of the Intergovernmental Panel on Climate Change. Geneva, Switzerland: IPCC.

Jacques, P. J., Dunlap, R. E., & Freeman, M. (2008). The organisation of denial: Conservative think tanks and environmental scepticism. *Environmental Politics, 17,* 349−385.

Kahan, D. M., Jenkins-Smith, H., & Braman, D. (2010). Cultural cognition of scientific consensus. *Journal of Risk Research, 14,* 147−174.

Kahan, D. M., Peters, E., Wittlin, M., Slovic, P., Ouellette, L. L., Braman, D., & Mandel, G. (2012). The polarizing impact of science literacy and numeracy on perceived climate change risks. *Nature Climate Change, 2*(10), 732−735.

Kaplan, J. T., Gimbel, S. I., & Harris, S. (2016). Neural correlates of maintaining one's political beliefs in the face of counterevidence. *Nature Scientific Reports, 6,* 39589.

Kasperson, R. E., Renn, O., Slovic, P., Brown, H. S., Emel, J., Goble, R., et al. (1988). The social amplification of risk: A conceptual framework. *Risk Analysis, 8*(2), 177−187.

Krosnick, J. A., Holbrook, A. L., Lowe, L., & Visser, P. S. (2006). The origins and consequences of democratic citizens' policy agendas: A study of popular concern about global warming. *Climatic Change, 77,* 7−43.

Kull, S., Ramsay, C., Weber, S., Lewis, E., Speck, M., Brouwer, M.,. . ., Medoff, A. (2007). *International polling on climate change.* <http://www.worldpublicopinion.org/pipa/pdf/dec07/CCDigest_Dec07_rpt.pdf> Accessed February 2014.

Kunda, Z. (1990). The case for motivated reasoning. *Psychological Bulletin, 108*(3), 480−498.

Lee, T. M., Markowitz, E. M., Howe, P. D., Ko, C. Y., & Leiserowitz, A. A. (2015). Predictors of public climate change awareness and risk perception around the world. *Nature Climate Change, 5*(11), 1014−1020.

Leiserowitz, A. (2008). *Public perception, opinion and understanding of climate change: Current patterns, trends and limitations.* New York: United Nations Development Programme.

Leiserowitz, A., Maibach, E., Roser-Renouf, C., Cutler, M., & Rosenthal, S. (2017). *Trump voters & global warming.* New Haven, CT: Yale Program on Climate Change Communication, Yale University and George Mason University. <http://climatechangecommunication.org/wp-content/uploads/2017/02/Trump-Voters-and-Global-Warming.pdf> Accessed 14.02.17.

Leiserowitz, A., Maibach, E., Roser-Renouf, C., Feinberg, G., & Howe, P. (2012). *Climate change in the American mind: Americans' beliefs and attitudes in September 2012.* New Haven, CT: Yale Project on Climate Change Communication, Yale University.

Leiserowitz, A., Maibach, E., Roser-Renouf, C., Feinberg, G., & Rosenthal, S. (2014). *Climate change in the American mind, April 2014.* <http://environment.yale.edu/climate-communication/files/Climate-Change-American-Mind-April-2014.pdf> Accessed May 2014.

Leiserowitz, A., Maibach, E., Roser-Renouf, C., Rosenthal, S., & Cutler, M. (2017). *Climate change in the American mind: November 2016.* New Haven, CT: Yale Program on Climate Change Communication, Yale University and George Mason University. <http://climatechangecommunication.org/wp-content/uploads/2017/01/Climate-Change-American-Mind-November-2016.pdf> Accessed 14.02.17.

Leviston, Z., Price, J., & Bishop, B. (2014). Imagining climate change: The role of implicit associations and affective psychological distancing in climate change responses. *European Journal of Social Psychology, 44*(5), 441−454.

Lewandowsky, S., Ballard, T., Oberauer, K., & Benestad, R. E. (2016). A blind expert test of contrarian claims about climate data. *Global Environmental Change, 39,* 91−97.

Lorenzoni, I., Leiserowitz, A., de Franca Doria, M., Poortinga, W., & Pidgeon, N. F. (2006). Cross-national comparisons of image associations with "Global Warming" and "Climate Change" among laypeople in the United States of America and Great Britain. *Journal of Risk Research*, *9*(3), 265–281.

Lorenzoni, I., Nicholson-Cole, S., & Whitmarsh, L. (2007). Barriers perceived to engaging with climate change among the UK public and their policy implications. *Global Environmental Change*, *17*, 445–459.

Lorenzoni, I., & Pidgeon, N. F. (2006). Public views on climate change: European and USA perspectives. *Climatic Change*, *77*, 73–95.

Maibach, E. W., Leiserowitz, A., Roser-Renouf, C., & Mertz, C. K. (2011). Identifying like-minded audiences for global warming public engagement campaigns: An audience segmentation analysis and tool development. *PLoS ONE*, *6*, e17571.

Markowitz, E., Hodge, C., & Harp, G. (2014). *Connecting on climate: A guide to effective climate change communication*. New York and Washington, DC: Center for Research on Environmental Decisions and EcoAmerica. Available from www.connectingonclimate.org.

McComas, K., & Shanahan, J. (1999). Telling stories about global climate change: Measuring the impact of narratives on issue cycles. *Communication Research*, *26*(1), 30–57.

McCright, A. M., & Dunlap, R. E. (2011). The politicization of climate change and polarization in the American public's views of global warming, 2001–2010. *The Sociological Quarterly*, *52*, 155–194.

Morton, T. A., Rabinovich, A., Marshall, D., & Bretschneider, P. (2011). The future that may (or may not) come: How framing changes responses to uncertainty in climate change communications. *Global Environmental Change*, *21*(1), 103–109.

Moser, S. C., & Dilling, L. (2011). Communicating climate change: Closing the science-action gap. In R. Norgaard, D. Schlosberg, & J. Dryzek (Eds.), *The Oxford handbook of climate change and society*. Oxford: Oxford University Press.

Myers, T. A., Maibach, E. W., Roser-Renouf, C., Akerlof, K., & Leiserowitz, A. A. (2013). The relationship between personal experience and belief in the reality of global warming. *Nature Climate Change*, *3*, 343–347.

Nilsson, A., von Borgstede, C., & Biel, A. (2004). Willingness to accept climate change strategies: The effect of values and norms. *Journal of Environmental Psychology*, *24*(3), 267–277.

Nisbet, M. C., & Myers, T. (2007). The polls—Trends twenty years of public opinion about global warming. *Public Opinion Quarterly*, *71*, 444–470.

O'Neill, S., Boykoff, M., Niermeyer, S., & Day, S. A. (2013). On the use of imagery for climate change engagement. *Global Environmental Change*, *23*, 413–421.

O'Neill, S., & Nicholson-Cole, S. (2009). "Fear won't do it": Promoting positive engagement with climate change through visual and iconic representations. *Science Communication*, *30*, 355–379.

Oreskes, N., & Conway, E. M. (2010). Defeating the merchants of doubt. *Nature*, *465*, 686–687.

Painter, J., & Ashe, T. (2012). Cross-national comparison of the presence of climate scepticism in the print media in six countries, 2007–10. *Environmental Research Letters*, *7*, 044005.

Palm, R., Lewis, G. B., & Feng, B. (2017). What causes people to change their opinion about climate change? *Annals of the American Association of Geographers*, *107*, 883–896.

Perkins S. (2010). Atmospheric science: The cold facts. *Nature Climate Change.* doi:10.1038/nclimate1008.

Peters, H.P., & Heinrichs, H. (2004). Expertise for the public: The science-journalism interface in German discourse on global climate change. In: Public communication of science and technology conference (PCST-8), Barcelona, Spain.

Petty, R. E., & Cacioppo, J. T. (1986). *The elaboration likelihood model of persuasion.* New York: Academic Press.

Pew Center. (2010). *Obama more popular abroad than at home, global image of U.S. continues to benefit: 22-Nation Pew Global Attitudes survey.* <http://pewglobal.org/files/2011/04/Pew-Global-Attitudes-Spring-2010-Report2.pdf> Accessed February 2014.

Pew Center. (2013). *GOP deeply divided over climate change.* <http://www.people-press.org/files/legacy-pdf/11-1-13%20Global%20Warming%20Release.pdf> Accessed April 2014.

Pidgeon, N. (2012). Public understanding of, and attitudes to, climate change: UK and international perspectives and policy. *Climate Policy, 12*(S1), S85–S106.

Poortinga, W., & Darnton, A. (2016). Segmenting for sustainability: The development of a sustainability segmentation model from a Welsh sample. *Journal of Environmental Psychology, 45,* 221–232.

Poortinga, W., & Pidgeon, N. F. (2003). *Public perceptions of risk, science and governance.* Norwich: UEA/MORI.

Poortinga, W., Pidgeon, N.F., Capstick, S., & Aoyagi, M. (2014). *Public attitudes to nuclear power and climate change in Britain two years after the Fukushima accident.* <www.ukerc.ac.uk/support/tiki-download_file.php?fileId = 3514> Accessed April 2014.

Poortinga, W., Spence, A., Whitmarsh, L., Capstick, S., & Pidgeon, N. (2011). Uncertain climate: An investigation into public scepticism about anthropogenic climate change. *Global Environmental Change, 21,* 1015–1024.

Postigo, J. C., Wells, G. B., & Cancino, P. C. (2013). *Social sciences at the crossroads: Global environmental change in Latin America and the Caribbean. Social science capacity in global environmental change research—World social science report 2013: Changing global environments.* Paris: United Nations Educational, Scientific and Cultural Organisation.

Ratter, B. M., Philipp, K. H., & von Storch, H. (2012). Between hype and decline: Recent trends in public perception of climate change. *Environmental Science & Policy, 18,* 3–8.

Reser J.P., Bradley G.L., Ellul M.C. (2014). Encountering climate change: 'Seeing' is more than 'believing'. *Wiley Interdisciplinary Reviews: Climate Change.* doi:10.1002/wcc.286.

Rudman, L. A., McLean, M. C., & Bunzl, M. (2013). When truth is personally inconvenient, attitudes change the impact of extreme weather on implicit support for green politicians and explicit climate-change beliefs. *Psychological Science, 24,* 2290–2296.

Sánchez-Cortés, M. S., & Chavero, E. L. (2011). Indigenous perception of changes in climate variability and its relationship with agriculture in a Zoque community of Chiapas, Mexico. *Climatic Change, 107*(3), 363–389.

Schwartz, M. (2010). *Majority of Americans continue to believe that global warming is real.* <https://woods.stanford.edu/sites/default/files/files/Krosnick-20090312_0.pdf> Accessed February 2014.

Schwartz, S. H. (1994). Are there universal aspects in the structure and contents of human values? *Journal of Social Issues, 50*(4), 19–45.

Shi, J., Visschers, V. H. M., Siegrist, M., & Arvai, J. (2016). Knowledge as a driver of public perceptions about climate change reassessed. *Nature Climate Change*, *6*(8), 759−762.

Smith, J. (2014). Counter-hegemonic networks and the transformation of global climate politics: Rethinking movement-state relations. *Global Discourse*, *4*, 120−138.

Smith, N., & Joffe, H. (2012). How the public engages with global warming: A social representations approach. *Public Understanding of Science*, *22*, 16−32.

Smith, N., & Leiserowitz, A. A. (2012). The rise of global warming skepticism: Exploring affective image associations in the United States over time. *Risk Analysis*, *32*(6), 1021−1032.

Spence, A., Poortinga, W., Butler, C., & Pidgeon, N. F. (2011). Perceptions of climate change and willingness to save energy related to flood experience. *Nature Climate Change*, *1*, 46−49.

Steentjes, K., Pidgeon, N., Poortinga, W., Corner, A., Arnold, A., Böhm, G., ... Tvinnereim, E. (2017). *European perceptions of climate change: Topline findings of a survey conducted in four European countries in 2016*. Cardiff: Cardiff University.

Steg, L., De Groot, J. I., Dreijerink, L., Abrahamse, W., & Siero, F. (2011). General antecedents of personal norms, policy acceptability, and intentions: The role of values, worldviews, and environmental concern. *Society and Natural Resources*, *24*(4), 349−367.

Steg, L., Dreijerink, L., & Abrahamse, W. (2005). Factors influencing the acceptability of energy policies: A test of VBN theory. *Journal of Environmental Psychology*, *25*(4), 415−425.

Swim, J. K., & Becker, J. C. (2012). Country contexts and individuals' climate change mitigating behaviors: A comparison of US versus German individuals' efforts to reduce energy use. *Journal of Social Issues*, *68*(3), 571−591.

Swim, J. K., & Whitmarsh, L. (2017). Climate change as a unique environmental problem. In L. Steg, A. van den Berg, & J. de Groot (Eds.), *Environmental psychology: An introduction*. Hoboken, New Jersey: Wiley-Blackwell.

Transatlantic Trends. (2007). Key findings 2007. <http://trends.gmfus.org/files/archived/doc/2007_english_key.pdf> Accessed February 2014.

Trumbo, C. W. (1996). Constructing climate change: Claims and frames in US news coverage of an environmental issue. *Public Understanding of Science*, *5*, 269−283.

Tvinnereim, E., & Fløttum, K. (2015). Explaining topic prevalence in answers to open-ended survey questions about climate change. *Nature Climate Change*, *5*(8), 744−747.

Tvinnereim, E., Liu, X., & Jamelske, E. M. (2017). Public perceptions of air pollution and climate change: Different manifestations, similar causes, and concerns. *Climatic Change*, *140*, 399−412.

Ungar, S. (2000). Knowledge, ignorance and the popular culture: Climate change versus the ozone hole. *Public Understanding of Science*, *9*, 297−312.

Upham, P., Whitmarsh, L., Poortinga, W., Purdam, K., Darnton, A., McLachlan, C., & Devine-Wright, P. (2009). *Public attitudes to environmental change: A selective review of theory and practice. A research synthesis for the living with environmental change programme*. UK, Swindon: Research Councils. Available from www.lwec.org.uk.

Washington Post. (2017). *Post-ABC poll: Nearly 6 in 10 oppose Trump scrapping Paris agreement*. <https://www.washingtonpost.com/news/energy-environment/wp/2017/06/05/post-abc-poll-nearly-6-in-10-oppose-trump-scrapping-paris-agreement/?utm_term = .ae46af13695a> Accessed 07.06.17.

Whitmarsh, L. (2008). Are flood victims more concerned about climate change than other people? The role of direct experience in risk perception and behavioural response. *Journal of Risk Research*, *11*, 351−374.

Whitmarsh, L. (2009). What's in a name? Commonalities and differences in public understanding of 'climate change' and 'global warming'. *Public Understanding of Science, 18*, 401−420.

Whitmarsh, L. (2011). Scepticism and uncertainty about climate change: Dimensions, determinants and change over time. *Global Environmental Change, 21*, 690−700.

Whitmarsh, L., & Corner, A. (2017). Tools for a new climate conversation: A mixed-methods study of language for public engagement across the political spectrum. *Global Environmental Change, 42*, 122−135.

Whitmarsh, L., Seyfang, G., & O'Neill, S. (2011). Public engagement with carbon and climate change: To what extent is the public 'carbon capable'? *Global Environmental Change, 21*, 56−65.

Wolf, J., & Moser, S. C. (2011). Individual understandings, perceptions, and engagement with climate change: Insights from in-depth studies across the world. *Wiley Interdisciplinary Reviews: Climate Change, 2*(4), 547−569.

Xue, W., Hine, D. W., Marks, A. D., Phillips, W. J., & Zhao, S. (2015). Cultural worldviews and climate change: A view from China. *Asian Journal of Social Psychology, 19*(2), 134−144.

Zaval, L., Keenan, E. A., Johnson, E. J., & Weber, E. U. (2014). How warm days increase belief in global warming. *Nature Climate Change, 4*, 143−147.

Climate change communication: Challenges, insights, and opportunities

3

Ezra M. Markowitz and Meaghan L. Guckian
University of Massachusetts Amherst, Amherst, MA, United States

3.1 Introduction

Despite the widely lauded, landmark Paris Agreement reached by the planet's nations in 2015, serious questions and doubts about the international community's ability to act in concert on climate change remain. The populist and largely isolationist political uprisings of 2016 (e.g., U.S. presidential election, "Brexit" in the United Kingdom) in particular highlight the continued challenges we collectively face in effectively confronting this challenging collective action problem. Although not accepted or identified universally as a key driver of these challenges, many scientists, policymakers, issue advocates, and others point to relatively weak public engagement with the issue as a core barrier to intra- and international action on climate change (e.g., Hulme, 2009; Weber & Stern, 2011). In the United States in particular, much attention has been paid to citizens' attitudes, beliefs, knowledge, and preferences (political and behavioral) about the issue (e.g., Kahan et al., 2012; Leiserowitz, 2006; Whitmarsh, 2011). Hundreds of public opinion polls and surveys have consistently revealed significant heterogeneity amongst Americans with respect to nearly every aspect of their engagement (e.g., cognitive, affective, behavioral) with climate change (e.g., Leiserowitz, Maibach, Roser-Renouf, Feinberg, & Rosenthal, 2016; Pew Research Center, 2016); this heterogeneity stands in stark contrast to the strong consensus that exists amongst scientists who study climate change and are intimately familiar with what is currently known to science about the phenomenon (see Cook et al., 2016; Pew Research Center, 2015).

Although issue advocates, academics, and others have called for a variety of responses to address the observed heterogeneity of public engagement with climate change, perhaps none has received as enthusiastic an embrace as the call for "better communication" of the issue. As Susanne Moser and others have detailed (e.g., McCright & Dunlap, 2010; Moser, 2010), efforts to engage the public on the issue of climate change through communication, often but not always with the aim of increasing support for ameliorative action, have a long history, reaching back at least three decades (e.g., James Hansen's congressional testimony in 1988; McKibben, 1989).

For the purposes of the present chapter, *climate change communication* (CCC) refers to any effort—explicit or otherwise—that aims to raise public awareness,

Psychology and Climate Change. DOI: https://doi.org/10.1016/B978-0-12-813130-5.00003-5

understanding, and/or active engagement with the issue (Moser, 2010). Such a broad definition of CCC is necessary because so many approaches to communicating with the public on this issue have been developed and implemented by a diverse array of communicators. These include "traditional" advertising campaigns (e.g., Environmental Defense Fund's "Train" ad) and one-off pieces of communication (e.g., Al Gore's *Inconvenient Truth*, Showtime's *Years of Living Dangerously*) as well as more participatory formal and informal activities and events (e.g., town meetings, future visioning and scenario planning exercises, public art installations). Of course, the everyday conversations we all have with family, friends, and acquaintances about climate change, rare as they may be (e.g., Geiger & Swim, 2016), represent another critically important, if informal, form of CCC (Leiserowitz, Maibach, Roser-Renouf, Rosenthal, & Cutler, 2017; Moser, 2010).

As concern over climate change has increased in recent years amongst many scientists, business owners, resource managers, and policymakers, the public's level of concern has stayed relatively stable or increased only slightly over the past decades according to reports by Gallup (Saad, 2017), Yale Program on Climate Change Communication (Leiserowitz et al., 2017), and the Pew Research Center (2015). This growing disconnect (Pew Research Center, 2015) has in turn driven interest in finding ways to make the issue more salient and pressing to a broader swath of the public. To many, this apparently stubborn gap highlights the shortcomings of many past and existing efforts to communicate the severity and pressing nature of the issue (e.g., CRED & ecoAmerica, 2014; but see McCright & Dunlap, 2010 for an alternative account). In an effort to better understand the shortcomings of extant CCC efforts, and in some cases to provide evidence-based suggestions for improvement, social scientists from a variety of disciplines including psychology, communications, political science, and sociology began studying how individuals respond to various types and forms of CCC (e.g., Cook, in press; O'Neill & Nicholson-Cole, 2009; Spence & Pidgeon, 2010; Sterman, 2008; Whitmarsh, 2009). Over the past 5−10 years, this multidisciplinary field of study has exploded (see Fig. 3.1), providing the evidence base for more considered and perhaps effective efforts at communicating this issue to the public. Multiple attempts to integrate these disparate findings into concrete recommendations for communicators "on the ground" now exist (e.g., Climate Outreach, 2015; Corner & Clarke, 2017; CRED & ecoAmerica, 2014; Moser, 2010; Taylor, 2012).

One of the most consistent and clear findings of this work is that disagreements about climate change (e.g., whether it is anthropogenic, whether it is a serious problem, whether we should take costly action to combat it) are very infrequent disagreements *over "the facts"* (Kahan et al., 2012). Instead, at their core, disagreements about climate change are fundamentally tied to the *implications the issue holds for society and the way it is organized,* including how we produce, use, and pay for energy and other resources (Hulme, 2009; Kahan, 2015). The implications of this core finding for increasing the effectiveness of CCC efforts are both profound and simple: throwing more and more facts about the problem at people is extremely unlikely to shift minds and hearts in any appreciable way.

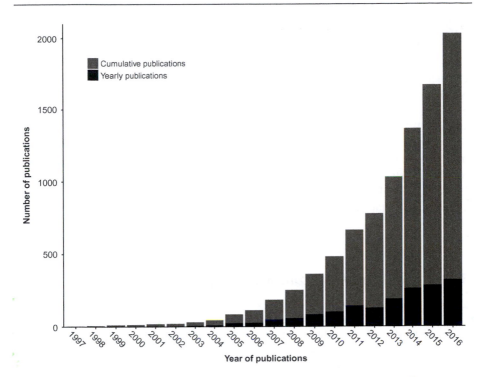

Figure 3.1 A Web of Science search was conducted to examine the growth of climate science communication research from 1997 to 2016. A topical search using the abridged search terms, climat* NEAR chang* AND communicat* allowed for broader inclusion of relevant articles (e.g., compared to title or keyword searches), as well as the inclusion of variations in the targeted search terms (e.g., communication versus communicating, etc.). Initial search returned $N = 3621$ entries; however, after manually screening for unrelated material (e.g., changes in business climates), as well as entries suggesting proscriptive communication needs, $N = 1709$ entries remained. Given the limitations of Web of Science and the search criteria, the above figure should be viewed as a conservative estimate characterizing growth in the field over the past two decades.

Indeed, as described in more detail below, this sort of deficit-model-based approach—one that assumes a lack of factual knowledge is the key barrier to greater issue engagement—may not only be ineffective, it may actually be detrimental to improving public engagement by causing counterproductive backfire effects (Cook, in press). This is particularly likely to happen among antagonistic and skeptical audiences (e.g., Hart & Nisbet, 2012). Instead, communicators need to develop new approaches to CCC that incorporate what we now know about the psychological and social factors that shape individuals' engagement with this issue (for a review, see Gifford, 2011; Swim et al., 2009). This means first understanding why climate change is in fact a very challenging issue to communicate about before incorporating evidence-supported best practices into CCC efforts.

3.2 Why is climate change communication so challenging?

Climate change is a uniquely challenging issue from a science communication and public engagement perspective; indeed, we might refer to it as a "perfect communications storm," much as Gardiner (2011) has referred to it as a "perfect moral storm." Why? Because it poses challenges on multiple fronts, from its inherent abstractness and complexity to the myriad social and psychological defense mechanisms it activates to the fact that its slow-moving nature makes it a challenge for journalists and media outlets to cover on a regular basis (Boykoff, 2011; Boykoff & Boykoff, 2007). Understanding these and other various challenges provides a useful starting point for those interested in developing more effective forms of CCC.

3.2.1 Challenge 1: The problem itself

Climate change is, as many advocates and communicators have long bemoaned, a slow-moving, long-term, complex, abstract phenomenon (IPCC, 2014). It is not an "in-your-face" type of problem (Gardiner, 2011): its impacts are diffuse and largely expected to occur in the future; relatively few people are directly impacted by its effects currently; attributing specific negative outcomes to climate change is challenging; it is largely a side-effect of normal, daily behavior, not intentionally caused; and it lacks many of the typical features that support engagement with and attention toward other societal risks, including obvious culprits, personally known victims, and a sense of urgency (Markowitz & Shariff, 2012). It is, in a word, deeply un-relatable at the personal level for most individuals (e.g., Spence, Poortinga, & Pidgeon, 2012).

These features of the phenomenon pose additional challenges from a communications and public engagement perspective. For example, it has been argued that media outlets' and journalists' financial incentives and institutional norms have in the past encouraged exaggeration of uncertainties that exist as well as the production of false narratives of equivalence between climate scientists and skeptics (Boykoff & Boykoff, 2007). There are also many other issues begging for the limited attention of the public. It does not grab front-page attention on a regular basis. Indeed, news coverage of climate change has been declining for the past decade (Nacu-Schmidt et al., 2016). In general, it is perceived as a low-importance issue relative to nearly all other challenges facing society, from economic development to global political instability to public health to most other environmental problems (Pew Research Center, 2014; Riffkin, 2014). Moreover, it is a challenging issue to keep people interested in over time, in part because the pace of change and new developments is quite slow compared to the time scales of days, weeks, months, and possibly a few years that people are used to thinking in. Thus, the "physical" features of the phenomenon itself pose significant challenges to communicators in terms of both capturing people's attention and keeping it long enough to truly engage them with the issue.

3.2.2 Challenge 2: Cultural conflict and polarization

Because climate change *is not* an immediately obvious and directly experienced phenomenon, people's understandings of and beliefs about the issue are largely mediated through the various messages and messengers they are most often exposed to (and their interpretations of those messages, see *Challenge 3*). Combined with extreme levels of elite polarization regarding climate change (Brulle, Carmichael, & Jenkins, 2012; Dunlap, McCright, & Yarosh, 2016) and deeply partisan media exposure patterns (Feldman, Myers, Hmielowski, & Leiserowitz, 2014; Jasny, Waggle, & Fisher, 2015; Williams, McMurray, Kurz, & Lambert, 2015), this basic fact goes a long way toward explaining how climate change has come to be the single most politically polarizing issue among American adults (Pew Research Center, 2016). Indeed, in terms of issue concern and engagement, the gap between Republicans and Democrats on climate change is as large or larger than it is for any other issues (see Pew Research Center, 2016).

This remarkable level of polarization highlights what may be the single most challenging, and stubborn, barrier to effective CCC, namely, the deep cultural conflict that exists around this issue. Climate change has become infused with deeply antagonistic political and group-identity meanings, such that "beliefs" about the issue have, some argue, essentially become proxies for political group membership and identity: what it means to be a "good" Republican is to be skeptical about the reality and urgency of climate change, whereas what it means to be a "good" Democrat is to see climate change as an existential threat in need of large-scale societal response (Kahan, 2015). These meanings have attached to the issue due to a number of interconnected factors: the implications the issue holds for the global economy; intentional efforts by vested interests to create uncertainty and division (Oreskes & Conway, 2011); and, well-meaning but counter-productive communications efforts by issue advocates over the past two decades (Nisbet, 2009). As a result, communicators' decisions about how to frame the issue, which audiences to engage, which messengers to employ, and which outcomes to target (e.g., attitude change, behavior, policy support) are fraught, to say the least.

The presence of this cultural divide on climate change strongly suggests that a one-size-fits-all approach to communication is extremely unlikely to work (CRED & ecoAmerica, 2014; ecoAmerica, 2016a). This in turn highlights the need for tailored communications efforts (Bolsen & Shapiro, in press), which are easy to call for in theory but challenging to implement in practice, for example, due to challenges involved in identifying appropriate audiences and cross-contamination of messages and channels (see Hine, Phillips, Driver, & Morrison, in press). Yet it is also clear that ignoring the cultural and group-identity underpinnings of disagreement over climate change is not an option for communicators interested in meaningfully engaging audiences (Feygina, Jost, & Goldsmith, 2010; Kahan, 2015).

3.2.3   Challenge 3: Psychological barriers to engagement and communication

Making matters worse, many of these challenging features of the problem itself (e.g., complexity, uncertainty, abstractness, political polarization) interact with the ways in which people's minds operate to further depress issue engagement and create even more barriers for communicators (Gifford, 2011; Markowitz & Shariff, 2012). For example, a number of recent studies suggest that persistent scientific uncertainties regarding climate change (e.g., timing and severity of impacts) can work to undermine people's issue engagement (Budescu, Por, & Broomell, 2012; Ho, Budescu, & Pu, in press; Joslyn & LeClerc, 2016), in part by activating cognitive mechanisms that promote wait-and-see attitudes (Sterman, 2008) and/or unrealistic optimism about future outcomes (Markowitz & Shariff, 2012). This suggests that communicators face significant challenges in deciding how to talk about what is known and what remains uncertain regarding climate change impacts; these problems are amplified by pervasive, and successful, efforts by certain organizations and vested interests to make the science around climate appear more uncertain than it in fact is (Dunlap & McCright, 2010; Oreskes & Conway, 2011).

As described in detail elsewhere (see Bolsen & Shapiro, in press; Gifford, 2011; Stoknes, 2015; Swim et al., 2009; Swim, Markowitz, & Bloodhart, 2012; Whitmarsh, 2009), a variety of basic, and primarily unconscious, psychological processes that powerfully shape everything from how people search for and process information, to the development of attitudes and risk perceptions, to how people ultimately make decisions, often work against the rapid and unbiased uptake of information and messages about climate change. For example, much research has revealed that people not only seek out information about climate change that reinforces their preexisting beliefs (e.g., Feldman et al., 2014), but also that they interpret new information they are exposed to in ways that promote polarization and attitude crystallization (e.g., Hart & Nisbet, 2012; Hart, Feldman, Leiserowitz, & Maibach, 2015; Kahan et al., 2012; Nyhan & Reifler, 2010). People tend to be more critical of and willing to counter-argue evidence they encounter that challenges their existing beliefs but are much less critical of supportive evidence (e.g., Lord, Ross, & Lepper, 1979). These unconscious biases pose a major challenge to communicators given the potent combination that currently exists in the United States of a fractured, politicized media landscape, and the deeply ingrained elite political polarization around climate change discussed above (McCright & Dunlap, 2011; Pew Research Center, 2016).

Work by Kahan, Braman, Gastil, Slovic, and Mertz (2007a) and Kunda (1990) on "identity-protective cognition" provides one plausible mechanism by which partisan differences in issue engagement, and hence receptivity to communication efforts, become entrenched and reinforced over time. According to Kahan, Braman, Slovic, Gastil, and Cohen (2007b), Kahan et al. (2012) and Kahan (2015), individuals are strongly motivated to form perceptions of risks, including those related to climate change, that support their overarching sense of who they are, that is, that reinforce their identity. Because our identities are closely tied to our social groups and preferences for how society is organized, a motivation to protect one's identity can result in different groups of people coming to see particular risks or issues, e.g., climate change, in highly divergent ways. However, understanding the role that "identity-protective cognition" may play in this domain also points the way toward possible "antidotes" to such polarization, as described in more detail below.

In addition to these directional or "motivated" psychological barriers to CCC, communicators face other cognitive and affective (emotional) challenges as well. For example, low issue salience and lack of direct, personal experience mean that climate change is simply not a top-of-mind issue for the vast majority of Americans, as described above; as such, simply getting people to pay attention to communications efforts is challenging. In addition, Lertzman (2015) and others have argued that when people *do* start paying attention to issue advocates, the problem can rapidly come to be perceived as overwhelming. In turn, this can lead people to emotionally and cognitively shut down and, in some cases, actively avoid learning more about the issue (see also Norgaard, 2011; Ungar, 2000). Thus, communicators also face a major hurdle in finding ways to engage audiences that simultaneously highlight the salience of the issue and need for immediate action while *not* making the situation appear hopeless (Feinberg & Willer, 2011). Work by O'Neill and Nicholson-Cole (2009) and O'Neill, Boykoff, Niemeyer, and Day (2013) suggests that such messages, including those that use visual imagery, are hard to come by (see also Chapman, Corner, Webster, & Markowitz, 2016). Indeed, much work in the risk communication literature across multiple domains highlights the critical need for communicators to support feelings of efficacy when discussing personally threatening issues (Hart & Feldman, 2016; Hornsey et al., 2015; Milfont, 2012; Witte & Allen, 2000), something not easily done in the context of climate change. This is particularly true in the current political climate.

3.3 Improving climate change communication efforts

In the face of so many varied, intertwined, and synergistic challenges to effectively engaging with nonexperts on the issue of climate change, many would be forgiven for giving up in despair. Yet a rapidly growing, multidisciplinary body of research and practice suggests that more effective approaches to climate communication *are* possible; indeed, scholars and practitioners are engaged in a wide variety of innovative efforts to effectively communicate about climate change (e.g., ecoAmerica's Let's Talk series, 2016b; Shaw et al., 2009; Southeast Climate Compact, n.d.). Many are finally moving beyond deficit model-based approaches (Ockwell, Whitmarsh, & O'Neil, 2009; Wibeck, 2014) and embracing the insights produced over the past decade by psychological, communications, public engagement, and other scholars on the ways in which individuals (dis)engage with this issue to improve communications efforts on the ground. Here we describe seven key considerations drawn from this growing and rapidly evolving evidence base (Table 3.1).

Table 3.1 **Seven insights to improve climate change communication**

Know what motivates the audience. Identify and understand how values, identities,
  worldviews, etc. differentially shape audiences' engagement with climate change and
  tailor communication efforts to their needs
Figure out what the audience already knows. Start where people are at: preexisting
  beliefs and experiences with climate change and climate-related events shape how
  individuals interpret and filter new information
Confront false information, do not reinforce it. Dislodge false beliefs with simple,
  factual alternatives, and leverage preemptive warning messages to prevent the uptake of
  misinformation
Find frames that "fit" audiences' needs. Package and connect climate change
  information to the needs and values that matter to your audiences (e.g., public health,
  responsibility, local impacts)
Highlight solutions. Encourage engagement and build individuals' feelings of efficacy
  and hopefulness by focusing on solutions
Tell stories. Use coherent narrative forms and include story elements such as characters
  and problem resolution to make messages more compelling and relatable
Leverage the right messengers and communication channels. Identify and work with
  existing social networks, communication channels, and trusted "in-group" messengers

3.3.1 Insight 1: Know what motivates the audience

A key tenet of persuasive communication—perhaps the most important one—is to
"know one's audience" (CRED & ecoAmerica, 2014). After all, how can one know
what pieces of information or ways of framing that information will be persuasive
or even how best to get the attention of the audience (e.g., through which channels)
without first knowing something about those individuals: what motivates them,
what they value, what their constraints and barriers are to greater issue engagement,
and, who they listen to and respect. One implication of attempting to address these
questions is that a "one-size-fits-all" approach to CCC is extremely unlikely to produce significant *positive* outcomes (see, e.g., Hart & Nisbet, 2012). In part, this is
due to the deeply antagonistic cultural meanings now attached to climate change
(see discussion of *Challenge 2*; also, Feygina et al., 2010; Kahan et al., 2012) and
in part to the simple fact that different people are motivated by different core
values, concerns, and needs (Rokeach, 1973). For example, individuals who are
strongly motivated by self-enhancement values are unlikely to respond positively to
exhortations to "sacrifice for the well-being of future generations." Conversely,
communication efforts that highlight the personal economic benefits of taking
action on climate change (e.g., reducing one's monthly energy bill) may actually
inhibit greater engagement among individuals who see this as a fundamentally
moral issue (Asensio & Delmas, 2015,2016). Thus, it has become readily apparent
that communicators need to tailor messages and outreach efforts to fit particular
audiences' needs and characteristics (Bostrom, Böhm, & O'Connor, 2013; Hine
et al., in press; Perkowitz, Speiser, Harp, Hodge, & Krygsman, 2014).

The first step in tailoring communication involves identifying subgroups within a population who share core values, motives, beliefs, and existing mental models, an approach often referred to as "audience segmentation" (Hine et al., 2014). Although still in its infancy, the use of audience segmentation tools to support CCC efforts is growing (Hine et al., 2016; Maibach, Roser-Renouf, & Leiserowitz, 2008, 2009; Perkowitz et al., 2014). In some ways, the concept is simple: people who share common beliefs, values, and motives should be more likely to respond consistently and predictably to particular ways of communicating about climate change. Thus, communicators should use existing tools often used by social marketers, psychologists, and others (e.g., latent class analysis, McCutcheon, 1987) to identify coherent subgroups within the larger public, opening up the possibility of developing communications messages and strategies that speak directly to those groups' core interests and concerns (Hines et al., 2014; Maibach, Leiserowitz, Roser-Renouf, & Mertz, 2011).

The most widely recognized and cited effort to do this in the climate change domain is the *Six Americas* project (Leiserowitz, Maibach, Roser-Renouf, Feinberg, & Howe, 2013; Maibach et al. 2009), which groups people into six distinct groups (e.g., "Alarmed," "Dismissive," "Disengaged") based on their existing beliefs and concerns about climate change, e.g., is it happening, is it a risk, is it human caused. Other researchers have similarly used climate change-specific beliefs and attitudes as the basis for categorizing individuals into groups that may respond differentially to various ways of framing the issue (e.g., Korkala, Hugg, & Jaakkola, 2014; Metag, Füchslinu, & Schäfer, 2015; Sibley & Kurz, 2013). However, such domain-specific, beliefs-based approaches to audience segmentation may not provide sufficient insight into the core motives and values of the different subgroups that have been identified (e.g., Corner, Whitmarsh, & Xenias, 2012), inhibiting the usefulness of such approaches in actually informing on-the-ground communication efforts. Instead, some researchers and practitioners have begun combining such issue-specific methods with a more traditional values-oriented, "psychographic" segmentation approach to identify subgroups that may respond in distinct ways to CCC efforts (e.g., Hine et al., 2016; Perkowitz et al., 2014; Poortinga & Darnton, 2016).

For communicators, the benefit of these approaches is that they can provide both deeper and broader insight into the values, motives, and cross-cutting concerns that communication approaches can tap into when developing messaging and engagement strategies (Hine et al., 2014; Whitmarsh, Lorenzoni, & O'Neill, 2012). For example, Hine et al. (2016) found that whereas certain messages engaged both dismissive and alarmed audiences, e.g., giving adaptation-specific advice, other messages increased engagement only amongst dismissive individuals, e.g., emphasizing local impacts (see also Bain, Hornsey, Bongiorno, & Jeffries, 2012; Benjamin, Por, & Budescu, 2016; Myers, Nisbet, Maibach, & Leiserowitz, 2012). Bain et al. (2012) similarly found that avoiding explicit mention of climate change and instead focusing on the societal, economic, or technological benefits of proenvironmental behavior increased climate-friendly action amongst dismissive individuals. And work by ecoAmerica (Perkowitz et al., 2014) has attempted to apply "psychographic" methods commonly used in marketing efforts to similarly help communicators better understand how different segments of the population are likely to respond to various ways of framing climate change, e.g., as an economic opportunity versus a public health threat versus a personal responsibility. For example, they find that "achievers"—relatively high-resource, self- and family-focused individuals who often act as opinion leaders in their communities ("VALS" project; Strategic Business Insights, n.d.)—tend to be only moderately concerned about climate change and likely to be most strongly motivated by family- and responsibility-oriented concerns. Thus, appeals or messages that highlight how climate change may threaten families' well-being and security may productively engage that group.

3.3.2 Insight 2: Figure out what audiences already know

Why does it matter that communicators know their audiences well? Because people interpret and filter new information about climate change through their preexisting beliefs (e.g., mental models) and values (Kahan et al., 2007a,b; Kaplan & Kaplan, 2009; Morgan, Fischoff, Bostrom, & Atman, 2001). Thus, the same message or piece of information may, and likely will, be interpreted in very different ways by individuals who hold opposing worldviews or who hold very different understandings of how the climate system operates. This extends even to people's own personal experiences with climate-related events (e.g., extreme weather events). Recent work suggests that how people understand and interpret such experiences with respect to climate change, whether they connect them to the larger issue or not, differs depending on their political identity (Deryugina, 2013; Egan & Mullin, 2012; Hamilton & Stampone, 2013). These findings, in turn, suggest that the recent trend amongst some scientists, advocates, and journalists toward connecting particular extreme events with climate change in the hope of increasing issue salience (e.g., Trenberth, Fasullo, & Shepherd, 2015) may actually backfire amongst skeptical individuals and groups (e.g., Chapman & Lickel, 2016). An alternative but related approach—highlighting how individuals and communities can prepare for the *next* major event—may be more likely to successfully engage a wider audience by circumventing problematic ideological entanglements, although this remains to be seen.

Knowing what people already believe about climate change can also improve communication efforts by helping communicators identify easily understood words and concepts, correct for common misconceptions, and build appropriate mental models where they are lacking (de Bruin & Bostrom, 2013). For example, recent research suggests that mental models and beliefs about the stability of the climate system and scientific consensus regarding climate change can work to dampen public support for ameliorative action (Cutler, Leiserowitz, & Rosenthal, 2017; Lewandowsky, Gignac, & Vaughan, 2013). Similarly, earlier work by Sterman and Sweeney (2007) showed how individuals' faulty reasoning about stock-and-flow systems, such as the climate system, can lead to preferences for a problematic wait-and-see approach to dealing with the problem. Together these findings suggest that communications efforts aimed at correcting such foundational beliefs and understandings of the climate system (e.g., "consensus messaging"; for a recent review see Cook, in press) could enhance certain audiences' motivation to take ameliorative action sooner rather than later (e.g., Lewandowsky et al., 2013). However, caution is warranted in using such messaging approaches, as recent work suggests that such messages may actually reinforce political polarization amongst highly knowledgeable individuals by increasing skepticism amongst highly educated conservatives (Cook & Lewandowsky, 2016), even as they increase positive engagement amongst liberals.

3.3.3 Insight 3: Confront false information, do not reinforce it

The prevalence and persistence of climate change myths and misinformation, such as the incorrect belief that there is a *lack* of scientific consensus, is problematic because such misinformation can interfere with the communication of accurate scientific information. In contrast to pure ignorance or knowledge deficits, the consequences of audiences relying on such engrained misinformation are even more troublesome because these beliefs are often held strongly (Leiserowitz, Maibach, Roser-Renouf, & Hmielowski, 2011) and may contribute to faulty decision-making that runs counter to society's and individuals' best interests. Thus, finding ways to neutralize misinformation is necessary; however, retracting myths or misinformation that has been embedded in individuals' minds is notoriously difficult. In part, this is due to the cognitive mechanisms that deter individuals from relinquishing steadfast convictions, processing unfamiliar or counter-attitudinal information, and ultimately updating beliefs when new evidence is encountered (for a review, see Lewandowsky, Ecker, Seifert, Schwarz, & Cook, 2012).

Simple retractions generally fail to dislodge false beliefs (e.g., Ecker, Lewandowsky, Swire, & Chang, 2011) and in some instances can even backfire or reinforce them (e.g., see Nyhan & Reifler, 2010; Lewandowsky et al., 2012). For example, our initial perceptions of others continue to affect our judgments of them even when we subsequently learn that the original information we had about them was incorrect (e.g., Ecker, Lewandowsky, Fenton, & Martin, 2014). One reason for this failure includes individuals' proclivity for messages that are consistent with their preexisting beliefs and that generally just "feel right"; thus, inconsistent information tends to be rejected (Schwarz, Sanna, Skurnik, & Yoon, 2007; Winkielman, Huber, Kavanagh, & Schwarz, 2012). Furthermore, rudimentary attempts to extricate misinformation may create gaps in the mental models that people have built and rely on; failing to fill the void may ultimately result in individuals falling back on faulty information (Ecker, Lewandowsky, & Tang, 2010; Lewandowsky et al., 2012).

Fortunately, recent research has identified specific strategies that communicators can use when correcting or debunking false beliefs. Two methods have shown promise: repeating retractions and filling the gaps created by the retracted misinformation with a factual alternative. Using multiple, repeated retractions can alleviate, if not eliminate, the effect of encoded misinformation by strengthening the efficacy of the retraction (Ecker et al., 2011; Lewandowsky et al., 2012). However, the extent of this effect is undermined by the persistence and strength of the initial misinformation encoding compared to subsequent retractions (Ecker et al., 2011). More promising in reducing the continued influence of misinformation is to fill the gap created by the retraction with a factual alternative (Johnson & Seifert, 1994). For the factual alternative to be successful it must be plausible, accurately account for causation (Seifert, 2002), be simple, sticky (compelling), and memorable (Heath & Heath, 2007), and ideally, both explain the origin and motivation behind the misinformation (Lewandowsky et al., 2012). For example, when debunking common climate myths, such as the *lack* of scientific consensus, communicators should lead with compelling third-party studies demonstrating 97% consensus and then warn about and refute the myth's line of argument (e.g., false signatories of the Oregon Petition; Cook & Lewandowsky, 2011). To avoid unintentional backfire effects, communicators should also seek to affirm rather than attack individuals' identities as well as foster skepticism about misinformation sources and intentions and use simple, brief rebuttals (Lewandowsky et al., 2012).

Even better than working to debunk existing false beliefs and misinformation is protecting people against their formation in the first place. This approach involves providing individuals with preemptive warning messages about why and how misinformation is presented in an effort to better equip people to recognize and dismiss false arguments (Compton, 2013; Lewandowsky et al., 2012). Recent research suggests that such "prebunking," sometimes also referred to as "inoculation," strategies can work to decrease the uptake of false information through a variety of mechanisms, including by decreasing the perceived trustworthiness of such information sources and their motivations (Cook, in press; Lewandowsky et al., 2012). To be most effective, prebunking messages should both explicitly warn individuals of the threat of misinformation as well as explain the techniques used in establishing those arguments (e.g., see Bolsen & Druckman, 2015). In the context of climate change-related misinformation, prebunking strategies have been found to neutralize misinformation when drawing attention to the flaws of the argument and/or pointing to actual scientific consensus (Cook, Lewandowsky, & Ecker, 2017). While empirical investigations into the inoculation effect are ongoing, others have extended these insights into practical interventions, including a video-based Massive Open Online Course (MOOC) titled, *Making Sense of Climate Science Denial* (Cook et al., 2015). However, it remains to be seen whether such techniques actually work in real-world settings, in which individuals are "exposed" to counter-messages continually; similarly, the necessary "dose" of correcting information is currently unknown and potentially quite challenging to "administer" in a competitive media landscape.

3.3.4   Insight 4: Find frames that "fit" audiences' needs

Knowing one's audience also provides the foundation for developing communications strategies and materials (e.g., messages) that "speak to" or leverage an audience's particular needs, values, mental models, etc. Issue "framing" is the most widely used approach to do just that, particularly in the climate change domain. Framing refers to the strategic use of specific words, images, and concepts (including metaphors) in an effort to increase the salience of certain aspects of an issue or problem and shape how individuals think about it (Druckman, 2001). Moser (2010) writes, "frames construct a problem, provide a perspective from which to interpret it ... and deeply influence how persuasive we find the information being communicated" (p. 39). Any complex issue, including climate change, can be framed in a multitude of ways. Nisbet (2009) and Nisbet and Mooney (2007) provide an overview of many of the frames most commonly associated with climate change, including morality (e.g., stewardship as obligation), conflict (e.g., fighting a "war" against climate change), and economic development (e.g., "green jobs").

Of particular relevance to framing CCC is the consideration of different aspects of the outcome (e.g., gains versus losses), which highlight the potential negative or positive consequences of inaction or action. Much of the communication on climate change to date has focused on the dire and dangerous implications of inaction, e.g., habitat degradation, sea level rise. Conversely, opponents of climate change and mitigation policies often refer to and highlight the *benefits* of living in a warmer world (Malone, 2009). Building on Kahneman and Tversky's (1979) classic work demonstrating individuals' aversion to losses, researchers have begun to explore how such gain and loss frames operate within the context of climate communication and engagement, in particular when coupled with messages of distance and uncertainty (Morton, Rabinovich, Marshall, & Bretschneider, 2011; Scannell & Gifford, 2013; Spence & Pidgeon, 2010). These studies tend to suggest that positive, localizing frames are more likely to support and build motivation to take action, although these effects are moderated by a number of other factors (e.g., discussion of uncertainty, audience characteristics).

A large body of research has emerged over the past decade that explores how issue framing and audience-message "fit" work to either support or inhibit productive issue engagement amongst various subgroups and audiences (see Bolsen & Shapiro, in press for a recent in-depth review). Highly influential work by Kahan et al. (e.g., Bliuc et al., 2015; Kahan et al., 2007a,b, 2012; Kahan, 2013) reveals that individuals' core values and social identities powerfully shape how information about climate change is interpreted and either accepted or rejected as valid. This is particularly true with respect to political identity, which has repeatedly been shown to moderate the effects of various climate change frames and engagement with the issue (e.g., Hart & Nisbet, 2012; McCright, Charters, Dentzman, & Dietz, 2016; Unsworth & Fielding, 2014). For example, Hart and Nisbet (2012) found that a message about the health impacts of climate change *increased* political polarization amongst their study participants when the victims of climate impacts were framed as socially distant (e.g., from another country), specifically by causing a boomerang effect among Republicans. On the other hand, studies such as the Bain et al. (2012) work discussed above highlight more productive ways of framing proclimate action, e.g., as supportive of economic and technological development, particularly when engaging with conservative audiences. For communicators, the critical takeaway is the need to identify possible frames for particular audiences and then test them thoroughly before wider dissemination.

3.3.5   Insight 5: Highlight solutions

Much of the existing work on framing, mental models, and risk communication more broadly (e.g., Witte & Allen, 2000) suggests that effective CCC *requires* a focus on solutions rather than solely highlighting impacts and causes (e.g., CRED & ecoAmerica, 2014). Although this makes intuitive sense, the vast majority of existing climate communication does just the opposite, highlighting the anthropogenic causes of the problem as well as the multitude of diverse and depressing anticipated impacts of unmitigated and continued climate change without a clear focus on what can be done to remedy the situation (see Hart & Feldman, 2014). The problem is that such negative, risk-oriented messaging, while likely aligning well with the motives and concerns of many climate communicators, tends to increase the salience of the issue at the cost of depressing individuals' feelings of efficacy and motivation to take action (e.g., Chapman et al., 2016; O'Neill et al., 2013). Moreover, and more importantly, such impacts-focused messaging leads many individuals and audiences to simply turn off from the issue, if not spiral into unproductive denial or feelings of hopelessness (Feinberg & Willer, 2011; Hulme, 2009). Such problematic messaging is perpetuated by the popular press and media (Painter, 2013), which inconsistently convey threat and efficacy messages while framing climate change impacts and actions (Hart & Feldman, 2014).

In contrast, when communicators highlight solutions, particularly those that align with peoples' values, worldviews, and preferred approaches to dealing with societal issues (see Kahan et al., 2007a,b), audiences are able to envision a positive and desirable future world and remain engaged with the issue. In turn, this can provide a concrete goal for individuals and communities to work toward, building both motivation to take action on the issue *and* a sense of personal and collective efficacy (Lee & Aaker, 2004; Roser-Renouf, Maibach, Leiserowitz, & Zhao, 2014; Witte, 1992).

Moreover, solutions-focused messages and outreach strategies allow individuals to worry about the issue in ways that promote rather than inhibit engagement and, often, to identify cobenefits of taking action sooner rather than later (e.g., improving air quality and public health), further building motivation to engage (Bain et al., 2016; Myers et al., 2012). Indeed, practitioners and communicators alike are engaging in meaningful efforts to generate detailed, coherent visualizations of future climate scenarios embedded with planning solutions at the local scale to increase both collective capacity as well as mitigative and adaptive policy support (Cohen et al., 2012; Shaw et al., 2009; Sheppard, 2012). This is an important and ripe area for future research, as it remains largely unknown exactly which combinations of concern-evoking, impacts-focused messages, and hope-inspiring, positive visions of the future are likely to be most effective.

3.3.6   Insight 6: Tell stories

Tailoring and framing messages and outreach efforts to match the needs, values, and existing beliefs of particular audiences is critically important (Bostrom et al.,

2013) but likely not sufficient to produce engaging, effective pieces of communication. As professional storytellers and masterful communicators know well (oftentimes intuitively), communication efforts are most effective when they *tell engaging stories.* But what constitutes a "story" and how does this look differently than what climate communicators are already doing? After all, many climate change advocates and communicators may feel as if they already are engaged in developing and telling stories.

Bringing together much of the work cited above with scholarship on narrative form and storytelling, Jones and Peterson (in press) suggest five strategies for telling effective stories about climate change. The first is both obvious and yet often overlooked by many climate communicators: use well-known narrative forms (e.g., quest, realistic fiction) and components (characters, plot, setting, conflict) to put communication efforts into story form as opposed to more commonly used forms such as press releases and fact sheets. Second, the specific components of the story, e.g., the problem that needs to be overcome and the context within which characters are acting, should be tailored to match audiences so that the overarching issue becomes more personally relevant and relatable. Third, the characters of the story (e.g., heroes, villains, victims, bystanders) also need to be relatable for audiences; this likely means developing different characters for different audiences. For example, farmers are more likely to be engaged by a story that involves other farmers acting as heroes to solve a problem versus one in which the hero is someone unknown or even disliked. Fourth, stories have a temporal component that causally links characters, plot, and setting and highlights people making progress toward overcoming a risk or challenge. Finally, and closely tied to Insight 5 (*Highlight Solutions*), climate change stories should have a clear point or takeaway linked to possible policy (or other) solutions to the challenge. Many of these suggestions can be seen at work in recent, high production-value climate communication efforts (e.g., Showtime's *Years of Living Dangerously*; Leonardo DiCaprio's *Before the Flood*).

3.3.7 Insight 7: Leverage the right messengers and communications channels

Finally, even the most perfectly framed, audience-tailored message or campaign has little chance of succeeding in engaging people when it (1) does not reach the intended audience and/or (2) is delivered by the wrong messenger. Put another way, effective engagement requires identifying and recruiting trusted messengers (i.e., "in-group" members) and communicating with audiences through the information channels they most often use. Of course, these are not always easy things to do, particularly when the aim is to communicate with disengaged or antagonistic audiences. For example, many outreach efforts rely on recruiting celebrities to serve as spokespersons (e.g., Showtime's *Years of Living Dangerously*; see also Anderson, 2011) and the use of social media and other web-based platforms to disseminate campaigns and messages. Although these approaches may work with certain groups (e.g., highly alarmed Millennials), they are less likely to work with other demographic groups and audiences (e.g., older adults, disengaged audiences); in general, it remains largely unknown, due to a lack of extant research, to what extent celebrities can be successfully used as effective messengers in the context of climate change. In contrast, ongoing efforts by Maibach and colleagues to recruit and train broadcast news meteorologists to integrate climate change-relevant information into the nightly newscast is an example of the type of approach that holds the potential to reach audiences who might otherwise not have much exposure to the issue (Placky et al., 2016; Zhao et al., 2014), both because these individuals have frequent, repeated access to their audiences and because they tend to be highly trusted.

Extant work across a number of disciplines further reinforces the importance of carefully selecting and cultivating messengers who are already trusted by target audiences (Corner et al., 2015; Kahan et al., 2007a,b; Nisbet & Kotcher, 2009), and a number of organizations have begun attempting to put these recommendations into practice (e.g., republicEn, MomentUs, Interfaith Power, & Light). These efforts are particularly important for engaging audiences unlikely to be reached by traditional approaches or whose defense mechanisms may be activated whenever they encounter campaigns or messaging developed and disseminated by mainstream environmental advocacy organizations.

3.4 Moving forward: New approaches and future directions

Although it can be frustrating for issue advocates to hear it, perhaps the clearest takeaway from the existing research is that effective climate communication and engagement requires communicators to truly "get to know" their intended audiences when developing materials and campaigns. Despite rapid growth of research on issue framing and climate change, for example, it remains unclear whether there are certain frames (e.g., public health, responsible management of resources, protection of future generations) that consistently improve public engagement with the issue, particularly when looking across audiences (Bolsen & Shapiro, in press). In part, this may be due to the fact that the broader communication and cultural environment into which climate communication efforts are being injected is constantly changing (witness, for example, the political turmoil across the globe in 2016 and 2017), which in turn affects how particular pieces of communication (e.g., a campaign, a documentary) are interpreted. Put another way, effective communication is conditional on both the audience and the broader context within which communication efforts take place, thus reinforcing the need to test how particular ways of talking about the issue may be interpreted and either used or ignored by audiences at a given point in time.

Indeed, despite the significant growth of CCC research in recent years (and its spreading dissemination among many issue advocates, policymakers, journalists, and others), it is clear that communicators continue to face significant challenges in effectively engaging diverse and oftentimes antagonistic, or simply apathetic, audiences with this issue. Moreover, many of the suggestions that come from the existing research base, e.g., tailoring, pilot testing messages, recruiting trusted in-group messengers, are difficult to put into place, particularly for organizations or individuals with limited budgets, capacity, time, and relevant expertise. Tailoring communication strategies to audiences' needs is particularly challenging, for a variety of reasons (Bostrom et al., 2013). One involves the problem of "cross-contamination": communication efforts intended to reach one particular audience are likely to be seen by others, potentially hindering the effectiveness of such tailoring efforts. Another is the practical cost involved in "getting to know" each audience well enough to craft effective messages, which may require conducting audience-specific precampaign research. And of course there is the challenge of being able to identify and accurately target the audience(s) to which any given individual belongs (Hine et al., in press).

3.4.1 A need for continued experimentation

All these challenges, particularly those related to audience tailoring, highlight the critical need for communicators and issue advocates to continue experimenting with techniques and approaches that may be able to engage multiple, diverse audiences simultaneously. The recommendation to use the tools and strategies of effective storytelling and careful choice of narrative form is one such approach (Jones & Peterson, in press). Another promising approach may involve the use of various social psychological tools to extend people's mental timelines, either to "bring the future into the present" or else to extend the present into the future, thus decreasing people's tendency to discount the future costs and benefits of today's (in)action on climate change. Indeed, recent work suggests that a variety of interventions, e.g., having people think about their own legacies (e.g., Zaval, Markowitz, & Weber, 2015), reminding them that the person they are now is the person they will be in the future (e.g., Hershfield, Cohen, & Thomson, 2012; Bartels & Urminsky, 2011), asking people to write letters to future others (Shrum, n.d.), can successfully engage diverse audiences in thinking and behaving more productively about the future. Critically, such approaches appear to increase engagement without worsening polarization along political or other cultural divides, although much more work is needed to determine the conditions under which such approaches will and will not be successful at supporting productive engagement with climate change (Vandenbergh & Raimi, 2015; Zaval et al., 2015).

Shifting climate communication from a traditional top-down approach—one in which an organization or individual develops all information to be communicated in advance of engaging with an audience—to a more bidirectional and needs-oriented model may also hold considerable promise moving forward (Brulle, 2010; Ockwell et al., 2009). Such approaches can take many different forms and are already being used in various settings. For example, the Citizens' Climate Lobby trains citizens to engage with (i.e., talk to) a variety of stakeholders and audiences, including other individuals in their local communities as well as elected officials and representatives. Taking a different approach, leaders of the ongoing Southeast Florida Regional Climate Change Compact have developed a model of highly involved community engagement and public participation that, specifically because of the process it sets out, has allowed diverse perspectives to coexist and overcome potential roadblocks. In large part, this has been accomplished by focusing on addressing the decision-making needs of all involved parties rather than focusing on "converting" people into "believers"; as a result, the focus for participants in the Compact has been on using the best available evidence (i.e., science) to make locally relevant and highly impactful decisions (Kahan, 2015), just as issue advocates hope will happen at all scales of action on climate change.

As past work has revealed, most people report that everyday conversations with trusted family, friends, coworkers, and acquaintances are highly influential in shaping their beliefs about and engagement with climate change. At the same time, people report engaging in few of these conversations in the course of their daily lives (e.g., Leiserowitz et al., 2017; Maibach, Leiserowitz, Rosenthal, Roser-Renouf, & Cutler, 2016). Together these findings suggest that there are potentially large gains to be made in improving outreach and issue engagement if advocates and communicators can develop "soft approaches" that increase the likelihood and civility of such interactions. One possible direction for future research and experimentation in this vein may be to explore different methods for intervening in existing social networks, both face-to-face and internet-based, in an effort to increase the salience of the issue and the frequency with which it comes up as a topic of discussion. This may be particularly powerful if done in ways that leverage existing network leaders to help promote such informal sharing of information about the issue with others (e.g., Hopper & Nielsen, 1991; Nisbet & Kotcher, 2009; Shapiro & Park, 2017; Chapter 4: Social construction of scientifically grounded climate change discussions).

In support of these and other novel approaches, social scientists have a critical role to play by pushing research in new directions. For example, little extant research has examined the key leverage points that communicators might be able to use to increase the incidence of everyday climate change conversations between nonexperts. These may include motivational, social, dispositional, and other factors that psychologists in particular are well-versed in studying in other contexts (e.g., Geiger & Swim, 2016). What may be required is simply a shift in researchers' conceptualization of climate-relevant behavior to also include the many forms of interpersonal communication that could be influential in shaping public engagement with the issue, e.g., talking with friends; signaling interest and concern implicitly and explicitly. Similarly, researchers can repurpose many of the existing paradigms in the literature to identify more and less effective ways of actually encouraging such communications behaviors amongst different groups and audiences. This will entail less of a focus on the *content* of messages and information being conveyed by people to one another and more of a focus on the *drivers* of such behaviors, though of course both could be studied simultaneously (e.g., Geiger & Swim, 2016; Geiger, Swim, & Fraser, 2017; Maki & Raimi, 2017; Swim, Fraser, & Geiger, 2014).

3.4.2   A need for evaluation and new partnerships

As the types and forms of CCC continue to expand, there is also a need for more evaluation-oriented work to be done by researchers. For example, the rapid growth in climate change-related public art installations both in the United States and abroad (e.g., *High Tide*, www.rosekennedygreenway.org/public-art/past-exhibitions/hightide/) represents a perfect opportunity for social scientists to partner with artists, public planners, and humanities scholars to examine how such informal pieces of climate communication influence audiences (see also Guy, Henshaw, & Heidrich, 2015; Nurmis, 2016). Such work could and should also identify how different forms of such public communication efforts differentially influence several audiences and various types of issue engagement (e.g., concern, efficacy, salience, apathy, decision-making). Similar assessment efforts are sorely needed (and beginning to emerge, e.g., Karlin & Johnson, 2011; Sakellari, 2015) with respect to the evergrowing number of documentary and feature films that either focus on climate change explicitly or else contain storylines and/or references to climate-relevant phenomena, e.g., extreme events, future climatic conditions.

3.4.3   Overcoming and avoiding polarization are key

Perhaps most critically, future research on and practice of CCC must find ways to effectively communicate the issue in ways that avoid further polarizing the issue; as Kahan (2015) has put it, communication and engagement strategies need to find ways to "disentangle" climate change knowledge and decision-making from antagonistic cultural commitments and identities if they are to be useful in terms of supporting productive collective action on this issue. Of course, doing so will be challenging given how tightly attitudes toward climate change have become enmeshed in cultural and societal conflicts as well as in the face of continued intentional efforts by vested interests to maintain such polarization (McCright & Dunlap, 2011; Oreskes & Conway, 2011). Moreover, vigilance in the form of continued research and ever-improving methods is required to ensure that communications recommendations are truly supported by rigorous evidence and that they are changed (and well communicated!) when new evidence emerges, e.g., regarding asymmetrical effects of consensus messaging on different audiences (Bolsen & Shapiro, in press). That being said, emerging and innovative efforts make us hopeful that such depolarizing and truly effective approaches to CCC are indeed possible.

3.5   Concluding thoughts

CCC is hard to do well and easy to do poorly. There are many potential pitfalls and relatively few unambiguous and universal recommendations to be found. And yet, clear progress has been made over the past few years toward improved communication and outreach efforts. This progress is, in some part, thanks to the ongoing efforts of researchers across the social sciences who have begun to carefully examine what motivates and inhibits public engagement with the issue, how people react to different types of climate change frames and stories, and what forms and modes of communication and outreach are likely to effectively engage diverse audiences. Perhaps most encouraging, though, is the continued diversification and experimentation around CCC that is currently under way. As researchers and communicators continue to push their efforts in new and innovative directions, the potential to truly shift public engagement with and discourse around this issue and to support better individual and collective climate-relevant decisions grows.

References

Anderson, A. (2011). Sources, media, and modes of climate change communication: The role of celebrities. *Wiley Interdisciplinary Reviews: Climate Change, 2*(4), 535−546.

Asensio, O. I., & Delmas, M. A. (2015). Nonprice incentives and energy conservation. *Proceedings of the National Academy of Sciences of the United States of America, 112* (6), E510−E515. Available from https://doi.org/10.1073/pnas.1401880112.

Asensio, O. I., & Delmas, M. A. (2016). The dynamics of behavior change: Evidence from energy conservation. *Journal of Economic Behavior & Organization, 126*, 196−212. Available from https://doi.org/10.1016/j.jebo.2016.03.012.

Bain, P. G., Hornsey, M. J., Bongiorno, R., & Jeffries, C. (2012). Promoting pro environmental action in climate change deniers. *Nature Climate Change, 2*(8), 600−603.

Bain, P. G., Milfont, T. L., Kashima, Y., Bilewicz, M., Doron, G., Garðarsdóttir, R. B., ... Corral-Verdugo, V. (2016). Co-benefits of addressing climate change can motivate action around the world. *Nature Climate Change, 6*(2), 154−157.

Bartels, D. M., & Urminsky, O. (2011). On intertemporal selfishness: How the perceived instability of identity underlies impatient consumption. *Journal of Consumer Research, 38*, 182−198.

Benjamin, D., Por, H. H., & Budescu, D. (2016). Climate change versus global warming: Who is susceptible to the framing of climate change? *Environment and Behavior, 49*(7), 745−770.

Bliuc, A. M., McGarty, C., Thomas, E. F., Lala, G., Berndsen, M., & Misajon, R. (2015). Public division about climate change rooted in conflicting socio-political identities. *Nature Climate Change, 5*(3), 226−229.

Bolsen, T., & Druckman, J. N. (2015). Counteracting the politicization of science. *Journal of Communication, 65*(5), 745−769.

Bolsen, T., & Shapiro, M.A. (In press). Strategic framing and persuasive messaging to influence climate change perceptions and decisions. In M.C. Nisbet (Ed.), *The Oxford Encyclopedia for Climate Change Communication*. Oxford and New York: Oxford University Press. https://doi.org/10.1093/acrefore/9780190228620.013.385.

Bostrom, A., Böhm, G., & O'Connor, R. E. (2013). Targeting and tailoring climate change communications. *Wiley Interdisciplinary Reviews: Climate Change, 4*(5), 447−455.

Boykoff, M. T. (2011). *Who speaks for the climate?: Making sense of media reporting of climate change*. Cambridge: Cambridge University Press.

Boykoff, M. T., & Boykoff, J. M. (2007). Climate change and journalistic norms: A case study of US mass-media coverage. *Geoforum, 38*(6), 1190−1204.

Brulle, R. J. (2010). From environmental campaigns to advancing the public dialog: Environmental communication for civic engagement. *Environmental Communication, 4* (1), 82–98.

Brulle, R. J., Carmichael, J., & Jenkins, J. C. (2012). Shifting public opinion on climate change: An empirical assessment of factors influencing concern over climate change in the US, 2002–2010. *Climatic Change, 114*(2), 169–188.

Budescu, D. V., Por, H. H., & Broomell, S. B. (2012). Effective communication of uncertainty in the IPCC reports. *Climatic Change, 113*(2), 181–200.

Center for Research on Environmental Decisions and ecoAmerica. (2014). Connecting on climate: A guide to effective climate change communication. New York and Washington, DC

Chapman, D. A., Corner, A., Webster, R., & Markowitz, E. M. (2016). Climate visuals: A mixed methods investigation of public perceptions of climate images in three countries. *Global Environmental Change, 41*, 172–182.

Chapman, D. A., & Lickel, B. (2016). Climate change and disasters how framing affects justifications for giving or withholding aid to disaster victims. *Social Psychological and Personality Science, 7*(1), 13–20.

Climate Outreach. (2015). *Communicating climate change uncertainty.* Oxford: Climate Outreach.

Cohen, S. J., Sheppard, S., Shaw, A., Flanders, D., Burch, S., Taylor, B., . . . Carmichael, J. (2012). Downscaling and visioning of mountain snow packs and other climate change implications in North Vancouver, British Columbia. *Mitigation and Adaptation Strategies for Global Change, 17*(1), 25–49.

Compton, J. (2013). Inoculation theory. In J. P. Dillard, & L. Shen (Eds.), *The Sage handbook of per-suasion: Developments in theory and practice* (pp. 220–237). Los Angeles, CA: Sage.

Corner, A., & Clarke, J. (2017). *Talking climate: From research to practice in public engagement.* United Kingdom: Palgrave Macmillan.

Corner, A., Roberts, O., Chiari, S., Völler, S., Mayrhuber, E. S., Mandl, S., & Monson, K. (2015). How do young people engage with climate change? The role of knowledge, values, message framing, and trusted communicators. *Wiley Interdisciplinary Reviews: Climate Change, 6*(5), 523–534.

Corner, A., Whitmarsh, L., & Xenias, D. (2012). Uncertainty, scepticism and attitudes towards climate change: Biased assimilation and attitude polarisation. *Climatic Change, 114*(3), 463–478.

Cook, J. (in press). Countering climate science denial and communicating scientific consensus. In M.C. Nisbet (Ed.), *The Oxford Encyclopedia for Climate Change Communication.* Oxford and New York: Oxford University Press. https://doi.org/ 10.1093/acrefore/9780190228620.013.314.

Cook, J., & Lewandowsky, S. (2011). *The debunking handbook.* St. Lucia, Australia: University of Queensland.

Cook, J., & Lewandowsky, S. (2016). Rational irrationality: Modeling climate change belief polarization using Bayesian networks. *Topics in Cognitive Science, 8*(1), 160–179.

Cook, J., Lewandowsky, S., & Ecker, U. K. (2017). Neutralizing misinformation through inoculation: Exposing misleading argumentation techniques reduces their influence. *PLoS ONE, 12*(5), e0175799.

Cook, J., Oreskes, N., Doran, P. T., Anderegg, W. R., Verheggen, B., Maibach, E. W., . . . Nuccitelli, D. (2016). Consensus on consensus: A synthesis of consensus estimates on human-caused global warming. *Environmental Research Letters, 11*(4), 048002.

Cook, J., Schuennemann, K., Nuccitelli, D., Jacobs, P., Cowtan, K., Green, S., et al. (2015). Denial101x: Making sense of climate science denial. *edX*. Retrieved from ⟨http://edx. org/understanding-climate-denial⟩.

Cutler, M., Leiserowitz, A., and Rosenthal, S. (2017). *Is nature stable, delicate, or random?* New Haven, CT: Yale Program on Climate Change Communication, Yale University.

de Bruin, W. B., & Bostrom, A. (2013). Assessing what to address in science communication. *Proceedings of the National Academy of Sciences, 110*(Suppl. 3), 14062–14068.

Deryugina, T. (2013). How do people update? The effects of local weather fluctuations on beliefs about global warming. *Climatic Change, 118*(2), 397–416.

Dunlap, R. E., & McCright, A. M. (2010). Climate change denial: Sources, actors and strategies. Routledge handbook of climate change and society. In C. Lever-Tracy (Ed.), *Routledge hand- book of climate change and society* (pp. 240–259). Abingdon, England: Routledge.

Dunlap, R. E., McCright, A. M., & Yarosh, J. H. (2016). The political divide on climate change: Partisan polarization widens in the US. *Environment: Science and Policy for Sustainable Development, 58*(5), 4–23.

Druckman, J. N. (2001). The implications of framing effects for citizen competence. *Political Behavior, 23*(3), 225–256.

ecoAmerica. (2014). *American climate values 2014: Psychographic and demographic insights*. Washington, DC: ecoAmerica.

ecoAmerica. (2016a). *15 Steps to create effective climate communications*. Washington, DC: ecoAmerica.

ecoAmerica. (2016b). *Let's talk health and climate: Communication guidance for health professionals*. Washington, DC: Climate for Health.

Egan, P. J., & Mullin, M. (2012). Turning personal experience into political attitudes: The effect of local weather on Americans' perceptions about global warming. *The Journal of Politics, 74*(3), 796–809.

Ecker, U. K., Lewandowsky, S., Fenton, O., & Martin, K. (2014). Do people keep believing because they want to? Preexisting attitudes and the continued influence of misinformation. *Memory & Cognition, 42*(2), 292–304.

Ecker, U. K., Lewandowsky, S., Swire, B., & Chang, D. (2011). Correcting false information in memory: Manipulating the strength of misinformation encoding and its retraction. *Psychonomic Bulletin & Review, 18*(3), 570–578.

Ecker, U. K., Lewandowsky, S., & Tang, D. T. (2010). Explicit warnings reduce but do not eliminate the continued influence of misinformation. *Memory & Cognition, 38*(8), 1087–1100.

Feldman, L., Myers, T. A., Hmielowski, J. D., & Leiserowitz, A. (2014). The mutual reinforcement of media selectivity and effects: Testing the reinforcing spirals framework in the context of global warming. *Journal of Communication, 64*(4), 590–611.

Feinberg, M., & Willer, R. (2011). Apocalypse soon? Dire messages reduce belief in global warming by contradicting just-world beliefs. *Psychological Science, 22*(1), 34–38.

Feygina, I., Jost, J. T., & Goldsmith, R. E. (2010). System justification, the denial of global warming, and the possibility of "system-sanctioned change". *Personality and Social Psychology Bulletin, 36*(3), 326–338.

Gardiner, S. M. (2011). *A perfect moral storm: The ethical tragedy of climate change*. Oxford, UK: Oxford University Press.

Geiger, N., & Swim, J. K. (2016). Climate of silence: Pluralistic ignorance as a barrier to climate change discussion. *Journal of Environmental Psychology, 47*, 79–90.

Geiger, N., Swim, J. K., & Fraser, J. (2017). Creating a climate for change: Interventions, efficacy and public discussion about climate change. *Journal of Environmental Psychology, 51*, 104−116.

Gifford, R. (2011). The dragons of inaction: Psychological barriers that limit climate change mitigation and adaptation. *American Psychologist, 66*(4), 290.

Guy, S., Henshaw, V., & Heidrich, O. (2015). Climate change, adaptation and Eco-Art in Singapore. *Journal of Environmental Planning and Management, 58*(1), 39−54.

Hamilton, L. C., & Stampone, M. D. (2013). Blowin' in the wind: Short-term weather and belief in anthropogenic climate change. *Weather, Climate, and Society, 5*(2), 112−119.

Hart, P. S., & Feldman, L. (2014). Threat without efficacy? Climate change on US network news. *Science Communication, 36*(3), 325−351.

Hart, P. S., & Feldman, L. (2016). The influence of climate change efficacy messages and efficacy beliefs on intended political participation. *PLoS ONE, 11*(8), e0157658.

Hart, P. S., Feldman, L., Leiserowitz, A., & Maibach, E. (2015). Extending the impacts of hostile media perceptions: Influences on discussion and opinion polarization in the context of climate change. *Science Communication, 37*(4), 506−532.

Hart, P. S., & Nisbet, E. C. (2012). Boomerang effects in science communication: How motivated reasoning and identity cues amplify opinion polarization about climate mitigation policies. *Communication Research, 39*(6), 701−723.

Heath, C., & Heath, D. (2007). *Made to stick: Why some ideas survive and others die.* Random House.

Hershfield, H. E., Cohen, T. R., & Thomson, L. (2012). Short horizons and tempting situations: Lack of continuity to our future selves leads to unethical decision making and behavior. *Organizational Behavior and Human Decision Processes, 117*, 298−310.

Hine, D. W., Phillips, W. J., Cooksey, R., Reser, J. P., Nunn, P., Marks, A. D., ... Watt, S. E. (2016). Preaching to different choirs: How to motivate dismissive, uncommitted, and alarmed audiences to adapt to climate change? *Global Environmental Change, 36*, 1−11.

Hine, D.W., Phillips, W.J., Driver, A.B. & Morrison, M. (in press). Audience segmentation and climate change communication. In M.C. Nisbet (Ed.), *The Oxford Encyclopedia for Climate Change Communication.* Oxford and New York: Oxford University Press. https://doi.org/10.1093/acrefore/9780190228620.013.390.

Hine, D. W., Reser, J. P., Morrison, M., Phillips, W. J., Nunn, P., & Cooksey, R. (2014). Audience segmentation and climate change communication: Conceptual and methodological considerations. *Wiley Interdisciplinary Reviews: Climate Change, 5*(4), 441−459.

Ho, E.H., Budescu, D.V., & Pu, H.H. (in press). Psychological challenges in communicating about climate change and its uncertainites. In M.C. Nisbet (Ed.), The Oxford Encyclopedia for Climate Change Communication. Oxford and New York: Oxford University Press. https://doi.org/10.1093/acrefore/9780190228620.013.381.

Hopper, J. R., & Nielsen, J. M. (1991). Recycling as altruistic behavior normative and behavioral strategies to expand participation in a community recycling program. *Environment and Behavior, 23*(2), 195−220.

Hornsey, M. J., Fielding, K. S., McStay, R., Reser, J. P., Bradley, G. L., & Greenaway, K. H. (2015). Evidence for motivated control: Understanding the paradoxical link between threat and efficacy beliefs about climate change. *Journal of Environmental Psychology, 42*, 57−65.

Hulme, M. (2009). *Why we disagree about climate change: Understanding controversy, inaction and opportunity.* Cambridge, UK: Cambridge University Press.

IPCC. (2014). *Climate change 2014: Synthesis report of the fifth assessment of the intergovernmental panel on climate change.* Geneva: IPCC.

Jasny, L., Waggle, J., & Fisher, D. R. (2015). An empirical examination of echo chambers in US climate policy networks. *Nature Climate Change, 5*(8), 782−786.

Johnson, H. M., & Seifert, C. M. (1994). Sources of the continued influence effect: When misinformation in memory affects later inferences. *Journal of Experimental Psychology: Learning, Memory, and Cognition, 20*(6), 1420.

Jones, M., & Peterson, H. (2017). Narrative persuasion and storytelling as climate communication strategies. *Oxford Research Encyclopedia of Climate Science.* Retrieved from: https://doi.org/10.1093/acrefore/9780190228620.001.0001/acrefore-9780190228620-e-384. (Accessed 21.02.18).

Joslyn, S. L., & LeClerc, J. E. (2016). Climate projections and uncertainty communication. *Topics in Cognitive Science, 8*(1), 222−241.

Kahan, D. M. (2013). Ideology, motivated reasoning, and cognitive reflection. *Judgment and Decision Making, 8,* 407−424.

Kahan, D. M. (2015). Climate-science communication and the measurement problem. *Advances in Political Psychology, 36,* 1−43.

Kahan, D. M., Braman, D., Gastil, J., Slovic, P., & Mertz, C. K. (2007a). Culture and identity-protective cognition: Explaining the white-male effect in risk perception. *Journal of Empirical Legal Studies, 4*(3), 465−505.

Kahan, D.M., Braman, D., Slovic, P., Gastil, J., & Cohen, G.L. (2007b). The second national risk and culture study: Making sense of-and making progress in-the American culture war of fact. SSRN eLibrary. ⟨http://ssrn.com/paper = 1017189⟩.

Kahan, D. M., Peters, E., Wittlin, M., Slovic, P., Ouellette, L. L., Braman, D., & Mandel, G. (2012). The polarizing impact of science literacy and numeracy on perceived climate change risks. *Nature Climate Change, 2*(10), 732−735.

Kahneman, D., & Tversky, A. (1979). Prospect theory: An analysis of decision under risk. *Econometrica: Journal of the Econometric Society,* 263−291.

Kaplan, S., & Kaplan, R. (2009). Creating a larger role for environmental psychology: The Reasonable Person Model as an integrative framework. *Journal of Environmental Psychology, 29*(3), 329−339.

Karlin, B., & Johnson, J. (2011). Measuring impact: The importance of evaluation for documentary film campaigns. *M/C Journal, 14*(6).

Korkala, E. A., Hugg, T. T., & Jaakkola, J. J. (2014). Awareness of climate change and the dietary choices of young adults in Finland: A population-based cross-sectional study. *PLoS ONE, 9*(5), e97480.

Kunda, Z. (1990). The case for motivated reasoning. *Psychological Bulletin, 108*(3), 480.

Lee, A. Y., & Aaker, J. L. (2004). Bringing the frame into focus: The influence of regulatory fit on processing fluency and persuasion. *Journal of Personality and Social Psychology, 86*(2), 205.

Leiserowitz, A. (2006). Climate change risk perception and policy preferences: The role of affect, imagery, and values. *Climatic Change, 77*(1), 45−72.

Leiserowitz, A., Maibach, E., Roser-Renouf, C., Feinberg, G., & Howe, P. D. (2013). *Global warming's six Americas in September 2012.* New Haven, CT: Yale Program on Climate Change Communication, Yale University.

Leiserowitz, A., Maibach, E., Roser-Renouf, C., Feinberg, G., & Rosenthal, S. (2016). *Climate change in the American mind: March, 2016.* New Haven, CT: Yale Program on Climate Change Communication, Yale University and George Mason University.

Leiserowitz, A., Maibach, E., Roser-Renouf, C., & Hmielowski, J. D. (2011). *Politics & global warming: Democrats, republicans, independents, and the Tea Party*. New Haven, CT: Yale Project on Climate Change Communication, Yale University and George Mason University.

Leiserowitz, A., Maibach, E., Roser-Renouf, C., Rosenthal, S., & Cutler, M. (2017). *Climate change in the American mind: November 2016*. New Haven, CT: Yale Program on Climate Change Communication, Yale University and George Mason University.

Lertzman, R. (2015). *Environmental melancholia: Psychoanalytic dimensions of engagement*. Abingdon, England: Routledge.

Lewandowsky, S., Ecker, U. K., Seifert, C. M., Schwarz, N., & Cook, J. (2012). Misinformation and its correction continued influence and successful debiasing. *Psychological Science in the Public Interest, 13*(3), 106−131.

Lewandowsky, S., Gignac, G. E., & Vaughan, S. (2013). The pivotal role of perceived scientific consensus in acceptance of science. *Nature Climate Change, 3*(4), 399−404.

Lord, C. G., Ross, L., & Lepper, M. R. (1979). Biased assimilation and attitude polarization: The effects of prior theories on subsequently considered evidence. *Journal of Personality and Social Psychology, 37*, 2098−2109.

Maibach, E., Leiserowitz, A., Rosenthal, S., Roser-Renouf, C., & Cutler, M. (2016). *Is there a climate "spiral of silence" in America?* New Haven, CT: Yale Program on Climate Change Communication, Yale University and George Mason University.

Maibach, E., Roser-Renouf, C., & Leiserowitz, A. (2009). *Global warming's Six Americas 2009: An audience segmentation analysis*. New Haven, CT: Yale Project on Climate Change, Yale University and George Mason University.

Maibach, E. W., Leiserowitz, A., Roser-Renouf, C., & Mertz, C. K. (2011). Identifying like-minded audiences for global warming public engagement campaigns: An audience segmentation analysis and tool development. *PLoS ONE, 6*(3), e17571.

Maibach, E. W., Roser-Renouf, C., & Leiserowitz, A. (2008). Communication and marketing as climate change-intervention assets: A public health perspective. *American Journal of Preventive Medicine, 35*(5), 488−500.

Maki, A., & Raimi, K. T. (2017). Environmental peer persuasion: How moral exporting and belief superiority relate to efforts to influence others. *Journal of Environmental Psychology, 49*, 18−29.

Malone, E. L. (2009). *Debating climate change: Pathways through argument to agreement*. New York, NY: Routledge.

Markowitz, E. M., & Shariff, A. F. (2012). Climate change and moral judgement. *Nature Climate Change, 2*(4), 243−247.

McCright, A. M., & Dunlap, R. E. (2010). Anti-reflexitivity: The American conservative movement's success in undermining climate science and policy. *Theory, Culture, and Society, 27*(2-2), 1−34.

McCright, A. M., & Dunlap, R. E. (2011). The politicization of climate change and polarization in the American public's views of global warming, 2001−2010. *The Sociological Quarterly, 52*(2), 155−194.

McCright, A. M., Charters, M., Dentzman, K., & Dietz, T. (2016). Examining the effectiveness of climate change frames in the face of a climate change denial counter−frame. *Topics in Cognitive Science, 8*(1), 76−97.

McKibben, B. (1989). *The end of nature*. New York, NY: Random House.

McCutcheon, A. L. (1987). Latent class analysis *(No. 64)*. Newbury Park, CA: Sage.

Metag, J., Füchslin, T., & Schäfer, M. S. (2015). Global warming's five Germanys: A typology of Germans' views on climate change and patterns of media use and information. *Public Understanding of Science, 26*(4), 434−451.

Milfont, T. L. (2012). The interplay between knowledge, perceived efficacy, and concern about global warming and climate change: A one-year longitudinal study. *Risk Analysis, 32*(6), 1003−1020.

Moser, S. C. (2010). Communicating climate change: History, challenges, process and future directions. *Wiley Interdisciplinary Reviews: Climate Change, 1*(1), 31−53.

Morgan, M. G., Fischoff, B., Bostrom, A., & Atman, C. J. (2001). *Risk communication: A mental model approach.* New York, NY: Cambridge University Press.

Morton, T. A., Rabinovich, A., Marshall, D., & Bretschneider, P. (2011). The future that may (or may not) come: How framing changes responses to uncertainty in climate change communications. *Global Environmental Change, 21*(1), 103−109.

Myers, T. A., Nisbet, M. C., Maibach, E. W., & Leiserowitz, A. A. (2012). A public health frame arouses hopeful emotions about climate change. *Climatic Change, 113*(3−4), 1105−1112.

Nacu-Schmidt, A., Andrew, K., Boykoff, M., Daly, M., Gifford, L., Luedecke, G., & McAllister, L. (2016). *World newspaper coverage of climate change or global warming, 2004−2016. Center for Science and Technology Policy Research, Cooperative Institute for Research in Environmental Sciences.* Retrieved from http://sciencepolicy.colorado.edu.

Nisbet, M. C. (2009). Communicating climate change: Why frames matter for public engagement. *Environment: Science and Policy for Sustainable Development, 51*(2), 12−23.

Nisbet, M. C., & Kotcher, J. E. (2009). A two-step flow of influence? Opinion-leader campaigns on climate change. *Science Communication, 30*(3), 328−354.

Nisbet, M. C., & Mooney, C. (2007). Framing science. *Science, 316*, 56.

Norgaard, K. M. (2011). *Living in denial: Climate change, emotions, and everyday life.* Cambridge, MA: MIT Press.

Nyhan, B., & Reifler, J. (2010). When corrections fail: The persistence of political misperceptions. *Political Behavior, 32*(2), 303−330.

Nurmis, J. (2016). Visual climate change art 2005−2015: Discourse and practice. *Wiley Interdisciplinary Reviews: Climate Change, 7*(4), 501−516.

Ockwell, D., Whitmarsh, L., & O'Neill, S. (2009). Reorienting climate change communication for effective mitigation: Forcing people to be green or fostering grass-roots engagement?. *Science Communication, 30*(3), 305−327.

O'Neill, S. J., Boykoff, M., Niemeyer, S., & Day, S. A. (2013). On the use of imagery for climate change engagement. *Global Environmental Change, 23*(2), 413−421.

O'Neill, S., & Nicholson-Cole, S. (2009). "Fear Won't Do It" promoting positive engagement with climate change through visual and iconic representations. *Science Communication, 30*(3), 355−379.

Oreskes, N., & Conway, E. M. (2011). *Merchants of doubt: How a handful of scientists obscured the truth on issues from tobacco smoke to global warming.* USA: Bloomsbury Publishing.

Painter, J. (2013). *Climate change in the media: Report risk and uncertainty.* Oxford: Reuters Institute for the Study of Journalism.

Perkowitz, R., Speiser, M., Harp, G., Hodge, C., & Krygsman, K. (2014). *ecoAmerica & Strategic Business Insights. American Climate Values 2014: Psychographic and demographic insights.* Washington, DC: ecoAmerica.

Pew Research Center. (2014). *Deficit reduction declines as policy priority.* Washington, DC: Author.

Pew Research Center. (2015). *Public and scientists views on science and society.* Washington, DC: Author.

Pew Research Center. (2016). *Partisanship and political animosity in 2016.* Washington, DC: Author.

Placky, B. W., Maibach, E., Witte, J., Ward, B., Seitter, K., Gardiner, N., … Cullen, H. (2016). Climate matters: A comprehensive educational resource program for broadcast meteorologists. *Bulletin of the American Meteorological Society, 97*(5), 709−712.

Poortinga, W., & Darnton, A. (2016). Segmenting for sustainability: The development of a sustainability segmentation model from a Welsh sample. *Journal of Environmental Psychology, 45,* 221−232.

Riffkin, R. (2014). *Climate change not a top worry in U.S.* Gallup Poll. Retrieved from: http://news.gallup.com/poll/167843/climate-change-not-top-worry.aspx.

Rokeach, M. (1973). *The nature of human values.* New York, NY: Free press.

Roser-Renouf, C., Maibach, E. W., Leiserowitz, A., & Zhao, X. (2014). The genesis of climate change activism: From key beliefs to political action. *Climatic Change, 125*(2), 163−178.

Saad, L. (2017). *Global warming concern at three-decade high in US.* Gallop Poll. Retrieved from: http://news.gallup.com/poll/206030/global-warming-concern-three-decade-high.aspx.

Sakellari, M. (2015). Cinematic climate change, a promising perspective on climate change communication. *Public Understanding of Science, 24*(7), 827−841.

Scannell, L., & Gifford, R. (2013). Personally relevant climate change: The role of place attachment and local versus global message framing in engagement. *Environment and Behavior, 45*(1), 60−85.

Schwarz, N., Sanna, L. J., Skurnik, I., & Yoon, C. (2007). Metacognitive experiences and the intricacies of setting people straight: Implications for debiasing and public information campaigns. *Advances in Experimental Social Psychology, 39,* 127−161.

Seifert, C. M. (2002). The continued influence of misinformation in memory: What makes a correction effective? *Psychology of Learning and Motivation, 41,* 265−292.

Shapiro, M. A., & Park, H. W. (2017). Climate change and YouTube: Deliberation potential in post-video discussions. *Environmental Communication, 12*(1), 1−17.

Shaw, A., Sheppard, S., Burch, S., Flanders, D., Wiek, A., Carmichael, J., … Cohen, S. (2009). Making local futures tangible—synthesizing, downscaling, and visualizing climate change scenarios for participatory capacity building. *Global Environmental Change, 19*(4), 447−463.

Sheppard, S. R. (2012). *Visualizing climate change: A guide to visual communication of climate change and developing local solutions.* Abingdon, England: Routledge.

Shrum, T. (n.d.). The salience of future climate impacts and the willingness to pay for climate change mitigation. Working paper.

Sibley, C. G., & Kurz, T. (2013). A model of climate belief profiles: How much does it matter if people question human causation? *Analyses of Social Issues and Public Policy, 13* (1), 245−261.

Southeast Florida Regional Climate Change Compact (n.d.). Southeast Florida regional climate change compact. Retrieved from: http://www.southeastfloridaclimatecompact.org/. (Accessed 21.02.18)

Spence, A., & Pidgeon, N. (2010). Framing and communicating climate change: The effects of distance and outcome frame manipulations. *Global Environmental Change, 20*(4), 656−667.

Spence, A., Poortinga, W., & Pidgeon, N. (2012). The psychological distance of climate change. *Risk Analysis, 32*(6), 957−972.

Sterman, J. D. (2008). Risk communication on climate: Mental models and mass balance. *Science, 322*(5901), 532−533.

Sterman, J. D., & Sweeney, L. B. (2007). Understanding public complacency about climate change: Adults' mental models of climate change violate conservation of matter. *Climatic Change, 80*(3), 213−238.

Stoknes, P. E. (2015). *What we think about when we try not to think about global warming: Toward a new psychology of climate action.* White River Junction, VT: Chelsea Green Publishing.

Strategic Business Insights. (n.d.). VALS. Retrieved from <www.strategicbusinessinsights.com/vals>.

Swim, J., Clayton, S., Doherty, T., Gifford, R., Howard, G., Reser, J., ... & Weber, E. (2009). Psychology and global climate change: Addressing a multi-faceted phenomenon and set of challenges. *A report by the American Psychological Association's task force on the interface between psychology and global climate change.* Washington: American Psychological Association.

Swim, J. K., Fraser, J., & Geiger, N. (2014). Teaching the choir to sing: Use of social science information to promote public discourse on climate change. *Journal of Land Use & Environmental Law, 30*(1), 91−117.

Swim, J. K., Markowitz, E. M., & Bloodhart, B. (2012). Psychology and climate change: Beliefs, attitudes and human contributions. In S. Clayton (Ed.), *The oxford handbook of environmental and conservation psychology.* New York, NY: Oxford University Press.

Taylor, B. (2012). *Climate solutions for a stronger America.* Breakthrough Strategies & Solutions.

Trenberth, K. E., Fasullo, J. T., & Shepherd, T. G. (2015). Attribution of climate extreme events. *Nature Climate Change, 5,* 725−730.

Ungar, S. (2000). Knowledge, ignorance and the popular culture: Climate change versus the ozone hole. *Public Understanding of Science, 9*(3), 297−312.

Unsworth, K. L., & Fielding, K. S. (2014). It's political: How the salience of one's political identity changes climate change beliefs and policy support. *Global Environmental Change, 27,* 131−137.

Vandenbergh, M.P., & Raimi, K.T. (2015). Climate change: Leveraging legacy. (Ecology LQ, 42,139.

Weber, E. U., & Stern, P. C. (2011). Public understanding of climate change in the United States. *American Psychologist, 66*(4), 315.

Wibeck, V. (2014). Enhancing learning, communication and public engagement about climate change − some lessons from recent literature. *Environmental Education Research, 20*(3), 387−411.

Williams, H. T., McMurray, J. R., Kurz, T., & Lambert, F. H. (2015). Network analysis reveals open forums and echo chambers in social media discussions of climate change. *Global Environmental Change, 32,* 126−138.

Whitmarsh, L. (2009). What's in a name? Commonalities and differences in public understanding of "climate change" and "global warming". *Public Understanding of Science, 18*(4), 401−420.

Whitmarsh, L. (2011). Skepticism and uncertainty about climate change: Dimensions, determinants and change over time. *Global Environmental Change, 21*(2), 690−700.

Whitmarsh, L., Lorenzoni, I., & O'Neill, S. (2012). *Engaging the public with climate change: Behaviour change and communication.* Abingdon, England: Routledge.

Winkielman, P., Huber, D. E., Kavanagh, L., & Schwarz, N. (2012). Fluency of consistency: When thoughts fit nicely and flow smoothly. *Cognitive Consistency: A Fundamental Principle in Social Cognition*, 89—111.

Witte, K. (1992). Putting the fear back into fear appeals: The extended parallel process model. *Communications Monographs*, *59*(4), 329—349.

Witte, K., & Allen, M. (2000). A meta-analysis of fear appeals: Implications for effective public health campaigns. *Health Education & Behavior*, *27*(5), 591—615.

Zaval, L., Markowitz, E. M., & Weber, E. U. (2015). How will I be remembered? Conserving the environment for legacy's sake. *Psychological Science*, *26*, 231—236.

Zhao, X., Maibach, E., Gandy, J., Witte, J., Cullen, H., Klinger, B. A., ... Pyle, A. (2014). Climate change education through TV weathercasts: Results of a field experiment. *Bulletin of the American Meteorological Society*, *95*(1), 117—130.

Social construction of scientifically grounded climate change discussions

Janet K. Swim[1], Nathaniel Geiger[1], Julie Sweetland[2] and John Fraser[3]
[1]Pennsylvania State University, University Park, PA, United States, [2]FrameWorks Institute, Washington, DC, United States, [3]New Knowledge Organization Ltd, New York, NY, United States

4.1 Social construction of scientifically grounded climate change discussions

The scientific assessment of the risks of climate change and ways to manage that risk has been accumulating for decades. This growth is evidenced by the more documentation and improved understanding of climate change causes and impacts over the last five versions of the United Nations Intergovernmental Panel on Climate Change (IPCC) reports on climate change (IPCC, 1990 to IPCC, 2013). However, despite the strength of information and accumulation of evidence leading to a high degree of scientific certainty about the phenomenon, there are still major gaps in the public's understanding of climate change. For example, many falsely link climate change to ozone holes but are unaware of links between climate change and ocean acidification, which suggests that they do not understand the role of changes in carbon cycle on both climate systems and ocean health (Capstick, Whitmarsh, Poortinga, Pidgeon, Upham, 2015; Swim, Geiger, Fraser & Pletcher, 2017). This discrepancy between the depth of scientific information about climate change and what lay people know about climate change suggests that most of the public's understanding of the topic is not founded upon a solid understanding of the scientific findings, but instead based upon its social construction (Berger & Luckmann, 1966). That is to say, the public understanding of climate change and associated risks are built through social processes, such as social interactions, that result in a shared perception of reality or events. Broadly speaking, public perceptions of climate change can be considered to include perceptions of knowledge about its causes and impacts, shared feelings about it, and beliefs about how the public can and should help mitigate and prepare inevitable consequences from human caused climate change.

Because of the social basis of perceptions of climate change, it is useful to focus on social interactions that influence these perceptions. The importance of interpersonal exchange of information on climate change opinions has been proposed through research on the role of social media on such opinions (Anderson, 2017).

Psychology and Climate Change. DOI: https://doi.org/10.1016/B978-0-12-813130-5.00004-7

Expressive activities, such as voicing one's opinions or concerns about climate change and social media consumption patterns, can influence perceptions of climate change. The tendency for conversations about climate change to stay within one's social network reinforces existing beliefs (e.g., Brady, Wills, Jost, Tucker, & Bavel, 2017). This research suggests that those interested in empowering the public to take action on climate, may wish to direct their efforts toward influencing the social construction of perceptions of climate change.

In the present chapter, we consider ways that conversations about climate change can help create socially shared perceptions of climate change that are both grounded in climate science and motivate social change. First, we describe the benefits of conversations in order to explain why we believe changing conversations is an effective conduit for social change, while also noting psychological barriers that prevent these conversations from occurring. Building on this foundation as well as on research on effective climate change messaging, we describe ways that conversations can be improved to both overcome barriers and yield benefits to public understanding and action. We then provide an example of how these recommendations can be used to influence public discourse on climate change: an intervention in which educators at informal science learning centers (mostly zoos and aquariums) were taught these general recommendations and encouraged to share this information with visitors to their informal science learning centers as well as with their professional and personal contacts. The goal of this intervention was to create a ripple effect that radiates out from these key influencers into public discourse, to encourage more engagement in the climate change challenge as evidenced by greater public understanding of the topic, improved public hope about the ability of individuals and communities in the US to address climate change, and more individual and group actions that have the goal of helping to reduce America's carbon footprint.

4.2 The importance of conversations

Carefully constructed conversations can provide opportunities for exposure to scientifically sound information and encourage deliberations that help the public interpret information about climate change. These conversations can address aspects of climate change that can make it hard to understand and the risks difficult to grasp. These aspects include the global nature of the problem, the presence of direct and indirect impacts from climate change, variations in the manifestation of the impacts in different regions of the world, and attributional ambiguity about causes and responsibility for enacting solutions (Pearson, Schuldt, & Romero-Canyas, 2016; Swim & Bloodhart, 2018; Swim & Whitmarsh, 2017). Conversations can pull together such information, and when guided by someone with knowledge about the topic, help interpret it. These guides are likely to be most useful when they are trusted sources.

Conversations can motivate action by overcoming lack of salience and minimization of the perceived importance of the risks posed by climate change. When individuals fail to engage in regular discourse about, and cognitive evaluation of, climate change, the importance of taking action to address the issue can be overshadowed by personal and political concerns that appear to require a more immediate response and are more likely to trigger automatic responses by the human brain (e.g., personal financial difficulties, crime; Marshall, 2014). This discounting can be accentuated by an optimism bias that can encourage people to think the risk of climate change is geographically distant and will occur elsewhere or later in time (Gifford et al., 2009; Milfont, Abrahamse, & McCarthy, 2011). Reducing psychological distance from climate change impacts can potentially increase concern (Fraser, Pantesco, Plemons, Gupta, & Rank, 2013; Jones, Hine, & Marks, 2017), although the conditions under which this happens are not well established (Brügger, Dessai, Devine-Wright, Morton, & Pidgeon, 2015). Yet, conversations can expose individuals to information about climate change, prompt reflection about the topic, and potentially facilitate a heightened awareness of the importance of the topic and the seriousness of the risk.

After the risk is understood, conversations can help develop and implement solutions. Conversations can generate novel or locally relevant ideas about how to address climate change. The ideas can translate into group actions by generating collective efficacy and providing social support (cf., van Zomeren, Leach, & Spears, 2012). Further, public commitment to participating in these solutions can increase social accountability for following up one's statements with action (Abrahamse & Steg, 2013). Conversations may also facilitate the development of coordinated responses to climate change, such as installing solar panels to be shared among a community, or mobilizing people to take part in politically oriented protests designed to highlight the need for action on climate change.

Ideas and social norms are disseminated through social diffusion processes such as interpersonal conversations. A meta-analysis confirms the importance of social processes as some of the strongest influences on adoption of pro-environmental behavior (Abrahamse & Steg, 2013). This meta-analysis suggests that opinion leaders have a particularly strong influence, likely through conversations with others (Abrahamse & Steg, 2013; see also Bloodhart, Swim, & Zawadzki, 2013; Burn, 1991; Geiger, Swim, & Glenna, 2017; Valente & Davis, 1999). These results support the two-step flow model of social influence, which proposes that the transmission of ideas from experts and mass media to the general public is facilitated through connections with community opinion leaders, who absorb new information and exert influence upon those that they interact with (Katz, 1957; Nisbet, Kotcher, 2009). Thus, interpersonal conversations about climate change are useful for facilitating engagement with the topic, and may be particularly relevant to promoting action when they occur between community opinion leaders and others in their community.

4.3   Barriers to conversations

The importance of conversations in facilitating action on climate change contrasts with the reality that much of the public does not engage in regular conversations about climate change (Leiserowitz, Maibach, Roser-Renouf, Feinberg, & Rosenthal, 2015). According to national survey data in 2016, a majority of Americans report that they either "rarely" (36%) or "never" (32%) discuss global warming with members of their personal social networks (i.e., family and friends). Further, the tendency to search the internet for the terms "global warming" and "climate change" declined from 2004 to 2014, with the peak years being from 2007 to 2010 (Lineman, Do, Kim, & Joo, 2015). This suggests that over the last decade the public is paying less attention to the topic, despite the increased scientific certainty and understanding of the complexities associated with the causes, impacts, and possible responses to climate change. Unfortunately, these discussions are often not sufficiently facilitated by educators in formal settings such as schools (Plutzer et al., 2016) and informal settings such as zoos and aquariums (Dilenschneider, 2017; Fraser & Sickler, 2009); Wijeratne, Van Dijk, Kirk-Brown, & Frost, 2014; Swim & Fraser, 2013) despite the high degree of public trust people place in these institutions to guide them on the topic (Dilenschneider, 2017; Fraser, Sickler, 2009).

4.3.1   Concerns about ability to discuss the topic

Lack of willingness to have a conversation can be a result of assumptions about one's audience leading to insecurity about one's ability to have an effective conversation. First, many falsely conclude that others are not concerned about the topic (Leviston, Walker, & Morwinski, 2012), likely because they attribute others' silence to lack of interest in the topic. In reality, this silence may be based on others' reactions to situational cues that promote the silence (Gawronski, 2004; Geiger, Swim, 2016). Second, misperceptions about one's audience can lead to self-presentation concerns. For example, many US college students are concerned about being perceived as incompetent if they were to bring up the topic, particularly when they believe that potential discussion partners hold different opinions from their own (Geiger, Swim, 2016). We suggest that these concerns about not being able to sound competent in a climate change discussion likely prevail across much of the general public, considering that much of the public poorly understands the basic mechanisms of climate change and is unable to connect the causes of climate change to the effects (Capstick et al., 2015; Swim *et al.* 2017; Volmert et al., 2013). In addition to these general concerns, people may also hold situation-specific concerns about discussing climate change. For example, trained educators at zoos and aquariums report concerns about boring others while communicating climate change (Swim & Fraser, 2014).

Together, beliefs about others' opinions and self-presentation concerns propagate a downward spiral of silence on the topic: individuals refrain from discussing climate change because they believe others are not interested, but individuals believe others are not interested because they do not hear others discussing climate change (Geiger, Swim, 2016; Noelle-Neumann, 1993). If an intervention is to be successful at ending the spiral of silence, it should provide accurate information about a particular audience's beliefs about climate change (Geiger & Swim, 2016) and improve self-assessed competency to talk about that topic (e.g., Geiger, Swim, & Fraser, 2017).

4.3.2   Emotional barriers

Lack of concern about climate change cannot sufficiently explain the general dearth of conversations. True, greater concern is associated with talking more about climate change (Leiserowitz et al., 2015; Swim & Geiger, 2017). However, even among the majority of Americans who express some degree of concern about climate change, less than half regularly discuss the topic (Leiserowitz et al., 2015; Swim, Geiger, 2017). Ironically, people may avoid talking about climate change not because they lack concern but because the perceived severity of the threat of climate change can be existentially and emotionally threatening (Fraser et al, 2013; Norgaard, 2011). According to interviews Norgaard (2011) conducted in her ethnographic research, the consequences of climate change are sufficiently aversive that Norwegians report preferring to talk about other topics, particularly issues they perceive they can influence. Thus, emotional experiences and intensity of these experiences can have a relevant effect on responses to climate change messages.

4.3.3   Conversation content

Individuals' lack of willingness to engage in conversations about climate change can be driven in part by insufficient knowledge to engage in a meaningful discussion. Even if scientifically accurate, default frames of the topic may be limited in scope, can be off-putting, or lead to unproductive outcomes. For example, one way to talk about oceans is that they are vast but this description can promote the appraisal that nature is tolerant of human impacts. Thus, framing the oceans as vast can discourage support for policies designed to address human-caused environmental degradation (cf. Steg & Sievers, 2000). As another example, a review of op-eds that referenced topics related to climate change published from 2009 to 2011 in the *New York, Times, Wall Street Journal, and USA Today* indicated that prototypically liberal moral frames of harm vs. care and equality of outcomes dominated comments relative to prototypically conservative moral frames of respect for authority, ingroup loyalty, and purity (Feinberg & Willer, 2013). Framing the issue in in terms of harm vs. care may create reactance or discourage interest among conservatives. These findings suggest the importance of evaluating the prevalence and effectiveness of frames that people commonly use to think about and discuss climate change in order to develop an intervention that can promote dialogue.

The content of conversations can also perpetuate misinformation. Conversations in which communicators ignore (or are not aware of) the current state of the science or focus on false scientific debates about whether human-caused climate change exists may propagate misinformation and demotivate action (Oreskes, Conway, 2011; Regan, 2007). Consumers of information may be misled by sources of information that either deliberately or inadvertently pass along misinformation. For example, when readers were told that news articles were selected by audiences, the articles were viewed more favorably than when the articles were described as selected by news editors, who traditionally have been gatekeepers of the quality of information (Sundar & Nass, 2001). This suggests that social validation of information can direct attention to socially appraised sources of information rather than sources of information appraised by an expert. If a dyad or group with strongly held yet factually incorrect beliefs about a topic engages in a discussion, an in-group discussion can reinforce their beliefs or lead them to believe even more extreme misinformation because they perceive their beliefs to be typical of the entire population rather than their smaller in-group. This phenomenon can enhance the beliefs that participants hold prior to their group discussion, a phenomenon known as group polarization (Isenberg, 1986). To prevent misleading polarization, conversations need to be infused with accurate content.

4.4 Improving conversations

Social psychological research, such as that reviewed above, coupled with research in communication, points to strategies to facilitate fact-based and productive conversations. Productive conversations are defined as being engaging, informative, staying on topic, building to action, and spreading to others. Below we describe elements of conversations that can help achieve these outcomes, elements that are connected to the training provided to educators in the intervention we report here. The elements follow a general arc of story beginning with an introduction that sets the stage and tone of the conversation, moves to the core story based on simplifying metaphors, and ends with a resolution that describes relatively simple community and collective actions.

4.4.1 Frame messages to engage audiences

Overarching frames--the context in which messages are situated—introduce topics and influence responses to messages (e.g., Corner, Markowitz, & Pidgeon, 2014; Lakoff, 2010). Effective frames can engage listeners, and promote or motivate action. In contrast, disengagement or even resistance may be met when frames do not align with an audience's values and moral principles. Many communicators are in search of effective frames that reach across audiences, are endorsed by most members of the public, or match the values of a particular target audience.

Empirical research can help in the selection of such frames. Examples of effective frames are those that encourage the vast majority of people to think compassionately and empathically about animals and humans, and thinking about one's impact on the future generations (Pfattheicher, Sassenrath, & Schindler, 2016;

Swim & Bloodhart, 2014; Zaval, Markowitz, & Weber, 2015). Research also points to matching frames with audience views of climate change (Maibach, Leiserowitz, Roser-Renouf, & Mertz, 2011). For example, frames that emphasize harmful impacts that will be a consequence of climate change on people are less effective at reaching conservative audiences than messages that emphasize technological solutions that can address the problem, reinforce conservative moral principles such as purity in the form of protecting air and water quality, or build on in-group loyalty in the form of patriotism (Feinberg & Willer, 2013; Wolsko, Ariceaga, & Seiden, 2016).

4.4.2 Provide an even toned conversation

The tone of conversation can determine the success of interpersonal exchanges (Kasperson et al., 1988; Renn, 2011). Expressing a rigid, dogmatic belief that one's beliefs are superior to others' beliefs may increase frustration with conversations and discourage future conversations without increasing the effectiveness of persuading the other (Maki, Raimi, 2017; Regan, 2007). In contrast, those who acknowledge the legitimacy of the other's viewpoint and focus on a give-and-take dialogue create more positive experiences that are also more influential (Maki, Raimi, 2017; Regan, 2007). Such a dialogue could still address misinformation by providing scientifically grounded information but couch these corrections within active listening and consideration of what others are thinking and feeling. Listening carefully to what a misinformed person is saying could not only help that person be more receptive but also help identify common logical fallacies. In these instances, rather than countering misinformation with accurate information, misinformation is likely best countered by identifying logical fallacies in the misinformation, such as cherry-picking data (Cook & Lewandowsky, 2011). Cook and Lewandowsky also argue that effective commuicators follow the identification of a fallacy by circling back to core messages grounded in science in order to mentally replace the misinformation with succinctly articulated accurate information. That is to say, a fallacy requires substitution in conversation with a simplified scientifically accurate replacement.

4.4.3 Create core science messages

Climate change education does not need to be complicated. Brief statements that provide information about how climate change works have been shown to change attitudes about the topic (Ranney & Clark, 2016). An ideal conversation will contribute to improved climate literacy by moving the general mental models of climate change to align with expert climate scientists' understanding of the phenomenon. This includes the goals of encouraging the public to understand causes and evidence of climate change, the consequences of climate change, and the mechanisms that connect the causes with evidence of climate change and its consequences (Volmert, 2014). Attending to causal processes could encourage people to think more in terms of systems, such as the carbon cycle, rather than disconnected attributes such as carbon dioxide or isolated consequences such as melting icebergs. *Systems thinking* (i.e. thinking holistically about complex systems rather than seeing all parts as disconnected from one another) can encourage people to see people, including themselves, as operating within the climate system. By situating a person within the system, they can better perceive themselves as a causal agent, someone who will experience predicted impacts, and, as part of a group, have the power to address the causes and impacts. Encouraging systems thinking can be helpful in climate change messaging because it is related to both risk perception and policy support (Lezak & Thibodeau, 2016).

In order to address both actual knowledge and competency related self-presentation concerns, the content in the core message should be easily understood. Explanatory metaphors and analogies can provide a means of conveying key climate change learning objectives (cf. Sopory & Dillard, 2002). Consistent with aligning expert and public understanding of climate change, an explanatory metaphor provides "a bridge between expert and public (that is, non-scientist) understandings" (p. 416) that highlights salient features of a complex or abstract concept and maps them onto more concrete and familiar objects, events, or processes (Kendall-Taylor & Haydon, 2016). Further, effective analogies should "(1) be factual and not misleading, (2) use a familiar domain to explain the unfamiliar, (3) be novel enough to capture interest, and (4) allow for correct extrapolations based on understanding of the known domain." (p. 3; Raimi, Stern, & Maki, 2017). Ideally, these messages would be tested for one's audience in order to assure that specific learning objectives are achieved (e.g., Raimi et al., 2017). An example of a tested effective metaphor for encouraging systems thinking is describing the "earth as our home" (Thibodeau, Frantz, & Berretta, 2017).

In order to encourage the social construction of climate change, effective messages would facilitate easy repetition of the message to others. Metaphors and analogies may help achieve this if they make the topic vivid and improve memory for the information (cf. Blondé & Girandola, 2016). As noted above, messages would ideally be tested to ensure that they are easy to recall and repeat.

The success of central climate change messages would be revealed in improved public understanding of the mechanisms that connect causes of climate change to evidence of climate change and understanding of how to mitigate risk from that change. Greater understanding of climate change can overcome self-presentation concerns about incompetence that prevent people from talking about climate change, particularly with audiences that they anticipate will disagree with their position on the topic (Geiger *et al.* 2017; Geiger, Swim, 2016). Further, if metaphors are selected that teach about climate change and have demonstrably been repeated accurately to others, there is a higher likelihood that people will repeat those core messages in other conversations.

4.4.4   Increase hope with doable solutions

Climate change messages were described earlier in this chapter as sometimes so emotionally disturbing that people prefer to not talk about it. In this sense, "catastrophizing" climate change has been described as counter-productive because the emotions produced from the message can lead to disengagement and denial (Foust & O'Shannon Murphy, 2009; O'Neill, Nicholson-Cole, 2009). As a result, some communicators may choose to avoid using disturbing images of climate change impacts as a way to avoid controversy. However, understanding changes in the climate that can be attributed to human development is central to explaining why the issue is of such proximate concern. Describing human activity that has disrupted the carbon cycle can help a listener understand why life on the planet is at more risk now than it has been in the past centuries, and that this risk is projected to increase over the next century (see IPCC, 2013 for details on projected climate risks).

Rather than avoiding discussion of impacts, research on fear appeals has demonstrated that messages can be improved if the impacts are paired with solutions that help people cope with the problem (Tannenbaum et al., 2015). For example, when the source of most carbon dioxide in the atmosphere is described as being from fossil fuels used to create electricity and transportation, it becomes clearer that people can engage in solutions to reduce the use of fossil fuels. Proposed climate communications solutions are more likely to lead to action when they are perceived as "doable", that is, when audience member perceive that they have the capacity to take action personally (known as self-efficacy) and the knowledge that if they take these actions, there result will be a desired outcome (known as response efficacy; Geiger et al. 2017; Norgaard, 2011). The importance of actions that make a difference is reflected in the New York Times journalist and Pulitzer prize winner Thomas Friedman's 2008 encouragement to "change your leaders not your light bulb" (Starosta, 2008). While energy-efficiency behaviors such as replacing inefficient lightbulbs can play an important part in reducing carbon emissions, the statement highlights that civic behavior has a higher likelihood of achieving the large-scale impacts necessary to counter the risks that will flow from climate change than do small-scale personal actions. People may not believe that they have the power to replace disliked political leaders, but wider public engagement with the challenge can also convince policy makers to commit more resources to the solution.

These findings demonstrate that effective climate messaging is a combination of literacy expansion and personal actions for learners that meet the "sweet spot." Inspiring climate communications combine actions that are small enough that individuals can do them, yet large enough to contribute to systemic difference. Examples include civic and community responses such as installing community solar panels, support for government development of public transportation, participating in coordinated neighborhood activities to reduce collective energy use, and talking about climate change as a problem that groups and organizations can help to solve through implementing these activities.

Evidence that messages have achieved their goals include the sense that the listener has the capacity to make a change in their own sphere of influence and increased hope about people's ability to address climate change (Chadwick, 2015). Hope can be a particularly relevant emotion to target because hope is an emotion associated with agency and expansive thinking, which can galvanize action

(Cavanaugh, Cutright, Luce, & Bettman, 2011; Ojala, 2012; Snyder, 2002). Thus, messages that instill hope in audiences can motivate commitment to engaging in actions, potentially those most similar to those recommended in messages, such as community level actions.

4.5   Applying research in practice

Given the importance of scientifically grounded conversations about climate change along with the relative dearth of such conversations, the National Network for Ocean and Climate Change Interpretation (NNOCCI), a partnership of climate scientists, communication scientists, and informal science educators, established the aspirational goal of promoting public engagement with climate change by changing the US public discourse on climate change and its impact on ocean systems. Changing the discourse refers to changing the way that the American public communicates about climate change so that it is consistent with scientific information and inspires hope and action in the public. Informal science learning centers were considered an ideal vector to reach this lofty goal because millions of people visit zoos, aquariums, and national parks in the US each year (Swim & Fraser, 2014), many visitors to these centers hold beliefs promoting receptivity to climate change messaging (Fraser, Sickler, 2009), many of these centers have conservation missions that have expanded to include climate change education (Swim & Fraser, 2014), and educators there are viewed as trusted source of information, perceived to be highly credible, and to not have a political agenda (Dilenschneider, 2017; Fraser et al, 2013).

The aspirational goal of changing the US discourse was transformed into an intervention training program designed to enhance the quantity and quality of public conversation about climate change in the US. It would do this by equipping informal science educators with communication skills that would allow the information they conveyed about climate change to filter into the general public through their contact with visitors at their centers, colleagues, friends, and family (see Fig. 4.1). The training program taught a set of clear, empirically tested ways of speaking about a changing climate that were depoliticized, easily understood, and readily repeated with fidelity, a strategy that could shift the conversation at informal science learning centers and spread across the nation. The communication skills taught were rooted in the core recommendations noted above (value framing, even tone, effective metaphors, and solutions that build hope).

4.5.1   Developing a core message

NNOCCI began when the New England Aquarium convened an interdisciplinary group of researchers and practitioners to take on the challenge of changing the conversation on climate change in their public programs and grew to include a larger range of communication and education experts. Education leaders at the New

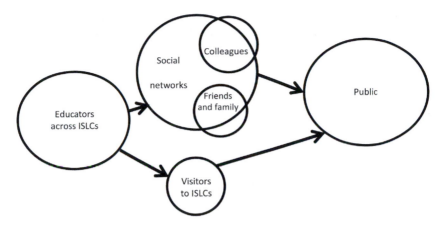

Figure 4.1 Vectors of change.

England Aquarium, Monterey Bay Aquarium, National Aquarium and the Association of Zoos and Aquariums wanted to raise awareness among visitors to informal science learning centers of climate change impacts with specific attention to the threats to marine life, but noted that staff needed greater capacity to guide such interactions with confidence. To bolster the communications strategy, this group of educators and advisors engaged climate change scientists, aquarium professionals, and an interdisciplinary group of communication researchers from FrameWorks Institute--a nonprofit think tank that conducts social science research to promote effective communications on social and scientific issues across a variety of topics. As the communications research and training partner for NNOCCI, FrameWorks Institute provided a theory of communication, empirically tested communications strategies and tools, and a curriculum for teaching professionals how to incorporate framing insights into their communications opportunities. NNOCCI then drew together a much larger team of advisors, social scientists and education researchers to build a robust training program to create a community of practice among interpreters from zoos, aquariums, nature centers, parks, and science centers located across the US.

4.5.2 Developing metaphors

Applied communications researchers at the FrameWorks Institute have, over time, found that metaphors can play an influential role in effectiveness of messages by giving people robust, accessible ways to think and talk about social and political issues. Metaphors offer a way for science communicators to describe key concepts succinctly and concisely yet maintain fidelity to the science. For instance, in a decade-long partnership with researchers associated with the National Scientific Council on the Developing Child, FrameWorks researchers generated and tested a number of metaphors for various scientific phenomena that have since found their way into news media, legislation, and everyday discourse (Shonkoff & Bales, 2011). For the present intervention, FrameWorks applied their experience and skills to developing climate change metaphors.

We present detailed information about FrameWorks design and testing used to translate science into metaphors in order to illustrate how social science information and methods were used in developing the training materials. FrameWorks deployed an iterative design process involving multiple cycles of testing, analysis, and refinement to select metaphors consistent and measurable results on public understanding of climate change (Volmert, 2014). The steps in this metaphor generation process were as follows.

1. *Identification of Instrumental Goals for Metaphor.*

   In this initial step, specific conceptual outcomes were established. Researchers first identified ways that the public talked about climate change, with a specific focus on tautologies and misconstruals. They used well-proven techniques from cognitive anthropology, qualitatively coding open-ended or natural language interviews where members of the public were asked to describe various aspects of climate change and ocean acidification (Quinn, 2005). These results were compared with coding of interviews with scientific experts on the same topics. This research identified strongly held conceptual models that were at odds with the ways that climate scientists talk about our changing climate (Volmert et al., 2013).

   These "gaps" in the public's knowledge and ability to talk about climate change served as communication goals that could be reached through the use of carefully-designed metaphors. As an example, the researchers' analyses revealed that the public lacked basic awareness of ocean acidification, and when pressed to guess what caused the phenomenon, many relied on dominant models of material pollution and "dumping" into the ocean as the cause of ocean acidification rather than carbon dioxide combining with water to create carbonic acid (Volmert et al, 2013). The analysis also revealed that people lacked a strong model of the climate as a system that included the ocean. Among other gaps, filling these two distinct "cognitive holes" became priorities for the development of two different metaphors.

2. *Generation of Multiple Candidate Metaphors.*

   In the next step of the metaphor generation process, an interdisciplinary team generated several possible source domain categories (e.g., mechanical systems, human body, and musical instruments) and within those categories, developed one or more metaphors that mapped well to the targeted climate science. As an example, one set of metaphors designed to address the exclusion of oceans from climate systems compared the role of the ocean in the climate to a hub, a scale, a spine, a brain, a skeleton, a foundation, and shock absorbers. These candidates were discussed, ranked, and refined by the team. Once a suitable set was decided upon, the metaphor candidates were written up in short paragraphs, with special care taken to ensure that the presentations of the candidates were parallel and minimally differing along the dimensions of tone, sentence structure, and length.

3. *Rapid Qualitative Testing*

   Following the development of the various explanatory metaphors, the researchers conducted on-the-street interviews to collect data on their effectiveness. Researchers recruited participants in public spaces and presented one of the metaphors orally. Participants' ability to reiterate the message were video- and audio-recorded by a professional videographer. The resulting data was coded and analyzed to identify which specific elements of the metaphors were functioning well, which were less successful in clarifying concepts and shifting perspectives, and which metaphors were ineffective and should be abandoned. In this step, the metaphor of climate's spine, where the ocean supports life on the planet, was adapted and extended into another metaphor, climate's heart, as a different way of conveying this idea.

4. *Experimental testing of messages.*

FrameWorks then tested a refined set of explanatory metaphors in an online quantitative experiment. The experiment queried 2,800 respondents drawn from a national online panel, who were randomly assigned to either a single message condition or a control group, and then asked to respond to a set of questions that probed knowledge, attitudes, and policy preferences. Data were weighted on the basis of gender, age, race, education and party identification to ensure that the sample was nationally representative. This step of the study provided an empirical basis for selecting tools that were most successful relative to a set of theoretically-driven outcome measures. Continuing the example with oceans as being a part of the climate system, in the end, experimental data was used to select two metaphors about the ocean (Climate's Spine and Climate's Heart) that were then taken into a final stage of empirical testing, described next.

5. *Persistence trials.*

After completion of the quantitative data to select effective metaphors, the research team conducted persistence trials of the final recommended set of metaphors to answer two general research questions: (1) can and do participants transmit the explanatory metaphor to other participants with a reasonable degree of fidelity? and (2) how do participants transmit the explanatory metaphor? In other words, the method examines how well the explanatory metaphors held up when "passed" between individuals, and how participants used and incorporated the metaphors in explanation to other participants. A comparison between how participants subsequently talk about climate change and whether they repeated the metaphor after hearing the Climate's Spine versus Climate's Heart metaphors revealed that the latter was a highly communicable, easily accessible tool that could be used to talk about the importance of oceans within the broader climate system, how oceans regulate climate, and how human activity is disrupting the ocean's' capacity to regulate climate effectively. The metaphor addressed the public's lack of basic understanding about what the climate system is, how it works, and the ocean's role within it. Below is an example of the use of the heart metaphor.

The ocean regulates the climate system the way your heart regulates the flow of blood throughout your body. The heart sustains the body by controlling the circulation of blood, making sure the right amount gets to all parts of the body — not too much and not too little. The ocean acts as the climate's heart, sustaining the climate by controlling the circulation of things like heat and humidity….. Burning fossil fuels damages the ocean's ability to maintain good circulation of heat and moisture. When we burn fossil fuels, we put a lot of stress on the ocean, which damages its ability to keep the climate stable — so sometimes the oceans pump too much heat and moisture through the system, sometimes too little. Burning fossil fuels weakens the ocean's ability to regulate the climate system (p. 13; Bales, Sweetland, & Volmert, 2015).

4.5.3 Reflection on the climate heart metaphor

The results of this research into the use of the Climate's Heart metaphor indicate that this simple metaphor:

- Conveys the centrality of oceans within the climate system: The metaphor is highly successful in communicating the importance of oceans for the proper functioning of the climate system;
- Facilitates thinking about how oceans can be harmed: Talking about the ocean as "the heart" of the climate produces the recognition that oceans, like hearts, are vulnerable to damage, and that this damage can have severe repercussions on a wider set of outcomes. The metaphor displaces assumptions that current changes to oceans are natural, and that if oceans are damaged they can simply repair themselves;
- Promotes thinking about the importance of preventative care: Just as hearts must be monitored and cared for to ensure their health and the health of the whole body, oceans must be monitored and cared for to ensure their health and the health of the climate; and
- Generates understanding of how oceans regulate climate: The concept of circulation opens up thinking about how oceans regulate climate by controlling the circulation of heat and moisture throughout the system.

4.5.4 Additional recommendations

Using the same methodology, other metaphors were developed for different aspects of the climate system (Bales et al., 2015; Volmert, 2014). These additional metaphors included the following: 1) differentiating between natural and human caused contribution of carbon dioxide as "regular" versus "rampant" levels of carbon dioxide, 2) a "heat trapping blanket" that gets thicker and thicker as a result of the accumulation of carbon dioxide in the atmosphere causing the planet to get warmer and warmer, and 3) "osteoporosis of the sea" which is a result of carbon dioxide combining with water to create carbonic acid that then eats away at sea creatures with calcium exteriors.

The same process was also used to select two ways to frame messages (Simon, Volmert, Bunten, & Kendall-Taylor, 2014). One recommended frame emphasized "protection" where people and places that we depend upon are protected thereby ensuring people's safety, risk reduction, and preserving habitats. This framing is reminiscent of research on loss aversion comparing people's preferences to avoid losses rather than achieve equivalent gains (Tversky & Kahneman, 1981). It also connects to research on moral principles of caring for others (Wolsko et al., 2016) and environmental concerns about the impact of environmental problems on people and the planet (Schultz, 2001). The second recommended frame focused on "responsible management" where people engage in step-by-step approaches to responsibly take care of environmental resources for long term planning and future generations. This frame, therefore, connects to a business approach to caring for the environment (Swim, Vescio, Dahl, & Zawadzki, 2017) and to legacy motives where people are asked to consider the impact of their current actions on future generations (Zaval et al., 2015). A frame that focused on scientific authorities was also tested. This framing argued for respecting scientific consensus, relying on scientists' findings and recommended solutions and supporting scientific research. Outcome measures suggested that "Scientific Authority" frame was not as effective as the other two frames so it was not recommended for further development.

4.6   Effects of training on educators and visitors to informal science learning centers

FrameWork's recommendations were integrated into a training program for 24 groups of educators at informal science learning centers. Each training program consisted of three in-person meetings over a six-month period with at-home exercises between the in-person trainings. The program ran for a total of seven years. Each training session included 10 pairs of educators and two climate scientists drawn from the faculty at Woods Hole Oceanographic Institute (WHOI). The training included learning about default ways that the public thinks about climate change, how to use metaphors and rhetoric tactics to avoid getting caught up in purposeless debates, and up-to-date training on science content provided by WHOI faculty. Participants were taught and practiced using recommended metaphors and the frames described above along with basic engagement tactics for deliberative dialogue (e.g., using reasonable tone and presenting community level solutions).

Three types of data provide support for the effectiveness of the NNOCCI training: data from the educators that attended the training, data from visitors to the educators' informal science learning centers, and data from members of the educators' social networks. These data sets represent the vectors of influence noted in Fig. 4.1. The first two data sets have been reported elsewhere so we provide highlights from these data sets and offer a more elaborated description of the third data set here. Given the multiple activities and experiences at the training, we cannot anchor the outcomes to any specific aspect of the program, but rather the overall suite of learning opportunities. We did, however, include measures designed to assess whether educators were using recommended communication techniques up to six months after the training concluded.

Educator data. Educator data focused on trainees' experiences with the training and changes pre-training to post-training on key outcome measures including their use of framing techniques, self-presentation concerns, and hope about their ability to meet their goals about talking about climate change. Data came from a pilot program where educators reflected on their training experience (Swim & Fraser, 2014), from educators' descriptions of their climate change communication efforts immediately before the training sessions, immediately after the training sessions, and six months following training completion (Geiger, Gasper & Swim, in preparation, Geiger, Swim, Fraser & Flinner, 2017), and from surveys at the end of the five year intervention where educators reflected on their membership in the community of practice developed by the intervention (Flinner, Fraser, Roberts, LaMarca, Swim, & Geiger, 2016). Following the training, informal educators felt less concern about talking about climate change and increased hope about their ability to talk about the issue. The value of the training was also revealed in educators being more likely to talk about climate change with visitors, colleagues, and friends and to use recommended messaging techniques.

Visitor data. Visitor data focused on the public's experiences with presentations at informal science learning centers. One set of data came from a national survey comparing three groups: 1) visitors to informal science learning centers that had sent educators to the training, 2) visitors to informal science learning centers that had not sent educators to the training and 3) members of the general public that had not attended an informal science learning centers (Swim et al., 2017). A second data set included on-site data collection from visitors who observed the educators' programs prior to the training with different visitors who observed the same educators six months after they had been trained (see Geiger et al., 2017). Results confirmed educators' reports that they tended to talk more about climate change and use recommended techniques more often following training (Geiger et al., 2017). Additionally, visitors had slight improvements in their knowledge of climate change and ocean acidification, were more hopeful about their ability to work with others to address climate change, felt more personally efficacious about talking about climate change, and were more likely to report intentions to engage in actions to address climate change (Swim et al., 2017).

4.6.1   Social network data

The third set of data was collected from members of educators' social networks. These data tested the social diffusion of the training beyond the visitor groups entailed by the job. We considered both formal networks (i.e., connections with coworkers in the same community of practice) and informal networks (i.e. connections with friends and family). We were interested in the formal networks because connections with co-workers could extend the reach of the training program. We were interested in informal networks because it could demonstrate that the training has a depth of personal impact and breadth of social impact that goes beyond the educator's job and place of employment.

Three-hundred seventy-seven friends, family, and colleagues who were connected to one of 116 educators completed a survey six months after the educator had completed the NNOCCI training program. Relative to the general public (but similar to the demographics of those who visit informal science learning centers, Geiger et al., 2017), women, whites, and political liberals were all overrepresented in our sample. See Appendix for more information about the sample.

In the survey, participants indicated recent changes in their conversations about climate change with the educator. More specifically, the survey assessed educators' communications about climate change—the frequency they talked about climate change over the previous six months, representing the time interval since they completed the training program; whether they used techniques recommended in the training; and their influence on network members' understanding of climate change, emotional responses and behaviors. After indicating the degree of influence the educator had on them, respondents indicated whether this influence reflected a change from before the educators' training. The measure of understanding included self-assessment of respondents' understanding of climate science, knowledge about sources of information about climate change (suggesting that they could success-fully seek additional information about climate change), knowing ways that communities could address climate change, and knowing ways to discuss climate change. Emotional reactions included feeling hopeful, helpless, bored, and anxious. The latter three were considered undesirable states for the purposes of the present research. See Appendix A for more information about measures.

Understanding and hope were of interest for three reasons. First, improved understanding and hope suggest that the training was addressing competency and emotional barriers to climate conversations, respectively. Second, if the effect of the training on educators accounted for the influence of educators on network members, then both the frequency and the use of recommended techniques should be associated with educators' influence on their network members' understanding of climate change and hope. Associations with understanding would suggest that the core messages were conveying the science as intended. Associations with hope would suggest that recommended solutions overcame emotional barriers to communication and action. Third, understanding and hope could motivate behavior. As noted above, our assessment of understanding included both understanding the science and understanding knowledge about actions. Together, these two components of understanding could motivate people to take such actions. If hope does suggest that solutions were more "doable" then people may be more persuaded to take actions.

With regard to network members observations of educators, on average, network members indicated that educators talked "occasionally" about climate change and "agreed" or "strongly agreed" that the educators used strategic framing techniques (see see weighted means in Table 4.1). Additionally, weighted percents indicate that over half reported that this was an increase over the previous six months which reflected the time between educators having completed the training and network members completing the survey. With regard to impact, weighted means also indicated that educators influenced network members' understanding of climate, hope about their ability to work with others to address climate change, and engagement in pro-environmental behaviors. Over half indicated an increase in influence in understanding and half indicated an increase in hope over the previous six months. A third indicated an increase in influence in pro-environmental behaviors. The lower percent may reflect greater difficulty in changing behaviors or more time needed to make such changes. In contrast, network members reported that the educators did not influence their negative feelings related to climate change (helpless, anxious, and disengaged) and only about 10% indicated that there was a change in educators influence on negative emotions. Changes over time in educator behavior and influence on network members did not significantly differ between educators' co-workers vs. friends and family, ps > .05.

The impact of educator behavior on understanding and hope and the subsequent impact of understanding and hope on behaviors result in the model illustrated in Figure 4.2. We conducted multilevel logistic regressions to test whether 1) changes in the frequency and way that the educators talked about climate change (as

Table 4.1 **Changes in conversations with educators**

	Weighted mean[a] [95% CI]	Weighted percent reporting an increase[a]	Weighted log odds of an increase in a respondent[b]
Reports of Conversations			
Frequency of discussion (0 = Never to 3 = Often)	2.12 [2.04, 2.20]	58%	0.34**
Use of strategic framing (−2 = Strongly Disagree to +2 = Strongly Agree)	1.65 [1.59, 1.70]	57%	0.29**
Reported Influence of Conversations			
Understanding of climate change (−2 = Strongly Disagree to +2 = Strongly Agree)	1.05 [0.97, 1.14]	59%	0.38**
Emotions (−1.5 = definitely do not feel this to +1.5 = definitely feel this)			
Hopeful	0.50 [0.44, 0.56]	49%	−0.04[(NS)]
Anxious[c]	−0.84[-0.90, −0.77]	10%	−2.23***
Helpless[c]	−0.80[-0.86, −0.73]	15%	−1.76***
Disengaged[c]	−1.15[-1.20, −1.10]	12%	−2.01***
Pro-environmental behaviors (−2 = Strongly Disagree to +2 = Strongly Agree)	0.61 [0.52, 0.70]	36%	−0.59***

Notes. CI = confidence interval. [(NS)] $p > .05$, *$p < .05$, ** $p < .01$, ***$p < .001$.
[a]Weighted means and weighted changes calculated through null (i.e., random intercept but no predictor variables) multilevel model to adjust for differences in number of participants who completed surveys for each interpreter.
[b]Log odds > 0 means more than half of educators increased. Log odds < 0 means less than half of educators increased.
[c]For negative emotions (anxious, helpless, disengaged), we assessed the percentage/probability of reporting a decrease in the emotion rather than an increase.

perceived by the network members) were related to network members' reports of changes in educators' influence on their understanding of climate change and hope about their ability to address climate change, and 2) these changes in understanding and hope were subsequently associated with changes in network members' reports that educators were influencing pro-environmental behaviors. We did not include negative emotions in the model because few indicated that changes in conversations

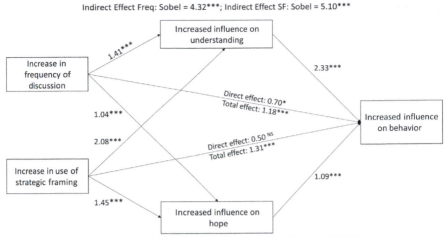

Figure 4.2 Process model for educator-induced change.
Notes: Logistic regressions were used for all analyses; coefficients represent log odds. Indirect Effect Freq = indirect effect of increased frequency of discussion on increased behavior that can be explained by the given mediator, Indirect Effect SF = indirect effect of increased use of strategic framing concepts on increased behavior that can be explained by the given mediator.

with network members had decreased these emotions and most indicated no changes in these emotions.

As shown in Fig. 4.2, an increase in educators' frequency of talking about climate change and use of strategic framing were positively associated with increase of educators' influence on network members' understanding of climate change and hope, ps < .001. Both changes in understanding of climate change and hope were subsequently positively associated with increased influence of educators on network members' pro-environmental behaviors, ps < .001. We used the procedures outlined in MacKinnon and Dwyer (1993) on conducting mediation analyses with dichotomous outcome variables to estimate indirect effects. Sobel tests revealed that all indirect effects were significantly greater than 0 (ps <.001), suggesting that relations between changes in the manner that educators discussed climate change and increased behavior among respondents could be explained by both increased understanding and hope among respondents. Additional analyses indicated that none of the paths in Fig. 4.2 differed between a) coworkers and b) friends/family.

In summary, the results of this rather large study revealed that those who participated in the NNOCCI training program were able to inspire those with whom they regularly interacted (i.e., those in their professional and personal social networks) into greater climate change engagement through educators' frequency and content of conversations about the topic. Over half of the contacts reported that educators had increased these activities since the training. The impact of educator behavior on

Table 4.2 **Demographics of survey respondents by sample source**

	Sample source	
	Friend/Family	**Colleague**
Political orientation		
Very Liberal	21%	25%
Liberal	42%	47%
Moderate	26%	24%
Conservative	10%	4%
Very Conservative	0%	1%
Gender		
Women	56%	73%
Men	44%	27%
Race/Ethnicity[a]		
White	99%	94%
Black	1%	2%
Middle Eastern	1%	0%
Hispanic	1%	3%
Asian	2%	3%
Native American	1%	1%
Pacific Islander	1%	0%

[a]Percentages add up to more than 100% because participants were able to select multiple ethnic origins.

behavioral engagement is attributable to the influence of educators on their network members' understanding of climate change and hope. When combined with results from data collected from educators and visitors, data from social network members suggest that the NNOCCI training program led to an overall increase in climate change engagement among a wide range of individuals who have contact with the educators. Since this increase in climate change engagement included increased discussion of climate change (Geiger et al., 2017), this training could result in ripple effects, affecting not only those who directly interact with training alumni but also those two or more degrees socially removed from those participating in the training program.

There are limitations in our analyses. First, the research design led to descriptive and correlational analyses. Given the lack of a control group, we cannot assert causality with regard to our process model shown in Fig. 4.2. Our descriptive findings could also have been skewed by respondents wishing to portray educators in a positive light and response bias: those who viewed the educator less favorably could have been less likely to respond to our invitation to complete the survey. We acknowledge these limitations but also note the convergence between these results and independent research assessing improvements in the educators' communication as viewed by visitors (Geiger et al., 2017), which suggests that these limitations may be minor and not impact the overall findings. The fact that similar conclusions can be drawn from analyses using diverse methodologies and sampling methods supports the validity of both sets of findings.

4.7 Conclusion

In this chapter, we have argued that interpersonal communications can be a vector for increasing public understanding and engagement in climate change actions, and that such communications can be improved both in terms of the frequency with which they occur and the content of the conversations. While the content was explicitly taught to educators at informal science learning centers, the strategies can be used in multiple contexts representing different opportunities for discussions by all members of the public. In the zoo context, conversations could be about the animals such as the pika, a rodent living in the alpine regions of mountains in the Western US that cannot survive in warm conditions. In the aquarium context, conversations could be about coral reefs that are less able to produce their skeletons where many other ocean species live. Outside informal science learning centers, conversations can be about families forced to move due to hurricanes whose intensity is increasing with warming water temperatures or about risks to food security and food cost due to changes in ability to raise crops and available water. Overall, the goal of this work is to create meaningful conversations that help scaffold the thinking of active learners from the general public by interpreting climate change and policy relevant information in ways that enhance their capacity to work toward solving the climate challenge. By making climate change causes and risks more salient and meaningful, interpreters at informal science learning centers can help communities develop and implement solutions.

Our research points to the importance of social influence on the social construction of climate change. Through seeding simplifying metaphors into meaningful conversations, it is possible to shift shared perceptions of climate change so they are more aligned to the discourse of climate change scientists. In this study, educators at informal science learning centers served as the touch point with the public with their social influence processes rippling and radiating out through their social networks. The impacts we report here on social networks are particularly significant for understanding the flow of information through social connections because these conversations were not specifically related to educators' work duties of talking with visitors to their institutions. The findings suggest that the training led most educators to voluntarily engage in more frequent and better conversations with those with whom they interacted in multiple domains of their life. Greater understanding of climate change prompted by information learned from informal science learning centers can increase efficacy about and frequency of discussion about climate change (Geiger et al., 2017). This study revealed the potential extended effects of educators' conversations as vectors for change throughout a community, continuing the spread of information to at least two degrees of separation from the educators.

Because this system of communication is also distributed across the entire United States, the social radiation of these concepts has a high likelihood of achieving national impact.

This chapter illustrated how interventions that employ principles from across the social sciences of psychology, sociology and communications can create social change. Our review and research demonstrate the effectiveness of grounding climate change literacy interventions in social sciences. The general principles about how to improve conversations noted here were identified, validated and reinforced through NNOCCI's efforts to integrate and apply recommended strategies in a training program. The results reinforce the argument that perceptions of climate change, including understanding the science, whether one can hope that their actions will matter, and what one should do, are socially constructed. Because these social constructions are developed by people within specific social contexts, they are open to reconstruction in ways that can align more closely to the scientific discourse and thereby promote engagement in science-based actions by members of the general public.

Appendix A   Details about study

Design and Participants. Educators provided contact information for a) up to five coworkers and b) up to five friends/family members that they believed would be willing to complete a survey six months after the completion of the educator's training program. One-hundred thirty-three educators who had participated in the NNOCCI training program between 2013 and 2015 (59% of all total educators) listed at least one person's contact information, for a total of 898 contacts (512 colleagues and 312 friends and family members). Five hundred and twenty of these individuals (315 colleagues, 205 friends/family) completed surveys (a 58% response rate) about their interactions with 120 educators. We removed 143 respondents who had skipped at least one entire section relevant to analyses (i.e., changes in discussions about climate change with the interpreter, strategic framing, understanding, hope, or civic behavior), leaving 377 respondents corresponding to 116 educators in the final dataset. (See Table 4.2 for demographics).

Network members completed questions about their education-related experiences with the educator who nominated them. The educator's name appeared on their survey when they answered the questions. We first assessed descriptive information about the conversations: whether network members perceived a change in the frequency that educators talked about climate change and ocean acidification and a change in the manner they talked about it, a change that would be consistent with the use of strategic framing. To do so, we asked participants to reflect on changes in educators' behaviors over the previous six months, corresponding to the time period between when the educators had completed their training and when the network members were asked to complete the survey.

First, respondents indicated the frequency the educator talked about climate change and ocean acidification over the previous six months (2 questions $\alpha = .68$) and whether the educator used strategic framing techniques (3 items, $\alpha = .78$; connected with their values, used easily understood metaphors, used a reasonable tone). After each of the frequency and strategic framing questions, network members indicated whether this reflected a decrease (-1), no change (0), or increase (1) in the educators' behaviors ($\alpha s = .75$ and $.90$, respectively).

Next, network members reported their agreement that their understanding of climate change (e.g., causes and impacts, and individual and community responses to address climate change on nine items, $\alpha = .95$) was a result of their interactions with the educator (on -3 "strongly disagree" to +3 "strongly agree" scale). Then they indicated whether their conversations with the educator made them feel hopeful (hopeful, confident, assured, optimistic, $\alpha = .87$; on 0 "not at all" to 4 "completely"). Using the same 0 to 4 scales, they indicated any changes in negative emotions: feeling helpless (helpless, powerless, lacking control, $\alpha = .91$), bored (indifferent, not caring, bored, $\alpha = .91$) and anxious (on edge, uneasy, nervous, $\alpha = .92$) about their ability to address climate change. Finally, network members reported their agreement that the educators prompted them to engage four civic pro-environmental behaviors ($\alpha = .93$, on -3 "strongly disagree" to +3 "strongly agree" scale).

Similar to above, they were asked whether these network driven consequences of the educators represented a decrease (-1), no change (0), or increase (1). With the exception of changes in negative emotions, very few (<1%) indicated a decrease in any outcomes over time, so all responses (except for changes in negative emotions) were dichotomized into (1) increase or (0) no increase. Scales corresponding to each of the above consequence were created (αs range from .87 to .99).

Acknowledgements

We would like to thank Kate Flinner for her help in tracking educators across the project. We would like to thank Anna Vargo for help in editing the chapter. This research was partially supported by NSF Grant DUE-1239775.

References

Abrahamse, W., & Steg, L. (2013). Social influence approaches to encourage resource conservation: A meta-analysis. *Global Environmental Change*, 23(6), 1773–1785.

Anderson, A. A. (2017). Social Media Use and Its Relationship to Climate Change Opinion, Knowledge, and Behavior. *Oxford Research Encyclopedias: Climate Science*. Available from https://doi.org/10.1093/acrefore/9780190228620.013.369. Retrieved July, 2017 from http://climatescience.oxfordre.com.

Bales, S.N., Sweetland, J., & Volmert, A. (2015, September). *How to Talk about Climate Change and the Ocean: A FrameWorks Message Memo*. *FrameWorks Institute*.

Retrieved from http://www.frameworksinstitute.org/assets/files/PDF_oceansclimate/cli-matechangeandtheocean_mm_final_2015.pdf

Berger, P. L., & Luckmann, T. (1966). *The Social Construction of Reality: A Treatise in the Sociology of Knowledge.* Garden City, NY: Anchor Books.

Blondé, J., & Girandola, F. (2016). Revealing the elusive effects of vividness: a meta-analysis of empirical evidences assessing the effect of vividness on persuasion. *Social Influence,* *11*(2), 111−129. Available from https://doi.org/10.1080/15534510.2016.1157096.

Bloodhart, B., Swim, J. K., & Zawadzki, M. J. (2013). Spreading the Eco-Message: Using Proactive Coping to Aid Eco-Rep Behavior Change Programming. *Sustainability, 5*(4), 1−19.

Brady, W. J., Wills, J. A., Jost, J. T., Tucker, J. A., & Bavel, J. J. V. (2017). Emotion shapes the diffusion of moralized content in social networks. *Proceedings of the National Academy of Sciences, 114*(28), 7313−7318. Available from https://doi.org/10.1073/pnas.1618923114.

Brügger, A., Dessai, S., Devine-Wright, P., Morton, T. A., & Pidgeon, N. F. (2015). Psychological responses to the proximity of climate change. *Nature Climate Change, 5* (12), 1031−1037. Available from https://doi.org/10.1038/nclimate2760.

Burn, S. M. (1991). Social psychology and the stimulation of recycling behaviors: The block leader approach. *Journal of Applied Social Psychology, 21*(8), 611−629.

Capstick, S., Whitmarsh, L., Poortinga, W., Pidgeon, N., & Upham, P. (2015). International trends in public perceptions of climate change over the past quarter century. *WIREs: Climate Change, 6*(1), 35−61.

Cavanaugh, L. A., Cutright, K. M., Luce, M. F., & Bettman, J. R. (2011). Hope, pride, and processing during optimal and nonoptimal times of day. *Emotion, 11*(1), 38−46. Available from https://doi.org/10.1037/a0022016.

Chadwick, A. E. (2015). Toward a theory of persuasive hope: effects of cognitive appraisals, hope appeals, and hope in the context of climate change. *Health Communication, 30*(6), 598−611. Available from https://doi.org/10.1080/10410236.2014.916777.

Cook, J., & Lewandowsky, S. (2011). *The Debunking Handbook.* St. Lucia, Australia: University of Queensland. Retrieved from https://www.skepticalscience.com/Debunking-Handbook-now-freely-available-download.html.

Corner, A. J., Markowitz, E., & Pidgeon, N. F. (2014). Public engagement with climate change: the role of human values. *Wiley Interdisciplinary Reviews: Climate Change, 5* (3), 411−422. Available from https://doi.org/10.1002/wcc.269.

Dilenschneider, C. (2017). *People trust museums more than newspapers. Here is why that matters right now (DATA).* Retrieved August, 2017 from https://www.colleendilen.com/2017/04/26/people-trust-museums-more-than-newspapers-here-is-why-that-matters-right-now-data/

Feinberg, M., & Willer, R. (2013). The Moral Roots of Environmental Attitudes. *Psychological Science, 24*(1), 56−62. Available from https://doi.org/10.1177/0956797612449177.

Foust, C. R., & O'Shannon Murphy, W. (2009). Revealing and Reframing Apocalyptic Tragedy in Global Warming Discourse. *Environmental Communication: A Journal of Nature and Culture, 3*(2), 151−167. Available from https://doi.org/10.1080/17524030902916624.

Fraser, J., Pantesco, V., Plemons, K., Gupta, R., & Rank, S. J. (2013). Sustaining the Conservationist. *Ecopsychology, 5*(2), 70−79. Available from https://doi.org/10.1089/eco.2012.0076.

Fraser, J., & Sickler, J. (2009). *Why Zoos and Aquariums Matter Handbook: Handbook of Research, Key Findings and Results from National Audience Survey.* Silver Spring, MD: Association of Zoos and Aquariums.

Flinner, K., Fraser, J., Roberts, S-J, LaMarca, N., Swim, J. & Geiger, N. (2016). NNOCCI community of practice, summative study: Survey findings. New Knowledge Publication #NSF.052.111.30. New York: New Knowledge Organization Ltd.

Gawronski, B. (2004). Theory-based bias correction in dispositional inference: The fundamental attribution error is dead, long live the correspondence bias. *European Review of Social Psychology,* *15*(1), 183−217. Available from https://doi.org/10.1080/10463280440000026.

Geiger, N., Gasper, K., Swim, J. K., & Fraser, J. Disentangling the roles of agency and pathways thinking in hope-related interventions: A multilevel modeling approach. Unpublished manuscript.

Geiger, N., & Swim, J. K. (2016). Climate of silence: Pluralistic ignorance as a barrier to climate change discussion. *Journal of Environmental Psychology,* *47*, 79−90. Available from https://doi.org/10.1016/j.jenvp.2016.05.002.

Geiger, N., Swim, J. K., & Fraser, J. (2017). Creating a climate for change: Interventions, efficacy and public discussion about climate change. *Journal of Environmental Psychology,* *51*, 104−116. Available from https://doi.org/10.1016/j.jenvp.2017.03.010.

Geiger, N., Swim, J. K., Fraser, J., & Flinner, K. (2017). Catalyzing public engagement with climate change through informal science learning centers. *Science Communication,* *39*(2), 221−249. Available from https://doi.org/10.1177/1075547017697980.

Geiger, N. & Swim, J.K., Glenna, L. (2017). Spread the green word: A social community perspective into environmentally sustainable behavior. Under review.

Gifford, R., Scannell, L., Kormos, C., Smolova, L., Biel, A., Boncu, S., & Uzzell, D. (2009). Temporal pessimism and spatial optimism in environmental assessments: An 18-nation study. *Journal of Environmental Psychology,* *29*(1), 1−12.

IPCC. (1990). In I. J. T. Houghton, G. J. Jenkins, & J. J. Ephraums (Eds.), *First assessment report (FAR). Report prepared for Intergovernmental Panel on Climate Change byWorking Group.* Cambridge, Great Britain, New York, NY, USA and Melbourne, Australia: Cambridge University Press.

IPCC. (2013). In T. F. Stocker, D. Qin, G.-K. Plattner, M. Tignor, S. K. Allen, J. Boschung, A. Nauels, Y. Xia, V. Bex, & P. M. Midgley (Eds.), *Climate Change 2013: The Physical Science Basis. Contribution of Working Group I to the Fifth Assessment Report of the Intergovernmental Panel on Climate Change.* Cambridge, United Kingdom and New York, NY, USA: Cambridge University Press, 1535 pp, doi:10.1017/CBO9781107415324.

Isenberg, D. J. (1986). Group polarization: A critical review and meta-analysis. *Journal of Personality and Social Psychology: Interpersonal Relations and Group Processes,* *50*(6), 1141−1151. Available from https://doi.org/10.1037/0022-3514.50.6.1141.

Jones, C., Hine, D. W., & Marks, A. D. G. (2017). The Future is Now: Reducing Psychological Distance to Increase Public Engagement with Climate Change. *Risk Analysis,* *37*(2), 331−341. Available from https://doi.org/10.1111/risa.12601.

Kasperson, R. E., Renn, O., Slovic, P., Brown, H. S., Emel, J., Goble, R., & Ratick, S. (1988). The Social Amplification of Risk: *A Conceptual Framework. Risk Analysis,* *8*(2), 177−187. Available from https://doi.org/10.1111/j.1539-6924.1988.tb01168.x.

Katz, E. (1957). The Two-Step Flow of Communication: An Up-To-Date Report on an Hypothesis. *Public Opinion Quarterly,* *21*, 61. Available from https://doi.org/10.1086/266687. (1, Anniversary Issue Devoted to Twenty Years of Public Opinion Research).

Kendall-Taylor, Nathaniel, & Haydon, Abigail (2016). Using metaphor to translate the science of resilience and developmental outcomes. *Public Understanding of Science*, *25*(5), 576−587.

Lakoff, G. (2010). Why it Matters How We Frame the Environment. *Environmental Communication: A Journal of Nature and Culture*, *4*(1), 70−81. Available from https://doi.org/10.1080/17524030903529749.

Leiserowitz, A., Maibach, E. W., Roser-Renouf, C., Feinberg, G., & Rosenthal, S. (2015). *Climate change in the American mind: March, 2015. Yale Project on Climate Change Communication*. New Haven, CT: Yale University and George Mason University. Retrieved from http://environment.yale.edu/climatecommunication/files/Global-Warming-CCAM-March-2015.pdf.

Leviston, Z., Walker, I., & Morwinski, S. (2012). Your opinion on climate change might not be as common as you think. *Nature Climate Change*, *3*(4), 334−337. Available from https://doi.org/10.1038/nclimate1743.

Lezak, S. B., & Thibodeau, P. H. (2016). Systems thinking and environmental concern. *Journal of Environmental Psychology*, *46*, 143−153. Available from https://doi.org/10.1016/j.jenvp.2016.04.005.

Lineman, M., Do, Y., Kim, J. Y., & Joo, G.-J. (2015). Talking about Climate Change and Global Warming: e0138996. *PLoS One*, *10*(9). Available from https://doi.org/10.1371/journal.pone.0138996.

MacKinnon, D. P., & Dwyer, J. H. (1993). Estimating mediated effects in prevention studies. *Evaluation Review*, *17*, 144−158.

Maibach, E. W., Leiserowitz, A., Roser-Renouf, C., & Mertz, C. K. (2011). Identifying Like-Minded Audiences for Global Warming Public Engagement Campaigns: An Audience Segmentation Analysis and Tool Development. *PLOS ONE*, *6*(3), e17571. Available from https://doi.org/10.1371/journal.pone.0017571.

Maki, A., & Raimi, K. T. (2017). Environmental peer persuasion: How moral exporting and belief superiority relate to efforts to influence others. *Journal of Environmental Psychology*, *49*, 18−29. Available from https://doi.org/10.1016/j.jenvp.2016.11.005.

Marshall, G. (2014). *Don't Even Think About It: Why Our Brains Are Wired to Ignore Climate Change*. New York, NY: Bloomsbury Publishing.

Milfont, T. L., Abrahamse, W., & McCarthy, N. (2011). Spatial and temporal biases in assessments of environmental conditions in New Zealand. *New Zealand Journal of Psychology*, *40*(2), 56−67.

Nisbet, M. C., & Kotcher, J. E. (2009). A Two-Step Flow of Influence?: Opinion-Leader Campaigns on Climate Change. *Science Communication*, *30*(3), 328−354. Available from https://doi.org/10.1177/1075547008328797.

Noelle-Neumann, E. (1993). *The Spiral of Silence: Public Opinion--Our Social Skin*. Chicago, IL: University of Chicago Press.

Norgaard, K. M. (2011). *Living in Denial: Climate change, Emotions, and Everyday Life*. Cambridge, MA: Massachusetts Institute of Technology.

Ojala, M. (2012). Hope and climate change: the importance of hope for environmental engagement among young people. *Environmental Education Research*, *18*(5), 625−642. Available from https://doi.org/10.1080/13504622.2011.637157.

O'Neill, S., & Nicholson-Cole, S. (2009). "Fear Won't Do It": Promoting Positive Engagement With Climate Change Through Visual and Iconic Representations. *Science Communication*, *30*(3), 355−379. Available from https://doi.org/10.1177/1075547008329201.

Oreskes, N., & Conway, E. M. (2011). *Merchants of Doubt: How a Handful of Scientists Obscured the Truth on Issues from Tobacco Smoke to Global Warming*. New York, NY: Bloomsbury Press.

Pearson, A. R., Schuldt, J. P., & Romero-Canyas, R. (2016). Social climate science: A new vista for psychological science. *Perspectives on Psychological Science*, *11*(5), 632−650.

Pfattheicher, S., Sassenrath, C., & Schindler, S. (2016). Feelings for the suffering of others and the environment: Compassion fosters proenvironmental tendencies. *Environment and Behavior*, *48*(7), 929−945. Available from https://doi.org/10.1177/0013916515574549.

Plutzer, E., McCaffrey, M., Hannah, A. L., Rosenau, J., Berbeco, M., & Reid, A. H. (2016). Climate confusion among U.S. teachers. *Science*, *351*(6274), 664−665. Available from https://doi.org/10.1126/science.aab3907.

Quinn, N. (2005). *Finding Culture in Talk: A Collection of Methods*. New York, NY: Palgrave- McMillan.

Raimi, K. T., Stern, P. C., & Maki, A. (2017). The Promise and Limitations of Using Analogies to Improve Decision-Relevant Understanding of Climate Change. *PLOS ONE*, *12*(1), e0171130. Available from https://doi.org/10.1371/journal.pone.0171130.

Ranney, M. A., & Clark, D. (2016). Climate Change Conceptual Change: Scientific Information Can Transform Attitudes. *Topics in Cognitive Science*, *8*(1). Available from https://doi.org/10.1111/tops.12187.

Regan, K. (2007). A role for dialogue in communication about climate change. In S. C. Moser, & L. Dilling (Eds.), *Creating a climate for change: Communicating climate change and facilitating social change* (pp. 213−222). New York, NY: Cambridge University Press, doi. org/10.1017/CBO9780511535871.016.

Renn, O. (2011). The social amplification/attenuation of risk framework: application to climate change. *Wiley Interdisciplinary Reviews: Climate Change*, *2*(2), 154−169. Available from https://doi.org/10.1002/wcc.99.

Schultz, P. W. (2001). The structure of environmental concern: Concern for self, other people, and the biosphere. *Journal of Environmental Psychology*, *21*(4), 327−339. Available from https://doi.org/10.1006/jevp.2001.0227.

Shonkoff, J., & Bales, S. N. (2011). Science does not speak for itself: Translating child development research for the public and its policymakers. *Child Development*, *82*, 17−32.

Simon, A., Volmert, A., Bunten, A., & Kendall-Taylor, N. (2014). The Value of Explanation: Using Values and Causal Explanations to Reframe Climate and Ocean Change *(A Frameworks Research Report)*. Washington, D.C: Frameworks Institute.

Snyder, C. R. (2002). Hope theory: Rainbows in the mind. *Psychological Inquiry*, *13*(4), 249−275.

Sopory, P., & Dillard, J. P. (2002). The Persuasive Effects of Metaphor: A Meta-Analysis. *Human Communication Research*, *28*(3), 382−419. Available from https://doi.org/10.1111/j.1468-2958.2002.tb00813.x.

Starosta, G. (2008). *Friedman Urges Audience: 'Change Your Leaders, Not Your Light Bulbs' | Sanford School of Public Policy*. Retrieved September 6, 2017, from http://news.sanford.duke.edu/news-type/news/2008/friedman-urges-audience-%E2%80%98change-your-leaders-not-your-light-bulbs%E2%80%99

Steg, L., & Sievers, I. (2000). Cultural Theory and Individual Perceptions of Environmental Risks. *Environment and Behavior*, *32*(2), 250−269. Available from https://doi.org/10.1177/00139160021972513.

Sundar, S. S., & Nass, C. (2001). Conceptualizing sources in online news. *Journal of Communication, 51*(1), 52−72. Available from https://doi.org/10.1111/j.1460-2466.2001.tb02872.x.

Swim, J. K., & Bloodhart, B. (2014). Portraying the Perils to Polar Bears: The Role of Empathetic and Objective Perspective-taking Toward Animals in Climate Change Communication. *Environmental Communication, 9*(4), 446−468. Available from https://doi.org/10.1080/17524032.2014.987304.

Swim, J.K. & Bloodhart, B. (2018). *Climate Change Justice and Intergroup Relations*. Paper under review.

Swim, J. K., & Fraser, J. (2013). Fostering hope in climate change educators. *Journal of Museum Education, 38*(3), 286−297.

Swim, J. K., & Fraser, J. (2014). Zoo and aquarium professionals' concerns and confidence about climate change education. *Journal of Geoscience Education, 62*(3), 495−501.

Swim, J. K., & Geiger, N. (2017). From Alarmed to Dismissive of Climate Change: A Single Item Assessment of Individual Differences in Concern and Issue Involvement. *Environmental Communication, 11*(4), 568−586. Available from https://doi.org/10.1080/17524032.2017.130840.

Swim, J. K., Geiger, N., Fraser, J., & Pletcher, N. (2017). Climate change education at nature-based museums. *Curator: The Museum Journal, 60*(1), 101−119. Available from https://doi.org/10.1111/cura.12187.

Swim, J.K., Vescio, T.K., Dahl, J.L., & Zawadzki, S.J. (2017). Gendered discourse on climate change discourse. Under review.

Swim, J. K., & Whitmarsh, L. (2017). Climate change as a unique environmental problem. In L. Steg, A. E. van den Berg, & J. I. M. de Groot (Eds.), *Environmental Psychology: An Introduction*. West Sussex, UK: BPS Blackwell & John Wily & Sons, Ltd.

Tannenbaum, M. B., Hepler, J., Zimmerman, R. S., Saul, L., Jacobs, S., Wilson, K., & Albarracín, D. (2015). Appealing to fear: A meta-analysis of fear appeal effectiveness and theories. *Psychological Bulletin, 141*(6), 1178−1204. Available from https://doi.org/10.1037/a0039729.

Thibodeau, P. H., Frantz, C. M., & Berretta, M. (2017). The earth is our home: systemic metaphors to redefine our relationship with nature. *Climatic Change, 142*(1−2), 287−300. Available from https://doi.org/10.1007/s10584-017-1926-z.

Tversky, A., & Kahneman, D. (1981). The framing of decisions and the psychology of choice. *Science, 211*(4481), 453−458. Available from https://doi.org/10.1126/science.7455683.

Valente, T. W., & Davis, R. L. (1999). Accelerating the diffusion of innovations using opinion leaders. *The Annals of the American Academy of Political and Social Science, 566*(1), 55−67.

Van Zomeren, M., Leach, C. W., & Spears, R. (2012). Protesters as "Passionate Economists": A dynamic dual pathway model of approach coping with collective disadvantage. *Personality and Social Psychology Review, 16*(2), 180−199.

Volmert, A. (2014). Getting to the Heart of the Matter: Using Metaphorical and Causal Explanation to Increase Public Understanding of Climate and Ocean Change *(A Frameworks Research Report)*. Washington, D.C: Frameworks Institute. Retrieved from http://www.frameworksinstitute.org/assets/files/PDF_oceansclimate/occ_metaphor_report.pdf.

Volmert, A., Baran, M., Kendall-Taylor, N., Lindland, E., Haydon, A., Arvizu, S., & Bunten, A. (2013). Just the Earth Doing Its Own Thing: Mapping the Gaps Between Expert and Public Understandings of Oceans and Climate Change *(A Frameworks Research*

Report). Washington, D.C: Frameworks Institute. Retrieved from http://www.frameworksinstitute.org/assets/files/cc_oceans_mtg.pdf.

Wijeratne, A. J. C., Van Dijk, P. A., Kirk-Brown, A., & Frost, L. (2014). Rules of engagement: The role of emotional display rules in delivering conservation interpretation in a zoo-based tourism context. *Tourism Management, 42*, 149–156. Available from https://doi.org/10.1016/j.tourman.2013.11.012.

Wolsko, C., Ariceaga, H., & Seiden, J. (2016). Red, white, and blue enough to be green: Effects of moral framing on climate change attitudes and conservation behaviors. *Journal of Experimental Social Psychology, 65*, 7–19. Available from https://doi.org/10.1016/j.jesp.2016.02.005.

Zaval, L., Markowitz, E. M., & Weber, E. U. (2015). How will I be remembered? Conserving the environment for the sake of one's legacy. *Psychological Science, 26*(2), 231–236. Available from https://doi.org/10.1177/0956797614561266.

A diversity science approach to climate change

Adam R. Pearson[1] and Jonathon P. Schuldt[2]
[1]Pomona College, Claremont, CA, United States, [2]Cornell University, Ithaca, NY, United States

5.1 A diversity science approach to climate change

For Latinos, our strong positions on questions pertaining to the importance of stewardship of our natural environment and conservation of resources reflect long-held cultural tenets taught to us not as environmentalism, but based more on common sense, economic necessity, and good citizenry.—Mark Magaña, President/Founder GreenLatinos

When Hurricane Katrina struck New Orleans in late August of 2005, virtually all inhabitants of the city were affected and displaced, but impacts fell disproportionately on racial and ethnic minority and low-income communities. Disparities were evident in a comparison of undamaged vs damaged areas, which had a higher proportion of Black and low-income residents (Masozera, Bailey, & Kerchner, 2007), in the slower rates of return to the city by Blacks compared to Whites (Fussell, Sastry, & VanLandingham, 2010), and in higher mortality rates (estimated at 1.7−4 times greater) among Black residents, relative to Whites (Brunkard, Namulanda, & Ratard, 2008). Events such as these highlight the significant social dimensions of natural disasters, such as hurricanes, that are projected to increase in intensity as the planet warms (Bolin, 2006; Knutson et al., 2010; Laska & Morrow, 2006). Yet, despite growing attention to inequity in climate-related impacts, and to racial and ethnic disparities within psychology generally, scholars have only recently begun to apply behavioral science approaches to understand the diversity of human responses to climate change in pluralistic societies.

This chapter reviews the insights and applications of diversity science to the psychological study of climate change. Although many identity dimensions are relevant to the study of diversity (e.g., age, religion, cultural diversity), in this chapter, we focus on racial, ethnic, and class differences in climate change engagement, consistent with the growing empirical literatures on these dimensions in the study of climate change (see Pearson, Ballew, Naiman, & Schuldt, 2017). We begin by considering why diversity matters for understanding public engagement with climate change and describe what a diversity science approach can contribute to current social science perspectives in this area. We then review empirical evidence for

Psychology and Climate Change. DOI: https://doi.org/10.1016/B978-0-12-813130-5.00005-9

racial, ethnic, and class differences in climate change attitudes, beliefs, and behavior that highlight the differing ways that groups engage with the issue. Next, we discuss social psychological processes that can enhance and hinder engagement among groups that remain substantially underrepresented within the environmental movement. We conclude by considering the implications of a diversity science approach for developing effective organizational practices and policies that seek to broaden public participation in environmental decision-making.

5.2   Why diversity matters for climate change

Due to increased transnational migration and demographic shifts within countries, many industrialized nations that contribute disproportionately to climate change and have the greatest influence on international policy-making, such as the United States and nations in Western Europe, are also becoming more diverse. Within the United States, racial and ethnic minorities accounted for over 92% of the nation's population growth in the decade from 2000 to 2010, with current estimates indicating that a majority of the under-18 US population will identify as a member of a racial or ethnic minority by 2020 (Colby & Ortman, 2015; Heimlich, 2011). Beyond the United States, similar demographic changes are projected for Europe and Australasia with the arrival of humanitarian entrants and skilled migrants, with migration set to increase as a result of climate change and its impacts in the coming decades (Piguet, Pécoud, & de Guchteneire, 2011; United Nations Development Programme, (2007). These shifting demographics underscore a need for research that can inform government and organizational efforts to broaden public participation in climate discourse and decision-making in increasingly diverse societies, and particularly among groups disproportionately affected by climate change.

Although climate change is a global threat, its impacts are not evenly distributed but instead fall disproportionately on the world's poor and politically disenfranchised (e.g., Miranda, Hastings, Aldy, & Schlesinger, 2011; Wilson, Richard, Joseph, & Williams, 2010). Members of socioeconomically disadvantaged groups, such as racial and ethnic minorities and the poor, experience harmful impacts of climate change at substantially greater levels than those of more advantaged groups, such as Whites and the more affluent (Cutter, Emrich, Webb, & Morath, 2009; United Nations Development Programme, (2007). To make matters worse, global inequality is expected to increase substantially within the next several decades as wealthier nations at higher latitudes, such as Canada and Scandinavia, stand to benefit economically from regional warming, whereas poorer nations closer to the equator will be negatively affected. The effects of climate change on global inequality may further exacerbate and compound climate disparities as poorer countries struggle to adapt to its effects (Burke, Hsiang, & Miguel, 2015).

Beyond fundamental issues of equity, there are other important reasons for studying factors that broaden and sustain public engagement on climate change. In particular, the well-documented political divide on climate change within the

United States and some European nations (see Dunlap, McCright, & Yarosh, 2016) and wavering public interest in climate change globally (Brulle, Carmichael, & Jenkins, 2012) present formidable challenges for organizations and policy-makers who are looking to build consensus and galvanize public support for adaptation and mitigation policies. Moreover, research on group decision-making suggests that diversity in teams promotes more effective problem solving and the development of more innovative solutions (e.g., Hong & Page, 2004; Levine et al., 2014)— precisely the kind of solutions needed to avert the worst effects of climate change. Understanding factors that enhance diversity in climate decision-making may, thus, not only address inequity by giving voice to groups disproportionately affected by climate change but also spur the development of new solutions that are urgently needed to help communities and nations adapt to a changing climate.

5.2.1 A diversity science approach

Insights from diversity science can help guide psychological inquiry on factors that shape public engagement on climate change. Diversity science represents an interdisciplinary approach that uses behavioral science methodologies to consider how people create, interpret, and maintain group differences, as well as the psychological and societal consequences of these distinctions (Plaut, 2010). Thus, a diversity science approach can help to illuminate key *motivational* underpinnings of environmental engagement (i.e., social psychological mechanisms) and the ways in which both intra- and intergroup processes can powerfully shape these motivations.

Diversity science, as an interdisciplinary approach, emerged from social psychology and organizational behavior to understand psychological processes underpinning racial and ethnic disparities within organizations and academia. The approach has since been applied to a wide range of fields, including healthcare, employment, education, criminal justice, and organizational behavior (for reviews, see Apfelbaum, Norton, & Sommers, 2012; Cheryan, Ziegler, Montoya, & Jiang, 2017; Dovidio, Gaertner, Ufkes, Saguy, & Pearson, 2016; Cohen, Garcia, & Goyer, 2017; Oyserman & Lewis, 2017; Plaut, 2010; Yeager & Walton, 2011). Importantly, within each of these domains, a diversity science approach considers how the perspectives of both majority and minority group members can contribute to intergroup disparities. In the following sections, we extend a diversity science framework to the domain of climate change communication and organizational practice to explore three core questions: What motivates people to join environmental professions, organizations, and initiatives? How do different ways of framing sustainability challenges influence *who* engages with climate change advocacy? And how do both majority and minority group perspectives shape environmental attitudes and collective action in increasingly diverse societies, such as the United States?

In their review of public opinion work on climate change, Wolf and Moser (2011) distinguish between climate change *understandings* (acquisition and use of knowledge about climate change), *perceptions* (e.g., subjective experience as well as interpretations of others' beliefs and actions), and *engagement* (a motivational state that can include cognitive, emotional, and/or behavioral dimensions) as distinct but complementary ways that individuals respond to climate change. In the following sections, we summarize research and theory that examine how social groups shape each of these dimensions, with a particular focus on psychological processes that may influence engagement at the collective level (e.g., activism and participation in environmental organizations). We begin by reviewing empirical research highlighting the key role of identity processes in climate change engagement and then turn to theoretical perspectives within psychology that offer additional insights into the ways that group memberships can impact engagement, particularly for members of traditionally underrepresented groups.

5.2.2   Identity-based approaches to climate change engagement

A growing body of research on environmental behavior suggests that social identities can affect both how people perceive environmental risks and how they engage with groups working to address them (Feygina, 2013; Fielding, Hornsey, & Swim, 2014; Pearson, Schuldt, & Romero-Canyas, 2016; Swim & Becker, 2012). Moreover, interventions that capitalize on social identity processes have been shown to be particularly effective at motivating cooperation in resource dilemmas (see Brewer & Silver, 2000; Ostrom, 1990; Van Vugt, 2009), and engagement with activist causes, generally (see Tyler & Blader, 2000).

According to the social identity model of collective action (van Zomeren, Postmes, & Spears, 2008; see also van Zomeren, Spears, & Leach, 2010), people take action when they identify with groups attempting to mobilize action, believe that their group's actions can be effective, and experience strong emotional reactions (e.g., feelings of injustice). For instance, a series of studies examining what motivates people to join local climate change initiatives found that the extent to which people identified with the group involved in the cause was a strong predictor of motivation to participate, over and above concerns about costs and benefits of participating (Bamberg, Rees, & Seebauer, 2015; see also Chapter 8: Environmental protection through societal change: What psychology knows about collective climate action—and what it needs to find out). In addition, whereas those who more strongly identified with the group showed intrinsic motivations to participate (e.g., viewing the group's goals as more important than one's personal reasons for participating), those with low levels of identification were more extrinsically motivated, focusing on personal costs and benefits of participating.

The group engagement model (Tyler & Blader, 2003) similarly posits that identity motivations are central to psychological and behavioral engagement with groups, and that perceptions of procedural justice (e.g., inclusion in decision-making processes, being recognized and treated with respect) are a primary mechanism through which people assess, establish, and maintain group ties. Process fairness provides people with reassurance that a group values and represents their interests, which in turn fosters a sense of connection and identification with the group, its members, and their goals. Including members of traditionally underrepresented groups as meaningful stakeholders in climate change decision-making is, thus, important not only for ensuring greater equity in decision-making (e.g., addressing problems that matter to these groups) but also for promoting solidarity with groups working to address climate change.

The unique complexity (e.g., implicating both biophysical and social systems), temporal features, and geographic scale of climate change that make it difficult to understand and predict can also directly impact social identity processes. Uncertainty about the causes and long-term effects of climate change is often viewed as a chief barrier to public mobilization (Barrett & Dannenberg, 2014; Budescu, Broomell, & Por, 2009; Pidgeon & Fischhoff, 2011). However, uncertainty can also *increase* collective action by enhancing identification with groups engaged in activist causes. Generally, people participate in social movements not only to effect social change but also to establish social identities and strengthen social ties with fellow group members (Hogg, 2007; Klandermans, 2004). High and enduring uncertainty due to economic collapse or natural disasters can lead people to seek and affiliate with groups that are ideologically more extreme, or make existing groups more extreme, to reduce the uncertainty (see Hogg, 2007). Thus, uncertainty surrounding climate change may heighten the importance of social identities and impact the strength of group ties in ways that may hinder or enhance collective efforts to address the problem.

Research on partisan influences provides additional evidence of the role of group identities (e.g., party affiliations) in shaping public opinion on climate change. People's beliefs and experiences, including their perceptions of other group members' beliefs, form an important basis for how they perceive social and political issues (Wood & Vedlitz, 2007). Individuals tend to adopt beliefs that are shared by members of salient ingroups and may resist revision of these beliefs when they are confronted with conflicting information (Kahan, Braman, Gastil, Slovic, & Mertz, 2007; McCright & Dunlap, 2011a; Schuldt & Roh, 2014). Similarly, the elite cues hypothesis (Krosnick, Holbrook, & Visser, 2000) suggests that people are especially likely to rely on information from high-status ingroup members (e.g., political leaders) when an issue is perceived to be complex or controversial. Consistent with these perspectives, several studies have shown that as education and science literacy increase within the US public, political polarization on climate change becomes *stronger*, suggesting that people process climate-related information in ways that reinforce their prior political stance (e.g., Hamilton, 2011).

5.3 Identity influences beyond partisan politics

Compared to partisan influences, considerably less attention has been paid to the role of nonpartisan social identities and group memberships, such as those related to race, ethnicity, and social class, that have also been shown to influence how people assess environmental risks (for reviews, see Ferguson, McDonald, & Branscombe, 2016; Pearson & Schuldt, 2015; Pearson et al., 2016; Schuldt & Pearson, 2016). Early studies often conflated environmental attitudes with specific behaviors, such as outdoor recreation (e.g., visits to national parks), membership in environmental organizations, and charitable donations. This measurement problem contributed to the belief that non-Whites were less concerned about the environment than Whites (for reviews, see Mohai, 2008; Macias, 2016b; and Taylor, 1989). Spurred largely by work in the environmental justice field over the past two decades, there has been a notable shift away from assessing environmental concern based primarily on attitudes toward *conservation* (e.g., protection of natural resources) to incorporating measures of environmental *risk*, and particularly perceived exposure to environmental hazards, such as health risks associated with industrial pollution that disproportionately affect Black and Latino communities (see Arp & Kenny, 1996; Bullard, Johnson, & Torres, 2011; Jones & Rainey, 2006; Macias, 2016a; Mohai, 2008; Mohai & Bryant, 1998).

5.3.1   Evidence for the roles of racial and ethnic identities

US opinion polls reveal a racial/ethnic gap in environmental concern—including about climate change, specifically—with non-White minorities expressing a level of concern that often exceeds that expressed by Whites (e.g., Dietz, Dan, & Shwom, 2007; Guber, 2013; Leiserowitz & Akerlof, 2010; Macias, 2016a; McCright & Dunlap, 2011a; Speiser & Krygsman, 2014; Whittaker, Segura, & Bowler, 2005; Williams & Florez, 2002). For instance, an analysis of US Gallup Polls between 2001 and 2010 revealed that relative to Whites, non-Whites reported greater concern that climate change would pose a serious threat within their lifetime (McCright & Dunlap, 2011a), and this racial/ethnic gap in concern remained when controlling for other variables found to correlate with climate change beliefs, including income, education, religiosity, and political orientation (see Guber, 2013). Similarly, using data from the 2010 General Social Survey (GSS), Macias (2016a) found that non-Whites expressed greater concern for climate change than Whites, controlling for effects of age, gender, household income, education, rural/urban location, and political ideology. Moreover, non-Whites' concerns about climate change exceeded concern for more localized issues, such as air pollution from cars and industry[1].

Research on ethnicity and acculturation processes also suggests a unique role of ethnic identities in climate change engagement. For instance, within the United States, Asians and Latinos, the fastest growing minority groups, consistently show the highest levels of concern about climate change among all racial and ethnic groups, and particularly among first-generation immigrants (e.g., Jones, Cox, & Navarro-Rivera, 2014; Leiserowitz & Akerlof, 2010; Macias, 2016a, 2016b). Social psychological research has identified distinct value orientations among these groups, such as a more interdependent, collectivistic orientation that prioritizes social harmony, respect, and concern for family and community over individuality and self-interest (Holloway, Waldrip, & Ickes, 2009)—values that are also

[1] For evidence of a similar gap in climate change beliefs, risk perceptions, and policy support with regard to gender, see Pearson et al. (2017).

associated with proenvironmental attitudes and behaviors (see Milfont, 2012). For instance, Schultz (2002) found that people from collectivist cultures generally have greater biospheric concerns than those from individualist cultures. These findings highlight the need for additional research that investigates key cultural factors that impact environmental attitudes and beliefs.

These gaps in concern translate to differences in policy support at both local and national levels. For instance, Blacks and Latinos typically express higher levels of support for national climate and energy policies than Whites, even when these policies incur a short-term cost (e.g., taxes). This includes proportionally higher support for regulating carbon emissions, improving fuel economy and household energy efficiency standards, and increasing taxes to mitigate climate change (see Fig. 5.1; Leiserowitz & Akerlof, 2010; see also Dietz et al., 2007; Leiserowitz, 2006; and Krygsman, Speiser, & Lake, 2016). A similar pattern is evident even among policy-makers, with research suggesting that Hispanic and African-American members of Congress are more likely than White members to vote proenvironmentally (Ard & Mohai, 2011).

Some scholars have argued that environmental beliefs, including skepticism about climate change, can serve an "identity-protective" function to buffer the status afforded by advantaged group memberships (Kahan et al., 2007). Individuals

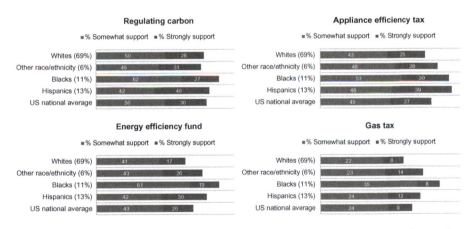

Figure 5.1 Percentage of US respondents supporting climate and energy policies by race/ethnicity, from Leiserowitz and Akerlof (2010). Items include support or opposition to regulating carbon as a pollutant; providing a government subsidy to replace household appliances that would cost the average household $5 a month in higher taxes; establishing an energy efficiency fund to help make buildings more energy efficient and teach Americans how to reduce their energy use; and increasing taxes on gasoline by 25 cents per gallon and returning the revenues to taxpayers. Results are based on a nationally representative survey of 2164 US adults. Racial/ethnic categories include Hispanics (13% of the sample), Blacks (11%), other race/ethnicity (6%), and Whites (69%). See Leiserowitz and Akerlof (2010) for additional survey items and methodology.

from higher status groups (e.g., White males) are especially likely to resist regulatory policies aimed at reducing environmental risks and perceive them as challenges to established social, economic, and political institutions (Feygina et al., 2010; McCright & Dunlap, 2011b). Policies aimed at mitigating climate change can represent a challenge to the status quo, which, in turn, may prompt responses to defend and legitimize those advantageous systems (e.g., denying climate change or its human causes; see Hennes, Ruisch, Feygina, Monteiro, & Jost, 2016).

Related work on the "White male effect" in environmental risk perception has highlighted the ways that gender, race, and political orientation can intersect to predict beliefs about climate change and support for mitigation policy. For instance, conservative White males are significantly more likely than other groups in the United States to deny the existence of climate change (Kahan, Jenkins-Smith, & Braman, 2011; Finucane, Slovic, Mertz, Flynn, & Satterfield, 2000; McCright & Dunlap, 2013). Complementing these findings, individuals from higher status groups who are also more likely to perceive prevailing group hierarchies as just and fair (e.g., conservative White males) are most likely to resist policies aimed at regulating environmental risks and to perceive them as threatening established social, economic, and political systems (Feygina *et al.* 2010; McCright & Dunlap, 2011a).

5.3.2   An attitude-participation gap in minority engagement

Although US minorities often report higher levels of environmental concern than their White counterparts, they nevertheless remain substantially underrepresented in environmental organizations and professions. For instance, an analysis of occupational disparities revealed that despite constituting 38% of the US population and nearly one-third of the US science, technology, engineering, and math (STEM) workforce, non-Whites account for only 10%–15% of environmental science professionals (Pearson & Schuldt, 2014). These findings mirror disparities in the US environmental sector more generally. A study of 293 US environmental nonprofits, government agencies, and grant-making foundations found that non-Whites comprised no more than 16% of staff in all three types of institutions (Taylor, 2014). Within academia, a similar picture emerges. A survey of US faculty across 17 environmental disciplines revealed only 11% minority representation, with a majority of faculty reporting having either one or no faculty of color in their department (Taylor, 2010).

Efforts to address disparities in the environmental sector have frequently focused on increasing the salience of environmental risks, and in so doing, appear to assume that low environmental awareness is the chief barrier to engagement—an assumption at odds with the high levels of risk awareness and environmental concern expressed by US racial and ethnic minorities and lower income individuals, discussed above (e.g., Dietz et al., 2007; Guber, 2013; Leiserowitz & Akerlof, 2010). Moreover, surveys reveal substantial numbers of racial and ethnic minorities who are qualified to work in the environmental sector (Taylor, 2010, 2014). Thus, other factors may be at play.

Although the above findings document a persistent and substantial attitude-participation gap in minority engagement, theoretically informed approaches aimed at bridging this gap are lacking. Much of the social science scholarship, to-date, has focused on key structural barriers, such as insular hiring practices and limited minority outreach, that impede the recruitment and retention of racial and ethnic minorities within the environmental sector (see Taylor, 2014; for a review). In the following sections, we explore complementary *psychological* processes that may contribute to the attitude-participation gap and represent additional pathways for intervention.

5.4   Motivational barriers across groups

Research suggests that differing group concerns—particularly related to differing levels of vulnerability to harms associated with environmental hazards—are central to understanding how majority and minority groups engage with the problem of climate change and assess its risks.

According to the differential vulnerability hypothesis, non-Whites in the United States may feel more vulnerable to the effects of climate change than Whites, in part, because of their less privileged position in society (Flynn, Slovic, & Mertz, 1994; Satterfield, Mertz, & Slovic, 2004). Consistent with this hypothesis, Adeola (2004) found that disproportionate exposure to environmental hazards predicted Blacks' greater perception of a wide range of environmental risks, including those associated with industrial emissions. Similarly, in a nationally representative U.S sample, Satterfield et al. (2004) found that the racial/ethnic gap in environmental concern was partially accounted for by non-Whites' greater awareness of disproportionate environmental hazards and greater perceived vulnerability—effects obtained independent of those of income, education, and political orientation (see also Mohai, 2003).

Similar effects have been documented for lower income individuals. Stokes, Wike, and Carle (2015) reported that Americans making less (vs more) than $50,000 a year were more likely to believe that climate change is a very serious problem and were more concerned that it would harm them personally. Whereas this result may partly reflect the economic means of wealthier individuals to adapt to threats posed by climate change (see Macias, 2016b; Semenza et al., 2008), poorer people may feel a heightened sense of vulnerability to negative impacts both because they lack financial means and because the places where they typically live and work are more vulnerable to climate impacts (Crona, Wutich, Brewis, & Gartin, 2013; Mirza, 2003; Swim et al., 2009).

These differences in risk perceptions mirror the reality that low-income and minority communities in many industrialized nations suffer disproportionately from a wide range of environmental hazards, as mentioned above. For instance, due to persistent racial segregation and discrimination in the real estate economy, US Blacks and Latinos are substantially more likely to live near hazardous industrial sites and high-pollution-emitting power plants (Bolin, Grineski, & Collins, 2005;

Bullard et al., 2011; Jones & Rainey, 2006; Mohai, 2008). As a result, non-Whites experience higher levels of smog exposure than equivalent-income Whites, with racial disparities in exposure up to 20 times greater than disparities by income (Clark, Millet, & Marshall, 2014).

5.4.1   Differential motives in climate change engagement

Given their greater vulnerability and awareness of inequities (Satterfield et al., 2004), racial and ethnic minorities and members of other socioeconomically disadvantaged groups may be motivated by concerns that are less rooted in political orientation (i.e., party identification or political ideology) compared to Whites and members of advantaged groups. Consistent with this reasoning, in a large nationally representative survey of the US public, we (Schuldt & Pearson, 2016) found that relative to Whites, racial and ethnic minorities' climate change views were less politically polarized (and also were more weakly correlated with their willingness to self-identify as an "environmentalist"). Most strikingly, political ideology, a variable that strongly predicts climate polarization in the United States, was substantially less predictive of the climate beliefs of non-Whites relative to Whites. This same pattern held across a range of related beliefs, including belief in the existence of climate change, perceptions of the scientific consensus, and support for mitigation efforts (regulating greenhouse gases). Thus, factors that strongly predict Whites' opinions on climate change and shape the dominant narrative about the partisan gap—namely, political orientation and self-identifying as an environmentalist —are relatively weak predictors for minorities.

Similar effects have also been obtained for socioeconomic status, whereby lower income and lower educated individuals also show weaker polarization of climate change opinions, relative to those with higher incomes and education levels (see Pearson et al., 2017; for a review). These findings suggest that, consistent with their heightened awareness of environmental risks, the climate change attitudes and beliefs of racial and ethnic minorities and of members of other socioeconomically disadvantaged groups may be less partisan and less ideologically driven compared to those of Whites and members of socioeconomically advantaged groups.

Notably, within the United States, there is also evidence of differential political polarization between advantaged and disadvantaged groups in the perceived dangers posed by climate change. Figs. 5.2 and 5.3 show the percentage of Whites vs non-White minorities and lower income vs higher income Americans, respectively, who indicated that the "rise in the world's temperature" is "extremely" or "very" dangerous from the 2000 and 2010 GSS. As seen in the figures, the concerns of Whites and higher income Americans grew more politically polarized over this time period, in line with the familiar trend seen in public opinion research and commonly reported in news media on climate change (see Dunlap et al., 2016). In sharp contrast, the concerns of non-Whites and lower income respondents showed little evidence of political polarization in either 2000 or 2010. Similar trends have been documented for educational attainment in the United States, with increasing

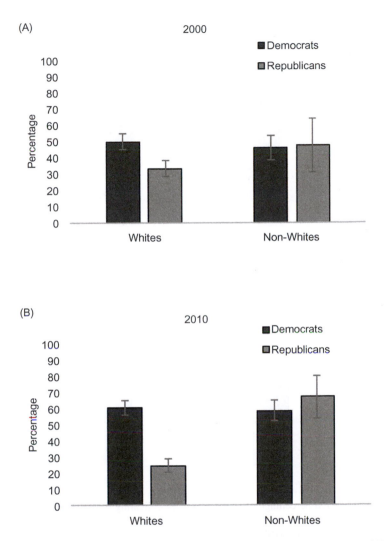

Figure 5.2 Weighted percentage of US respondents indicating the "rise in the world's temperature" is "extremely" or "very dangerous" by race and party affiliation in 2000 (A) and 2010 (B). Error bars represent 95% confidence intervals.
Source: General Social Survey.

polarization of climate opinions among more educated Americans between 2001 and 2016 (see Dunlap et al., 2016).

Taken together, these findings suggest that advantaged and disadvantaged group members' responses to climate change may be rooted in different motivations and concerns, with partisan perspectives and ideological concerns more strongly accounting for the responses of the former, and concerns about equity, health, and

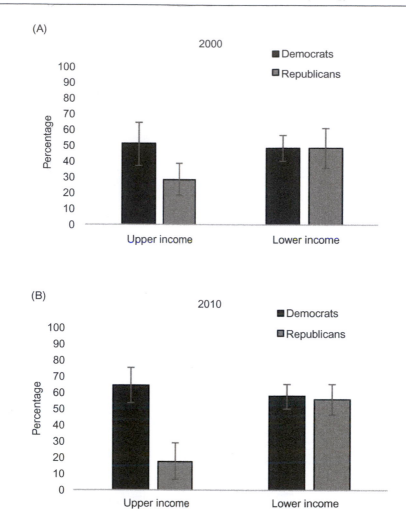

Figure 5.3 Weighted percentage of US respondents indicating the "rise in the world's temperature" is "extremely" or "very" dangerous by total household income and party affiliation in 2000 (A) and 2010 (B). Upper and lower income categories approximate the bottom and top quintiles (i.e., ≤ \$17,499 vs ≥ \$75,000 in 2000; ≤ \$22,499 vs ≥ 110,000 in 2010). Error bars represent 95% confidence intervals. *Note:* Question wording referenced "greenhouse effect" in 2000 and "climate change" in 2010.

community impacts more strongly influencing the responses of the latter. Consistent with this perspective, Ehret, Sparks, and Sherman (2017) found that higher levels of education led to increased attention to and awareness of elite political cues (e.g., partisan news media, political candidate speeches), which was associated with the stronger adherence to partisan positions on climate change and the environment. In contrast, as previously noted, members of disadvantaged groups show greater awareness of the risks of climate change and their vulnerability to its impacts and indicate stronger support for climate policies as a consequence.

These findings have important implications for efforts to broaden public engagement on climate change. Groups for whom the issue of climate change is less politically charged, such as racial and ethnic minorities and members of socioeconomically disadvantaged groups, represent key audiences for bridging partisan disagreements and building policy consensus. Social psychological research suggests that intersectional or "dual identity" groups (e.g., non-White and lower income conservatives) are uniquely positioned to act as a communication gateway between groups that represent the respective sources of their dual identity and have the potential to garner trust from both groups. Levy, Saguy, van Zomeren, and Halperin (2017), for instance, found that the mere presence of a group with a dual identity (Israeli Arabs) can lead to reduced conflict and improved intergroup relations, even in high conflict settings. The presence of individuals with intersecting identities can also disrupt stereotypical and heuristic modes of thinking and can signal to oppositional groups that a common identity with shared perspectives, incorporating viewpoints of both groups, is possible (see Gaertner & Dovidio, 2000).

Strategic messaging that focuses on political disagreements at the expense of other concerns (e.g., disproportionate impacts of climate change, unequal access to green jobs) may be relatively ineffective for engaging members of disadvantaged groups, whose views on the issue may be less partisan-driven (Schuldt & Pearson, 2016). Researchers and practitioners would also be wise not to mistake some minority groups' lower identification as "environmentalists"—a term that may signal other identity-relevant information, such as race or class membership (see the next section)—with a lack of concern about climate change or other environmental issues.

5.4.2   Stereotypic representations as barriers to engagement

Research on variability in disparities across different science and engineering fields may offer insights into factors that perpetuate environmental occupational disparities, as well as impede broader engagement with environmental organizations and professions more generally. A look at research on gender disparities in science and engineering is illustrative. In their comprehensive review, Cheryan et al. (2017) identify two key factors that reduce women's sense of belonging and contribute to larger disparities (greater male representation) in engineering fields compared to math and the life sciences: stronger gender stereotypes (e.g., masculinity) associated with engineering, and limited early exposure to female role models in engineering compared to math and life sciences. Below, we examine evidence that each of these general factors—stereotypes and limited representation of role models—may undermine minority engagement within the environmental sector.

Public perceptions of scientists as white and male have remained largely unchanged within US society over the past half century (Steinke et al., 2007). However, recent findings suggest environmental STEM fields may face a dual burden, contending with both STEM *and* environment-specific stereotypes that may contribute to uniquely high disparities in environmental fields. In an online survey of US adults (Pearson & Schuldt, 2015), participants indicated the extent to which they associated the terms "environmentalist," "scientist," and "engineer" with each of four racial/ethnic groups: White/European Americans, Black/African-Americans, Latinos, and Asian Americans, using 7-point scales (1 = not at all to 7 = very much). Only the category White was rated significantly above the scale midpoint (4) for the term "environmentalist," t (167) = 9.74, P <.001, and Whites were more strongly associated with the term environmentalist compared to all other groups (all pairwise Ps <.001). All other non-White racial and ethnic categories were significantly below the scale midpoint [ts from −6.42 (vs Black/African-Americans) to −2.10 (Asian Americans), Ps <.04], indicating a dissociation between these groups and the term "environmentalist." In contrast, Asian Americans were positively associated with the terms "scientist" and "engineer," relative to the midpoint (ts > 5.45, Ps <.001), and Blacks were more strongly associated with these terms (albeit still below the scale midpoint) than with the term "environmentalist" (Ps <.01). Moreover, both White and non-White participants more strongly associated Whites with the term environmentalist than all other racial and ethnic groups (all paired-sample Ps <.001).

A recent nationally representative survey lends additional support for these findings and highlights the unique challenges facing environmental organizations and advocacy groups. In a representative survey of US adults conducted April−May of 2016, we (Pearson et al., 2017) found that both Whites and non-Whites strongly associated "environmentalists" with the racial category White. Moreover, both groups *dissociated* non-White minority groups (Blacks, Latinos, and Asians) with the category "environmentalists" relative to the midpoint of the scale. We also found strong consensus in class stereotypes related to income and education, such that the term "environmentalist" was associated with being moderately wealthy and highly educated. These class stereotypes were similarly widely shared and varied little by respondent race/ethnicity, income, or education level.

Theory and research suggest that stereotypes can operate as powerful cues to belonging, signaling whether a group or domain is compatible with one's social identity. According to the identity-based motivation framework (IBM; Oyserman, Fryberg, & Yoder, 2007), people are particularly likely to engage in behaviors that are seen as congruent with their racial group identity ("ingroup-defining") and to avoid behaviors that are seen as incongruent with their identity. Oyserman *et al.* (2007) found that lower income African-American and Latino youth perceive healthy eating and exercise as identity incongruent and consequently expressed lower motivation to engage in these behaviors when their racial/ethnic identity was made salient. Additional studies have directly linked stereotype accessibility to identity congruence. When African-Americans and Latinos were prompted to consider stereotypes about their ingroups as self-defining, they showed decreased preferences for healthy foods and increased preferences for unhealthy foods (Rivera, 2014). Thus, factors beyond awareness of climate change and its risks, such as stereotypic associations with the terms "environmentalist" and "environmentalism," which may evoke concerns about the compatibility of one's identity with those in environmental organizations, may also contribute to disparities in the environmental sector (see Jones, 2002; Mohai, 2003).

Race and class-based stereotypes may also extend to notions of the "environment" and "environmentalism" in ways that similarly impede public outreach efforts. For instance, the use of nonurban imagery and a common focus on the preservation of natural and uninhabited spaces in conservation advocacy may signal that the perspectives and concerns of nonrepresented groups—and particularly those in urban areas—are not valued. Indeed, studies of environmental media reveal a strikingly narrow range of imagery used to depict the environment in both online and print media. For instance, in their analysis of the first 400 Google image search results for the word "ecosystems," Medin and Bang (2014) found that 393 (98.2%) did not include humans, 4 (1%) had humans within the ecosystem, and 3 (.8%) had humans outside looking in. Moreover, they found that European American (but not Native American) narratives in children's books tend to position human beings as apart from nature, rather than as part of it. Such depictions may unwittingly alienate individuals for whom environmental issues are also urban issues with significant human dimensions.

Psychological research on stereotyping and identity threat can help guide the development of interventions to combat environmental stereotypes and their transmission. Low representation of minority groups in environmental organizations, and particularly among those in leadership roles, may perpetuate stereotypic beliefs about environmental groups as noninclusive and, in turn, undermine minorities' identification with nondiverse environmental groups and their initiatives. In one experiment examining gender disparities in STEM (Murphy, Steele, & Gross, 2007), university students were shown one of two versions of a 7-min promotional video for an upcoming science and engineering leadership conference that depicted either a gender-balanced or a gender-unbalanced (3:1, male to female) ratio of attendees. Compared to those in the gender-balanced condition, women in the gender-unbalanced condition showed elevated stress and reported a lower sense of belonging and less interest in attending the conference. Thus, visible cues of low representation can reinforce notions that women do not belong in a stereotypically male-dominated domain. Nevertheless, stereotypic beliefs are malleable. In one experiment, simply reading a short (200-word) news article that computer scientists no longer fit the male stereotype significantly increased women's career interests in computer science (Cheryan, Plaut, Handron, & Hudson, 2013; see also Cheryan, Plaut, Davies, & Steele, 2009). Similar studies testing the malleability of environmental stereotypes represent a promising avenue for future research.

Finally, early exposure to science through both formal (e.g., secondary education) and informal learning environments (e.g., news media, entertainment, museums) has been shown to predict professional engagement later in life. Access to field-specific coursework—a primary means through which people may be exposed to ingroup role models—has been shown to predict reduced gender disparities (Cheryan et al., 2017). Nevertheless, early exposure may also *widen* disparities if this exposure reinforces cultural stereotypes and undermines a sense of belonging for members of underrepresented groups. Thus, future research might examine how early experiences with both formal and informal environmental education and experiences may exacerbate or reduce existing disparities, as well as the stereotype processes that are presumed to mediate these disparities.

5.4.3 Perceptual barriers and norm-based messaging

Misperceptions of group norms related to Whites' and non-Whites' environmental engagement may also impede diversity efforts within the climate movement. Numerous studies document the power of social norms in guiding sustainability-related behavior (Miller & Prentice, 2016). Individuals are more likely to avoid littering, conserve energy, and save water when a majority of others in close proximity do the same (Nolan, Schultz, Cialdini, Goldstein, & Griskevicius, 2008). Moreover, normative influence can outweigh cost savings in driving conservation behavior. In one field experiment, making energy-conscious choices visible to others (a nonfinancial reputational incentive) was more effective at increasing participation in an energy blackout prevention program in California than a $25 monetary incentive, leading to over four times the rate of compliance (Yoeli, Hoffman, Rand, & Nowak, 2013).

Work on identity threat and IBM suggests that minority group members may be particularly sensitive to norms that signal what behaviors are appropriate and preferred by their group (Oyserman & Lewis, 2017; Oyserman et al., 2007). When behaviors are believed to be normative (i.e., what "people like me" do), minority individuals are more likely to engage in personal, political, and social causes (Oyserman et al., 2007). In the absence of such normative information, people may look to the visible representations of their group in organizations and decision-making (e.g., the group memberships of those in leadership roles within the environmental sector; Taylor, 2014). Moreover, research suggests that norm conformity can occur even when the perceived norm is stigmatizing for members of a particular social group, and when members of the stigmatized group are motivated to avoid conforming. For instance, in a field experiment in rural India, Hoff and Pandey (2006) provided unacquainted schoolchildren with a monetary incentive to solve as many simple puzzles as possible out of a set of 15. In one version of the experiment, children's caste membership was made public before completing the puzzle task. When the participants' caste was publicly known, the motivation and performance of lower caste students (but not of other students) declined markedly compared to a condition in which the caste was unknown, consistent with the low achievement stereotype of lower caste groups. Thus, when individuals are identified as members of a stigmatized group, they may respond behaviorally by conforming to stereotypic beliefs, even when they are motivated to avoid doing so (e.g., when counterstereotypic actions are incentivized).

Given the positive connotations associated with proenvironmentalism (Steg & Vlek, 2009), being perceived as a member of a group that is relatively unconcerned about the environment (compared to other groups) may be similarly stigmatizing and, to the extent that these perceptions are internalized among minority group, may impede engagement among groups that are negatively stereotyped within the environmental sphere (e.g., non-Whites and those with lower income and education levels). We explore these normative influence processes below.

Despite evidence that salient group norms can shape behavior, few studies have investigated whether perceptions of attitudinal and behavioral ingroup norms around environmentalism (e.g., which groups are most concerned about climate change) vary among different racial and ethnic groups. Negative consequences of *misperceiving* ingroup norms, such as holding the belief that one's private views deviate from the consensus views of one's group (i.e., "pluralistic ignorance;" Prentice & Miller, 1993)—are well-documented. These include attitudinal and behavioral conformity to the perceived ingroup norm (Botvin, Botvin, Baker, Dusenbury, & Goldberg, 1992; Prentice & Miller, 2003), feelings of alienation and disidentification with a particular domain (Prentice & Miller, 1993), and reduced willingness to share opinions about contentious topics. Research investigating pluralistic ignorance in the context of climate change has documented self-silencing among those most concerned about the issue (Geiger & Swim, 2016), and recent survey findings suggest that self-silencing in discussions around climate change may be particularly common among non-Whites: In a nationally representative sample, whereas 53% of Whites reported being willing to admit differing viewpoints about climate change in discussions with family and friends, only 26% of Blacks and 34% of Latinos report a similar willingness to do so (Speiser & Krygsman, 2014). Thus, documenting the nature and extent of pluralistic ignorance in the context of climate change among racial and ethnic minority groups remains a critical avenue for future research.

Initial evidence for the importance of perceived ingroup norms in non-Whites' climate change engagement was obtained in a study with a racially and socio-economically diverse online sample of US adults (Pearson et al., 2017)[2]. In this study, ingroup pluralistic ignorance about climate change (operationalized as self-minus perceived racial/ethnic ingroup concern, controlling for mean levels of self-concern) was assessed, along with perceived individual and collective efficacy about climate change and environmental citizenship (social, economic, and political engagement with environmental organizations and initiatives). Environmental efficacy (Ojala, 2012) included items assessing individual efficacy (e.g., "I think that I myself can contribute to the improvement of the climate change situation") and collective efficacy (e.g., "I believe that together we can do something about the climate threat"), rated on a scale from 1 (*Strongly Disagree*) to 7 (*Strongly Agree*). Environmental citizenship (Stern, Dietz, Abel, Guagnano, & Kalof, 1999) included summed yes/no responses to seven questions (e.g., "In the last twelve months, have

---

[2] The sample consisted of 406 MTurk respondents; age ranged from 18 to 77 years (M_{age} = 34.8). The sample was 29.6% White (n = 120), 24.1% Black/African-American (n = 98), 20.4% Latin/Hispanic (n = 83), 15.5% Asian/Asian American (n = 63), and 10.3% "other" (n = 42). About half of participants (47.6%) had either an Associate's or Bachelor's degree and a majority (51.8%) indicated an annual income of $40,000 or less.

you read any newsletters, magazines or other publications written by environmental groups?"; "Boycotted or avoided buying the products of a company because you felt that company was harming the environment?"; "Voted for a candidate in an election at least in part because he or she was in favor of strong environmental protection?").

When controlling for political ideology, across all respondent groups, a greater perceived gap between self and ingroup concern predicted lower efficacy beliefs about climate change (beta = $-.15$, $P = .006$), and lower environmental citizenship (beta = $-.26$, $P < .001$), with stronger effects shown for racial and ethnic minority respondents. Moreover, when self and perceived ingroup concern about climate change were included simultaneously in regression analyses that included the same covariates, perceived ingroup concern about climate change predicted Asian (beta = .32, $P = .03$), Black (beta = .23, $P = .02$), and Hispanic (beta = .27, $P = .02$) respondents' environmental citizenship and was the sole significant predictor of Hispanics' and Asians' citizenship, in contrast, among Whites, only self-reported concern predicted. Whites' environmental citizenship (beta = .28, $P = .01$). Moreover, these effects could not be explained by differences in intergroup attitudes (Wolsko, Park, & Judd, 2006), political ideology (liberalism−conservatism), or socially desirable responding (Dunton & Fazio, 1997), and remained significant when these variables were included as covariates in the models.

These findings suggest that perceived ingroup attitudinal norms about climate change may shape non-Whites' perceptions of individual and collective efficacy around climate change and undermine their engagement with environmental organizations and initiatives. Norms-based interventions appear especially promising for motivating environmental engagement among individuals from more collectivistic cultures, such as individuals from East Asian countries and US Hispanics and Latinos. For instance, Eom, Kim, Sherman, and Ishii (2016) found that whereas environmental concern predicted proenvironmental consumer choices among European Americans but not Japanese, perceived ingroup norms were the stronger predictor among Japanese. Thus, future studies should also consider the broader cultural orientations of different demographic groups in assessing the potential effectiveness of norm-based messaging in environmental outreach and advocacy work.

5.5   Implications for organizational outreach and policy

The research reviewed in the previous section suggests that the lack of diversity in the environmental domain may be rooted, in part, in different motivational barriers that exist across majority and minority groups. These differing motivations, in turn, may be shaped by persistent and pervasive racial, ethnic, and class stereotypes and differing levels of visible representation in the environmental sector among majority and minority groups. Recognition of these barriers affords new pathways for interventions. For instance, messages that accurately reflect the high levels of concern among non-White and lower income groups and key contributions of people of color, and especially those within leadership roles (see Green 2.0's "Leadership at Work" initiative for a notable example), may be particularly effective for engaging groups that remain underrepresented in environmental discourse and decision-making.

5.5.1 Diversity messaging to promote inclusion

Within organizations, "colorblind" messaging that focuses on member similarities and avoids issues of race and ethnicity can signal that these identities are not valued and, in turn, can fuel distrust of these organizations, particularly when they have low diversity. In a series of experiments, Purdie-Vaughns, Steele, Davies, Ditlmann, and Crosby (2008) showed Black professionals corporate brochures that depicted either many or few minority staff-members, coupled with an organizational mission statement emphasizing colorblindness or one emphasizing the value of diversity. Participants were then asked for their opinions about the organization. Those exposed to a colorblind message, when that message was also coupled with images depicting low minority representation, were less comfortable envisioning themselves as an employee, less trusting of the organization's management, and more concerned about how others in the organization would treat them.

Whites' attempts to be colorblind can alienate minorities, who generally seek acknowledgement of their racial identity, and fuel interracial distrust. For instance, Apfelbaum, Sommers, and Norton (2008) found that although avoidance of race in conversations was seen by Whites as a favorable strategy for promoting positive interracial interactions, in practice, the failure to acknowledge race in conversations, when relevant, resulted in *greater* perceptions of racial prejudice by Black interaction partners. Moreover, racial colorblindness extends to perceptions of environmental impacts and government responses to those impacts. For instance, whereas a large majority (71%) of African-American respondents attributed the disproportionate effects of Hurricane Katrina on minority communities to the persistence of racial inequality in the United States, only 32% of Whites believed the same (Doherty, 2015). Similarly, whereas two-thirds (66%) of African-Americans indicated that the government's response to Hurricane Katrina would have been faster if most of the victims had been Whites, just 17% of Whites agreed.

These findings highlight a problem for environmental organizations that seek to diversify their memberships or broaden their appeal, but fail to sufficiently address disparities in environmental impacts or the potentially differing needs and concerns of underrepresented communities. By contrast, *multicultural* organizational practices, which seek to acknowledge both differences as well as shared perspectives among members and prospective members, can foster mutual understanding and promote a sense of belonging among members of historically marginalized groups. At the same time, messaging that emphasizes differences alone can be viewed as coercive. *Tailored inclusion* that highlights the dual identities of minority groups, connecting subgroup identities with broader American society, may be a more effective approach when developing inclusive messaging for advocacy and community outreach (see Lewis & Oyserman, 2016). At present, limited research has examined messaging on diversity in the context of environmental issues - a critical avenue for future psychological scholarship.

5.5.2   Bridging science and practice: Insights from public health

Psychologists are uniquely positioned to develop behavioral interventions that are "wise" to both the social contexts and underlying psychological processes that shape adaptation and mitigation behavior (see Walton, 2014; Clayton et al., 2015). To maximize their impact, behavioral interventions need to be appropriately tailored for different audiences and sensitive to their social context, and to set in motion new thought processes or behaviors that can be sustained over time (Cohen et al., 2017; Cunningham & Card, 2014). In developing these interventions, scholars and practitioners may benefit from incorporating insights from evidence-based approaches that have seen real-world success outside of the domain of climate change.

For instance, like the problem of climate change, the HIV/AIDS epidemic is global in reach, has both biophysical and social causes, and disproportionately affects communities of color and other socioeconomically disadvantaged groups (Pellowski, Kalichman, Matthews, & Adler, 2013). Research on health disparities related to the HIV epidemic highlights not only ways in which risks can be effectively communicated to different segments of the public but also ways that organizations can involve at-risk groups in decision-making processes that can influence public policy. Through initiatives such as the "Face of AIDS" and the "Global Village" that emphasize social dimensions of the epidemic, the International AIDS Conference—a global forum of scientists, practitioners, and communities directly affected by HIV—has successfully pressured governments and corporations to seek universal global access to preventive treatments and to collaborate in developing evidence-based solutions (Brecher & Fisher, 2013).

Psychological research on health disparities also offers a powerful blueprint for understanding *how* to design, evaluate, and effectively disseminate interventions to effect behavior change that may prove useful for combating climate change (e.g., reducing energy use; Swim, Geiger, & Zawadzki, 2014) and helping communities adapt to its impacts. For example, research suggests that highlighting "healthy" in the domain of food consumption can backfire, making healthy food less identity congruent for minority groups (Gomez & Torelli, 2015). Similarly, emphasizing protection of the natural environment (e.g., nonurban spaces) in the context of climate change may undermine the identity-congruence of climate actions among historically marginalized groups who may view the issue primarily through the lens of public health, economics, and community engagement (see Bullard et al., 2011). Practically, initiatives such as the US Center for Disease Control's High Impact HIV/AIDS Prevention Project and Prevention Research Synthesis (PRS) Project provide working models for the effective delivery of behavioral interventions to mitigate health risks among disproportionately affected groups that might be productively translated to the climate context. The PRS includes an online

compendium of nearly 100 evidence-based behavioral interventions and best practices, with intervention materials packaged into user-friendly kits that are freely
accessible to state and local governments (effectiveinterventions.org; see Norton,
Amico, Cornman, Fisher, & Fisher, 2009). Presently, no similar programs exist for
evaluating and broadly disseminating climate-related behavioral interventions to
different segments of the public—an important direction for future psychological
research (see Brecher & Fisher, 2013).

5.6 Conclusion

As this chapter and the others in this volume make clear, climate change is not only
a formidable technical challenge but also a complex social challenge that will
require multifaceted social solutions. We have focused on the opportunities
afforded by adopting a diversity science approach to climate change, one that
leverages the extensive literature on group processes within social and organizational psychology, to explore how social identities impact environmental engagement, including on the issue of climate change. Although racial and ethnic
disparities within the environmental movement are well-documented (see Taylor,
2014), the approach we describe here highlights key psychological processes (e.g.,
differing group motives, stereotypic representations, and normative perceptions)
that may contribute to these disparities and impede efforts to broaden public
engagement on climate change. Importantly, these processes also point to promising
pathways for future research and intervention.

Our hope is that this approach offers a blueprint of the types of diversity-related
questions that may be examined from the perspective of social psychological
research and theory. For example, what types of messages are best for changing
misconceptions about low minority concern? What kinds of media are most effective for enhancing environmental advocacy and professional engagement among
underrepresented minority groups? Moreover, our review focused primarily on
racial and ethnic disparities; however, identity-based approaches may be similarly
fruitful for understanding a broader range of identity factors, such as gender and
religious identities, which have also been shown to predict how people perceive
and respond to climate change and organizations working to address it (e.g.,
Pearson et al., 2017).

The differential impacts of climate change pose a unique challenge for motivating sustained collective action on the issue. Collective threats can enhance the
salience of shared aspects of identity in ways that motivate cooperation (Dovidio
et al., 2004). Nevertheless, cooperation can be difficult to sustain over time, and
particularly in the face of inequities that highlight group differences (Aquino,
Steisel, & Kay, 1992; also Piff, Kraus, Côté, Cheng. & Keltner, 2010). Identifying
the conditions under which people form and maintain shared identities around
threats that expose and exacerbate societal inequities is thus a critical question for
future research. Moreover, few studies have examined *which* identity dimensions

(e.g., perceived similarity vs group investment; see Masson & Fritsche, 2014) matter for climate engagement, or examined causal effects of identity on climate risk perceptions—another important area for psychological inquiry.

Research on social disparities in the context of climate change has the potential not only to inform policy but also yield new insights about group processes. For example, understanding racial/ethnic and class disparities in environmental STEM may inform our understanding of factors contributing to *heterogeneity* in disparities, generally, across STEM fields—an emerging direction for STEM diversity research (see Cheryan et al., 2017). More generally, the context of climate change provides an opportunity to examine how stereotyping and identity processes shape self-perceptions and collective action within a politicized and moralized domain (Steg & Vlek, 2009).

Finally, the global reach of climate change highlights an urgent need for research beyond the United States and other industrialized nations to examine how group dynamics influence climate change understanding and action in regions that shoulder a disproportionate burden of climate impacts. Despite the need for international cooperation and consensus-building, cross-national empirical research on racial, ethnic, and socioeconomic diversity is currently lacking (see Pearson et al., 2017). Moreover, few studies have explored ways in which nonpartisan identities, such as race/ethnicity and social class, may interact to influence climate change engagement. In addition to highlighting the importance of considering justice and equity motives in environmental decision-making, our review suggests that racial and ethnic minorities and members of other disadvantaged and disproportionately-affected groups represent critical audiences for bridging growing partisan disagreements on climate change. Increasing attention to these factors, and the role of diversity more generally in climate change communication and public advocacy, can enhance understanding of key barriers to participation in climate discourse and decision-making and help pave the way for a more inclusive and influential climate movement for the 21st century.

Acknowledgements

Preparation of this chapter was supported by a David L. Hirsch III and Susan H. Hirsch Research Initiation Grant awarded to the first author.

References

Adeola, F. O. (2004). Environmentalism and risk perception: Empirical analysis of black and white differentials and convergence. *Society & Natural Resources, 17*, 911–939.

Ard, K., & Mohai, P. (2011). Hispanics and environmental voting in the US Congress. *Environmental Practice, 13*, 302–313.

Arp, W., & Kenny, C. (1996). Black environmentalism in the local community context. *Environment and Behavior, 28*, 267−282.

Apfelbaum, E. P., Norton, M. I., & Sommers, S. R. (2012). Racial color blindness: Emergence, practice, and implications. *Current Directions in Psychological Science, 21* (3), 205−209.

Apfelbaum, E. P., Sommers, S. R., & Norton, M. I. (2008). Seeing race and seeming racist? Evaluating strategic colorblindness in social interaction. *Journal of Personality and Social Psychology, 95*(4), 918−932.

Aquino, K., Steisel, V., & Kay, A. (1992). The effects of resource distribution, voice, and decision framing on the provision of public goods. *Journal of Conflict Resolution, 36* (4), 665−687.

Barrett, S., & Dannenberg, A. (2014). Sensitivity of collective action to uncertainty about climate tipping points. *Nature Climate Change, 4*, 36−39.

Bamberg, S., Rees, J., & Seebauer, S. (2015). Collective climate action: Determinants of participation intention in community-based pro-environmental initiatives. *Journal of Environmental Psychology, 43*, 155−165.

Bolin, R. (2006). Race, class, and disaster vulnerability. In E. L. Quarantelli, & R. Dynes (Eds.), *Handbook of disaster research* (pp. 113−129). New York: Springer.

Bolin, B., Grineski, S. E., & Collins, T. W. (2005). Geography of despair: Environmental racism and the making of south Phoenix, Arizona, USA. *Human Ecology Review, 12*(2), 155−167.

Botvin, G. J., Botvin, E. M., Baker, E., Dusenbury, L., & Goldberg, C. J. (1992). The false consensus effect: Predicting adolescents' tobacco use from normative expectations. *Psychological Reports, 70*(1), 171−178.

Brecher, J., & Fisher, K. (2013). Climate protection can learn from the AIDS movement. *Nature Climate Change, 3*, 850−851.

Brewer, M. B., & Silver, M. D. (2000). Group distinctiveness, social identification, and collective mobilization. *Self, Identity, and Social Movements, 13*, 153−171.

Brulle, R. J., Carmichael, J., & Jenkins, J. C. (2012). Shifting public opinion on climate change: An empirical assessment of factors influencing concern over climate change in the US, 2002−2010. *Climatic change, 114*, 169−188.

Brunkard, J., Namulanda, G., & Ratard, R. (2008). Hurricane Katrina deaths, Louisiana, 2005. *Disaster Medicine and Public Health Preparedness, 2*(04), 215−223.

Budescu, D. V., Broomell, S., & Por, H. (2009). Improving communication of uncertainty in the reports of the Intergovernmental Panel on Climate Change. *Psychological Science, 20*, 299−308.

Bullard, R. D., Johnson, G. S., & Torres, A. O. (2011). *Environmental health & racial equity in the United States: Building environmentally just, sustainable, & livable communities.* Washington, DC: American Public Health Association.

Burke, M., Hsiang, S. M., & Miguel, E. (2015). Global non-linear effect of temperature on economic production. *Nature, 527*, 235−239.

Cheryan, S., Plaut, V. C., Davies, P. G., & Steele, C. M. (2009). Ambient belonging: How stereotypical cues impact gender participation in computer science. *Journal of Personality and Social Psychology, 97*(6), 1045−1060.

Cheryan, S., Plaut, V. C., Handron, C., & Hudson, L. (2013). The stereotypical computer scientist: Gendered media representations as a barrier to inclusion for women. *Sex Roles, 69*(1-2), 58−71.

Cheryan, S., Ziegler, S., Montoya, A. M., & Jiang, L. (2017). Why are some STEM fields more gender balanced than others? *Psychological Bulletin, 143*, 1−35.

Clark, L. P., Millet, D. B., & Marshall, J. D. (2014). National patterns in environmental injustice and inequality: Outdoor NO_2 air pollution in the United States. *PLoS ONE, 9*(4), e94431.

Clayton, S., Devine-Wright, P., Stern, P. C., Whitmarsh, L., Carrico, A., Steg, L., ... Bonnes, M. (2015). Psychological research and global climate change. *Nature Climate Change, 5*(7), 640–646.

Cohen, Geoffrey L., Garcia, J., & Parker Goyer, J. (2017). Turning point: Targeted, tailored, and timely psychological intervention. In Andrew J. Elliot, Carol S. Dweck, & David S. Yeager (Eds.), *Handbook of competence and motivation* (2nd Ed, pp. 657–686). New York, NY: Guilford Press.

Colby, S. L., & Ortman, J. M. (2015). *Projections of the size and composition of the U.S. population: 2014 to 2060*. United States Census Bureau. Retrieved from https://www.census.gov/content/dam/Census/library/publications/2015/demo/p25-1143.pdf.

Crona, B., Wutich, A., Brewis, A., & Gartin, M. (2013). Perceptions of climate change: Linking local and global perceptions through a cultural knowledge approach. *Climatic Change, 119*(2), 519–531.

Cunningham, S. D., & Card, J. J. (2014). Realities of replication: Implementation of evidence-based interventions for HIV prevention in real-world settings. *Implementation Science, 9*(1), 5.

Cutter, S.L., Emrich, C.T., Webb, J.J., & Morath, D. (2009). Social vulnerability to climate variability hazards: A review of the literature. Report to Oxfam America. Retrieved from http://adapt.oxfamamerica.org/resources/Literature_Review.pdf.

Dietz, T., Dan, A., & Shwom, R. (2007). Support for climate change policy: Social psychological and social structural influences. *Rural Sociology, 72*, 185–214.

Doherty, C. (2015). *Remembering Katrina: Wide racial divide over government's response*. Pew Research Center. Retrieved from http://www.pewresearch.org/fact-tank/2015/08/27/remembering-katrina-wide-racial-divide-over-governments-response/.

Dovidio, J. F., ten Vergert, M., Stewart, T. L., Gaertner, S. L., Johnson, J. D., Esses, V. M., ... Pearson, A. R. (2004). Perspective and prejudice: Antecedents and mediating mechanisms. *Personality and Social Psychology Bulletin, 30*, 1537–1549.

Dunlap, R. E., McCright, A. M., & Yarosh, J. H. (2016). The political divide on climate change: Partisan polarization widens in the US. *Environment: Science and Policy for Sustainable Development, 58*(5), 4–23.

Dunton, B. C., & Fazio, R. H. (1997). An individual difference measure of motivation to control prejudiced reactions. *Personality and Social Psychology Bulletin, 23*(3), 316–326.

Ehret, P. J., Sparks, A. C., & Sherman, D. K. (2017). Support for environmental protection: An integration of ideological-consistency and information-deficit models. *Environmental Politics, 26*(2), 253–277.

Eom, K., Kim, H. S., Sherman, D. K., & Ishii, K. (2016). Cultural variability in the link between environmental concern and support for environmental action. *Psychological Science, 27*(10), 1331–1339.

Ferguson, M. A., McDonald, R. I., & Branscombe, N. R. (2016). Global climate change: A social identity perspective on informational and structural interventions. In S. McKeown, R. Haji, & N. Ferguson (Eds.), *Understanding peace and conflict through social identity theory, Peace Psychology Book Series.* (pp. 145–164). Springer, Cham.

Feygina, I., Jost, J. T., & Goldsmith, R. E. (2010). System justification, the denial of global warming, and the possibility of "system-sanctioned change". *Personality and Social Psychology Bulletin, 36*(3), 326–338.

Feygina, I. (2013). Social justice and the human−environment relationship: Common systemic, ideological, and psychological roots and processes. *Social Justice Research, 26,* 363−381.

Fielding, K. S., Hornsey, M. J., & Swim, J. K. (2014). Developing a social psychology of climate change. *European Journal of Social Psychology, 44,* 413−420.

Finucane, M. L., Slovic, P., Mertz, C. K., Flynn, J., & Satterfield, T. A. (2000). Gender, race, and perceived risk: The 'white male' effect. *Health, Risk & Society, 2,* 159−172.

Flynn, J., Slovic, P., & Mertz, C. K. (1994). Gender, race, and perception of environmental health risks. *Risk Analysis, 14,* 1101−1108.

Fussell, E., Sastry, N., & VanLandingham, M. (2010). Race, socioeconomic status, and return migration to New Orleans after Hurricane Katrina. *Population and Environment, 31*(1-3), 20−42.

Gaertner, S. L., & Dovidio, J. F. (2000). *Reducing intergroup bias: The common ingroup identity model.* New York: Psychology Press.

Geiger, N., & Swim, J. K. (2016). Climate of silence: Pluralistic ignorance as a barrier to climate change discussion. *Journal of Environmental Psychology, 47,* 79−90.

Gomez, P., & Torelli, C. J. (2015). It's not just numbers: Cultural identities influence how nutrition information influences the valuation of foods. *Journal of Consumer Psychology, 25*(3), 404−415.

Guber, D. L. (2013). A cooling climate for change? Party polarization and the politics of global warming. *American Behavioral Scientist, 57,* 93−115.

Hamilton, L. C. (2011). Education, politics and opinions about climate change evidence for interaction effects. *Climatic Change, 104,* 231−242.

Heimlich, R. (2011). *Minorities account for nearly all US population growth.* Pew Research Center. Retrieved from http://www.pewresearch.org/fact-tank/2011/03/30/minorities-account-for-nearly-all-u-s-population-growth/.

Hennes, E. P., Ruisch, B. C., Feygina, I., Monteiro, C. A., & Jost, J. T. (2016). Motivated recall in the service of the economic system: The case of anthropogenic climate change. *Journal of Experimental Psychology: General, 145*(6), 755−771.

Holloway, R. A., Waldrip, A. M., & Ickes, W. (2009). Evidence that a simpático self-schema accounts for differences in the self-concepts and social behavior of Latinos versus Whites (and Blacks). *Journal of Personality and Social Psychology, 96*(5), 1012−1028.

Hogg, M. A. (2007). Uncertainty-identity theory. In M. P. Zanna (Ed.), *Advances in experimental social psychology* (Vol. 39, pp. 69−126). San Diego, CA: Academic.

Hong, L., & Page, S. E. (2004). Groups of diverse problem solvers can outperform groups of high-ability problem solvers. *Proceedings of the National Academy of Sciences of the United States of America, 101,* 16385−16389.

Hoff, K., & Pandey, P. (2006). Discrimination, social identity, and durable inequalities. *American Economic Review, 96,* 206−211.

Jones, R. E. (2002). Blacks just don't care: Unmasking popular stereotypes about concern for the environment among African-Americans. *International Journal of Public Administration, 25,* 221−251.

Jones, R. E., & Rainey, S. A. (2006). Examining linkages between race, environmental concern, health, and justice in a highly polluted community of color. *Journal of Black Studies, 36,* 473−496.

Jones, R.P., Cox, D., & Navarro-Rivera, J. (2014). *Believers, sympathizers, and skeptics: Why Americans are conflicted about climate change, environmental policy and science: Findings from the PRRI/AAR religions, values, and climate change survey.* Retrieved from https://www.prri.org/wp-content/uploads/2014/11/2014-Climate-Change-FINAL1-1.pdf.

Kahan, D. M., Braman, D., Gastil, J., Slovic, P., & Mertz, C. K. (2007). Culture and identity-protective cognition: Explaining the white-male effect in risk perception. *Journal of Empirical Legal Studies, 4*, 465–505.

Kahan, D. M., Jenkins-Smith, H., & Braman, D. (2011). Cultural cognition of scientific consensus. *Journal of Risk Research, 14*, 147–174.

Klandermans, B. (2004). The demand and supply of participation: Social-psychological correlates of participation in social movements. In D. Snow, S. Soule, & H. Kriesi's (Eds.), *The Blackwell companion to social movements* (pp. 360–379). New York, NY: Blackwell.

Knutson, T. R., McBride, J. L., Chan, J., Emanuel, K., Holland, G., Landsea, C., . . . Sugi, M. (2010). Tropical cyclones and climate change. *Nature Geoscience, 3*(3), 157–163.

Krosnick, J. A., Holbrook, A. L., & Visser, P. S. (2000). The impact of the Fall 1997 debate about global warming on American public opinion. *Public Understanding of Science, 9*, 239–260.

Krygsman, K., Speiser, M., & Lake, C. (2016). *Let's talk climate: Messages to motivate U.S. Latinos*. Washington, DC: Lake Research Partners and ecoAmerica.

Laska, S., & Morrow, B. H. (2006). Social vulnerabilities and Hurricane Katrina: An unnatural disaster in New Orleans. *Marine Technology Society Journal, 40*, 16–26.

Levine, S. S., Apfelbaum, E. P., Bernard, M., Bartelt, V. L., Zajac, E. J., & Stark, D. (2014). Ethnic diversity deflates price bubbles. *Proceedings of the National Academy of Sciences of the United States of America, 111*, 18524–18529.

Levy, A., Saguy, T., van Zomeren, M., & Halperin, E. (2017). Ingroups, outgroups, and the gateway groups between: The potential of dual identities to improve intergroup relations. *Journal of Experimental Social Psychology, 70*, 260–271.

Leiserowitz, A. (2006). Climate change risk perception and policy preferences: The role of affect, imagery, and values. *Climatic Change, 77*, 45–72.

Leiserowitz, A., & Akerlof, K. (2010). *Race, ethnicity and public responses to climate change*. New Haven, CT: Yale Project on Climate Change, Yale University and George Mason University.

Lewis, N. A., Jr., & Oyserman, D. (2016). Using identity-based motivation to improve the nation's health without breaking the bank. *Behavioral Science and Policy, 2*(2), 25–38.

Macias, T. (2016a). Environmental risk perception among race and ethnic groups in the United States. *Ethnicities, 16*(1), 111–129.

Macias, T. (2016b). *Ecological* assimilation: Race, ethnicity, and the inverted gap of environmental concern. *Society & Natural Resources, 29*(1), 3–19.

Masozera, M., Bailey, M., & Kerchner, C. (2007). Distribution of impacts of natural disasters across income groups: A case study of New Orleans. *Ecological Economics, 63*(2), 299–306.

Masson, T., & Fritsche, I. (2014). Adherence to climate change-related ingroup norms: Do dimensions of group identification matter? *European Journal of Social Psychology, 44* (5), 455–465.

Miranda, M. L., Hastings, D. A., Aldy, J. E., & Schlesinger, W. H. (2011). The environmental justice dimensions of climate change. *Environmental Justice, 4*(1), 17–25.

McCright, A. M., & Dunlap, R. E. (2011a). Cool dudes: The denial of climate change among conservative white males in the United States. *Global Environmental Change, 21*, 1163–1172.

McCright, A. M., & Dunlap, R. E. (2011b). The politicization of climate change and polarization in the American public's views of global warming, 2001–2010. *The Sociological Quarterly*, *52*, 155–194.

McCright, A. M., & Dunlap, R. E. (2013). Bringing ideology in: The conservative white male effect on worry about environmental problems in the USA. *Journal of Risk Research*, *16*, 211–226.

Milfont, T. L. (2012). Cultural differences in environmental engagement. In S. Clayton (Ed.), *The Oxford handbook of environmental and conservation psychology* (pp. 181–201). New York, NY: Oxford University Press.

Miller, D. T., & Prentice, D. A. (2016). Changing norms to change behavior. *Annual Review of Psychology*, *67*, 339–361.

Medin, D. L., & Bang, M. (2014). The cultural side of science communication. *Proceedings of the National Academy of Sciences of the United States of America*, *111*, 13621–13626.

Mirza, M. M. Q. (2003). Climate change and extreme weather events: Can developing countries adapt? *Climate Policy*, *3*(3), 233–248.

Mohai, P. (2003). Dispelling old myths: African American. *Environment: Science and Policy for Sustainable Development*, *45*, 10–26.

Mohai, P. (2008). Equity and the environmental justice debate. *Research in Social Problems and Public Policy*, *15*, 21–49.

Mohai, P., & Bryant, B. (1998). Is there a "race" effect on concern for environmental quality? *Public Opinion Quarterly*, *62*, 475–505.

Murphy, M. C., Steele, C. M., & Gross, J. J. (2007). Signaling threat: How situational cues affect women in math, science, and engineering settings. *Psychological Science*, *18*(10), 879–885.

Nolan, J. M., Schultz, P. W., Cialdini, R. B., Goldstein, N. J., & Griskevicius, V. (2008). Normative social influence is underdetected. *Personality and Social Psychology Bulletin*, *34*, 913–923.

Norton, W. E., Amico, K. R., Cornman, D. H., Fisher, W. A., & Fisher, J. D. (2009). An agenda for advancing the science of implementation of evidence-based HIV prevention interventions. *AIDS and Behavior*, *13*, 424–429.

Ojala, M. (2012). How do children cope with global climate change? Coping strategies, engagement, and well-being. *Journal of Environmental Psychology*, *32*, 225–233.

Ostrom, E. (1990). *Governing the commons: The evolution of institutions for collective action*. Cambridge, England: Cambridge University Press.

Oyserman, D., Fryberg, S., & Yoder, N. (2007). Identity-based motivation and health. *Journal of Personality and Social Psychology*, *93*, 1011–1027.

Oyserman, D., & Lewis, N. A., Jr. (2017). Seeing the destination AND the path: Using identity-based motivation to understand and reduce racial disparities in academic achievement. *Social Issues and Policy Review*, *11*(1), 159–194.

Pearson, A. R., Ballew, M. T., Naiman, S., & Schuldt, J. P. (2017). Race, class, gender and climate change communication. *Oxford Encyclopedia of Climate Change Communication*. Available from https://doi.org/10.1093/acrefore/9780190228620.013.412.

Pearson, A.R., Schuldt, J.P., Romero-Canyas, R., Ballew, M.T., & Larson-Konar, D. *Stereotypes drive consensus in false beliefs about minority and low-income Americans' environmental engagement among the US public*. Unpublished Manuscript. Claremont, CA.

Pearson, A. R., & Schuldt, J. P. (2014). Facing the diversity crisis in climate science. *Nature Climate Change*, *4*, 1039–1042.

Pearson, A.R., & Schuldt, J.P. (2015). Beyond politics: Which identities matter for climate beliefs?. In: *Talk presented at the annual meeting of the Association for Psychological Science*. New York, NY.

Pearson, A. R., Schuldt, J. P., & Romero-Canyas, R. (2016). Social climate science: A new vista for psychological science. *Perspectives on Psychological Science, 11*, 632–650.

Pellowski, J. A., Kalichman, S. C., Matthews, K. A., & Adler, N. (2013). A pandemic of the poor: Social disadvantage and the US HIV epidemic. *American Psychologist, 68*(4), 197–209.

Pidgeon, N., & Fischhoff, B. (2011). The role of social and decision sciences in communicating uncertain climate risks. *Nature Climate Change, 1*, 35–41.

Piff, P. K., Kraus, M. W., Côté, S., Cheng, B. H., & Keltner, D. (2010). Having less, giving more: The influence of social class on prosocial behavior. *Journal of Personality and Social Psychology, 99*(5), 771–784.

Piguet, E., Pécoud, A., & de Guchteneire, P. (2011). *Migration and climate change*. Cambridge, UK: Cambridge University Press.

Plaut, V. C. (2010). Diversity science: Why and how difference makes a difference. *Psychological Inquiry, 21*, 77–99.

Prentice, D. A., & Miller, D. T. (1993). Pluralistic ignorance and alcohol use on campus: Some consequences of misperceiving the social norm. *Journal of Personality and Social Psychology, 64*(2), 243–256.

Purdie-Vaughns, V., Steele, C. M., Davies, P. G., Ditlmann, R., & Crosby, J. R. (2008). Social identity contingencies: How diversity cues signal threat or safety for African Americans in mainstream institutions. *Journal of Personality and Social Psychology, 94*(4), 615–630.

Rivera, L. M. (2014). Ethnic-racial stigma and health disparities: From psychological theory and evidence to public policy solutions. *Journal of Social Issues, 70*(2), 198–205.

Satterfield, T. A., Mertz, C. K., & Slovic, P. (2004). Discrimination, vulnerability, and justice in the face of risk. *Risk Analysis, 24*, 115–129.

Semenza, J. C., Hall, D. E., Wilson, D. J., Bontempo, B. D., Sailor, D. J., & George, L. A. (2008). Public perception of climate change: Voluntary mitigation and barriers to behavior change. *American Journal of Preventive Medicine, 35*, 479–487.

Schuldt, J. P., & Pearson, A. R. (2016). The role of race and ethnicity in climate change polarization: Evidence from a US national survey experiment. *Climatic Change, 136*(3-4), 495–505.

Schuldt, J. P., & Roh, S. (2014). Of accessibility and applicability. How heat-related cues affect belief in "global warming" versus "climate change.". *Social Cognition, 32*, 217–238.

Schultz, P. W. (2002). *Inclusion with nature: The psychology of human-nature relations*. *Psychology of sustainable development* (pp. 61–78). US: Springer.

Speiser, M., & Krygsman, K. (2014). *American climate values 2014: Insights by racial and ethnic groups*. Washington, DC: Strategic Business Insights and ecoAmerica.

Steg, L., & Vlek, C. (2009). Encouraging pro-environmental behaviour: An integrative review and research agenda. *Journal of Environmental Psychology, 29*(3), 309–317.

Steinke, J., Lapinski, M. K., Crocker, N., Zietsman-Thomas, A., Williams, Y., Evergreen, S. H., & Kuchibhotla, S. (2007). Assessing media influences on middle school–aged children's perceptions of women in science using the Draw-A-Scientist Test (DAST). *Science Communication, 29*(1), 35–64.

Stern, P. C., Dietz, T., Abel, T. D., Guagnano, G. A., & Kalof, L. (1999). A value-belief-norm theory of support for social movements: The case of environmentalism. *Human Ecology Review, 6*(2), 81–97.

Stokes, B., Wike, R., & Carle, J. (2015). *Global concern about climate change, broad support for limiting emissions.* Pew Research Center. Retrieved from http://www.pewglobal.org/files/2015/11/Pew-Research-Center-Climate-Change-Report-FINAL-November-5-2015.pdf.

Swim, J., Clayton, S., Doherty, T., Gifford, R., Howard, G., Reser, J., et al. (2009). *Psychology and global climate change: Addressing a multi-faceted phenomenon and set of challenges. A report by the American Psychological Association's task force on the interface between psychology and global climate change.* Washington, DC: American Psychological Association.

Swim, J. K., & Becker, J. C. (2012). Country contexts and individuals' climate change mitigating behaviors: A comparison of US versus German individuals' efforts to reduce energy use. *Journal of Social Issues, 68,* 571−591.

Swim, J. K., Geiger, N., & Zawadzki, S. J. (2014). Psychology and energy-use reduction policies. *Policy Insights from the Behavioral and Brain Sciences, 1,* 180−188.

Taylor, D. E. (1989). Blacks and the environment: Towards an explanation of the concern and action gap between blacks and whites. *Environment and Behavior, 21,* 175−205.

Taylor, D.E. (2010). Race, gender, and faculty diversity in environmental disciplines. In: *Environment and social justice: An international perspective, research in social problems and public policy* (Vol. 18) (pp. 385−407). Bingley, UK: Emerald Group Publishing Limited.

Taylor, D.E. (2014). *The state of diversity in environmental organizations: Mainstream NGOs, foundations & government agencies.* Green 2.0 Working Group.

Tyler, T. R., & Blader, S. L. (2000). *Cooperation in groups: Procedural justice, social identity, and behavioral engagement.* Philadelphia, PA: Psychology Press.

Tyler, T. R., & Blader, S. L. (2003). The group engagement model: Procedural justice, social identity, and cooperative behavior. *Personality and Social Psychology Review, 7*(4), 349−361.

United Nations Development Programme. (2007). *U.N. Human Development Report 2007/ 2008: Fighting climate change. Human solidarity in a divided world.* New York, NY: Palgrave Macmillan.

Van Vugt, M. (2009). Averting the tragedy of the commons using social psychological science to protect the environment. *Current Directions in Psychological Science, 18,* 169−173.

Van Zomeren, M., Postmes, T., & Spears, R. (2008). Toward an integrative social identity model of collective action: A quantitative research synthesis of three sociopsychological perspectives. *Psychological Bulletin, 134*(4), 504.

Van Zomeren, M., Spears, R., & Leach, C. W. (2010). Experimental evidence for a dual pathway model analysis of coping with the climate crisis. *Journal of Environmental Psychology, 30,* 339−346.

Walton, G. M. (2014). The new science of wise psychological interventions. *Current Directions in Psychological Science, 23,* 73−82.

Whittaker, M., Segura, G. M., & Bowler, S. (2005). Racial/ethnic group attitudes toward environmental protection in California: Is "environmentalism" still a white phenomenon? *Political Research Quarterly, 58,* 435−447.

Williams, B. L., & Florez, Y. (2002). Do Mexican Americans perceive environmental issues differently than Caucasians: A study of cross-ethnic variation in perceptions related to water in Tucson. *Environmental Health Perspectives, 110*(Suppl 2), 303−310.

Wilson, S. M., Richard, R., Joseph, L., & Williams, E. (2010). Climate change, environmental justice, and vulnerability: An exploratory spatial analysis. *Environmental Justice, 3* (1), 13−19.

Wolf, J., & Moser, S. C. (2011). Individual understandings, perceptions, and engagement with climate change: Insights from in-depth studies across the world. *Wiley Interdisciplinary Reviews: Climate Change, 2,* 547–569.

Wolsko, C., Park, B., & Judd, C. M. (2006). Considering the tower of Babel: Correlates of assimilation and multiculturalism among ethnic minority and majority groups in the United States. *Social Justice Research, 19*(3), 277–306.

Wood, B. D., & Vedlitz, A. (2007). Issue definition, information processing, and the politics of global warming. *American Journal of Political Science, 51,* 552–568.

Yoeli, E., Hoffman, M., Rand, D. G., & Nowak, M. A. (2013). Powering up with indirect reciprocity in a large-scale field experiment. *Proceedings of the National Academy of Sciences of the United States of America, 110,* 10424–10429.

Yeager, D. S., & Walton, G. M. (2011). Social-psychological interventions in education: They're not magic. *Review of Educational Research, 81,* 267–301.

Part II

Responding to Climate Change

Contributions of psychology to limiting climate change: Opportunities through consumer behavior

6

Kimberly S. Wolske[1] and Paul C. Stern[2,3]
[1]University of Chicago, Chicago, IL, United States, [2]Social and Environmental Research Institute, Northampton, MA, United States, [3]Norwegian University of Science and Technology, Trondheim, Norway

6.1 Introduction

Limiting anthropogenic contributions to climate change is one of the greatest global challenges of this century. According to one recent analysis, achieving a 66% probability of keeping global mean temperature rise to below 2°C, a target commonly selected for reducing the likelihood of catastrophic outcomes, would require energy-related carbon dioxide emissions to peak by 2020 and to fall by more than 70% from today's levels by 2050. According to this analysis, achieving this target "would require an unparalleled ramp up of all low-carbon technologies in all countries" (International Energy Agency & International Renewable Energy Agency, 2017, p. 7).

Meeting or even approaching this target will require major and rapid change in most domains of human activity, including not only the technological but also the economic, policy, and sociocultural, and at all levels of social organization from the individual to the international. Because the challenge is both pressing and long-term, contributions can come from human activities at all time scales, from everyday energy use to changes that take decades to complete, such as replacing capital equipment stocks, raising new generations with reduced consumption tendencies, reducing urban sprawl, and developing innovative technologies.

The ultimate effect of any of these changes will inevitably depend on multiple conditions in society and economy. For example, a new technology that can reduce greenhouse gas emissions associated with a desired service such as home heating or personal transport will not have the intended effect unless people and organizations adopt the technology in large numbers. And that will not happen unless policies are adequately supportive, financial conditions are attractive, and the potential adopters believe that the new technology will actually provide the desired service without excessive cost or other undesired consequences. Because the ultimate effect of any effort to reduce the drivers of climate change is multiply determined, the potential

Psychology and Climate Change. DOI: https://doi.org/10.1016/B978-0-12-813130-5.00007-2

of any effort needs to be evaluated after taking into account the full range of factors likely to determine its effects.

This sort of evaluation is not always done. More commonly, specialists in one field, such as technology, law, or a physical or social science, make presumptions about the impact of the efforts they propose, without adequately considering other factors in the larger system. As a result, the innovation's impact often falls far short of expectations. An example from the domain of new technology is the programmable thermostat, which was developed with advanced engineering (and government support), but without much attention to users' likely responses. The result has been widespread adoption of the technology, but suboptimal use, and much less reduction of energy use for home heating and cooling than anticipated (US EIA, 2013a; Peffer, Perry, Pritoni, Aragon, & Meier, 2013; Pritoni, Meier, Aragon, Perry, & Peffer, 2015).

A narrow focus starting with psychology has equally serious shortcomings. An example is research on household energy conservation, which began in response to the energy crisis of the 1970s and has been the subject of extensive research over nearly four decades (for reviews see Abrahamse, Steg, Vlek, & Rothengatter, 2005; Delmas, Fischlein, & Asensio, 2013; Frederiks, Stenner, & Hobman, 2015). This research typically focuses on actions that reduce direct consumption of energy in homes with existing equipment—behaviors such as turning off lights, that are frequently repeated but that have limited potential for reducing emissions from the household sector compared to less frequent actions such as replacing the existing equipment with more efficient alternatives. The most promising of such studies, which examine the effects of providing feedback to households about their electricity consumption, typically find reductions of between 2% and 12% (Allcott, 2011b; Ayres, Raseman, & Shih, 2013; Fischer, 2008; Karlin, Zinger, & Ford, 2015), an amount that comprises an even smaller percentage of a household's total carbon footprint, which typically also includes direct use of fossil fuels for such purposes as transportation and home heating.

Psychologists can potentially make larger contributions if they target behaviors for intervention in terms of two criteria: the potential climate impact of the behavior and the potential of psychological concepts to improve uptake of that behavior (Stern, 2017). This is the approach we take in this chapter. We hope in this way to point psychologically grounded researchers in directions that are promising in terms of climate objectives and not only disciplinary ones. We seek to identify some of the most promising ways psychology can contribute, both on its own and more importantly, in collaboration with other scientific fields and with practical knowledge.

6.1.1 Behaviors that influence climate change

Psychology is fundamentally the study of individual behavior and its determinants. Individuals contribute to climate change and can contribute to transformations to limit climate change in a variety of ways, any of which might be appropriate objects of psychological research and analysis (Stern, 2014). First and most obviously, individuals consume fossil fuel-based energy directly, to heat and cool homes and water, to power home appliances and motor vehicles, and so forth. Such consumption makes them responsible for emissions of greenhouse gases from their homes, their motor vehicles, and from the production and distribution of the energy sources they use. They can reduce emissions by using their energy-consuming equipment less intensively, by adopting and maintaining household equipment that produces desired services with more efficient energy consumption, or by replacing fossil fuels that supply those services with renewable energy.

Second, individuals cause greenhouse gas emissions indirectly. One route is via nonenergy actions that shape future energy choices, such as by having children or by choosing a home, which indirectly affects demand for motorized travel and home energy. Another indirect route is through the purchase of nonenergy consumer goods and services that have fossil fuel consumption in their life cycles, from the mining of raw materials through the disposal of product wastes. Consumers may be unaware of the effects of the emissions from the life cycles of consumer products, but if they could know the emissions associated with alternative purchases, they might make that product attribute a consideration in their purchases. This is an objective of carbon labeling efforts of consumer products (Cohen & Vandenbergh, 2012; Shewmake, Cohen, Stern, & Vandenbergh, 2015), and it provides an emerging opportunity for interventions using psychological principles (e.g., Isley, Stern, Carmichael, Joseph, & Arent, 2016).

Third, individuals can influence climate change indirectly in their roles as citizens, by promoting or opposing government actions to develop, promote, or incentivize various technologies and energy sources or to shape energy needs by influencing the shape of human settlements and transportation systems. Public reactions to energy technologies and policies have attempted to exercise influence on the progress of nuclear energy systems for half a century (Rosa & Dunlap, 1994) and more recently have sought influence on policy in areas such as shale gas development (e.g., Small et al., 2014). Psychological concepts such as risk perception (e.g., Fischhoff, Slovic, Lichtenstein, Read, & Combs, 1978; Freudenburg & Rosa, 1984) and policy framing (e.g., Pidgeon, Lorenzoni, & Poortinga, 2008) are relevant here. Psychology can contribute, along with other social science disciplines, by suggesting ways to improve communication and decision-making processes for resolving policy disputes in ways that will affect the future course of climate change (e.g., Sidortsov, 2014; Stern, 2013).

Fourth, individuals can influence climate change indirectly in their roles as employees or managers in organizations that affect greenhouse gas emissions through direct energy consumption or through fossil fuel consumption in product and service supply chains of which they are a part. There are large opportunities in this domain, as organizations account for 60% of energy use worldwide and have considerable potential for reducing fossil fuel consumption (Lovins & Rocky Mountain Institute, 2011; Stern et al., 2016; US EIA, 2013b; Vandenbergh & Gilligan, 2015).

In the rest of this chapter, we focus primarily on behaviors of the first type—direct individual and household energy use. We choose this focus because that is where the great bulk of the psychological research has been conducted and because the implications of individual and household behavior for greenhouse gas emissions are most directly measurable with these behaviors. Moreover, there are opportunities for psychological concepts to make a much larger contribution to limiting climate change through these behaviors than they have to date.

6.1.2 Identifying target behaviors

In our view, a useful way to integrate the technical and behavioral aspects of change in greenhouse gas emissions is with the concept of reasonably achievable emissions reduction (RAER; Dietz, Gardner, Gilligan, Stern, & Vandenbergh, 2009). RAER has been defined as the mathematical product of the technical potential of an innovation, which is the amount of emissions reduction that would be achieved if the innovation were universally adopted, and behavioral plasticity, which is the proportion of potential users who could be induced to adopt the innovation. The RAER concept makes explicit the interactive nature of technical innovation and behavior with respect to reducing emissions and clarifies both the potential and the challenges of different options to reduce emissions from choices by individual consumers.

In Table 6.1, technical potential for the United States was estimated in 2009 from the number of households that had not yet undertaken the indicated behavioral change multiplied by a technical estimate of the amount of emissions reductions that would result from that behavioral change in an average household. Behavioral plasticity was estimated based on data on the most successful documented efforts to actually change the behavior. Behavioral plasticity is not a natural constant: More effective efforts to change behavior result in higher plasticity estimates, and an important objective of research on behaviors that affect greenhouse gas emissions is to identify ways of increasing behavioral plasticity, particularly for behaviors with high technical potential.

Table 6.1 covers consumer behaviors of five types, all of them direct influences on energy consumption: home weatherization and upgrading to efficient heating and cooling equipment (W), acquiring more energy-efficient major household equipment (home appliances other than heating and cooling) and motor vehicles (E), maintaining such equipment (M), adjusting water temperatures in home equipment (A), and changing daily energy-using behaviors (D). These types of behavior differ in their frequency and their cost, and also in the RAER they can achieve. In particular, the behaviors with the highest RAER are in the W and E categories: They involve infrequent actions, some of them quite expensive when first undertaken, which yield long-lasting savings in energy consumption and in total cost. As we show below, the vast majority of psychological research on household energy-consuming behaviors has been directed at types of behavior, particularly types A and D, that have low technical potential.

Other types of consumer behavior, not covered by the table, can also affect fossil energy consumption, greatly in some instances. Adoption of renewable energy technologies (R), such as residential photovoltaic energy systems (PV) or household participation in community renewable energy developments, can have a major impact by replacing all fossil-fueled electricity in the home and, in combination with electric vehicle technology, major portions of fossil energy use for travel. Also, given appropriate information, consumers can make choices that reduce the

Table 6.1 Technical potential, behavioral plasticity, and 10-year reasonably achievable emissions reduction (RAER, in millions of metric tons of carbon, MtC) estimated from 17 household actions in the USA

Behavior change	Category	Technical potential for emissions reduction (MtC)[a]	Behavioral plasticity[b] (%)	RAER[c] (MtC)	RAER[c] (% of individual or household emissions)
Weatherization	W	25.2	90	21.2	3.39
HVAC equipment	W	12.2	80	10.7	1.72
Low-flow showerheads	E	1.4	80	1.1	0.18
Efficient water heater	E	6.7	80	5.4	0.86
Appliances	E	14.7	80	11.7	1.87
Low-rolling resistance tires	E	7.4	80	6.5	1.05
Fuel-efficient vehicle	E	56.3	50	31.4	5.02
Change HVAC air filters	M	8.7	30	3.7	0.59
Tune up AC	M	3.0	30	1.4	0.22
Routine auto maintenance	M	8.6	30	4.1	0.66
Laundry temperature	A	0.5	35	0.2	0.04
Water heater temperature	A	2.9	35	1.0	0.17
Standby electricity	D	9.2	35	3.2	0.52
Thermostat setbacks	D	10.1	35	4.5	0.71
Line drying	D	6.0	35	2.2	0.35
Driving behavior	D	24.1	25	7.7	1.23
Carpooling and trip-chaining	D	36.1	15	6.4	1.02
Totals		233		123	20

Note: Categories are heating, ventilation, and air conditioning (HVAC) and *weatherization*, together designated as (W), more efficient vehicles and nonheating and cooling *equipment* (E), equipment *maintenance* (M), equipment *adjustments* (A), and *daily* use behaviors (D). *RAER,* reasonably achievable emissions reduction.
[a]Effect of change from the current level of penetration to 100% penetration, corrected for double-counting.
[b]Percentage of the relevant population that has not yet adopted an action that will adopt it by year 10 with the most effective interventions.
[c]Reduction in national CO_2 emissions at year 10 due to the behavioral change from plasticity, expressed in MtC/year saved and as a percentage of total US individual/household sector emissions (%I/H). Both estimates are corrected for double counting.
Adapted from: Dietz, T., Gardner, G.T., Gilligan, J., Stern, P.C., & Vandenbergh, M.P. (2009). Household actions can provide a behavioral wedge to rapidly reduce US carbon emissions. *Proceedings of the National Academy of Sciences of the United States of America, 106*(44), 18452–18456. https://doi.org/10.1073/pnas.0908738106.

life-cycle fossil energy use (L) in the products and services they buy (Isley et al., 2016). For example, consumers can choose foods that require less energy to produce and transport. These two types of behavior were not included in the 2009 analysis, but the potential of type R is now considerable and the potential of type L may become more so.

Psychologists may have focused on behaviors of equipment adjustment (type A) and daily energy-using (type D) behaviors out of an intuitive sense that psychological factors are key to changing them and that they might be readily altered via interventions familiar from psychological research, such as providing appropriately framed information, social support, social comparison, or appeals to values. In fact, this intuition is supported by research on these types of behavior, as discussed below. But by focusing on these behaviors, psychologists have restricted their attention to behaviors that can have relatively little effect on limiting climate change, as indicated by the RAER statistic. Psychologists may hope that what works for behaviors of type A or D will work as well for behaviors with higher technical potential, but this is typically not the case, as we also discuss below.

In the sections that follow, we briefly describe four classes of determinants known to influence energy-related behaviors (Steg, 2008; see also Steg, Perlaviciute, & van der Werff, 2015; Stern, 2008) and then review available evidence regarding the importance of these variables with different types of mitigation behaviors. Throughout the discussion, we use the RAER statistic as a guiding framework, focusing on the behaviors that are likely to result in the largest reductions in greenhouse gas emissions.

6.2 Determinants of behavior

6.2.1 Knowledge

Whether or not people act to limit climate change may depend on their understanding of climate change and the behaviors that can address it. There is evidence of systematic misunderstandings of which actions affect climate change and of the size of the effects. For example, some research indicates that people believe (incorrectly) that increased recycling makes a meaningful contribution to limiting climate change (Semenza et al., 2008; Whitmarsh, 2009). In addition, the relative potency of personal actions to limit climate change is often misunderstood. In a US survey that asked respondents to list the most effective thing they could do to conserve energy, only 12% of participants described household energy efficiency improvements; 55% described curtailment behaviors that involve changing daily routines, most often turning off lights (Attari, DeKay, Davidson, & Bruine de Bruin, 2010). This cognitive bias toward highly visible yet often low-impact behaviors has long been observed (e.g., Kempton, Harris, Keith, & Weihl, 1985; Kempton & Montgomery, 1982) and suggests that without further intervention, even individuals who are motivated to address climate change via energy use may focus their efforts on low-impact actions. This may be counterproductive overall, if individuals' limited time and attention are devoted to low-impact actions instead of high-impact ones.

In addition to knowing the relative effectiveness of different action strategies, people must know something about the energy systems they interact with in order to use them optimally. As discussed below, common misunderstandings about home heating and cooling systems, vehicle fuel efficiency ratings, and driving behaviors can lead individuals to inadvertently act in ways that are more carbon-intensive than they might wish.

6.2.2 Personal dispositions and motivations

Psychology often seeks to explain behavior by examining underlying motivations. In the context of climate change, people may act out of broad concern for the environment. The value-belief-norm (VBN) theory of proenvironmental behavior (Stern, 2000; Stern, Dietz, Abel, Guagnano, & Kalof, 1999) has been widely used to study a variety of behaviors affecting greenhouse gas emissions from travel-mode choice (Lind, Nordfjærn, Jørgensen, & Rundmo, 2015), to interest in solar panels (Wolske, Stern, & Dietz, 2017), to support for energy policies (Steg, Dreijerink, & Abrahamse, 2005). VBN proposes that environmental behavior is the indirect outcome of acting on deeply held values, typically those that demonstrate concern beyond one's immediate self-interest. These include altruism toward other humans as well as altruism toward the environment. Values are theorized to influence worldviews about the relationship of humans and nature, which, in turn, influence-specific beliefs about the consequences of environmental problems and actions. In line with Schwartz's norm activation model (Schwartz, 1977), when individuals perceive that environmental conditions threaten things they value and feel a sense of personal responsibility to address those threats, they are more likely to experience a sense of moral obligation (a personal norm) to take action. VBN suggests then that people are more likely to engage in energy-saving behaviors to the extent that they feel a moral obligation either to reduce fossil fuel use or to address climate change.

Efforts to reduce fossil energy consumption may also flow from self-interested motives. Reducing home energy use and transportation fuel costs have obvious financial benefits. Likewise, weatherization upgrades can increase thermal comfort and create a healthier home. People may also pursue energy consumption-reducing behaviors as a means to enhance their social status (Gneezy, Imas, Brown, Nelson, & Norton, 2011; Griskevicius, Tybur, & Van den Bergh, 2010; Noppers, Keizer, Bolderdijk, & Steg, 2014). Driving a hybrid vehicle or installing solar panels may also be a way of signaling one's environmental self-identity or the affluence associated with what may be perceived as luxury goods.

Adoption of energy efficient and renewable energy technologies may also be explained by consumers' openness to new experiences and ideas. According to Rogers' (2003) diffusion of innovations (DOIs) theory, individuals who typically seek out novelty are more likely to adopt innovative goods and services and to do so before others. Recent studies suggest this trait may be especially important for explaining early adoption of eco-innovations such as alternative fuel vehicles (Jansson, 2011) and solar PV (Chen, 2014; Wolske et al., 2017).

6.2.3   Behavior-specific beliefs, attitudes, and habits

Whether individuals choose to engage in a specific behavior may depend on how they weigh its costs and benefits. The theory of planned behavior (TPB, Ajzen, 1991) offers a useful framework. TPB proposes that intentions to engage in a behavior are the outcome of three factors: *attitudes* about the behavior, *subjective norms* (i.e., social pressure), and *perceived behavioral control* (i.e., perceived ability to enact the behavior). Each of these, in turn, is influenced by specific beliefs. Attitudes form in response to beliefs about the consequences of the behavior, subjective norms are based on beliefs about what valued peer groups think, and perceived behavioral control arises from beliefs about the feasibility of a behavior and one's personal capabilities. TPB has successfully explained variance in a wide range of climate-related intentions and behaviors including purchase of energy-efficient light bulbs (Harland, Staats, & Wilke, 1999), public transportation use (Bamberg, Ajzen, & Schmidt, 2003), and interest in adopting solar panels (Korcaj, Hahnel, & Spada, 2015; Wolske et al., 2017). Variables from DOI theory nicely complement TPB for explaining interest in innovative energy technologies such as solar PV and alternative fuel vehicles. Similar to behavioral beliefs and attitudes in TPB, DOI posits that an innovation is more likely to be adopted the more it is perceived to have favorable characteristics. These include a *relative advantage* over prior practices, low *complexity* to learn and use, *compatibility* with existing values and routines, the ability to adopt on a *trial basis*, and *observable* evidence that others have adopted the innovation successfully.

Numerous types of beliefs have been associated with households' financial investments to reduce energy consumption (Balcombe, Rigby, & Azapagic, 2013; Kastner & Stern, 2015). These include perceptions about expected net consequences for the household (e.g., financial costs and benefits, convenience, changes to the comfort and esthetics of one's home, independence in energy supply, and changes in social status) as well as consequences to others or the environment (e.g., limiting climate change, reducing dependence on foreign fossil fuels, and improving the environment for future generations). How people evaluate these consequences may also be a function of their underlying dispositions. For example, individuals with strong proenvironmental personal norms may be less deterred by the inconvenience of certain actions.

Habits and interventions to change them are a familiar topic for psychological research. However, as Table 6.1 makes clear, they are relevant only to daily energy-using behaviors (type D), which together have RAER of less than 20% of all the potential of the behaviors in the table. Among these behaviors, the ones with the greatest technical potential concern travel routines, which have not been studied much by psychologists and likely are highly dependent on contextual factors such as the availability of alternative forms of transportation, as well as on intrapersonal factors.

6.2.4   Contextual influences

Actions that affect a household's contribution to climate change may be influenced by a variety of contextual factors, many of which are outside of the household's control. For some behaviors, supportive policies that reduce costs, make the behavior more convenient, and provide necessary infrastructure are critical. Replacing personal vehicle trips in spatially dispersed communities with alternative forms of transportation may be quite challenging without a public transit system, bicycle paths, or good sidewalks. Similarly, the decision to get rooftop solar panels may hinge on policies that affect the financial cost of solar power (e.g., net metering, financial incentives, property taxes), and the ease of getting solar panels installed (e.g., local permitting practices). For energy investments such as home insulation and renewable energy systems, access to appropriate vendors and skilled labor may be a limiting factor.

Other aspects of the social and informational environment may also matter. Actions may be affected by social support from peers (as suggested by TPB), or in the case of more costly investments, perceptions that others have successfully adopted them (as suggested by DOI). The information that consumers rely upon may also be influenced by the trustworthiness of the source. Friends and family are often a preferred information channel, but the recommendations of perceived experts such as sales people, contractors, and service technicians may also have significant weight.

Finally, the extent to which individuals are interested and able to engage in different mitigation behaviors may depend on contextual factors within the home. While demographic variables such as age, gender, and education tend to have inconsistent and weak relationships with behavior, certain socioeconomic factors have been shown to have greater influence. Larger households and higher income levels, for example, strongly predict greater overall home energy consumption (Abrahamse & Steg, 2009; Brandon & Lewis, 1999; Frederiks et al., 2015; Lutzenhiser & Lutzenhiser, 2006). As might be expected, household income can also influence financial investments to reduce energy use, such as adoption of energy-efficient heating and cooling equipment, alternative fuel vehicles, and renewable energy systems. Likewise, renters may have limited opportunities to influence major appliance choice or home weatherization. Even in owner-occupied homes with sufficient financial resources, potential barriers remain. Disagreements among family members about home comfort, esthetics, or even household spending may block change. Homes of a certain age or construction type may be incompatible with weatherization upgrades or new technologies. Geographic location and climate factors may make some technologies impractical.

6.3   Influencing consumer energy behavior: What does psychology know?

6.3.1   Adoption of renewable energy and efficient vehicle technologies

6.3.1.1   Renewable energy technologies (R)

We begin by looking at a class of household behaviors that shows perhaps the greatest promise for reducing greenhouse gas emissions: adoption of renewable energy technologies (R). These technologies include, among others, solar thermal water heaters, solar PV, pellet heaters, geothermal systems, and microwind turbines. Although the amount of achievable greenhouse gas reductions varies by technology, each is designed to replace fossil fuels for major household energy uses such as water heating; space heating and cooling; electricity for appliances, lighting, and electronics; and when PV are used to power electric vehicles, transportation.

Renewable energy technologies typically involve high upfront costs and structural changes to homes. As such, their adoption is affected by contextual factors such as access to capital and tolerance for financial risk. Literature reviews find that adopters tend to be wealthier, have larger households or homes, and have achieved higher levels of education (Balcombe et al., 2013; Kastner & Stern, 2015). Other contextual factors such as the availability of supportive government incentives and policies also appear to be highly correlated with adoption. Uptake of residential solar PV, for example, dramatically increased in many countries after favorable incentives such as feed-in-tariffs, income tax credits, and net metering policies were introduced (Balcombe et al., 2013; Stern, Wittenberg, Wolske, & Kastner, 2018).

Interest in renewable energy technologies appears to be strongly determined by the specific beliefs and attitudes households have about these technologies (Kastner & Stern, 2015; Wolske et al., 2017). Perceived tradeoffs between upfront capital costs and financial benefits are especially influential. Perceptions that solar PV would lead to personal financial gains, for example, are among the strongest predictors of intentions to adopt or to contact an installer (Korcaj et al., 2015; Wolske et al., 2017). Among adopters and households who rejected renewable energy technologies, capital costs and long payback periods are often cited as the most significant barriers (Balcombe et al., 2013; Caird & Roy, 2010; Caird, Roy, & Herring, 2008; Jager, 2006). Some evidence indicates, however, that early adopters do not explicitly consider payback periods (Schelly, 2014b) but rather view these technologies as long-term investments that can help with retirement planning and rising energy costs (Rai, Reeves, & Margolis, 2016; Schelly, 2014a, 2014b).

Other beliefs besides financial ones may facilitate or hinder adoption. Common barriers include concerns about esthetic changes to the home, uncertainty about the reliability and performance of the technology, the inconvenience of making major modifications to the house or property, and the need for future maintenance (Balcombe et al., 2013; Caird & Roy, 2010; Caird et al., 2008; Claudy, Peterson, & O'Driscoll, 2013; Stern et al., 2018; Wolske et al., 2017). Motivations may include reducing climate change, greater independence from electricity suppliers, and the desire to promote a "green" self-image (Caird & Roy, 2010; Caird et al., 2008; Claudy et al., 2013; Korcaj et al., 2015; Leenheer, de Nooij, & Sheikh, 2011).

The extent to which individuals hold these beliefs may depend on underlying personal dispositions. Research on potential PV adopters in the United States indicates that individuals who are more innovative and have stronger proenvironmental norms are more likely to have favorable beliefs about PV, which in turn influence intention to contact an installer (Wolske et al., 2017). Research on early adopters of renewable energy systems shows that they are often characterized by both their enthusiasm for the technology (Labay & Kinnear, 1981; Schelly, 2014b) and their concern for the environment (Haas, Ornetzeder, Hametner, Wroblewski, & Hübner, 1999; Jager, 2006). While the ultimate decision to install a renewable energy system may depend mostly on economic factors, some have suggested that environmental concern motivates people to learn more about these technologies and help sustains their interest throughout the decision-making process (Jager, 2006; Keirstead, 2007).

Social influence has also been shown to have a positive influence on renewable energy technology adoption, especially solar PV. Several studies have demonstrated that the more concentrated PV installations are in a region, the greater the likelihood that additional installations will occur (Bollinger & Gillingham, 2012; Graziano & Gillingham, 2015; Müller & Rode, 2013). Peer effects appear to operate both passively through observation of nearby installations and actively through direct engagement with existing adopters. In the United States, seeing nearby PV installations and talking with adopters has been found to shorten the decision period for adoption and spark initial interest in the technology (Rai et al., 2016; Rai & Robinson, 2013). In Sweden, Palm (2017) found that nearby installations were only influential if potential adopters also spoke to an acquaintance with PV. The effect of talking to existing PV adopters was not to generate interest in the technology but rather to confirm its benefits, reduce uncertainties, and get information about incentives and installers. Other trusted sources of information may also fulfill this role, including renewable energy advocacy groups (Schelly, 2014b), local electricity utilities (Palm, 2016), and solar community organizations (Noll, Dawes, & Rai, 2014).

Households increasingly have opportunities to adopt renewable energy systems without directly making capital investments or changing the physical conditions of their homes. For example, Germany has offered incentives for households to participate in community solar PV projects that can be constructed away from the homes of those involved. This enables homes that are poorly situated for PV to switch to solar power. In many countries, and in some US jurisdictions, electricity customers are now allowed to choose among electricity suppliers and thus pay for renewable power if they want, again without making physical changes to their homes. Even renters in many places have this opportunity. These options considerably increase the potential penetration of renewable energy.

6.3.1.2   Energy-efficient and alternative-fuel vehicles

Passenger cars, sport utility vehicles, light-duty trucks, and minivans account for approximately 16% of US greenhouse gas emissions (Center for Sustainable Systems, 2016; US EPA, 2016). Energy-efficient vehicles, which use less petroleum per mile driven, and alternative fuel vehicles, which replace petroleum with less carbon-intensive fuels, are two strategies for reducing these emissions. Alternative fuel vehicles include both vehicles with traditional combustion engines that burn fuels with smaller climate impacts (e.g., biodiesel or natural gas) as well as electric vehicles. Electric vehicles can further be divided into several classes: hybrid electric vehicles that pair traditional internal combustion engines with regenerative braking, plug-in hybrid electric vehicles that extend the range of the battery by allowing it to be recharged, and plug-in battery electric vehicles that run entirely on electricity and must be recharged more frequently than hybrids. Of the various vehicle types, plug-in hybrids and battery electric vehicles have considerable potential to reduce carbon emissions[1] (McLaren *et al.* 2016), but, as we discuss below, some of the biggest barriers to adoption.

Most research on alternative fuel vehicle purchasing has focused on the economic and contextual factors that influence adoption. Analyses based on purchasing data of alternative fuel vehicles indicate that their adoption is driven primarily by rising fuel costs, government incentives that reduce upfront costs (Diamond, 2009; Gallagher & Muehlegger, 2011), and in the case of electric vehicles, the number of charging stations available (Sierzchula, Bakker, Maat, & van Wee, 2014). The form of the incentive also matters. In the United States, state sales tax waivers have a stronger impact on hybrid purchasing than income tax credits—even when the magnitude of the waiver is smaller—suggesting that consumers are more attentive to incentives that have immediate and transparent effects on the purchase price (Gallagher & Muehlegger, 2011). (In the United States, income tax credits offer their benefits in the year after the purchase.) Other evidence confirms that the timing of alternative fuel vehicle purchases aligns with the availability of incentives (Sallee, 2011), with sales dropping once incentives are removed (Tabuchi, 2017).

Lack of knowledge and understanding about life cycle costs has been cited as a significant barrier to purchasing of fuel-efficient vehicles (Lane & Potter, 2007; Rezvani, Jansson, & Bodin, 2015). While consumers tend to be knowledgeable about fuel costs at the pump, research shows that few people take into consideration the full costs of owning, operating, and maintaining a vehicle when comparison shopping (Allcott, 2011a; Lane & Potter, 2007; Rezvani et al., 2015; Sovacool & Hirsh, 2009). As Lane and Potter (2007) suggest, this may be because people assume that cars of the same class (e.g., four-door sedans) have similar fuel economy. US studies indicate that people systematically misinterpret miles-per-gallon (MPG) ratings (Larrick & Soll, 2008). Most people incorrectly believe that MPG scale linearly such that a difference of 1 MPG between two inefficient vehicles (e.g., getting 10 or 11 MPG) has the same impact on fuel consumption as a 1-MPG difference between two highly efficient cars (e.g., 40 vs 41 MPG). In fact, MPG have a curvilinear relationship, such that the impact of a 1-MPG difference

[1] Although plug-in electric vehicles, on average, reduce greenhouse emissions relative to conventional vehicles, actual achievable reductions depend on factors such as the carbon intensity of the electricity source and the time of day that recharging occurs (Elgowainy et al., 2010; McLaren, Miller, O'Shaughnessy, Wood, & Shapiro, 2016).

decreases as fuel efficiency increases. Coined the "MPG Illusion,"[2] this bias may lead consumers to overlook small differences in MPG among vehicles with lower fuel efficiency ratings (e.g., vans and trucks), when in fact those differences are substantial—and likewise overvalue cars at the high end of the spectrum, where small gains in MPG matter less (Allcott, 2011a).

Even when consumers are provided with a knowledge-related decision aid at the point of purchase, information about total operating costs may not affect purchasing behavior. In an experimental study by Allcott and Knittel (2017), car shoppers were approached at the dealership and shown the annual and lifetime fuel costs of the customer's current car as compared to the three vehicles the person was considering buying. To make the comparisons concrete, the lifetime fuel savings associated with the most efficient vehicle were compared to other purchases such as the number of iPads or trips to Hawaii that could be purchased. When the researchers contacted shoppers months later, no differences were found between the treatment and control conditions in terms of the average fuel efficiency of the cars purchased. The results suggest that lifetime cost considerations were outweighed by other factors.

Several studies have looked more specifically at the psychological determinants of alternative fuel vehicle adoption, particularly plug-in electric vehicles. Literature reviews by Rezvani et al (2015) and Lane and Potter (2007) identify several categories of beliefs that influence the decision (or intention) to adopt electric vehicles: financial considerations, inconvenience, concerns about performance, perceived environmental benefits, and symbolic attributes. As with renewable energy technologies, the high purchase price and long payback period associated with electric vehicles is a deterrent to many. Practical concerns about the limited range of all-electric battery electric vehicles, the time needed for batteries to recharge, as well as safety concerns about slow acceleration when driving are barriers. Some consumers may delay considering electric vehicles for fear that currently available technologies will quickly become obsolete. Evidence about the role of perceived environmental benefits is mixed, with some adopters describing environmental concerns as a motivation for their purchase, and other consumers expressing doubts about electric vehicles' environmental benefits (Rezvani et al., 2015). Consumers may also be deterred by the small size or style of some electric vehicles or be concerned about their slow operation (Graham-Rowe et al., 2012). In general, believing energy-efficient vehicles involve sacrificing performance, comfort, or pleasure has been shown to decrease intentions to adopt (Nayum & Klöckner, 2014).

Personal dispositions may shape consumers' beliefs about alternative fuel vehicles, as well as the attributes they pay attention to when shopping. Some studies have linked alternative fuel vehicle adoption to consumer innovativeness (Heffner, Kurani, & Turrentine, 2007; Jansson, 2011). Adopters in Sweden were found to rate

---

[2] Allcott (2011a, p. 98) provides a concrete example of the MPG illusion: "[C]onsider two pairs of vehicles. The first pair is two vans, one rated at 11 MPG and the other at 13 MPG, and the second pair is two cars rated at 29 and 49 MPG. Many people intuitively believe that conditional on gas price and miles driven, the difference in fuel costs between the second pair is much larger, because the difference in MPG is much larger. In fact, the fuel cost differences are almost exactly the same: The difference between each pair of vehicles in gallons of gasoline consumed per mile driven is 0.014."

alternative fuel vehicles as more compatible with their needs, less complex, and more advantageous than nonadopters did (Jansson, 2011). Other work finds that individuals with stronger proenvironmental norms perceive the functional attributes of electric vehicles more favorably (Schuitema, Anable, Skippon, & Kinnear, 2013). These views, in turn, positively predict beliefs about the symbolic and hedonic benefits of electric vehicles, which predict intentions to buy. Jansson, Marell, & Nordlund (2010, 2011) found that VBN variables, especially proenvironmental norms, had predictive value in explaining past adoption of alternative fuel vehicles as well as willingness to adopt them in the future. Intentions to adopt electric vehicles are also correlated with beliefs that adoption will enhance environmental identity and social status (Noppers et al., 2014).

Different attitudes may be important to understanding why people do not buy battery electric vehicles. Using a market segmentation approach, Nayum, Klöckner, and Mehmetoglu (2016) compared battery electric vehicle adopters in Norway with conventional car owners. While battery electric vehicle owners had higher ratings on personal norms and beliefs about the benefits of these vehicles, these variables had less discriminatory power than attitudes about performance and convenience, with owners of larger cars rating these as particularly important to their decision-making. In a survey of potential electric vehicle adopters, Egbue and Long (2012) similarly found that while environmental considerations were important, beliefs about cost and performance mattered more.

With financial and performance considerations being of primary importance to many shoppers, car dealerships may play a vital role in shaping consumer perceptions. However, the technology may have advanced faster than the ability of dealerships to market it. A study by Matthews, Lynes, Riemer, Del Matto, and Cloet (2017) found that in visits to 24-certified electric vehicle dealerships in Ontario, Canada, only 13 had an electric vehicle on the lot available to test drive, and in those dealerships, between a quarter to one-third of sales associates provided inaccurate information about available subsidies.

6.3.2 Improving energy efficiency of equipment in the home

6.3.2.1 Home weatherization (W)

Improving the building envelope of one's home and upgrading to more efficient heating and cooling systems are among the most effective strategies a household can take to reduce its climate change impact (see Table 6.1). Compared to energy-related behaviors with lower potential climate impact, however, they have received much less research attention from psychologists.

Kastner and Stern (2015) examined 26 empirical studies to identify the determinants of major energy-related investments that involve physically altering residential homes, including both retrofit measures (e.g., added insulation) and renewable energy systems. With the exception of wood pellet heaters, few differences were found between the determinants of different types of investments. In line with past research (Black, Stern, & Elworth, 1985), demographic variables and personal dispositions of the decision-maker, including environmental attitudes, were found to be less important than the perceived consequences of investing. Beliefs about investment costs and energy savings, increases in thermal comfort, and benefits to the environment were most commonly associated with decisions to invest in insulation measures. These findings complement earlier work by Caird et al. (2008). In their study of UK residents, concerns about capital costs and slow payback periods were the most common barriers to home efficiency improvements; increasing comfort and warmth while saving money and energy were cited as the primary motivations for adoption.

Other contextual factors may influence the timing of weatherization upgrades. Several studies suggest that homeowners are more likely to upgrade heating and cooling systems, appliances, and home insulation when undergoing other renovations (Judson & Maller, 2014; Noonan, Hsieh, & Matisoff, 2015) or after moving (Caird et al., 2008). Ethnographic research from Australia suggests, however, that even among households who self-identify as pursuing "green renovations," energy efficiency is often secondary to concerns about improving thermal comfort, reducing future costs, or changing the layout of a home to accommodate other needs (Judson & Maller, 2014).

6.3.2.2   Efficient appliances (E)

Appliances are responsible for approximately 18% of household electricity consumption in the United States (US EIA, 2017). While upgrading to more efficient models is a relatively straightforward way for households to reduce their climate change impacts and save money, energy consumption does not appear to be top of mind for most when shopping (Gaspar & Antunes, 2011). In a study of UK consumers, for example, price, brand, and reliability were reported as primary considerations; only 19% of respondents listed energy efficiency as a leading factor in their decision making (Yohanis, 2012). In the United States, Zhao, Bell, Horner, Sulik, and Zhang (2012) investigated what factors might lead consumers to consider purchasing energy-efficient and renewable energy goods such as Energy Star appliances, efficient heating and cooling systems, and solar panels. Initial costs and potential financial savings were ranked as having the greatest influence on decision-making followed by the availability of tax credits. Environmental benefits, cutting-edge technology, and access to low-interest financing were seen as much less important. Some evidence suggests that energy-efficient purchasing may be more likely among individuals who already engage in energy curtailment behaviors (Gaspar & Antunes, 2011) or who have purchased efficient appliances in the past (Nguyen, Lobo, & Greenland, 2016).

One reason energy efficiency may be overlooked is that people fail to consider lifetime costs when comparison shopping. The price premium associated with more efficient goods can often be recouped over time through energy savings, but this fact may not be obvious to consumers in the store. Considerable research has consequently focused on strategies for making lifetime costs more transparent to consumers, usually through on-product labels. While hypothetical discrete choice experiments suggest that presenting information about total operating costs may be effective (Deutsch, 2010; e.g., Heinzle, 2012; Newell & Siikamäki, 2014), evidence from field studies is less clear. Though not focused on appliances, Allcott and Taubinsky (2015) tested the effects of presenting the lifetime costs for incandescent and compact fluorescent light bulbs to customers of a hardware store; the information had no effect on purchasing decisions. In a similar study, Kallbekken, Sælen, and Hermansen (2013) used a factorial design to experimentally test the effects of presenting lifetime energy costs on refrigerators and tumble driers and training sales staff about the energy consumption of those products. No treatment effects were found for refrigerators, perhaps because of the small difference in lifetime costs between efficient and less efficient models. For tumble driers, only the combined treatment of label plus trained staff led to more efficient purchasing, suggesting that the sales staff helped to make the information more salient.

Other contextual factors may influence the decision-making process. Appliance shopping most often occurs in response to other events: the old appliance breaks or the household moves and must equip a new home (Gaspar & Antunes, 2011). Under these circumstances, people may have limited time and attention to research efficient options. Young, Hwang, McDonald, and Oates (2010) found this to be true even among self-identified "green consumers." "Green" shoppers also struggled to make efficient choices in the face of price constraints and the desire to factor in other criteria such as brand, size, appearance, and reliability.

6.3.3   Behavioral changes with existing technology: Travel

Behavioral changes with existing technology generally have lower RAERs than adoption of efficient or renewable energy technologies. Many behavioral changes are frequently repeated, and they typically involve low financial burden. We first examine such behaviors in the travel domain and then those in homes.

6.3.3.1   Eco-friendly driving (D) and vehicle maintenance (M)

Small changes in the way people drive and maintain their motor vehicles can have significant, cumulative impacts on transportation-related emissions (see Table 6.1). Eco-friendly driving behaviors include chaining trips to reduce miles driven and driving within the speed limit to optimize fuel efficiency. Drivers can also maximize fuel efficiency by maintaining tire pressure, changing air filters as needed, and investing in low-rolling resistance tires. Psychological research on these behaviors, however, is quite sparse.

The evidence available indicates that people often lack accurate knowledge of the potential energy savings associated with these behaviors (Attari et al., 2010). In an experimental study in the Netherlands, Dogan, Bolderdijk, and Steg (2014) tested the effectiveness of different informational messages on intentions to engage in six eco-driving behaviors. Participants were told about either the carbon savings or the financial benefits of each behavior. As compared to a control group, both messages were equally effective at increasing intentions. However, when asked to rate how worthwhile eco-driving seemed, those exposed to the environmental frame had significantly higher ratings than the financial frame. A related study found that people perceived they would feel better about themselves for complying with an environmental appeal to check tire pressure than a financial one (Bolderdijk, Steg, Geller, Lehman, & Postmes, 2013). In a follow-up field experiment, customers at a fueling station saw one of four signs encouraging them to get a free tire pressure check, three of which described either the environmental, financial, or safety reasons for doing so. Customers exposed to the environmental sign were significantly more likely to respond. Collectively, these studies indicate that, unlike energy-related investment behaviors, the populations studied do not think about eco-driving or minor car maintenance with a financial mindset; behavior change is more likely if interventions tap motivations related to an individual's self-concept.

6.3.3.2   *Travel mode choice (D)*

Another way households can reduce their travel-related emissions is to choose less carbon intensive modes of travel such as walking, biking, carpooling, or using public transportation instead of traveling alone in private motor vehicles. Given the diversity of these behaviors, a comprehensive review of their determinants is beyond the scope of this chapter. We focus here on key insights related to decisions to reduce car use and use public transportation. Most psychological research in this domain uses cross-sectional surveys to examine correlates of existing car use (or nonuse) and/or intentions to reduce driving. In a metaanalysis of 23 studies that examined car use as a function of TPB variables and habit, Gardner and Abraham (2008) found intentions to drive and past habit had the strongest relationships to car use, followed by perceptions about the difficulty of noncar travel (perceived behavioral control). Subjective norms to reduce car use and attitudes about the environmental impacts of different travel modes had significant but smaller effects on both intentions and behavior. More recent studies have confirmed the importance of attitudinal factors, perceived behavioral control, and past habit to travel mode choice (e.g., Abrahamse, Steg, Gifford, & Vlek, 2009; Galdames, Tudela, & Carrasco, 2011; Thøgersen, 2006).

Personal norms may also be a factor in travel mode choice (Abrahamse et al., 2009; Bamberg, Hunecke, & Blöbaum, 2007; Nordlund & Garvill, 2003), especially among individuals who have already committed to driving less or using public transportation (e.g., Lind et al., 2015). In a market segmentation study, Anable (2005) found strong proenvironmental norms were a defining characteristic both of individuals who had intentionally given up their cars and "aspiring environmentalists" who had strong intentions to use alternative modes. A large segment of "complacent car addicts"—people who were dependent on their cars but recognized it was possible to use alternative modes—were distinguished by their *lack* of moral obligation and awareness of consequences; they did not perceive barriers to changing transit modes but lacked the motivation to do so.

Other evidence points to the importance of contextual factors such as distance between home and work and the availability of high quality transportation alternatives. For example, in a metaanalysis of 22 studies, Neoh, Chipulu, and Marshall

(2017) found that the strongest predictors of carpooling behavior were situational factors such as employer size (which increases the pool of potential car sharers), transportation costs, reserved carpool parking, and the availability of high-occupancy vehicle lanes. In a longitudinal analysis of UK households, Clark, Chatterjee, and Melia (2016) found that car commuting patterns were fairly stable over time; commute mode changes primarily occurred when changing jobs or residences resulted in a shorter commute or improved access to public transport. Under these circumstances, individuals with stronger environmental attitudes were more likely to switch modes of transportation. Verplanken, Walker, Davis, and Jurasek (2008, p. 125) suggest that such contextual changes "can activate ecological values and beliefs, which thus guide the process of (re)negotiating proenvironmental behaviors." More research is needed to understand whether travel mode preferences factor into larger life decisions such as choice of job or residence, or whether travel behavior simply follows from them.

6.3.4 Behavioral changes with existing technology: Frequent behaviors in the home (D)

Much of the research on in-home behaviors to curtail carbon emissions has examined reducing overall levels of ongoing energy use in homes, rather than specific behaviors, such as turning off electronics and appliances on standby power or using less hot water when bathing and cleaning. We review what is known about reducing overall household energy use through such curtailment actions and then examine the determinants of one specific, relatively high-impact everyday action for which there is empirical evidence available: thermostat settings.

6.3.4.1 Household curtailment behaviors

As there have been several previous reviews of the determinants of household energy use reductions and the types of interventions that are effective at promoting them without technological change (e.g., Abrahamse et al., 2005; Delmas et al., 2013; Steg, 2008; Stern, 1992), this review is brief. Research suggests that individuals typically lack accurate knowledge of how much energy different activities in their homes use (Kempton & Montgomery, 1982; Mizobuchi & Takeuchi, 2013). When asked to estimate the energy consumption associated with different actions, most people overestimate the benefits of highly visible behaviors such as turning off lights while underestimating the impact of appliances, electronics, and hot water usage (Attari et al., 2010). Many interventions have consequently focused on making energy use more salient and transparent. In particular, providing feedback on total household energy consumption or savings has proved to be an effective strategy, delivering 5%−12% in energy savings depending on how the feedback is given (Fischer, 2008; Karlin et al., 2015). When provided frequently (e.g., real-time, daily, or weekly), feedback on energy usage can make individuals more aware of their consumption, prompt conservation behavior, and help them learn the relative impact of different actions (Abrahamse et al., 2005; Darby, 2001; Faruqui,

Sergici, & Sharif, 2010; Fischer, 2008; Grønhøj & Thøgersen, 2011; Tiefenbeck et al., 2016; Winett, Neale, & Grier, 1979). The effects on energy consumption may be amplified if the feedback is given in combination with a conservation goal (Abrahamse, Steg, Vlek, & Rothengatter, 2007; Becker, 1978; McCalley & Midden, 2002) or price signals related to electricity price changes (Newsham & Bowker, 2010). Home energy reports that compare a household's energy consumption to its neighbors are also generally effective in US studies (Allcott, 2011b; Ayres et al., 2013), though more so for political liberals than conservatives (Costa & Kahn, 2013b). Two metaanalyses suggest, however, that comparative feedback results in lower savings compared to other types of feedback (Karlin et al., 2015) or information (Delmas et al., 2013).

Other research has examined the underlying motivations for engaging in curtailment behaviors. Using voter registration and utility data, Costa and Kahn (2013a) found evidence that California households with liberal political party affiliations use less energy than conservatives living in comparable homes. This finding may reflect the tendency of liberals to have stronger proenvironmental values and attitudes (McCright, 2011). Strong proenvironmental norms have been found to predict self-reported curtailment behaviors such as shorter shower times (van der Werff & Steg, 2015) and lower hot water temperatures (Black et al., 1985). Other evidence suggests, however, that the effects are indirect: Environmental norms and beliefs do not explain added variance in household energy consumption if attitude measures from TPB are controlled (Abrahamse & Steg, 2009).

Several studies suggest that interventions are more effective at encouraging energy conservation if they call on prosocial motives rather than financial ones. In a series of multi-month field experiments, Asensio and Delmas (2015, 2016) demonstrated that providing feedback about the environmental and public health consequences associated with a household's energy use was more effective at reducing consumption than messages about potential monetary savings. Households in the prosocial treatment conditions reduced energy consumption by 8%−10% compared to control groups, whereas the monetary framings did not result in significant savings. A recent meta-analysis suggests that monetary information may even be detrimental, causing households to increase energy consumption (Delmas et al., 2013).

6.3.4.2   Thermostat settings

Past research suggests that consumers underestimate the energy savings achievable through thermostat setbacks (Attari et al., 2010). Misconceptions about how home heating and cooling systems operate may also keep households from conditioning their homes efficiently (Peffer, Pritoni, Meier, Aragon, & Perry, 2011; Pritoni et al., 2015). Confirming earlier work by Kempton (1986), Pritoni et al. (2015) found that people may waste energy because they mistakenly think thermostats control indoor temperatures like the knob on a gas stove: By setting the temperature higher, they expect their homes to warm up faster. Other misconceptions include believing that the thermostat sets the temperature of the air coming out of the system, and that it takes more energy to bring a home back to a desired temperature after a setback period than to heat it at a constant temperature.

Confusion about heating controls themselves may also be a barrier to effective action. Programmable thermostats—which were introduced to the market to help automate setbacks—have grown increasingly complex, allowing users to set schedules for different days of the week and for multiple times of the day. Evidence indicates that programing features are often underutilized or overridden, as many do not know how to change settings or are afraid to do so for fear of overheating or overcooling their homes (US EIA, 2013a; Nevius & Pigg, 2000; Peffer et al., 2011; Pritoni et al., 2015; Sachs et al., 2012). Research in the United Kingdom suggests that households with radiators face similar frustrations as the settings on thermostatic radiator valves are not calibrated to actual temperatures (Caird et al., 2008).

Among households who report regularly setting back their thermostats, a sense of moral obligation appears to be a primary motivator (Black et al., 1985; Wolske, 2011). Studies have also examined beliefs about the benefits and consequences of setting back thermostats. Not surprisingly, households are less likely to adjust their thermostats if concerned about thermal comfort (Becker, Seligman, Fazio, & Darley, 1981; Pedersen, 2008; Wolske, 2011). The inconvenience of remembering to adjust the thermostat or learning to use its programing features may also be a deterrent, though this may be less of a barrier for individuals who have favorable attitudes toward energy conservation (Nevius & Pigg, 2000). While evidence is scarce, believing that thermostat adjustments could save money does not appear to prompt changes in behavior (Black et al., 1985).

A number of contextual variables may influence heating and cooling choices. Several economic studies have shown, for example, that renters use more energy for space conditioning when utilities are included in their rent than when they pay for utilities directly (Gillingham, Harding, & Rapson, 2012). In rentals and owner-occupied homes alike, households whose members have different schedules and comfort preferences may struggle to maintain a setback routine or to find an agreeable temperature (Karjalainen, 2007; Pritoni et al., 2015).

Though few interventions have specifically targeted space-conditioning behaviors, some studies indicate that encouraging households to set specific conservation goals and providing detailed information about potential energy savings or emissions reductions could encourage greater setback behavior (McCalley & Midden, 2003; Wolske, 2011). Additional research is needed to understand the long-term efficacy of these strategies.

6.4 Conclusions and research agenda

The structure of this review follows the argument of Stern (2017) that social science can become more influential in societal transitions affecting climate change if it selects research topics (1) with large potential for change in physical terms and (2) for which its contributions can add value beyond what can be achieved using concepts from other fields. This review thus differs from many psychological reviews of environmentally significant behavior by focusing on behaviors first in terms of their potential importance for limiting climate change and only afterward on the psychological constructs that might explain variation and change in the behaviors. Thus, our discussion and these conclusions are organized around principles previously advanced for achieving what has been called the behavioral wedge (Dietz et al., 2009)—the portion of desired reductions in greenhouse gas emissions that can be achieved through changes in individual and household consumer behaviors. The first of these principles is to prioritize high-impact actions (Stern, Gardner, Vandenbergh, Dietz, & Gilligan, 2010; Vandenbergh, Stern, Gardner, Dietz, & Gilligan, 2010). These fall primarily in the categories of weatherization (W), equipment efficiency (E), and renewable energy technology (R).

A very limited body of research has examined the nontechnological and nonfinancial determinants of such actions (see, e.g., Kastner & Stern, 2015). Thus, conclusions must be drawn carefully and tentatively and may have greater value as offering promising directions for further research than as definitive results. One conclusion, however, flows quite strongly from the available research. The behaviors with the greatest potential impact for affecting climate change—primarily choices about adopting equipment with large lifetime effects on greenhouse gas emissions—have different major determinants from the behaviors most often studied by psychologists, which have relatively small climate impact. Very broadly speaking, for choices about the high-impact actions, considerations of financial cost and return, long payback periods, and, in some cases, trustworthy information about various aspects of the performance, reliability, and practicality of the equipment in the potential adopters' situations appear to be important determinants of decisions. Personal characteristics of consumers, especially values, environmental attitudes, and other attributes typically examined in psychological research tend to have weaker direct influences, though their indirect influences, such as through initial interest in the action, may be important.

This does not mean, however, that psychological and related social science concepts are unimportant. It has long been recognized that for expensive, high-impact household energy actions, there can be huge variations in households' responses to identical financial incentives. As reported three decades ago, responses to financial incentives for home weatherization actions varied tenfold across utility companies offering identical incentives—even when these incentives provided for the great majority of the initial costs (Stern et al., 1986). The variation was apparently due to differences in implementation of the incentive programs. It suggests that nontechnological and noneconomic factors affecting the target consumers are among the important determinants of the extent to which the potential emissions reductions from these behaviors is actually achieved and that psychological research focused on household behaviors with high RAER can add considerable value beyond what technological and economic studies offer.

An examination of the research on these behaviors and the associated work identifying design principles for programs to change them (Stern et al., 2010; Vandenbergh et al., 2010; Stern et al., 2018) suggests the following tentative conclusions, which also point to a research agenda:

1. Financial incentives are important, but other factors can make a huge difference in their effects. Incentive programs can be much more effective when they are supplemented with initiatives to address the nonfinancial barriers to action, as we elaborate below.
2. High-impact household actions are often two-step decisions, one step resulting in giving the action serious attention and the second resulting in decision and action. Even with strong incentives, marketing is commonly needed to convince target households to consider major actions. Expensive mass media advertising may or may not be effective. Informal marketing through social networks or efforts at potential points of purchase may be more cost-effective. For newer technologies such as renewable energy technologies and alternative fuel vehicles, targeting likely "early adopters" such as innovative or environmentally-minded consumers may be effective.
3. In the decision phase, it is important to provide valid information from credible sources at points of decision. Once a new option is being considered, it may be most effective to target marketing efforts to the times and places of decision and to engage the people who interact directly with consumers at those times and places (motor vehicle dealers, home improvement contractors, salespeople in appliance stores, real estate agents, etc.). For these people to be effective agents of change, they need to have valid and credible information at their disposal and they may need special training or incentives to change their own routines.
4. To be effective, information about the choice and its benefits should be kept simple, as well as valid and credible. It should be designed to overcome or bypass common misunderstandings that research has found to be associated with the particular choices at hand, and it should include attributes of the choice that are important to consumers but absent from many technological and economic analyses, such as effects on comfort, health, home appearance, and social status. Some important information might appear on well-designed labels on products or homes; some might best come as advice from trusted information sources. One-stop shopping, and minimization of paperwork and delay in delivering incentives, can make a substantial difference. With home energy efficiency, "instant rebates are more convenient than mail-in ones; rebates are more convenient than tax credits; and tax credits are more convenient than most loan-based programs" (Stern et al., 2010, p. 4848). Structuring programs so that they require opting out rather than opting in may be a promising approach.
5. Choice architecture, such as careful framing of the options and selection of default options, provides a promising approach to simplifying the complex decisions involved in high-impact consumer choices and thus increasing the likelihood that choices reduce emissions while remaining consistent with consumer preferences (Kunreuther & Weber, 2014).
6. Programs are more effective when they provide credible quality assurance so that adopters gain confidence that they will actually get the promised benefits. This may be accomplished, for example, by certifying contractors for home improvements and offering contractual guarantees of performance for renewable energy systems.

The relative importance of these influences and principles will need to be determined and are likely to be different for different actions, in different economic and policy contexts, and perhaps for different consumer segments. Most psychology-based research on proenvironmental behavior has focused on "average" effects, but in the domain of high-cost, high-impact energy investments, the field may do well to borrow market segmentation strategies from consumer psychology. A handful of studies have already proven this approach to be insightful for understanding alternative fuel vehicle purchasing behavior (Nayum et al., 2016), travel behavior (Anable, 2005), and household energy curtailment and efficiency measures (Sütterlin, Brunner, & Siegrist, 2011).

The usefulness of available psychological and other social science theories will also need to be determined. The most appropriate combination of explanatory concepts may vary with the type of behavior and its policy context. For example, in a study of interest in adoption of residential PV in the United States, three theories, including DOI theory, which is not usually included in psychological studies, all indicated some explanatory power (Wolske et al., 2017). Future research on high-impact household actions is likely to contribute to a better understanding of the theories that are applicable to different types of behaviors and choice contexts, of the relationships among theories, and of the economic concepts that are important in explaining environmentally important household actions. Such integrative approaches may also help identify segments of consumers that are likely to respond to different product attributes, thus informing segment-based approaches to influencing choice.

Psychology has only scratched the surface of the contributions it can make to limiting climate change through the actions of households as consumers. It has demonstrated its ability to contribute through studies of several types of household action that have relatively small potential for limiting climate change. It can contribute much more going forward by applying its concepts and methods to higher-impact consumer behaviors and helping to achieve RAER that are not achieved by current policies and programs. To do so, however, it needs to pay more attention to understanding the psychological influences specific to high-impact behaviors (e.g., the importance of reducing cognitive effort in the face of complex choices) and to engage more in collaboration with specialists in other fields, including technology design, consumer choice, and economics. Psychology also needs to be cognizant that influences on choice vary in different policy contexts. On a generational time scale, psychology can contribute even further through studies to facilitate major societal transitions, such as to electrically powered vehicle fleets and to community designs that reduce the need for motorized transport, both in developed and developing countries.

Acknowledgment

The authors have contributed equally to the paper; the listed order of authorship was determined by lot.

References

Abrahamse, W., & Steg, L. (2009). How do socio-demographic and psychological factors relate to households' direct and indirect energy use and savings?. *Journal of Economic Psychology*, *30*(5), 711−720. Available from https://doi.org/10.1016/j.joep.2009.05.006.

Abrahamse, W., Steg, L., Gifford, R., & Vlek, C. (2009). Factors influencing car use for commuting and the intention to reduce it: A question of self-interest or morality?. *Transportation Research Part F: Traffic Psychology and Behaviour, 12*(4), 317−324. Available from https://doi.org/10.1016/j.trf.2009.04.004.

Abrahamse, W., Steg, L., Vlek, C., & Rothengatter, T. (2005). A review of intervention studies aimed at household energy conservation. *Journal of Environmental Psychology, 25*, 273−291.

Abrahamse, W., Steg, L., Vlek, C., & Rothengatter, T. (2007). The effect of tailored information, goal setting, and tailored feedback on household energy use, energy-related behaviors, and behavioral antecedents. *Journal of Environmental Psychology, 27*(4), 265−276. Available from https://doi.org/10.1016/j.jenvp.2007.08.002.

Ajzen, I. (1991). The theory of planned behavior. *Organizational Behavior and Human Decision Processes, 50*, 179−211.

Allcott, H. (2011a). Consumers' perceptions and misperceptions of energy costs. *American Economic Review, 101*(3), 98−104.

Allcott, H. (2011b). Social norms and energy conservation. *Journal of Public Economics, 95* (9−10), 1082−1095. Available from https://doi.org/10.1016/j.jpubeco.2011.03.003.

Allcott, H., & Knittel, C. (2017). *Are consumers poorly-informed about fuel economy? Evidence from two experiments* (No. Working Paper 23076). NBER. Retrieved from http://www.nber.org/papers/w23076.

Allcott, H., & Taubinsky, D. (2015). Evaluating behaviorally motivated policy: Experimental evidence from the lightbulb market. *American Economic Review, 105*(8), 2501−2538.

Anable, J. (2005). "Complacent car addicts" or "aspiring environmentalists"? Identifying travel behaviour segments using attitude theory. *Transport Policy, 12*(1), 65−78. Available from https://doi.org/10.1016/j.tranpol.2004.11.004.

Asensio, O. I., & Delmas, M. A. (2015). Nonprice incentives and energy conservation. *Proceedings of the National Academy of Sciences of the United States of America, 112* (6), E510−E515. Available from https://doi.org/10.1073/pnas.1401880112.

Asensio, O. I., & Delmas, M. A. (2016). The dynamics of behavior change: Evidence from energy conservation. *Journal of Economic Behavior & Organization, 126*(Part A), 196−212. Available from https://doi.org/10.1016/j.jebo.2016.03.012.

Attari, S. Z., DeKay, M. L., Davidson, C. I., & Bruine de Bruin, W. (2010). Public perceptions of energy consumption and savings. *Proceedings of the National Academy of Sciences of the United States of America, 107*(37), 16054−16059.

Ayres, I., Raseman, S., & Shih, A. (2013). Evidence from two large field experiments that peer comparison feedback can reduce residential energy usage. *The Journal of Law, Economics, and Organization, 29*(5), 992−1022. Available from https://doi.org/10.1093/jleo/ews020.

Balcombe, P., Rigby, D., & Azapagic, A. (2013). Motivations and barriers associated with adopting microgeneration energy technologies in the UK. *Renewable and Sustainable Energy Reviews, 22*, 655−666. Available from https://doi.org/10.1016/j.rser.2013.02.012.

Bamberg, S., Ajzen, I., & Schmidt, P. (2003). Choice of travel mode in the theory of planned behavior: The roles of past behavior, habit, and reasoned action. *Basic and Applied Social Psychology, 25*(3), 175−187. Available from https://doi.org/10.1207/S15324834BASP2503_01.

Bamberg, S., Hunecke, M., & Blöbaum, A. (2007). Social context, personal norms and the use of public transportation: Two field studies. *Journal of Environmental Psychology, 27*(3), 190−203. Available from https://doi.org/10.1016/j.jenvp.2007.04.001.

Becker, L. J. (1978). Joint effect of feedback and goal setting on performance: A field study of residential energy conservation. *Journal of Applied Psychology*, *63*(4), 428–433.

Becker, L. J., Seligman, C., Fazio, R. H., & Darley, J. M. (1981). Relating attitudes to residential energy use. *Environment and Behavior*, *13*(5), 590–609. Available from https://doi.org/10.1177/0013916581135004.

Black, J. S., Stern, P. C., & Elworth, J. T. (1985). Personal and contextual influences on household energy adaptations. *Journal of Applied Psychology*, *70*(1), 3–21. Available from https://doi.org/10.1037/0021-9010.70.1.3.

Bolderdijk, J. W., Steg, L., Geller, E. S., Lehman, P. K., & Postmes, T. (2013). Comparing the effectiveness of monetary versus moral motives in environmental campaigning. *Nature Climate Change*, *3*(4), 413–416. Available from https://doi.org/10.1038/nclimate1767.

Bollinger, B., & Gillingham, K. (2012). Peer effects in the diffusion of solar photovoltaic panels. *Marketing Science*, *31*(6), 900–912. Available from https://doi.org/10.1287/mksc.1120.0727.

Brandon, G., & Lewis, A. (1999). Reducing household energy consumption: A qualitative and quantitative field study. *Journal of Environmental Psychology*, *19*(1), 75–85. Available from https://doi.org/10.1006/jevp.1998.0105.

Caird, S., & Roy, R. (2010). Adoption and use of household microgeneration heat technologies. *Low Carbon Economy*, *1*(2), 61–70.

Caird, S., Roy, R., & Herring, H. (2008). Improving the energy performance of UK households: Results from surveys of consumer adoption and use of low- and zero-carbon technologies. *Energy Efficiency*, *1*(2), 149. Available from https://doi.org/10.1007/s12053-008-9013-y.

Center for Sustainable Systems. (2016). *Personal transportation factsheet* (No. CSS01-07). University of Michigan. Retrieved from http://css.snre.umich.edu/factsheets/personal-transportation-factsheet.

Chen, K. K. (2014). Assessing the effects of customer innovativeness, environmental value and ecological lifestyles on residential solar power systems install intention. *Energy Policy*, *67*, 951–961. Available from https://doi.org/10.1016/j.enpol.2013.12.005.

Clark, B., Chatterjee, K., & Melia, S. (2016). Changes to commute mode: The role of life events, spatial context and environmental attitude. *Transportation Research Part A: Policy and Practice*, *89*, 89–105. Available from https://doi.org/10.1016/j.tra.2016.05.005.

Claudy, M. C., Peterson, M., & O'Driscoll, A. (2013). Understanding the attitude-behavior gap for renewable energy systems using behavioral reasoning theory. *Journal of Macromarketing*, *33*(4), 273–287. Available from https://doi.org/10.1177/0276146713481605.

Cohen, M. A., & Vandenbergh, M. P. (2012). The potential role of carbon labeling in a green economy. *Energy Economics*, *34*(1), S53–S63. Available from https://doi.org/10.1016/j.eneco.2012.08.032.

Costa, D. L., & Kahn, M. E. (2013a). Do liberal home owners consume less electricity? A test of the voluntary restraint hypothesis. *Economics Letters*, *119*(2), 210–212. Available from https://doi.org/10.1016/j.econlet.2013.02.020.

Costa, D. L., & Kahn, M. E. (2013b). Energy conservation "nudges" and environmentalist ideology: Evidence from a randomized residential electricity field experiment. *Journal of the European Economic Association*, *11*(3), 680–702. Available from https://doi.org/10.1111/%28ISSN%291542-4774/issues.

Darby, S. (2001). Making it obvious: Designing feedback into energy consumption. In: P. Bertoldi, A. Ricci, & A. de Almeida (Eds.), *Energy efficiency in household appliances and lighting* (pp. 685–696). Berlin: Springer. Available from https://doi.org/10.1007/978-3-642-56331-1_73.

Delmas, M. A., Fischlein, M., & Asensio, O. I. (2013). Information strategies and energy conservation behavior: A meta-analysis of experimental studies from 1975 to 2012. *Energy Policy, 61*, 729–739. Available from https://doi.org/10.1016/j.enpol.2013.05.109.

Deutsch, M. (2010). The effect of life-cycle cost disclosure on consumer behavior: Evidence from a field experiment with cooling appliances. *Energy Efficiency, 3*(4), 303–315. Available from https://doi.org/10.1007/s12053-010-9076-4.

Diamond, D. (2009). The impact of government incentives for hybrid-electric vehicles: Evidence from US states. *Energy Policy, 37*(3), 972–983. Available from https://doi.org/10.1016/j.enpol.2008.09.094.

Dietz, T., Gardner, G. T., Gilligan, J., Stern, P. C., & Vandenbergh, M. P. (2009). Household actions can provide a behavioral wedge to rapidly reduce US carbon emissions. *Proceedings of the National Academy of Sciences of the United States of America, 106* (44), 18452–18456. Available from https://doi.org/10.1073/pnas.0908738106.

Dogan, E., Bolderdijk, J. W., & Steg, L. (2014). Making small numbers count: Environmental and financial feedback in promoting eco-driving behaviours. *Journal of Consumer Policy, 37*(3), 413–422. Available from https://doi.org/10.1007/s10603-014-9259-z.

Egbue, O., & Long, S. (2012). Barriers to widespread adoption of electric vehicles: An analysis of consumer attitudes and perceptions. *Energy Policy, 48*, 717–729. Available from https://doi.org/10.1016/j.enpol.2012.06.009.

Elgowainy, A., Han, J., Poch, L., Wang, M., Vyas, A., Mahalik, M., & Rousseau, A. (2010). Well-to-wheels analysis of energy use and greenhouse gas emissions of plug-in hybrid electric vehicles *(No. ANL/ESD/10-1)* (p. 154) Argonne, Illinois: Argonne National Laboratory. Retrieved from https://energy.gov/eere/fuelcells/downloads/well-wheels-analysis-energy-use-and-greenhouse-gas-emissions-plug-hybrid.

Faruqui, A., Sergici, S., & Sharif, A. (2010). The impact of informational feedback on energy consumption—A survey of the experimental evidence. *Energy, 35*(4), 1598–1608. Available from https://doi.org/10.1016/j.energy.2009.07.042.

Fischer, C. (2008). Feedback on household electricity consumption: A tool for saving energy? *Energy Efficiency, 1*(1), 79–104. Available from https://doi.org/10.1007/s12053-008-9009-7.

Fischhoff, B., Slovic, P., Lichtenstein, S., Read, S., & Combs, B. (1978). How safe is safe enough? A psychometric study of attitudes towards technological risks and benefits. *Policy Sciences, 9*(2), 127–152. Available from https://doi.org/10.1007/BF00143739.

Frederiks, E. R., Stenner, K., & Hobman, E. V. (2015). The socio-demographic and psychological predictors of residential energy consumption: A comprehensive review. *Energies, 8*(1), 573–609. Available from https://doi.org/10.3390/en8010573.

Freudenburg, W. R., & Rosa, E. A. (1984). Public reaction to nuclear power: Are there critical masses? *(Vol. 93)*. Westview Press Inc.

Galdames, C., Tudela, A., & Carrasco, J.-A. (2011). Exploring the role of psychological factors in mode choice models by a latent variables approach. *Transportation Research Record: Journal of the Transportation Research Board, 2230*, 68–74. Available from https://doi.org/10.3141/2230-08.

Gallagher, K. S., & Muehlegger, E. (2011). Giving green to get green? Incentives and consumer adoption of hybrid vehicle technology. *Journal of Environmental Economics and Management, 61*(1), 1–15. Available from https://doi.org/10.1016/j.jeem.2010.05.004.

Gardner, B., & Abraham, C. (2008). Psychological correlates of car use: A meta-analysis. *Transportation Research Part F: Traffic Psychology and Behaviour*, *11*(4), 300−311. Available from https://doi.org/10.1016/j.trf.2008.01.004.

Gaspar, R., & Antunes, D. (2011). Energy efficiency and appliance purchases in Europe: Consumer profiles and choice determinants. *Energy Policy*, *39*(11), 7335−7346. Available from https://doi.org/10.1016/j.enpol.2011.08.057.

Gillingham, K., Harding, M., & Rapson, D. (2012). Split incentives in residential energy consumption. *The Energy Journal; Cleveland*, *33*(2), 37−62.

Gneezy, A., Imas, A., Brown, A., Nelson, L. D., & Norton, M. I. (2011). Paying to be nice: Consistency and costly prosocial behavior. *Management Science*, *58*(1), 179−187. Available from https://doi.org/10.1287/mnsc.1110.1437.

Graham-Rowe, E., Gardner, B., Abraham, C., Skippon, S., Dittmar, H., Hutchins, R., & Stannard, J. (2012). Mainstream consumers driving plug-in battery-electric and plug-in hybrid electric cars: A qualitative analysis of responses and evaluations. *Transportation Research Part A: Policy and Practice*, *46*(1), 140−153. Available from https://doi.org/10.1016/j.tra.2011.09.008.

Graziano, M., & Gillingham, K. (2015). Spatial patterns of solar photovoltaic system adoption: The influence of neighbors and the built environment. *Journal of Economic Geography*, *15*(4), 815−839. Available from https://doi.org/10.1093/jeg/lbu036.

Griskevicius, V., Tybur, J. M., & Van den Bergh, B. (2010). Going green to be seen: Status, reputation, and conspicuous conservation. *Journal of Personality and Social Psychology*, *98*(3), 392−404. Available from https://doi.org/10.1037/a0017346.

Grønhøj, A., & Thøgersen, J. (2011). Feedback on household electricity consumption: Learning and social influence processes. *International Journal of Consumer Studies*, *35*(2), 138−145. Available from https://doi.org/10.1111/j.1470-6431.2010.00967.x.

Haas, R., Ornetzeder, M., Hametner, K., Wroblewski, A., & Hübner, M. (1999). Socio-economic aspects of the Austrian 200 kwp-photovoltaic-rooftop programme. *Solar Energy*, *66*(3), 183−191. Available from https://doi.org/10.1016/S0038-092X(99)00019-5.

Harland, P., Staats, H., & Wilke, H. A. M. (1999). Explaining proenvironmental intention and behavior by personal norms and the theory of planned behavior. *Journal of Applied Social Psychology*, *29*(12), 2505−2528. Available from https://doi.org/10.1111/j.1559-1816.1999.tb00123.x.

Heffner, R. R., Kurani, K. S., & Turrentine, T. S. (2007). Symbolism in California's early market for hybrid electric vehicles. *Transportation Research Part D: Transport and Environment*, *12*(6), 396−413. Available from https://doi.org/10.1016/j.trd.2007.04.003.

Heinzle, S. L. (2012). Disclosure of energy operating cost information: A silver bullet for overcoming the energy-efficiency gap?. *Journal of Consumer Policy*, *35*(1), 43−64. Available from https://doi.org/10.1007/s10603-012-9189-6.

International Energy Agency, & International Renewable Energy Agency. (2017). *Executive summary. Perspectives for the energy transition: Investment needs for a low-carbon energy system* (pp. 5−16). International Energy Agency and International Renewable Energy Agency. Retrieved from http://www.irena.org/DocumentDownloads/Publications/Perspectives_for_the_Energy_Transition_2017.pdf.

Isley, S. C., Stern, P. C., Carmichael, S. P., Joseph, K. M., & Arent, D. J. (2016). Online purchasing creates opportunities to lower the life cycle carbon footprints of consumer products. *Proceedings of the National Academy of Sciences of the United States of America*, *113*(35), 9780−9785. Available from https://doi.org/10.1073/pnas.1522211113.

Jager, W. (2006). Stimulating the diffusion of photovoltaic systems: A behavioural perspective. *Energy Policy*, *34*(14), 1935−1943. Available from https://doi.org/10.1016/j.enpol.2004.12.022.

Jansson, J. (2011). Consumer eco-innovation adoption: Assessing attitudinal factors and perceived product characteristics. *Business Strategy and the Environment*, *20*(3), 192−210. Available from https://doi.org/10.1002/bse.690.

Jansson, J., Marell, A., & Nordlund, A. (2010). Green consumer behavior: Determinants of curtailment and eco-innovation adoption. *Journal of Consumer Marketing*, *27*(4), 358−370. Available from https://doi.org/10.1108/07363761011052396.

Jansson, J., Marell, A., & Nordlund, A. (2011). Exploring consumer adoption of a high involvement eco-innovation using value-belief-norm theory. *Journal of Consumer Behaviour*, *10*(1), 51−60. Available from https://doi.org/10.1002/cb.346.

Judson, E. P., & Maller, C. (2014). Housing renovations and energy efficiency: Insights from homeowners' practices. *Building Research & Information*, *42*(4), 501−511. Available from https://doi.org/10.1080/09613218.2014.894808.

Kallbekken, S., Sælen, H., & Hermansen, E. A. T. (2013). Bridging the energy efficiency gap: A field experiment on lifetime energy costs and household appliances. *Journal of Consumer Policy*, *36*(1), 1−16. Available from https://doi.org/10.1007/s10603-012-9211-z.

Karjalainen, S. (2007). Gender differences in thermal comfort and use of thermostats in everyday thermal environments. *Building and Environment*, *42*(4), 1594−1603. Available from https://doi.org/10.1016/j.buildenv.2006.01.009.

Karlin, B., Zinger, J. F., & Ford, R. (2015). The effects of feedback on energy conservation: A meta-analysis. *Psychological Bulletin*, *141*(6), 1205−1227. Available from https://doi.org/10.1037/a0039650.

Kastner, I., & Stern, P. C. (2015). Examining the decision-making processes behind household energy investments: A review. *Energy Research & Social Science*, *10*, 72−89. Available from https://doi.org/10.1016/j.erss.2015.07.008.

Keirstead, J. (2007). Behavioural responses to photovoltaic systems in the UK domestic sector. *Energy Policy*, *35*(8), 4128−4141. Available from https://doi.org/10.1016/j.enpol.2007.02.019.

Kempton, W. (1986). Two theories of home heat control. *Cognitive Science*, *10*(1), 75−90.

Kempton, W., Harris, C. K., Keith, J. G., & Weihl, J. S. (1985). Do consumers know "what works" in energy conservation? In: J. Byrne, D. A. Schulz, & M. B. Sussman (Eds.), *Families and the Energy Transition* (pp. 115−133). New York: Haworth Press, Inc.

Kempton, W., & Montgomery, L. (1982). Folk quantification of energy. *Energy*, *7*(10), 817−827.

Korcaj, L., Hahnel, U. J. J., & Spada, H. (2015). Intentions to adopt photovoltaic systems depend on homeowners' expected personal gains and behavior of peers. *Renewable Energy*, *75*, 407−415. Available from https://doi.org/10.1016/j.renene.2014.10.007.

Kunreuther, H., & Weber, E. U. (2014). Aiding decision making to reduce the impacts of climate change. *Journal of Consumer Policy*, *37*(3), 397−411. Available from https://doi.org/10.1007/s10603-013-9251-z.

Labay, D. G., & Kinnear, T. C. (1981). Exploring the consumer decision process in the adoption of solar energy systems. *Journal of Consumer Research*, *8*(3), 271−278.

Lane, B., & Potter, S. (2007). The adoption of cleaner vehicles in the UK: Exploring the consumer attitude−action gap. *Journal of Cleaner Production*, *15*(11−12), 1085−1092. Available from https://doi.org/10.1016/j.jclepro.2006.05.026.

Larrick, R. P., & Soll, J. B. (2008). The MPG illusion. *Science*, *320*(5883), 1593−1594. Available from https://doi.org/10.1126/science.1154983.

Leenheer, J., de Nooij, M., & Sheikh, O. (2011). Own power: Motives of having electricity without the energy company. *Energy Policy*, *39*(9), 5621−5629. Available from https://doi.org/10.1016/j.enpol.2011.04.037.

Lind, H. B., Nordfjærn, T., Jørgensen, S. H., & Rundmo, T. (2015). The value-belief-norm theory, personal norms and sustainable travel mode choice in urban areas. *Journal of Environmental Psychology*, *44*, 119−125. Available from https://doi.org/10.1016/j.jenvp.2015.06.001.

Lovins, A. B., & Rocky Mountain Institute. (2011). *Reinventing fire: Bold business solutions for the new energy era*. VT: Chelsea Green, White River Junction.

Lutzenhiser, L., & Lutzenhiser, S. (2006). Looking at lifestyle: The impacts of American ways of life on energy/resource demands and pollution patterns. *Proceedings of the 2006 American Council for an Energy Efficient Economy, summer study on energy efficiency in buildings* (Vol. 7, pp. 163−176). Washington, DC: ACEEE Press. Retrieved from http://aceee.org/files/proceedings/2006/data/papers/SS06_Panel7_Paper14.pdf.

Matthews, L., Lynes, J., Riemer, M., Del Matto, T., & Cloet, N. (2017). Do we have a car for you? Encouraging the uptake of electric vehicles at point of sale. *Energy Policy*, *100*, 79−88. Available from https://doi.org/10.1016/j.enpol.2016.10.001.

McCalley, L. T., & Midden, C. J. H. (2002). Energy conservation through product-integrated feedback: The roles of goal-setting and social orientation. *Journal of Economic Psychology*, *23*(5), 589−603. Available from https://doi.org/10.1016/s0167-4870(02)00119-8.

McCalley, L. T., & Midden, C. J. H. (2003). Goal setting and feedback: The programmable thermostat as a device to support conservation behavior in the user. *Proceedings of the Human Factors and Ergonomics Society Annual Meeting*, *47*(5), 797−800. Available from https://doi.org/10.1177/154193120304700502.

McCright, A. M. (2011). Political orientation moderates Americans' beliefs and concern about climate change. *Climatic Change*, *104*(2), 243−253. Available from https://doi.org/10.1007/s10584-010-9946-y.

McLaren, J., Miller, J., O'Shaughnessy, E., Wood, E., & Shapiro, E. (2016). Emissions associated with electric vehicle charging: Impact of electricity generation mix, charging infrastructure availability and vehicle type. *(No. NREL/TP-6A20-64852)* (p. 28) Golden, CO: National Renewable Energy Laboratory. Retrieved from http://www.nrel.gov/docs/fy16osti/64852.pdf.

Mizobuchi, K., & Takeuchi, K. (2013). The influences of financial and non-financial factors on energy-saving behaviour: A field experiment in Japan. *Energy Policy*, *63*, 775−787. Available from https://doi.org/10.1016/j.enpol.2013.08.064.

Müller, S., & Rode, J. (2013). The adoption of photovoltaic systems in Wiesbaden, Germany. *Economics of Innovation and New Technology*, *22*(5), 519−535. Available from https://doi.org/10.1080/10438599.2013.804333.

Nayum, A., & Klöckner, C. A. (2014). A comprehensive socio-psychological approach to car type choice. *Journal of Environmental Psychology*, *40*, 401−411. Available from https://doi.org/10.1016/j.jenvp.2014.10.001.

Nayum, A., Klöckner, C. A., & Mehmetoglu, M. (2016). Comparison of socio-psychological characteristics of conventional and battery electric car buyers. *Travel Behaviour and Society*, *3*, 8−20. Available from https://doi.org/10.1016/j.tbs.2015.03.005.

Neoh, J. G., Chipulu, M., & Marshall, A. (2017). What encourages people to carpool? An evaluation of factors with meta-analysis. *Transportation*, *44*(2), 423−447. Available from https://doi.org/10.1007/s11116-015-9661-7.

Nevius, M.J., & Pigg, S. (2000). Programmable thermostats that go berserk? Taking a social perspective on space heating in Wisconsin. *Proceedings of the 2000 ACEEE summer study on energy efficiency in buildings* (pp. 8.233−244). Retrieved from https://www. researchgate.net/publication/266495558_Programmable_Thermostats_ that_Go_Berserk_Taking_a_Social_Perspective_on_Space_Heating_in_Wisconsin.

Newell, R. G., & Siikamäki, J. (2014). Nudging energy efficiency behavior: The role of information labels. *Journal of the Association of Environmental and Resource Economists, 1*(4), 555−598. Available from https://doi.org/10.1086/679281.

Newsham, G. R., & Bowker, B. G. (2010). The effect of utility time-varying pricing and load control strategies on residential summer peak electricity use: A review. *Energy Policy, 38*(7), 3289−3296. Available from https://doi.org/10.1016/j.enpol.2010.01.027.

Nguyen, T. N., Lobo, A., & Greenland, S. (2016). Pro-environmental purchase behaviour: The role of consumers' biospheric values. *Journal of Retailing and Consumer Services, 33*, 98−108. Available from https://doi.org/10.1016/j.jretconser.2016.08.010.

Noll, D., Dawes, C., & Rai, V. (2014). Solar Community Organizations and active peer effects in the adoption of residential PV. *Energy Policy, 67*, 330−343. Available from https://doi.org/10.1016/j.enpol.2013.12.050.

Noonan, D. S., Hsieh, L.-H. C., & Matisoff, D. (2015). Economic, sociological, and neighbor dimensions of energy efficiency adoption behaviors: Evidence from the U.S residential heating and air conditioning market. *Energy Research & Social Science, 10*, 102−113. Available from https://doi.org/10.1016/j.erss.2015.07.009.

Noppers, E. H., Keizer, K., Bolderdijk, J. W., & Steg, L. (2014). The adoption of sustainable innovations: Driven by symbolic and environmental motives. *Global Environmental Change, 25*, 52−62. Available from https://doi.org/10.1016/j.gloenvcha.2014.01.012.

Nordlund, A. M., & Garvill, J. (2003). Effects of values, problem awareness, and personal norm on willingness to reduce personal car use. *Journal of Environmental Psychology, 23*(4), 339−347. Available from https://doi.org/10.1016/S0272-4944(03)00037-9.

Palm, A. (2016). Local factors driving the diffusion of solar photovoltaics in Sweden: A case study of five municipalities in an early market. *Energy Research & Social Science, 14*, 1−12. Available from https://doi.org/10.1016/j.erss.2015.12.027.

Palm, A. (2017). Peer effects in residential solar photovoltaics adoption—A mixed methods study of Swedish users. *Energy Research & Social Science, 26*, 1−10. Available from https://doi.org/10.1016/j.erss.2017.01.008.

Pedersen, M. (2008). Segmenting residential customers: Energy and conservation behaviors. *Proceedings of the 2008 ACEEE summer study on energy efficiency in buildings* (pp. 7-229−241). Retrieved from http://aceee.org/files/proceedings/2008/data/papers/7_671.pdf.

Peffer, T., Perry, D., Pritoni, M., Aragon, C., & Meier, A. (2013). Facilitating energy savings with programmable thermostats: Evaluation and guidelines for the thermostat user inter-face. *Ergonomics, 56*(3), 463−479. Available from https://doi.org/10.1080/00140139.2012.718370.

Peffer, T., Pritoni, M., Meier, A., Aragon, C., & Perry, D. (2011). How people use thermo-stats in homes: A review. *Building and Environment, 46*(12), 2529−2541. Available from https://doi.org/10.1016/j.buildenv.2011.06.002.

Pidgeon, N. F., Lorenzoni, I., & Poortinga, W. (2008). Climate change or nuclear power— No thanks! A quantitative study of public perceptions and risk framing in Britain. *Global Environmental Change, 18*(1), 69−85. Available from https://doi.org/10.1016/j.gloenvcha.2007.09.005.

Pritoni, M., Meier, A. K., Aragon, C., Perry, D., & Peffer, T. (2015). Energy efficiency and the misuse of programmable thermostats: The effectiveness of crowdsourcing for under-standing household behavior. *Energy Research & Social Science, 8*, 190−197. Available from https://doi.org/10.1016/j.erss.2015.06.002.

Rai, V., Reeves, D. C., & Margolis, R. (2016). Overcoming barriers and uncertainties in the adoption of residential solar PV. *Renewable Energy, 89,* 498–505. Available from https://doi.org/10.1016/j.renene.2015.11.080.

Rai, V., & Robinson, S. A. (2013). Effective information channels for reducing costs of environmentally-friendly technologies: Evidence from residential PV markets. *Environmental Research Letters, 8*(1), 014044. Available from https://doi.org/10.1088/1748-9326/8/1/014044.

Rezvani, Z., Jansson, J., & Bodin, J. (2015). Advances in consumer electric vehicle adoption research: A review and research agenda. *Transportation Research Part D: Transport and Environment, 34,* 122–136. Available from https://doi.org/10.1016/j.trd.2014.10.010.

Rogers, E. M. (2003). *Diffusion of Innovations (5th Edition).* New York: Simon and Schuster.

Rosa, E. A., & Dunlap, R. E. (1994). Poll trends: Nuclear power: Three decades of public opinion. *The Public Opinion Quarterly, 58*(2), 295–324.

Sachs, O., Tiefenbeck, V., Duvier, C., Qin, A., Cheney, K., Akers, C., & Roth, K. (2012). *Field evaluation of programmable thermostats (No. DOE/GO-102012-3804).* United States: U.S. Department of Energy, Energy Efficiency & Renewable Energy Retrieved from . Available from http://www.cse.fraunhofer.org/hs-fs/hub/55819/file-12977701-pdf/docs/ba_field_eval_thermostats.pdf.

Sallee, J. M. (2011). The surprising incidence of tax credits for the Toyota Prius. *American Economic Journal: Economic Policy, 3*(2), 189–219.

Schelly, C. (2014a). Implementing renewable energy portfolio standards: The good, the bad, and the ugly in a two state comparison. *Energy Policy, 67,* 543–551. Available from https://doi.org/10.1016/j.enpol.2013.11.075.

Schelly, C. (2014b). *Residential sol*ar electricity adoption: What motivates, and what matters? A case study of early adopters. *Energy Research & Social Science, 2,* 183–191. Available from https://doi.org/10.1016/j.erss.2014.01.001.

Schuitema, G., Anable, J., Skippon, S., & Kinnear, N. (2013). The role of instrumental, hedonic and symbolic attributes in the intention to adopt electric vehicles. *Transportation Research Part A: Policy and Practice, 48,* 39–49. Available from https://doi.org/10.1016/j.tra.2012.10.004.

Schwartz, S. H. (1977). Normative influences on altruism. In: L. Berkowitz (Ed.), *Advances in experimental social psychology* (Vol. 10, pp. 221–279). New York: Academic Press.

Semenza, J. C., Hall, D. E., Wilson, D. J., Bontempo, B. D., Sailor, D. J., & George, L. A. (2008). Public perception of climate change: Voluntary mitigation and barriers to behavior change. *American Journal of Preventive Medicine, 35*(5), 479–487. Available from https://doi.org/10.1016/j.amepre.2008.08.020.

Shewmake, S., Cohen, M. A., Stern, P. C., & Vandenbergh, M. P. (2015). Carbon triage: A strategy for developing a viable carbon labelling system. In: L. A. Reisch, & J. Thøgersen (Eds.), *Handbook of Research on Sustainable Consumption* (pp. 285–299). Northampton, MA: Edward Elgar Publishing, Inc. Retrieved from https://www.elgaronline.com/view/9781783471263.00030.xml.

Sidortsov, R. (2014). *Reinventing ru*les for environmental risk governance in the energy sector. *Energy Research & Social Science, 1,* 171–182. Available from https://doi.org/10.1016/j.erss.2014.03.013.

Sierzchula, W., Bakker, S., Maat, K., & van Wee, B. (2014). The influence of financial incentives and other socio-economic factors on electric vehicle adoption. *Energy Policy, 68,* 183–194. Available from https://doi.org/10.1016/j.enpol.2014.01.043.

Small, M. J., Stern, P. C., Bomberg, E., Christopherson, S. M., Goldstein, B. D., Israel, A. L., & Zielinska, B. (2014). Risks and risk governance in unconventional shale gas development. *Environmental Science & Technology*, *48*(15), 8289–8297. Available from https://doi.org/10.1021/es502111u.

Sovacool, B. K., & Hirsh, R. F. (2009). Beyond batteries: An examination of the benefits and barriers to plug-in hybrid electric vehicles (PHEVs) and a vehicle-to-grid (V2G) transition. *Energy Policy*, *37*(3), 1095–1103. Available from https://doi.org/10.1016/j.enpol.2008.10.005.

Steg, L. (2008). Promoting household energy conservation. *Energy Policy*, *36*(12), 4449–4453. Available from https://doi.org/10.1016/j.enpol.2008.09.027.

Steg, L., Dreijerink, L., & Abrahamse, W. (2005). Factors influencing the acceptability of energy policies: A test of VBN theory. *Journal of Environmental Psychology*, *25*(4), 415–425. Available from https://doi.org/10.1016/j.jenvp.2005.08.003.

Steg, L., Perlaviciute, G., & van der Werff, E. (2015). Understanding the human dimensions of a sustainable energy transition. *Frontiers in Psychology*, *6*, 1–17. Available from https://doi.org/10.3389/fpsyg.2015.00805.

Stern, P. C. (1992). What psychology knows about energy conservation. *American Psychologist*, *47*(10), 1224–1232.

Stern, P. C. (2000). Toward a coherent theory of environmentally significant behavior. *Journal of Social Issues*, *56*(3), 407–424.

Stern, P. C. (2008). Environmentally significant behavior in the home. In: A. Lewis (Ed.), *The Cambridge handbook of psychology and economic behaviour* (1st ed., pp. 363–382). New York: Cambridge University Press.

Stern, P. C. (2013). Design principles for governing risks from emerging technologies. In: T. Dietz, & A. K. Jorgenson (Eds.), *Structural human ecology: Risk, energy and sustainability* (pp. 91–118). Pullman, WA: Washington State University Press.

Stern, P. C. (2014). *Individual and* household interactions with energy systems: Toward integrated understanding. *Energy Research & Social Science*, *1*, 41–48. Available from https://doi.org/10.1016/j.erss.2014.03.003.

Stern, P. C. (2017). How can social science research become more influential in energy transitions? *Energy Research & Social Science*. Available from https://doi.org/10.1016/j.erss.2017.01.010.

Stern, P. C., Aronson, E., Darley, J. M., Hill, D. H., Hirst, E., Kempton, W., & Wilbanks, T. J. (1986). The effectiveness of incentives for residential energy conservation. *Evaluation Review*, *10*(2), 147–176. Available from https://doi.org/10.1177/0193841X8601000201.

Stern, P. C., Dietz, T., Abel, T., Guagnano, G. A., & Kalof, L. (1999). A value-belief-norm theory of support for social movements: The case of environmentalism. *Human Ecology Review*, *6*(2), 81–97.

Stern, P. C., Gardner, G. T., Vandenbergh, M. P., Dietz, T., & Gilligan, J. (2010). Design principles for carbon emissions reduction programs. *Environmental Science and Technology*, *44*(13), 4847–4848.

Stern, P. C., Janda, K. B., Brown, M. A., Steg, L., Vine, E. L., & Lutzenhiser, L. (2016). Opportunities and insights for reducing fossil fuel consumption by households and organizations. *Nature Energy*, *1*, 16043. Available from https://doi.org/10.1038/nenergy.2016.43.

Stern, P. C., Wittenberg, I., Wolske, K. S., & Kastner, I. (2018). Household production of photovoltaic energy: Issues in economic behavior. In: A. Lewis (Ed.), *Cambridge handbook of psychology and economic behavior* (2nd ed., pp. 541–566). New York, NY: Cambridge University Press.

Sütterlin, B., Brunner, T. A., & Siegrist, M. (2011). Who puts the most energy into energy conservation? A segmentation of energy consumers based on energy-related behavioral characteristics. *Energy Policy*, *39*(12), 8137−8152. Available from https://doi.org/10.1016/j.enpol.2011.10.008.

Tabuchi, H. (2017). Behind the quiet state-by-state fight over electric vehicles. *The New York Times*. Retrieved from https://www.nytimes.com/2017/03/11/business/energy-environment/electric-cars-hybrid-tax-credits.html.

Thøgersen, J. (2006). Understanding repetitive travel mode choices in a stable context: A panel study approach. *Transportation Research Part A: Policy and Practice*, *40*(8), 621−638. Available from https://doi.org/10.1016/j.tra.2005.11.004.

Tiefenbeck, V., Goette, L., Degen, K., Tasic, V., Fleisch, E., Lalive, R., & Staake, T. (2016). Overcoming salience bias: How real-time feedback fosters resource conservation. *Management Science*. Available from https://doi.org/10.1287/mnsc.2016.2646.

US EIA. (2013a, May 6). Residential energy consumption survey, housing characteristics tables, table HC6.1 space heating usage by type of housing unit. Retrieved from http://www.eia.gov/consumption/residential/data/2009/hc/hc6.1.xls.

US EIA. (2013b). *International energy outlook*. Retrieved from https://www.eia.gov/outlooks/ieo/pdf/0484(2013).pdf

US EIA. (2017, February 28). How is electricity used in U.S. homes? Retrieved from https://www.eia.gov/tools/faqs/faq.php?id = 96&t = 3.

US EPA. (2016). *Inventory of U.S. greenhouse gas emissions and sinks: 1990−2014*. Retrieved from https://www.epa.gov/sites/production/files/2016-04/documents/us-ghg-inventory-2016-main-text.pdf.

van der Werff, E., & Steg, L. (2015). One model to predict them all: Predicting energy behaviours with the norm activation model. *Energy Research & Social Science*, *6*, 8−14. Available from https://doi.org/10.1016/j.erss.2014.11.002.

Vandenbergh, M. P., & Gilligan, J. A. (2015). Beyond gridlock. *Columbia Journal of Environmental Law*, *40*(2), 217−303.

Vandenbergh, M.P., Stern, P.C., Gardner, G.T., Dietz, T., & Gilligan, J.M. (2010). *Implementing the behavioral wedge: Designing and adopting effective carbon emissions reduction programs* (SSRN Scholarly Paper No. ID 1617426). Rochester, NY: Social Science Research Network. Retrieved from http://papers.ssrn.com/abstract = 1617426.

Verplanken, B., Walker, I., Davis, A., & Jurasek, M. (2008). Context change and travel mode choice: Combining the habit discontinuity and self-activation hypotheses. *Journal of Environmental Psychology*, *28*(2), 121−127. Available from https://doi.org/10.1016/j.jenvp.2007.10.005.

Whitmarsh, L. (2009). Behavioural responses to climate change: Asymmetry of intentions and impacts. *Journal of Environmental Psychology*, *29*(1), 13−23.

Winett, R. A., Neale, M. S., & Grier, H. C. (1979). Effects of self-monitoring and feedback on residential electricity consumption. *Journal of Applied Behavior Analysis*, *12*(2), 173−184.

Wolske, K. S. (2011). Encouraging climate-friendly behaviors through a community energy challenge: The effects of information, feedback, and shared stories *(Unpublished doctoral dissertation)*. Ann Arbor, MI: University of Michigan.

Wolske, K. S., Stern, P. C., & Dietz, T. (2017). Explaining interest in adopting residential solar photovoltaic systems in the United States: Toward an integration of behavioral theories. *Energy Research & Social Science*, *25*, 134−151.

Yohanis, Y. G. (2012). Domestic energy use and householders' energy behaviour. *Energy Policy*, *41*, 654−665. Available from https://doi.org/10.1016/j.enpol.2011.11.028.

Young, W., Hwang, K., McDonald, S., & Oates, C. J. (2010). Sustainable consumption: Green consumer behaviour when purchasing products. *Sustainable Development*, *18*(1), 20–31. Available from https://doi.org/10.1002/sd.394.

Zhao, T., Bell, L., Horner, M. W., Sulik, J., & Zhang, J. (2012). Consumer responses towards home energy financial incentives: A survey-based study. *Energy Policy*, *47*, 291–297. Available from https://doi.org/10.1016/j.enpol.2012.04.070.

Understanding responses to climate change: Psychological barriers to mitigation and a new theory of behavioral choice

7

Robert Gifford, Karine Lacroix and Angel Chen
University of Victoria, Victoria, BC, Canada

The dimensions and impacts of climate change are massive; the importance of this topic is widely recognized, from the Nobel Prize given to the Intergovernmental Panel on Climate Change, to the 2015 global summit in Paris that led to an agreement by all the important countries of the world (except one), to the high-level national and international debates about possible solutions, to the formation of hundreds of local, municipal, and regional grass roots groups devoted to finding solutions.

Human health is already affected through the increased range of tropical disease vectors, and the very landscape is changing through the increase in the frequency of extreme events, such as the burning in 2009 of about 450,000 ha (1100,000 A) on Australia's Black Saturday (Wikipedia, n.d.), a 2011 Texas wildfire that scorched an area the size of Connecticut (CNN Wire Staff, 2011). As this is written, 36,000 residents of British Columbia have been evacuated in the face of about 220 active wildfires (http://www.cbc.ca/news/canada/british-columbia/b-c-wildfires-evacuations-relief-1.4197826). Climate change will affect almost every person and animal on the planet in one way or another. Perhaps no other problem today is more important for so many people and other living beings.

Some individuals in every society are changing their behavior and that of others in response to climate change, but humans in the aggregate continue to produce greenhouse gases in *increasing* quantities (Intergovernmental Panel on Climate Change, 2014). Most experts conclude that although some changes cannot be avoided, given the amount of greenhouse gases already in the atmosphere, over the next several decades humans collectively can either decelerate the rate of change or increase the temperature even more than has already occurred. Mitigation is the enormous challenge.

Fortunately, environmental psychologists and allied researchers have developed considerable knowledge about what it takes to change behavior (e.g., Sussman, Gifford, & Abrahamse, 2016). Understanding the drivers of sustainable (and unsustainable) behavior is increasingly important for the future of humans and many other species (Kahle & Gurel-Atay, 2014). As the APA Task Force on Climate Change (Swim et al., 2011) pointed out, psychologists and allied social scientists

Psychology and Climate Change. DOI: https://doi.org/10.1016/B978-0-12-813130-5.00006-0

are (or should be, as behavior experts) at the forefront of climate change, as those best qualified to understand the choices and behavioral tendencies of the now-7.3 billion actors whose everyday choices either ameliorate or worsen the damage already done. Former U.S. President Obama sought help for climate change in the form of a social and behavioral science research unit.

7.1   Why aren't we taking (more) action?

Many people are concerned about climate change, but they often engage in behavior that is detrimental to the environment or fail to engage in behavior necessary to ameliorate or prevent these problems. Much of the work in environmental psychology has focused on individuals' environmental knowledge, concern, and values, which are notoriously inconsistent, and usually weak correlates with proenvironmental behavior (e.g., Chaiken & Stangor, 1987; Finger, 1994; Vining & Ebreo, 2002). In a classic metaanalysis of 128 studies, the relations between knowledge and attitudes, attitudes and intentions, and intentions and environmentally responsible behavior were weak at the best (Hines, Hungerford, & Tomera, 1987). A more recent metaanalysis found that the overlap between reported and actual behavior is merely 21% (Kormos & Gifford, 2014). Self-reports of behavior are notably inaccurate, but this accounts for only part of the attitude-behavior gap. Several methodological and theoretical explanations for the "attitude-behavior gap" have been offered, including levels of specificity for attitude-behavioral measurement, direct vs vicarious experience with attitude objects (Newhouse, 1990), conflicts among motives (Kollmuss & Agyeman, 2002), and the low-cost/high-cost model (Diekmann & Preisendöerfer, 1992), which propose that even when people care about the environment, they may choose to engage in less effortful behavior, such as recycling, but continue to engage in high-cost behaviors such as driving, whose contributions to climate change outweigh the beneficial impact of recycling.

When obstacles for environmental behavior are considered and statistically controlled, the correlation between attitude and behavior strengthens (e.g., Corraliza & Berenguer, 2000; Kaiser & Gutscher, 2003). Several scholars have investigated perceived barriers to environmental behavioral change. For example, Blake (1999) identified three major barriers: intrapersonal (e.g., attitude and temperament), lack of felt responsibility, and lack of practicability (e.g., perceived shortages of time, money, or information).

In some cases, the bases for inaction are structural, that is, beyond an individual's reasonable control. For example, having a low income limits one's ability to purchase solar panels, living in a rural area usually means that public transport does not exist as an option to driving, and living in a region with very cold winters greatly restricts one's ability to reduce home heating-based energy use. Of course, if local or national governments do not support these structural improvements, they are part of the problem. However, many individuals do have the financial and structural capacity to act, but do not, or do much less than they could. Thus, the question remains: What limits more widespread proenvironmental behavior on the part of individuals, whether those are everyday citizens, Chief executive officer (CEOs), senior government officials, or other important carbon players, for whom such actions *are* feasible? Fully understanding the perceived, or psychological, barriers requires a more comprehensive perspective—one that recognizes the wide variety of potential constraints that may render proenvironmental values, attitudes, and intentions inert.

Recently, Gifford (2011) introduced a comprehensive list of 30 psychological barriers, called the dragons of inaction, grouped into 7 categories. This chapter describes updated work with the dragons of inaction and is organized as follows: First, it reviews these seven categories of psychological barriers to climate change mitigation and adaptation (limited cognition, ideologies, significant others, sunk costs, discredence, perceived risk, and limited behavior).

Second, it reviews studies that focus on measuring the dragons of inaction, particularly in the context of the main greenhouse gas-heavy behavioral domains, such as household energy use and mitigative food choices.

Third, based on that work, we introduce the Dragons of Inaction Psychological Barriers (DIPBs) instrument, designed for investigating the climate change and sustainable behavior domains.

Finally, we discuss how the barriers can be practically applied to designs of behavior change interventions, provide insights to future research directions, and form a key part of a new theoretical framework called the theory of behavioral choice (TBC).

7.2 Psychological barriers: The dragons of inaction

If so many are concerned about the environment and climate change, why aren't more citizens more engaged in actions that would help to ameliorate the problems? Of course, many citizens have taken some steps in this direction, and some have taken many steps. Nevertheless, as a whole, humans continue to degrade the environment and produce massive quantities of greenhouse gases. The current levels of atmospheric CO_2 are at a historic high.

In order to begin the process of discovering all of the important psychological barriers, Gifford (2011) assembled a compendium of 30 factors that may serve as obstacles to behavior change for climate change and sustainability. That "intuitive" list stemmed from having to respond to journalists' reasonable question: "If so many people are in favor of the environment, why is so little being done?" Dragons were dredged from the literature and slowly grew in number from 7 to 10 and more over several years of giving presentations and hearing of valuable new suggestions from audience members. As of the publication of the 2011 paper, they are as follows, as shown in Table 7.1. Several new dragons have been discovered since that

Table 7.1 The dragons of inaction as of 2011

Limited cognition	Ideologies	Comparisons with others	Sunk costs	Discredence	Perceived risks	Limited behavior
Ancient brain	Worldviews	Social comparison	Financial investments	Mistrust	Functional	Tokenism
Ignorance	Suprahuman powers	Social norms and networks	Behavioral momentum	Perceived program inadequacy	Physical	Rebound effect
Environmental numbness	Technosalvation	Perceived inequity	Conflicting values, goals, and aspirations	Denial	Financial	
Uncertainty	System justification		Place attachment[a]	Reactance	Social	
Judgmental discounting					Psychological	
Optimism bias					Temporal	
Perceived behavioral control/self-efficacy						

[a]Lack of place attachment was discussed in Gifford (2011), but accidentally omitted from this table.

could not be included in the present investigations[1], and more may be discovered in the future.

7.2.1 *Limited cognition*

Humans are less rational than once believed, before cognitive dissonance was introduced to psychology (Festinger, 1957), or Tversky and Kahneman (1974) demonstrated to economists that the "rational man" model was inaccurate. The science fiction writer Robert Heinlein wrote—using the gender language of the time—that "Man is not a rational animal, he is a rationalizing animal" (Heinlein, 1949, p. 59). This is as true for thinking about climate change and environmental issues as it is in other behavior domains. Seven "genera" of the "dragons of inaction" (psychological barriers) represent the territory of limited human rationality about behavior change related to sustainability and climate change.

Ancient brain. The human brain has not evolved much in thousands of years. At the time it reached its current physical development, our ancestors were mainly concerned with their immediate tribe, immediate risks, proximate exploitable resources, and the present. These here-and-now concerns are incompatible with solving climate and environmental problems, which often involve distant risks and delayed impacts. Our ancient brain obviously is *capable* of dealing with the slow impact of global climate change, but it is not top-of-mind.

Ignorance. By now almost no one is unaware of the many disturbing environmental realities. However, many individuals are paralyzed by their lack of knowledge about (1) *which* actions to take, (2) *how* to undertake actions that they know about, and (3) the *relative benefits* of different actions.

Environmental numbness. Our life spaces (Lewin, 1935) include far more sensory cues than we can successfully monitor, so we attend to a few selected cues that seem important. Thus, people are often unaware of problematic environmental changes, such as those in the climate or the environment. Another kind of environmental numbness occurs when environmental danger messages from the media, the government, or scientists are too similar or too frequent: They are no longer seen as news and are ignored, and, as a consequence, the underlying behavior does not change.

Uncertainty. Perceived or real environmental uncertainty, such as when climate scientists present a range of future temperature increases, or fisheries officials proclaim a range of probable sizes of an ocean fish stock, reduces the frequency of proenvironmental or sustainable behavior. This was demonstrated in a fishing microworld experiment: As uncertainty about the number of fish available for catching rose, the degree of overharvesting increased (Hine & Gifford, 1997). That

---

[1] The 30 dragons have increased to 36, and the newer ones have not yet been integrated into the current studies. These are: Authority Rules (forced to burn carbon by a superior), Confirmation Bias (choosing to attend to media that support one's antienvironmental views), Contrarian Personality (a person is against "whatever you got"), Time is Money (when individuals think of their time in terms of earnings, they tend to burn carbon), splitting Judgmental Discounting into Spatial and Temporal Discounting, and splitting Lack of Perceived Control/Self-Efficacy into separate dragons.

is, many individuals interpret uncertainty in ways that will serve their self-interest. For example, those who still believe that global warming may not be occurring, and desire a fuel-inefficient vehicle for other reasons, may well purchase one, justifying their behavior by citing the "possibility" that climate change "may not" be real.

Judgmental discounting. People tend to undervalue geographically and temporally distant risks. In an 18-nation study (Gifford et al., 2009), respondents tended to believe that environmental conditions were worse in countries other than their own—and, of course, people in those *other* countries believed the same thing about countries distant from *their* own. If a problem is presumed to be worse elsewhere, people are less motivated to improve their own environment. If it is said to have an impact in the future, motivation to act now is less.

Optimism bias. Optimism generally is healthy; personal and societal progress largely depends on it, but optimism can be overdone. For example, many falsely believe that they have a lower risk of cardiovascular disease than their peers, which of course will tend to hinder their health-promoting actions. Relevant to the present topic, individuals tend to underestimate their own objective risk from 22 environmental hazards (Schmidt & Gifford, 1989), which presumably dampens their motivation to engage in actions to mitigate those hazards.

Lack of perceived behavioral control. Climate change is a global problem, so many believe that, as individuals, they can do nothing about it, which of course blunts their motivation to act. Without a sense of self-efficacy (e.g., Bandura, 1977), an important motivation for action is missing.

7.2.2 Ideologies

Some broad belief systems (political, religious, and others) influence many aspects of a person's life in ways that can act as strong barriers to environmental behavior change.

Political worldviews. One source of inaction on global warming is unfettered belief in free-enterprise capitalism, proponents of which tend to exploit natural resources as quickly and fully as technology and available capital permit. This economic approach leads to greater greenhouse gas emissions than would a more sustainable approach to development (e.g., Heath & Gifford, 2006).

System justification. This is the tendency to defend the societal status quo. Climate action in the form of regulatory changes might influence the economic context, which some fear will threaten their comfortable lifestyle. This results in opposition to regulatory change and less personal proenvironmental action.

Suprahuman powers. Some individuals engage in little or no climate-positive action because they believe that a religious deity or Mother Nature (as a secular deity) is in complete control. Inaction is the result.

Technosalvation. Technological innovation clearly has improved the standard of living of many people. It obviously also can help with environmental problems. However, if individuals believe that engineers alone can and will solve all climate and sustainability problems, this absolves them from taking action.

7.2.3 Significant others

Humans are social animals; we often compare our situation to that of others and act accordingly. These comparisons can affect whether people act on climate, or not.

Social norms. People look to others to derive their norms about what is the "proper" course of action. Descriptive norms are what individuals believe, from scanning their environments, to be typical behavior; prescriptive norms are what individuals are told represent proper behaviors. Norms can be a force for progress in environmental issues, but they can also be forces for regress or inaction. If significant others, family, friends, or other nations are not doing their part (or *believed* to not be doing their part), individuals are likely to decide that they should not exert environmental efforts either.

Social comparison. Explicit comparisons made with another person or entity form a slightly different dragon of inaction. "If X is doing it (or *not* doing it), then maybe I should do it, too (or not, as the case may be)?"

Perceived inequity. Perceived inequity takes social comparison a step further. Individuals not only notice a difference between their choices and those of others, they assess the difference as being unfair. "Why should I change if *they* won't change?" Well-known persons, organizations, or other nations are cited as environmental foot-draggers, and these are used to justify one's own nonaction on perceived fairness grounds.

7.2.4 Sunk costs

Investments of money, time, and in behavior patterns can be valuable—unless they are harmful to the environment.

Financial investments. Once invested in something, dispensing with it can be difficult. If one has purchased a car and is now paying for its insurance and other costs, why should this cozy portable "living room" be left at home? Owning shares in an oil company will create cognitive dissonance about environmental actions; it can be easier to change one's mind about climate change than to divest oneself of oil stocks.

Behavioral momentum. Many habits are extremely resistant to change. Some that contribute to most environmental degradation (e.g., driving, diet, residential energy use, and flying) have a great deal of behavioral momentum.

Conflicting goals and aspirations. Everyone has multiple goals, many of which clash with the goal to improve one's environmental choices. Being willing to combat climate change, for example, is not compatible with aspirations such as buying a larger house or the latest electronic gadget. The larger house is a sunk cost in the sense that it normally means a continuing fixed increase in one's household energy costs.

Place attachment. Individuals may be more likely to care for a place to which they feel attachment than for one they do not. Place attachment is complex (Scannell & Gifford, 2010a), but can act as an impediment to action, in some contexts more than others. For example, being emotionally attached to a place might lead to opposition to green energy in the form of proposed new wind turbines in one's vicinity (more than another resident whose attachment to the same place is weaker). In this sense, one's attachment to a place is a commitment that forms a sunk cost. However, for the rootless or restless person who has little or no tendency to form place attachments, always being on the move is a kind of sunk cost in terms of the resulting commitment to use transportation energy.

7.2.5   Discredence

When individuals have a preexisting disbelief in experts or authorities, they are unlikely to take direction from them. For example, if scientists and politicians are disbelieved about the environment as a matter of course, suggestions from them to be more environmentally sustainable are likely to be ignored.

Mistrust. Trust is essential for healthy relationships. When it is absent, as it is between some citizens and scientists or government officials, resistance to their behavior-change suggestions will follow.

Perceived program inadequacy. Policymakers have implemented many programs designed to encourage climate-friendly behavior. However, citizens choose whether to accept these offers, and some will decide that the program is "not good enough" for their participation.

Reactance. Some people strongly react against policy that seems to threaten their freedom. This can go beyond mere inaction into actively choosing climate-harmful actions of products to spite policymakers.

Denial. Mistrust and reactance easily slide into denial. This may include denial that climate change is occurring, or that it has any anthropogenic cause, or that one's own actions are exacerbating climate change. Mitigative actions are unlikely to follow.

7.2.6   Perceived risk

Changing any important behavior holds at least six kinds of potential risk. Broadly speaking, people are risk-averse, so each of the six risk species below can act as a "drag on"[2] climate action.

Functional risk. Will it work? If one purchases, for example, an electric vehicle, it might, as a relatively new technology, have battery or range problems. Similar rationalizations can be offered about many new green technologies.

Physical risk. Some adaptations may have, or be perceived as having, danger to self or family. Is this electric car as crash-safe as the SUV that I sold to buy it? Cycling is great for climate change, but it may result in a visit to an emergency room.

Financial risk. Green solutions require capital outlays. How long is the payback? If the product becomes a fixed part of a residence (e.g., solar panels), will I recoup the installation costs or accrue enough energy savings before moving?

[2] One of the reasons for the choice of beings to use as a metaphor for justifying inaction.

Social risk. Others notice our choices. This leaves us open to judgment by our friends and colleagues, which could lead to damage to one's reputation. If I become a vegetarian, will my significant others push back, or my acquaintances deride me behind my back? If I don't fly home, will my family think that I no longer love them?

Psychological risk. Those who are teased, criticized, rebuked, or even bullied by their significant others, colleagues, or schoolmates for making some green choices, risk damage to their self-esteem in addition to the social loss. It's easier to ease off on that green behavior.

Temporal risk. The time spent planning a green course of action might fail to produce the desired results. Most people spend considerable time deciding whether to buy an electric vehicle, become a vegetarian, or plan how to cycle to work or school. What if it doesn't work out? The time was wasted, and time is valuable, and so some will not take this "risk."

7.2.7 Limited Behavior

Many people are engaged in at least minimal proenvironmental action. However, most people could do more. How do we justify doing less than we should?

Tokenism. Some proenvironmental behaviors are easy to adopt but have little impact on the big problems. "I recycle, so I've done my part." The ease of adopting some green behaviors means that these actions tend to be chosen over actions with higher effort costs but are more mitigative.

The rebound effect. After some mitigating effort has been made, the gain sometimes is diminished or erased by subsequent actions. For example, after acquiring a more fuel-efficient vehicle, owners tend to drive them farther (e.g., Linn, 2016). The net climate effect is negative. These 30 species of dragons include many, if not most, of the psychological barriers, or rationalizations or justifications, for not engaging in (more) proenvironmental behavior. Collectively, these dragons are a powerful group that presumably help to explain why most people agree that "there's a problem but" ... and that is the operative word that prevents concern from leading to action: *but*.

A reasonable question is whether these seven genera, which were proposed on an intuitive basis, are valid in an empirical sense. This is the question we raise in the next section.

7.3 Developing an instrument for measuring psychological barriers

Psychological barriers might help enhance existing theories of proenvironmental behavior by providing an explanation for the value-action gap or the intention-behavior gap (e.g., TBC discussed further in this chapter). The three studies described in this section are part of a continuous effort to improve understanding of (perceived) barriers and develop a useful structure and psychometrically sound measurement model. These studies have focused on barriers in the major climate-relevant behavior domains, in both student and community populations (e.g., Chen & Gifford, 2015; Gifford & Chen, 2017; Lacroix & Gifford, online). Constructing and validating sound psychological barrier scales also has practical value for designing policy and programs.

Gifford (2011) theorized psychological barriers were measured in approximately the same way in each study. Participants were first presented with a list of proenvironmental behaviors and asked to "pick a behavior that you or others believe should be done to help the environment, but which you are not doing right now, or are not doing enough." They were then presented with a series of barrier items and asked how much each was true for them on 7-point Likert scales, from "strongly disagree" to "strongly agree."

Barrier scales and items were analyzed after each study [e.g., interitem correlations, reliability indices, principal-component analyses (PCAs)]. Each new study allowed the authors to improve on the barrier measurements, remove less-useful items, and clarify items as needed. Two of these studies are described here, followed by a third that presents a revised barrier measurement model (i.e., the DIPBs instrument; Lacroix, Gifford, & Chen, Submitted).

An example from the food domain. In the first study, 251 Canadians were asked about the psychological barriers they face when making climate-positive food choices (Gifford & Chen, 2017). Climate-positive food-choice intentions were measured using six items (e.g., eat less meat, purchase organic food). Thirty-six barrier items were used to measure the psychological barriers, created to represent Gifford's (2011) list of dragon species and additional food specific barrier items.

Barrier components were extracted using PCA. Four were retained: Denial, Conflicting Goals and Aspirations, Interpersonal Influences, and Tokenism, which suggests that a four-factor structure is appropriate for the food domain. Of the four, Interpersonal Influences was the only one that was not significantly related to reported food choices. This may have been caused by the relatively weak reliability of the Interpersonal Influences component ($\alpha = .66$) or perhaps because, although eating is inevitably a social practice, the impact of social influences on food choices is less-often noticed.

Using confirmatory factory analyses, the fit of the four-factor model was compared with that of a seven-factor model, based on the original seven categories described in Gifford (2011), and with a unidimensional model. Both the four-factor and the seven-factor models demonstrated good model fit, although the seven-factor model was slightly better. The authors conclude that both models are equally valuable. The seven-factor model is more comprehensive, but some of its scales had low reliability. The four-factor model was more parsimonious and the scales more reliable.

An example from the energy domain. In a second study, 151 residents of British Columbia were asked about the psychological barriers they face when attempting to adopt household energy-saving behavior (Lacroix & Gifford, online). These behaviors were measured using 11 items (e.g., "I switch off the television and computer when not in use"). Five (i.e., Limited Cognition, Ideologies, Comparisons with Others, Sunk Costs, and Discredence) of the seven theorized (Gifford, 2011) barrier categories were included in this study based on their presumed suitability to the study's energy objectives. These were measured using multiple items per barrier.

Barrier components were extracted using PCA. Six components were retained: Denial, Conflicting Goals and Aspirations, Interpersonal Influences, Mission Impossible, Technosalvation, and Ignorance (i.e., not knowing how to change). The latter was the only component not significantly correlated with the energy conservation behaviors measured in the study. The energy conservation behaviors included in the study were low-cost ones; perhaps participants knew how to implement these energy conservation behaviors. The Ignorance barrier might apply more to difficult, high-cost behaviors.

Some differences and some similarities emerged between the two studies. The food domain study attempted to measure all seven theorized barrier categories (i.e., from Gifford, 2011). However, it did so using mostly single-item measures for the specific barrier manifestations. The energy domain study attempted to measure only five of seven barrier categories but used multiple-item measures. Both studies measured the barriers in only one behavior domain. Nonetheless, three of the retained barrier components were the same in both studies; Denial, Conflicting Goals and Aspirations, and Interpersonal Influences. Additional components were found, but may have differed because of the different measurement approaches used in each study (e.g., single-item vs multiple-item measures, including only five of the even barrier components). This called for additional analyses using multiple items to measure a comprehensive set of barriers.

A revised barriers scale. The above studies provided the groundwork for a third study designed to address their limitations (Lacroix, Gifford, & Chen, Submitted). The previous two studies were domain specific (food and energy). One objective of this third study (Lacroix, Gifford, & Chen, Submitted) was to provide a comprehensive but parsimonious measurement of psychological barriers to proenvironmental behavior that could be used across multiple domains. The study included proclimate behaviors from six major climate-relevant domains (i.e., food choices, energy use, transportation, waste and disposal, purchasing, and water conservation).

New items were added to supplement the hypothesized barrier factors; the resulting 65-item instrument, intended to cover all the barriers in Gifford's (2011) taxonomy using multiple items per barrier, was tested in a Canadian community sample ($n = 380$). Exploratory factor analyses were conducted to discover the barrier constructs underlying the set of barrier items. Six factors emerged. To reduce the number of items used to measure each barrier factor, so as to create a relatively short, efficient set of scales, four items were selected to represent each factor, using factor loadings, corrected interitem correlations, and reliabilities (alpha). The items were also chosen to ensure that as many of the specific hypothesized barriers (cf. Table 7.1, above) as possible were retained, while eliminating items that shared considerable variance, in the service of parsimony and the practical usability of the instrument. The six-factor barrier structure was validated using confirmatory factory analyses using a new sample.

7.4 The Dragons of Inaction Psychological Barriers (DIPB) instrument

This revised six-factor instrument, with four items per factor, explained 57% of the variance in psychological barriers. Each barrier factor had good internal reliability (i.e., alphas between .79 and .86). The barrier factors are as follows: No Need to Change, Conflicting Goals and Aspirations, Interpersonal Relations, Government and Industry, Tokenism, and Lacking Knowledge.

Overall, this experimentally derived six-factor instrument is quite similar to the originally theorized seven-factor structure (Fig. 7.1). However, some of the 2011 barrier categories were combined to form a new factor (i.e., Ideologies and

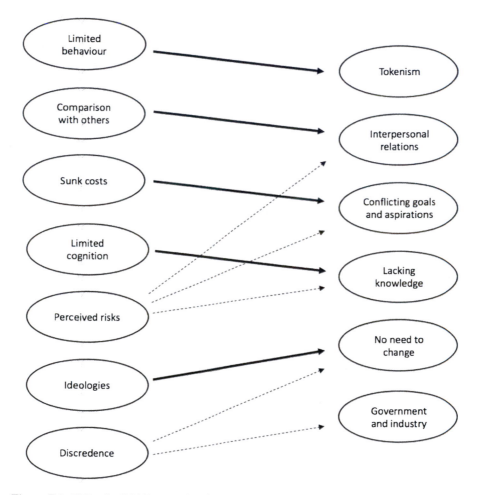

Figure 7.1 Gifford's (2011) seven barrier categories (left) in relation to the DIPB instrument (right). *DIPB*, Dragons of Inaction Psychological Barrier.

Discredence were combined to form the new No Need to Change factor), some were separated from their original group to form their own factor (e.g., perceived program inadequacy now forms the Government and Industry factor), and some barrier categories were eliminated, but their items redistributed elsewhere (i.e., Perceived Risks were redistributed into the Interpersonal Relations, Conflicting Goals and Aspirations, and the Lacking Knowledge factors). Many of the original barrier categories remain practically unchanged except for their names (i.e., Comparison with Others, Sunk Costs, and Limited Behavior). The revised six categories of psychological barriers to proenvironmental behavior are described next.

No Need to Change (AKA Mission Unnecessary). This barrier represents a belief that proenvironmental behavior is not necessary, because a person believes either that there is no environmental problem or that the problem will resolve itself. In the case of climate change, for example, those who are susceptible to this barrier tend to deny that it is occurring or that it is human-caused. If they do accept that the climate is changing, they believe that the problem will resolve itself through technological advancement, suprahuman powers (e.g., a religious deity), or through nature's resilience. Often, these individuals have a general mistrust of climate scientists and authorities or believe there is no need to act because the environmental risks are geographically or temporally distant.

In terms of the barriers taxonomy initially presented by Gifford (2011), this category encompasses mistrust, denial, reactance, technosalvation, suprahuman control, lack of self-efficacy, system justification, optimism bias, and confirmation bias. A prototypical item is "There is no need for change because I don't believe that a serious environmental problem exists."

Conflicting Goals and Aspirations (AKA Mission Contested). Some individuals recognize the need to change but cite financial or time constraints. Generally, they perceive a conflict between their other goals and engaging in proenvironmental behavior (e.g., wanting a bigger or more luxurious car, but also wanting to keep fuel consumption low). They may believe that changing their behavior will negatively impact their lifestyle or well-being and therefore are unwilling to change. Also, they might simply prefer to engage in climate-negative activities that they enjoy. Of the theorized specific barriers presented by Gifford (2011), financial investment, behavioral momentum, temporal and financial perceived risks, and conflicting goals barriers typically fall into this category. A prototypical item is "Making this change would interfere too much with my other goals in life."

Interpersonal relations (AKA Mission Others). Some people would like to change, but they wait for others to change first or they fear that their family or friends would not approve of the proenvironmental behavior. Within the Gifford (2011) taxonomy, social comparison, social norms, and perceived social risk typically fall into this category. A prototypical item is "Making this change would be criticized by those around me."

Government and industry (AKA Mission Upstairs). Some individuals would like to change, but they believe that it is not *their* responsibility to act. They believe that for them to make sacrifices when industry is causing most of environmental problems is unfair. These individuals often believe that the government should take

charge and make it easier for them to change by implementing incentives and programs. The perceived program inadequacy barrier (Gifford, 2011) applies to this
category. A prototypical item is "It's the government's responsibility to regulate
this change."

Tokenism (AKA Mission Accomplished). Generally, this group of barriers
applies to individuals who recognize that changes are necessary to address environmental problems. In fact, many of them have already made changes in their own
lives. The objective positive impact of these changes might be inconsequential, but
once they have adopted one or two proenvironmental actions, they believe that they
have done enough. The tokenism and rebound effect barriers (Gifford, 2011)
typically fall into this category. A prototypical item is "I've already made sacrifices
to solve environmental problems, so there is no need for me to do more."

Lacking Knowledge (AKA Mission Confused). Finally, some individuals
would like to change but report that they do not know how. This barrier probably
applies to behaviors that are easier to change, although this hypothesis will need to
be tested. Of the specific theorized barriers (Gifford, 2011), perceived functional
risks, ignorance, and environmental numbness fit into this category. A prototypical
item is "I would like to change, but I'm not sure where to begin."

More research is needed to understand the impact of these dragons. Why? It is
partly needed to enhance theory and fundamental knowledge, but also to learn
where, in the pursuit of optimal policy and regulations, to most efficiently invest
scarce societal resource funds and efforts. Evidence-based, targeted policy is
efficient. The next section expands on this theme.

7.5   Practical applications

Identifying psychological barriers to proenvironmental behavior is key to the design
of successful behavior change interventions. The DIPB will enable researchers to
conduct behavior-specific investigations to establish barrier probabilities for each
behavior and for different groups of individuals. Once these psychological barriers
have been identified, program designers can begin to "slay the dragons" more
efficiently through public campaigns, policies, and programs.

A reasonable starting point is to consider whether all dragons impede all constructive behaviors for all individuals. The very probable short answer is "no." I
(RG) have proposed a three-dimensional "Rubik's cube" model for this: Dragons x
Behaviors x Persons. First, one can safely speculate that different individuals (age,
culture, wealth, personality, motivation, etc.) will employ different justifications
(dragons) to excuse their actions for different behaviors. Further, the different major
behavior domains (domestic energy use, food choices, transportation, and the
acquisition and disposal of material goods) probably will elicit different justifications. Bearing this three-dimensional model in mind, some examples of strategies
for addressing each of the six experimentally derived psychological barrier factors
are described next.

In the context of climate change, the No Need to Change (Mission Unnecessary) barrier factor is often associated with climate change denial or skepticism about its causes. The gateway belief model (van der Linden, Leiserowitz, Feinberg, & Maibach, 2015) suggests one potential avenue for addressing the barrier. According to this model, highlighting the scientific consensus on climate change (i.e., that 97% of climate scientists agree it is happening and human-caused) increases the belief in climate change, which subsequently increases support for climate action (van der Linden et al., 2015; van der Linden, Leiserowitz, & Maibach, 2016; van der Linden, Leiserowitz, Rosenthal, & Maibach, 2017).

The Conflicting Goals and Aspirations (Mission Contested) barrier factor is often associated with perception that one's current behavioral habits are too difficult to change (Gifford & Chen, 2017; Lacroix & Gifford, online; Lacroix, Gifford, & Chen, Submitted). To the extent that the conflicting goals are habit-driven, some tools (e.g., implementation intention) are available for changing habits (Danner, Aarts, Papies, & de Vries, 2011; Gardner, Lally, & Wardle, 2012; Gardner, Sheals, Wardle, & McGowan, 2014; Turton, Bruidegom, Cardi, Hirsch, & Treasure, 2016). If time or inconvenience also is a barrier, these efforts could be combined with structural changes for more effective programs (e.g., improving public transportation). For changes that seem too difficult, way of increasing self-efficacy should be explored.

Highlighting the power of social norms can help to address the Interpersonal Relations (Mission Others) barrier factor. For example, informing household residents that they were consuming more electricity than most of their neighbors decreased their energy consumption (Schultz, Nolan, Cialdini, Goldstein, & Griskevicius, 2007). Modeling proper composting behavior increased composting in school cafeterias and public restaurants (Sussman & Gifford, 2013; Sussman, Greeno, Gifford, & Scannell, 2013). Efforts to increase social support may create more effective interventions.

The Tokenism (Mission Accomplished) barrier factor highlights the importance of emphasizing efforts to change high-impact behaviors (Capstick, Lorenzoni, Corner, & Whitmarsh, 2014; Schultz & Kaiser, 2012; Stern, Gardner, Vandenbergh, & Dietz, 2010; Chapter 6: Contributions of psychology to limiting climate change: Opportunities through consumer behavior). In the context of climate change, behaviors like flying less, eating less meat, and driving less or driving a more fuel-efficient car have a relatively higher potential to reduce greenhouse gas emissions than others (Lacroix, Gifford, & Chen, Submitted; Wynes & Nicholas, 2017). Research aimed at strengthening proenvironmental intentions toward less-impactful behavior still has its place, especially because it contains potential for these behaviors to spillover onto other behaviors. The Tokenism barrier is more likely to be surmounted (and positive spillover facilitated) when environmental motivation, attitude, and identity are stronger (Lanzini & Thøgersen, 2014; Schultz & Kaiser, 2012; Stern, 2011; Thøgersen & Crompton, 2009).

Positive spillover is also more likely when new skills have been learned. The promotion of self-efficacy (Bandura, 1977) is one potential avenue for addressing the Lacking Knowledge (Mission Confused) barrier factor. Generally, interventions that target self-efficacy should focus on strengthening individuals' perceptions of the benefits of change, and increasing their performance abilities (Anderson, Winett & Wojcik, 2007; Cherry, 2015; Haverstock & Forgays, 2012; Jancey et al., 2014; Janda & Trocchia, 2001; Lea, Crawford & Worsley, 2006; Menezes et al., 2015).

7.6   Future research directions

Using the DIPB should help to shed light on several questions that remain unanswered. For example, research might compare the perception of psychological barriers across public and private domains. Does the Interpersonal Relations (Mission Others) barrier more strongly hinder behaviors that occur outside one's home, and are thus more visible (e.g., using public transit), than behavior that takes place in private (e.g., wearing sweaters to conserve household energy)? The perception of psychological barriers might vary between individuals according to their values, worldviews, perceptions of social norms, or their financial situation. These psychological barriers may also be situation-dependent, that is, interact with structural barriers (e.g., the availability of alternative transportation).

Future research also could compare the influence of these barriers between easier and more difficult proenvironmental behaviors. One might hypothesize that a lack of knowledge about how to become a vegan (i.e., Mission Confused) is more common than not knowing how to change a lightbulb. Similarly, expecting the government to regulate a behavior (i.e., Mission Upstairs) might be more applicable for high-cost behaviors.

Once one has overcome some initial barriers, tokenism might hinder further action (Gifford, 2011). This hints at the possibility that at least some barriers are subject to a temporal or causal sequence. As another example of this, the first DIPB barrier, No Need for Change, characterizes individuals who do not see a need for change, whereas the remaining five barrier factors characterize the thinking of individuals who recognize that climate change exists and would like to do more to help, but nevertheless do too little. Future research should unpack the temporal sequence of barriers.

Future research might also investigate the interactions between psychological barriers. For example, does decreasing the perception of one barrier change the perception of other barriers? One might expect that once individuals accept that a given environmental problem exists and considers changing their behavior, they might become more conscious of the social norm surrounding that behavior. In other words, barriers might spill over (either negatively or positively) onto other barriers.

7.7   Incorporating psychological barriers into a new model of behavior choice

One of the most important future challenges for dealing with climate change is to develop a validated theory of human response to these environmental challenges.

Understanding that one can fruitfully build on existing work, we are developing a TBC that should improve upon the often-used, but often-criticized, theory of planned behavior (TPB; Ajzen, 2011). Promoting sustainable behavior is not easy, so an optimal model of the phenomenon in question is crucially important.

What influences pro- and anticlimate choices and behaviors? Which are most and least powerful? How do these influences relate to one another? The general reasoned-action approach (Fishbein & Ajzen, 2010) is the latest version of the theoretical ideas of the earlier theory of reasoned action (Fishbein & Ajzen, 1975) and TPB (Ajzen, 1985). It offers an integrative framework for the prediction and change of human social behavior. It has stimulated over a thousand empirical studies since 1975.

Essentially, Fishbein and Ajzen (2010) propose that human behavior can best be predicted from a person's *intentions*. Intention is the cognitive representation of a person's readiness to perform a given behavior, and it is considered to be the immediate antecedent of behavior. This intention is said to be determined by three influences: *attitude* toward the specific behavior, *subjective norms*, and *perceived behavioral control*.

The approach has been the target of much criticism and debate, and Ajzen (2011) recently replied to many of the reactions and reflections. Most critics accept the theory's basic reasoned action assumptions but question its sufficiency or inquire into its limiting conditions. The TPB is reasonably good at accounting for behavioral intentions, but a number of critiques have highlighted its shortcomings (e.g., Aarts & Dijksterhuis, 2000; Wegner, 2002).

Based on a review of the TPB's strengths and weaknesses, and of other research, including our research on barriers, we propose, and are in the midst of testing, a new model called the TBC (see Figure 7.2). The goal for the TBC is to rectify the main shortcomings of the TPB and thereby serve as a superior predictor of behavioral choices. The TBC shares some constructs with the TPB (which, after all, is a reasonable model) but adds four elements: desire to enact (or NOT to enact) a particular behavior, perceived (i.e., psychological) barriers, structural (i.e., objective, external) barriers, and reported behavior.

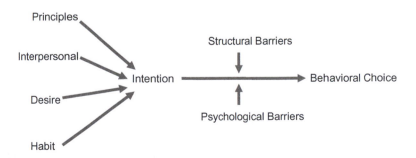

Figure 7.2 The theory of behavioral choice.

The work we have discussed above illustrates the importance of *perceived barriers*. In addition, some people face truly objective, external *structural barriers* (how can one choose public transit in a town that does not have any? How can one install solar panels as a poor person, or even as a middle-class renter?). Barriers of either sort seem to us to explain why individuals have intentions that are not turned into behaviors. "I would do that, but ..." leads directly to one or more perceived or structural barriers.

Reported behavior is included in the TBC because of the clear distinction between actual and reported behavior that was demonstrated in our recent metaanalysis: Across numerous proenvironmental behaviors, the correlation between reported and observed actual behavior was $r = .46$, representing a 21% overlap (Kormos & Gifford, 2014).

Desire is not clearly part of the TPB, but as one of the authors (RG) discovered from a listener at one of his presentations who asked "What if I just *want* to fly to Costa Rica?", this volitional element deserves some discussion. The extended model of goal-directed behavior (EMGB; Perugini & Conner, 2000) was one attempt to gain a better understanding of cognitive and affective decision-making processes. It deliberately extended the TPB and the model of goal-directed behavior (MGB; Perugini & Bagozzi, 2001) by focusing on behavioral volition and linking those volitions to goals. Perugini and Bagozzi (2001) posit that behavioral desire mediates the effects of the TPB antecedents (attitude, subjective norm, and perceived behavioral control) on behavioral intention.

An extension of the MGB to the EMGB (its extended version) incorporates two additional elements, goal desire and goal perceived feasibility. However, a recent study (van de Vreede, 2006) concluded that perhaps the EMGB is too unwieldy to be effective. Although it is admirably inclusive, it lacks parsimony. Some of the proposed mediations did not occur. The TBC aims to find a balance between the inclusion of all usefully predictive elements with no superfluous elements.

The knowledge gained during the development and validation of the TBC model can be applied by policymakers and nongovernment organizations to enhance the degree of climate-positive behavior in the community. By demonstrating how each element of the model influences individuals' intentions to act (or not act) in climate-positive ways, and determining how perceived and objective obstacles interfere with the transition from intention to action, these studies will serve as a guide for creating policies and practices that maximize the frequency of climate-positive behavior choices in the general population.

7.8 Conclusion

This chapter outlines the case for, and development of, a comprehensive and psychometrically sound instrument (the DIPB) for assessing the psychological barriers that hinder individuals from helping to mitigate the impacts of climate change and acting more sustainably. We also offer a new model (the TBC) that incorporates these psychological barriers, structural barriers, desire, and the distinction between actual and reported behavior into a model that should improve upon earlier models of behavior by increasing the range of influences while remaining reasonably parsimonious.

The DIPB and TBC aim to assist in efforts to deal with what is perhaps the *most* important current and future challenge, climate change. As someone said whose job it was to deal with all the important issues of our time, "There's one issue that will define the contours of this century more dramatically than any other, and that is the urgent and growing threat of a changing climate" (Barack Obama, UN Climate Change Summit, September 23, 2014).

Given that recent changes to the climate have mainly been caused by the collective behavior choices of 7.2 billion individuals, one obvious way forward is to increase our understanding of climate-related behavioral choices. One way to accomplish this is to create a useful predictive model for understanding those choices. Such a framework, in turn, needs reliable and valid measures. Improved models of human decision-making will serve as a crucial platform for community leaders and members of the community to craft policies that will soften the impact of an already changing climate for the generations to come. We hope that the DIPB and the TBC will be of use for this very important challenge.

References

Aarts, H., & Dijksterhuis, A. (2000). Habits as knowledge structures: Automaticity in goal-directed behavior. *Journal of Personality and Social Psychology, 78*, 53−63.

Ajzen, I. (1985). From intentions to actions: A theory of planned behavior. In J. Kuhl, & J. Beckman (Eds.), *Action-control: From cognition to behavior* (pp. 11−39). Heidelberg, Germany: Springer.

Ajzen, I. (2011). *The* theory of planned behavior: Reactions and reflections. *Psychology & Health, 26*, 1113−1127. Available from https://doi.org/10.1080/08870446.2011.613995.

Anderson, E. S., Winett, R. A., & Wojcik, J. R. (2007). Self-regulation, self-efficacy, outcome expectations, and social support: Social cognitive theory and nutrition behavior. *Annals of Behavioral Medicine, 34*, 304−312. Available from https://doi.org/10.1007/BF02874555.

Bandura, A. (1977). Self-efficacy: Toward a unifying theory of behavioral change. *Psychological Review, 84*, 191−215.

Blake, J. (1999). Overcoming the value-action gap in environmental policy: Tensions between national policy and local experience. *Local Environment, 4*, 257−278.

Capstick, S., Lorenzoni, I., Corner, A., & Whitmarsh, L. (2014). Prospects for radical emissions reduction through behavior and lifestyle change. *Carbon Management, 5*, 429−445. Available from https://doi.org/10.1080/17583004.2015.1020011.

Chaiken, S., & Stangor, C. (1987). Attitudes and attitude change. *Annual Review of Psychology, 38*, 575−630.

Chen, A., & Gifford, R. (2015). "I wanted to cooperate, but...": Justifying suboptimal cooperation in a commons dilemma. *Canadian Journal of Behavioral Science/Revue*

Canadienne Des Sciences Du Comportement, 47, 282—291. Available from https://doi.org/10.1037/cbs0000021.

Cherry, E. (2015). I was a teenage vegan: Motivation and maintenance of lifestyle movements. *Sociological Inquiry, 85,* 55—74. Available from https://doi.org/10.1111/soin.12061.

CNN Wire Staff. (2011). Wildfires rip through sun-scorched Texas. *CNN.* Retrieved from http://www.cnn.com/2011/US/09/05/texas.fires/index.html.

Corraliza, J. A., & Berenguer, J. (2000). Environmental values, beliefs and actions: A situational approach. *Environment and Behavior, 32,* 832—848.

Danner, U. N., Aarts, H., Papies, E. K., & de Vries, N. K. (2011). Paving the path for habit change: Cognitive shielding of intentions against habit intrusion. *British Journal of Health Psychology, 16,* 189—200. Available from https://doi.org/10.1348/2044-8287.002005.

Diekmann, A., & Preisendöerfer, P. (1992). Persönliches Umweltverhalten. Diskrepanzenzwischen Anspruch und Wirklichkeit [Personal environmental behavior: Discrepancies between claims and reality]. *Kölner Zeitschrift für Soziologie und Sozialpsychologie, 44,* 226—251.

Festinger, L. (1957). *A theory of cognitive dissonance.* Evanston, IL: Row, Peterson.

Finger, M. (1994). From knowledge to action? Exploring the relationships between experiences, learning and behavior. *Journal of Social Issues, 50,* 141—160.

Fishbein, M., & Ajzen, I. (1975). *Belief, attitude, intention and behavior: An introduction to theory and research.* Reading, MA: Addison Wesley.

Fishbein, M., & Ajzen, I. (2010). *Predicting and changing behavior: The reasoned action approach.* New York: Taylor & Francis.

Gardner, B., Lally, P., & Wardle, J. (2012). Making health habitual: The psychology of "habit-formation" and general practice. *The British Journal of General Practice, 62,* 664—666. Available from https://doi.org/10.3399/bjgp12X659466.

Gardner, B., Sheals, K., Wardle, J., & McGowan, L. (2014). Putting habit into practice, and practice into habit: A process evaluation and exploration of the acceptability of a habit-based dietary behavior change intervention. *International Journal of Behavioral Nutrition and Physical Activity, 11,* 135. Available from https://doi.org/10.1186/s12966-014-0135-7.

Gifford, R. (2011). The dragons of inaction: Psychological barriers that limit climate change mitigation and adaptation. *American Psychologist, 66,* 290—302.

Gifford, R., & Chen, A. (2017). Why aren't we taking action? Psychological barriers to climate-positive food choices. *Climatic Change, 140,* 165—178. Available from https://doi.org/10.1007/s10584-016-1830-y.

Gifford, R., Scannell, L., Kormos, C., Smolova, L., Biel, A., Boncu, S., ... Uzzell, D. (2009). Temporal pessimism and spatial optimism in environmental assessments: An 18-nation study. *Journal of Environmental Psychology, 29,* 1—12.

Haverstock, K., & Forgays, D. K. (2012). To eat or not to eat. A comparison of current and former animal product limiters. *Appetite, 58,* 1030—1036. Available from https://doi.org/10.1016/j.appet.2012.02.048.

Heath, Y., & Gifford, R. (2006). Free-market ideology and environmental degradation: The case of belief in global climate change. *Environment and Behavior, 38,* 48—71.

Heinlein, R. A. (1949). Gulf (part 2). *Astounding Stories.* (Magazine).

Hine, D. W., & Gifford, R. (1997). What harvesters really think about in commons dilemma situations: A grounded theory analysis. *Canadian Journal of Behavioral Science, 29,* 180—194.

Hines, J. M., Hungerford, H., & Tomera, A. (1987). Analysis and synthesis of research on responsible environmental behavior: A meta-analysis. *Journal of Environmental Education, 18*, 1−8.

Intergovernmental Panel on Climate Change. (2014). *Summary for policymakers. Climate change 2014: Mitigation of climate change. Contribution of Working Group III to the fifth assessment report of the Intergovernmental Panel On Climate Change* (pp. 1−30). United Kingdom and New York, NY: Cambridge University Press.

Jancey, J. M., Dos Remedios Monteiro, S. M., Dhaliwal, S. S., Howat, P. A., Burns, S., Hills, A. P., & Anderson, A. S. (2014). Dietary outcomes of a community based intervention for mothers of young children: A randomised controlled trial. *International Journal of Behavioral Nutrition and Physical Activity, 11*, 120. Available from https://doi.org/10.1186/s12966-014-0120-1.

Janda, S., & Trocchia, P. J. (2001). Vegetarianism: Toward a greater understanding. *Psychology and Marketing, 18*, 1205−1240. Available from https://doi.org/10.1002/mar.1050.

Kahle, L. R., & Gurel-Atay, E. (2014). *Communicating sustainability for the green economy.* Armonk, NY: M. E. Sharpe.

Kaiser, F. G., & Gutscher, H. (2003). The proposition of a general version of the theory of planned behavior: Predicting ecological behavior. *Journal of Applied Social Psychology, 33*, 586−603.

Kollmuss, A., & Agyeman, J. (2002). Mind the gap: Why do people act environmentally and what are the barriers to pro-environmental behavior?. *Environmental Education Research, 8*, 239−260.

Kormos, C., & Gifford, R. (2014). The validity of self-report measures of proenvironmental behavior: A meta-analytic review. *Journal of Environmental Psychology, 40*, 359−371. Available from https://doi.org/10.1016/j.jenvp.2014.09.003.

Lacroix, K., & Gifford, R. (online). Psychological barriers to energy-conservation behavior: The role of worldviews and climate change risk perception. *Environment and Behavior.* https://doi.org/10.1177/0013916517715296.

Lacroix, K., Gifford, R., & Chen, A. (Submitted). Psychological barriers to pro-environmental behavior: Structural validity of the dragons of inaction scale.

Lanzini, P., & Thøgersen, J. (2014). Behavioral spillover in the environmental domain: An intervention study. *Journal of Environmental Psychology, 40*, 381−390. Available from https://doi.org/10.1016/j.jenvp.2014.09.006.

Lea, E. J., Crawford, D., & Worsley, A. (2006). Consumers' readiness to eat a plant-based diet. *European Journal of Clinical Nutrition, 60*, 342−351. Available from https://doi.org/10.1038/sj.ejcn.1602320.

Lewin, K. (1935). *A dynamic theory of personality.* New York: McGraw-Hill.

Linn, J. (2016). The rebound effect for passenger vehicles. *The Energy Journal, 37*, 257−288.

Menezes, M. C., de, Mingoti, S. A., Cardoso, C. S., Mendonça, R., de, D., & Lopes, A. C. S. (2015). Intervention based on the transtheoretical model promotes anthropometric and nutritional improvements—A randomized controlled trial. *Eating Behaviors, 17*, 37−44. Available from https://doi.org/10.1016/j.eatbeh.2014.12.007.

Newhouse, N. (1990). Implications of attitude and behavior research for environmental conservation. *Journal of Environmental Education, 22*, 26−32.

Perugini, M., & Bagozzi, R. P. (2001). The role of desires and anticipated emotions in goal-directed behaviors: Broadening and deepening the theory of planned behavior. *British Journal of Social Psychology, 40*, 79−98.

Perugini, M., & Conner, M. (2000). Predicting and understanding behavioral volitions: The interplay between goals and behaviors. *European Journal of Social Psychology, 30,* 705−731.

Scannell, L., & Gifford, R. (2010a). Defining place attachment: A tripartite organizing framework. *Journal of Environmental Psychology, 30,* 1−10.

Schmidt, F. N., & Gifford, R. (1989). A dispositional approach to hazard perception: The environmental appraisal inventory. *Journal of Environmental Psychology, 9,* 57−67.

Schultz, P. W., & Kaiser, F. G. (2012). Promoting pro-environmental behavior. In S. Clayton (Ed.), *The Oxford handbook of environmental and conservation psychology* (pp. 556−580). New York, NY: Oxford University Press.

Schultz, P. W., Nolan, J. M., Cialdini, R. B., Goldstein, N. J., & Griskevicius, V. (2007). The constructive, destructive, and reconstructive power of social norms. *Psychological Science, 18,* 429−434.

Stern, P. C. (2011). Contributions of psychology to limiting climate change. *American Psychologist, 66,* 303−314. Available from https://doi.org/10.1037/a0023235.

Stern, P. C., Gardner, G. T., Vandenbergh, M. P., & Dietz, T. (2010). Design principles for carbon emissions reduction programs. *Environmental Science & Technology, 44,* 4847−4848.

Sussman, R., & Gifford, R. (2013). Be the change you want to see: Modeling food composting in public places. *Environment and Behavior, 45,* 323−343. Available from https://doi.org/10.1177/0013916511431274.

Sussman, R., Gifford, R., & Abrahamse, W. (2016). *Social mobilisation: How to encourage action on climate change.* White Paper for the Pacific Institute for Climate Solutions, University of Victoria.

Sussman, R., Greeno, M., Gifford, R., & Scannell, L. (2013). The effectiveness of models and prompts on waste diversion: A field experiment on composting by cafeteria patrons. *Journal of Applied Social Psychology, 43,* 24−34. Available from https://doi.org/10.1111/j.1559-1816.2012.00978.x.

Swim, J. K., Stern, P. C., Doherty, T., Clayton, S., Reser, J. P., Weber, E. U., ... Howard, G. S. (2011). Psychology's contributions to understanding and addressing global climate change mitigation and adaptation. *American Psychologist, 66,* 241−250.

Thøgersen, J., & Crompton, T. (2009). Simple and painless? The limitations of spillover in environmental campaigning. *Journal of Consumer Policy, 32,* 141−163. Available from https://doi.org/10.1007/s10603-009-9101-1.

Turton, R., Bruidegom, K., Cardi, V., Hirsch, C. R., & Treasure, J. (2016). Novel methods to help develop healthier eating habits for eating and weight disorders: A systematic review and meta-analysis. *Neuroscience and Biobehavioral Reviews, 61,* 132−155. Available from https://doi.org/10.1016/j.neubiorev.2015.12.008.

Tversky, A., & Kahneman, D. (1974). Judgment under uncertainty: Heuristics and biases. *Science, 185*(4157), 1124−1131. Available from https://doi.org/10.1126/science.185.4157.1124.

van de Vreede, G. (2006). *Understanding farmers' intentions to carry out agricultural nature management.* Unpublished Master's thesis, Leiden University.

van der Linden, S., Leiserowitz, A., & Maibach, E.W. (2016). *Communicating the scientific consensus on human-caused climate change is an effective and depolarizing public engagement strategy: Experimental evidence from a large national replication study* (SSRN Scholarly Paper No. ID 2733956). Rochester, NY: Social Science Research Network. Retrieved from https://papers.ssrn.com/abstract = 2733956.

van der Linden, S., Leiserowitz, A., Rosenthal, S., & Maibach, E. (2017). Inoculating the public against misinformation about climate change. *Global Challenges*. Available from https://doi.org/10.1002/gch2.201600008.

van der Linden, S., Leiserowitz, A. A., Feinberg, G. D., & Maibach, E. W. (2015). The scientific consensus on climate change as a gateway belief: Experimental evidence. *PLoS ONE, 10*, e0118489. Available from https://doi.org/10.1371/journal.pone.0118489.

Vining, J., & Ebreo, A. (2002). Emerging theoretical and methodological perspectives on conservation behavior. In R. B. Bechtel, & A. Churchman (Eds.), *Handbook of environmental psychology* (2nd ed., pp. 541−558). New York: Wiley.

Wegner, D. M. (2002). *The illusion of conscious will.* Cambridge, MA: MIT Press.

Wikipedia (n.d.). *Black Saturday bushfires.* Retrieved from https://en.wikipedia.org/wiki/Black_Saturday_bushfires#Overall_statistics.

Wynes, S., & Nicholas, K. A. (2017). The climate mitigation gap: Education and government recommendations miss the most effective individual actions. *Environmental Research Letters, 12*, 74024. Available from https://doi.org/10.1088/1748-9326/aa7541.

Environmental protection through societal change: What psychology knows about collective climate action—and what it needs to find out

Sebastian Bamberg[1], Jonas H. Rees[2] and Maxie Schulte[1]
[1]Bielefeld University of Applied Sciences, Bielefeld, Germany, [2]Bielefeld University, Bielefeld, Germany

> *If you want to go quickly, go alone. If you want to go far, go together.*
> —*African proverb*

Global environmental problems collected under the umbrella of climate change present formidable challenges to societies worldwide and cannot be solved by single states alone. For example, the Paris summit goal of restricting global warming to 1.5°C can only be realized by reducing total carbon emissions *across the globe* by 80% before 2050. Such an overwhelming goal can only be reached by deep-structural changes in the ways in which we all produce and consume, especially rich nations like the USA and the EU that have been industrialized for longer. Thus the challenge is no longer how to make our individual life styles "greener" but how to transform sociotechnical systems and social practices in central societal domains such as mobility, housing, agrofood, heating, and lighting for each and everyone. In other words, societal problems such as climate change can only be addressed by changing societies themselves rather than just individuals in these societies. Such transformations will only be successful if all relevant actors (e.g., companies and industry lines, politicians and administrators, consumers, civil society, researchers/engineers) participate and these change processes will probably take decades to unfold.

In the past, alongside neoclassical and behavioral economics, environmental psychology has contributed considerably to the debates on sustainable production and consumption. However, in recent years, sociologists and political scientists have begun questioning whether mainstream individualistic psychology has anything to contribute to the intensifying debate about developing effective strategies to achieve the described fundamental societal transformations. According to Geels, McMeekin, Mylan, and Southerton (2015), one reason for this skepticism is the close association of mainstream individualistic psychology with a position within

Psychology and Climate Change. DOI: https://doi.org/10.1016/B978-0-12-813130-5.00008-4

the sustainable production and consumption debate he calls the *reformistic position*. This position views consumers mainly as disconnected individuals equipped with sets of preferences on which they draw when making purchase decisions. Under the general banner of "proenvironmental behavior change," the reformistic position proposes intervention approaches such as social marketing (McKenzie-Mohr, 2000) and choice architectures from behavioral economics (Thaler & Sunstein, 2008). These approaches investigate how consumers can be motivated or incentivized to purchase eco-innovations, focusing on the role of eco-labels, information campaigns, prices, subsidies, and subliminal signals (Barr & Prillwitz, 2014; McMeekin & Southerton, 2012).

The problem with these approaches is not that they do not work—in fact, they work fine and their effectiveness in achieving *individual behavior change* is well documented (e.g., Abrahamse, Steg, Vlek, & Rothengatter, 2005; Möser & Bamberg, 2008). However, their aim is not the fundamental societal transition desperately needed for realizing the existential climate protection goals but merely to increase consumer acceptance of eco-innovations by fostering environmental consciousness and encouraging consumers to choose environmentally friendly products for their purchases, whether by offering market incentives or penalties (through preferential pricing strategies for greener products), or by appealing to attitudes through information and marketing campaigns (Bamberg & Möser, 2007).

The reformist position has several weaknesses, which have been addressed in detail elsewhere (Jackson, 2009; Scholl, Rubik, Kalimo, Biedenkopf, & Söebech, 2010; Schor, 2010). We emphasize two issues that are particularly pertinent for the current chapter. First, policies (e.g., tax reduction for low emission cars, licensed eco-labels for household appliances) based on the reformist position tend to focus on short-term efficiency gains rather than on long-term changes in sociotechnical systems and practices. However, this "tinkering" with market instruments makes little difference when the fundamental focus of markets is to expand consumption of resources. Second, the intellectual basis of the reformist position is rather narrow, based on theories that focus on individual decisions and actions. Scholars have therefore suggested broadening the social science base of research in this area (Fedrigo & Hontelez, 2010; Scholl et al., 2010). In particular, it is important to pay more attention to the embeddedness of individual consumers and companies in social (e.g., groups, norms, routines, conventions) and politicoeconomic structures (such as the institutional embeddedness of markets).

Thus, environmental psychology is confronted with the fundamental question of whether the individualistic behavior change approach provides the only or even the most adequate strategy psychological research can contribute to the aim of transforming societal sociotechnological systems. It is our conviction that psychology, especially social psychology, has more to offer. This is the rationale and motivation for writing this chapter: We are convinced that a shift in analysis is necessary, away from individual behavior and goodwill to examining the role of collective action in achieving societal change (for similar arguments in the more general context of societal change see also Dixon, Levine, Reicher, & Durrheim, 2012; Wright, 2009; Wright & Baray, 2012). Besides a focus on changing individuals' hearts and minds, more research should be devoted to studying how, when, and why people take collective action to create a better society.

Identification or *social identification* is a powerful driver of societal change: Being part of a group can empower us and make us realize that we can achieve more when we act together as opposed to acting alone. Identification with a group or its aims can not only evoke strong emotions such as outrage, anger, but also shame and guilt. Social identification encourages us to display commitment to the cause of changing society, to connect to like-minded people, to form coalitions with similar groups. Finally and crucially, social identification itself motivates us to act together in order to achieve our social and political goals (Craig & Richeson, 2012; Klandermans, 1997; Tajfel & Turner, 1979; Wright & Baray, 2012).

8.1 The social psychology of climate change

Social psychology in particular "has a long tradition of theory and research that is relevant to addressing key climate change questions" (Fielding, Hornsey, & Swim, 2014, p. 413). This is true for contexts such as attitudes and attitude change (Borden & Francis, 1978; Dunlap, 1975), behavior (Ajzen & Fishbein, 1980; for a metaanalysis, see Bamberg & Möser, 2007), social influence (Cialdini, Reno, & Kallgren, 1990; Goldstein, Cialdini, & Griskevicius, 2008), and inter- and intragroup behavior (Harth, Leach, & Kessler, 2013), where social psychological research is either immediately relevant for or has even been directly linked with environmental behavior and climate change. As one prominent example, Cialdini et al. (1990) investigated the role of social norms for individuals' environmental behavior and found that littering was significantly less likely in clean settings implying an "antilittering norm" or that hotel guests were more likely to reuse towels when they were presented with certain types of norms (Goldstein et al., 2008).

The common denominator of all this work—and arguably the core idea of social psychology in general—is that human behavior in many situations can only be understood as *social* behavior, or behavior that is embedded in a wider social context. In this sense, we express attitudes because they help us define social categories we care about; we show certain behaviors because we believe socially relevant others expect such behaviors from us or because these behaviors help us demonstrate our membership in social groups. In turn, the social groups we belong to shape the way we see the world around us. For example, we tend to adopt a certain view on climate change depending on which political category we identify with (Kahan, 2015). Feeling psychologically connected to or identifying with groups can also empower us when we realize that we are part of "something bigger," that we can "make a difference." Together, we might be able to achieve goals we would never be able to reach as single individuals. We might feel pride when thinking about how our group protects the environment (Harth et al., 2013), but we might also feel guilt when confronted with the amount of our national greenhouse gas emissions (Ferguson & Branscombe, 2010). All of these processes—beliefs about what we can achieve *because we are part of a group*, emotions we experience *because we feel connected to a certain social category*, and the underlying *identification with particular groups*—can only be understood when we take into account that individuals are socially embedded.

In this sense, the current chapter takes a genuinely social psychological approach to climate behavior by focusing on the group dynamics involved in the context of climate protection. We will take a closer look at the psychological factors underlying individuals' engagement in collective action. As the study of collective climate action has only developed recently, we will briefly summarize what we know from research in the area of collective protest first and outline an influential model, the social identity model of collective action (SIMCA) (Van Zomeren, Postmes, & Spears, 2008), developed in that context. We will then use the model and its recent modifications, as well as some thoughts on the specific context of environmental behavior (as opposed to social protest) to develop a preliminary model of collective climate action. After summarizing the psychological drivers that motivate activists or individuals identified with specific groups to engage in collective climate protection, we take a closer look at how individuals become activists in the first place. Such processes can start with the very basic experience of a normative conflict between the way things are and the way things should be, but we will also discuss practical interventions on how to get people engaged, e.g., through group discussions. In the final section of the chapter, we take a closer look at the various psychological outcomes of participation in collective climate protection action. There is growing evidence that ongoing participation in collective actions can stimulate personal development in new directions. These include not only direct benefits from participating such as the formation of new friendships, gaining new organizational skills and knowledge but also more fundamental psychological benefits such as feelings of empowerment, increased self-esteem and self-confidence.

8.2   Conceptualizing group-based behavior: The social identity model of collective action

In social psychology, sociology, and related disciplines, there is a rich theoretical basis and long tradition of research on the phenomenon of collective action. Traces reach back as far as to Le Bon's (1895) *The crowd* (e.g., Drury & Stott, 2012). One of many reasons why scholars in the field have been fascinated with the specific phenomenon of collective action is that, for example, in the context of social inequality and societal change, it "is consistently described as the more effective way to reduce inequality and to establish social justice" (Becker & Wright, 2011, p. 63).

Put differently, groups of people are more successful at achieving change than single individuals. Historically, collective action has always been a motor of societal change.

In a characteristic definition, Wright, Taylor, and Moghaddam (1990) define that a person engages in collective action "any time that she or he is acting as a representative of the group and the action is directed at improving the conditions of the entire group" (p. 995). This definition seems to presume at least a basic identification with a certain group that one is, or has chosen to become, part of. Although a group can also be formed on the basis of more flexible criteria such as shared opinions (we will come back to the concept of such *opinion-based groups* further below), we will focus for now on social groups with clearly defined boundaries between members and nonmembers—the type of groups that have been investigated in most previous research. Sticking close to the past literature and established concepts is important because research on collective climate action has only begun to develop more recently, and a great deal of previous research on collective action has been conducted in the context of social protest and social inequality. Much of this previous research has linked participation in collective action to the social identification with certain groups (Drury & Reicher, 2009; Klandermans, 1997; McGarty, Bliuc, Thomas, & Bongiorno, 2009; Stürmer & Simon, 2004; Van Zomeren et al., 2008). Results show quite consistently that individuals' intention to engage or even actual engagement in collective action, for example, protest on behalf of a certain disadvantaged group, is strongly dependent upon the social identification with that particular group.

Identifying with a group, in other words, is generally regarded as one of the main motivations for individuals to engage on behalf of that group, but it can also stimulate other psychological drivers of collective action such as collective efficacy beliefs or group-based emotions. In their influential SIMCA (Fig. 8.1), Van Zomeren et al. (2008), Van Zomeren, Postmes, Spears, and Bettache (2011), and Van Zomeren, Saguy, and Schellhaas (2013) therefore consider social identity to be not only the single most important motivation for collective action but also the crucial link between two other pathways leading to collective action: Social identity

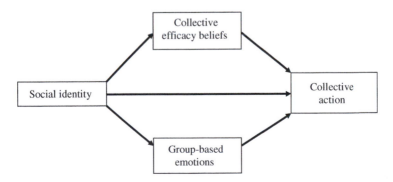

Figure 8.1 The social identity model of collective action.

feeds into both collective efficacy beliefs and group-based emotions as both are conceptually rooted in the identification with the group. In this sense, social identity also links the two pathways we will introduce next.

While social identity serves as a conceptual "bridge" between the two other constructs (Van Zomeren et al., 2008), the "rational" pathway based on efficacy beliefs and the "emotional" pathway based, e.g., on anger, are both rooted in research that we will briefly summarize in the following paragraphs. We will see that all three constructs are moderate and reliable predictors of collective action intention in nonclimate contexts. In exploring if and how the SIMCA can be adapted to collective *climate* action, however, we shall see that the model is readily applicable to this context but that its roots in collective protest necessitate some modifications before arriving at a first conceptualization specifically for collective climate protection action.

8.2.1   The "rational" pathway: Efficacy beliefs and collective action

One of the classic theories in the context of collective action or, more specifically, social protest is resource mobilization theory (McCarthy & Zald, 1977). The theory's basic premise is that social protest is a *rational* way for disadvantaged groups to advance their collective interests and to have their demands considered by more powerful groups. According to this rational perspective, objective resources such as number of group members or financial support should help facilitate the formation and organization of social movements. Empirical research, however, soon found that subjective perceptions about the group's capabilities are much more important than the group's objective resources. This subjective sense of available resources has been termed *collective efficacy* and is often also conceptualized as the individual's expectations about what the group is able to achieve through collective action (Bandura, 1997; Mummendey, Kessler, Klink, & Mielke, 1999). A host of collective action literature has accumulated showing that the higher the perceived collective efficacy, the more motivated people generally are to participate in collective action. This also leads to a classic paradox of collective action research, the free-rider problem, that we will come back to later: If a group works toward a common good such as climate protection and if my perception is that the group can achieve this goal, why would I care to join that group over spending my free time on the couch watching television (Olson, 1965)?

What is important to keep in mind for now is that the "rational" pathway to collective action seems to lead through collective efficacy beliefs. In their meta-analysis, Van Zomeren et al. (2008) found an averaged random effect correlation of $r = .34$, i.e., a moderate association, between collective efficacy and collective action.

8.2.2 The "emotional" pathway: Anger, shame, and collective action

There are different emotions that individuals may experience when being confronted with the problem of climate change. While the positive effects of pleasant emotions such as anticipated pride for behaviors in line with one's personal environmentally friendly norm (Onwezen, Antonides, & Bartels, 2013) or hope for constructive change (Ojala, 2012) have recently been documented, social psychological research has traditionally focused on the productive potential of negative emotions in response to the perception of an unjust status quo or to climate change. It is important to keep in mind that the perspective we are discussing is a group-based one. Consequently, we focus on *group-based emotions*, i.e., emotions that are experienced because of one's association or identification with a group (Doosje, Branscombe, Spears, & Manstead, 1998; Rees, Klug, & Bamberg, 2015). More specifically, Smith (1993) argued that whenever "group membership is salient, the group functions as a part of the self, and therefore [. . .] situations appraised as self-relevant trigger emotions just as they always do" (p. 303). Of course it is still an individual experiencing the emotion (e.g., group-based pride because the national greenhouse gas emissions have recently decreased drastically, or group-based shame in the face of environmental pollution in one's neighborhood). However, each individual experiences emotions as a member of specific groups and these group-based emotions may differ from the corresponding individual-level emotions in terms of determinants, consequences, and the ways in which they are regulated (Smith, Seger, & Mackie, 2007). Such differences are important because, conceptually, it will be group-based emotions and not individual-level emotions driving collective forms of behavior.

In its original form, the SIMCA focuses on how engaging in collective action can be motivated by group-based emotions, e.g., anger resulting from unfair collective disadvantage. This "emotional" pathway is rooted in relative deprivation theory (Walker & Smith, 2002), which suggests that the affective component of perceived deprivation predicts collective action intentions better than the cognitive component (Dubé-Simard & Guimond, 1986). The theory further proposes that individuals, when confronted with perceived disadvantage, will first appraise whether this disadvantage is group-level, then whether it is just or unjust. A resulting perception of unjust group-level disadvantage leads to group-based anger, which in turn motivates individuals to take collective action. Van Zomeren et al. (2008) found an averaged correlation of $r = .35$, i.e., a moderate association, between group-based anger and collective action.

However, whereas the "rational" pathway we reviewed above may translate from the protest context to the environmental context in a rather straightforward manner—individuals should be motivated to engage in collective climate action to the extent that they believe such group-based efforts will achieve their goals—emotions in the face of group-based environmental destruction may be different from those experienced in the face of group-based disadvantage: After all, each of us contributes to the problem of climate change more or less via our carbon footprint. It is therefore much more difficult to identify a well-defined "outgroup" to be angry at in this context. While a specific outgroup may be considered responsible for the disadvantage of my own group in certain contexts (e.g., an adversary group in conflictual contexts, or a more powerful group in contexts of oppression), *everyone* is more or less responsible for the problem of climate change. Instead of other-related moral emotions such as anger and outrage, self-related moral emotions such as guilt and shame may therefore be more important in motivating environmental behaviors (Böhm, 2003; Pfister & Böhm, 2001; Rees et al., 2015). It is also noteworthy that behaviors such as engaging in neighborhood-based climate protection initiatives differ from traditional protest through their self-critical focus. Instead of changing an unjust status quo, they aim at critically reflecting own behaviors or repairing damage that has been done. Again, because of their links with prosocial, reparative behaviors, emotions such as guilt and shame seem to lend themselves as alternatives to the classic anger-conceptualization of the "emotional" pathway (Rees & Bamberg, 2014).

8.2.3   The "social identity" factor: Bridging several gaps at once

Both of the pathways to action we discussed so far could be applied on the individual level or conceptualized through an individualistic lens. The rational pathway could be conceptualized as part of an individual-level cost—benefit calculation; emotions such as anger or outrage might be group-based but are still essentially experienced as an individual. Both pathways would lead to, e.g., environmentally friendly behavior because of individualistic efficacy beliefs and based on individual-level emotions (see Box 8.1) with engagement in a climate protection initiative potentially just being one such behavior. Social embeddedness would then simply be a by-product of individual-level processes. In fact, many "activist careers" may well have started because of individualistic motivations and considerations.

Such a conceptualization, however, would neglect the crucial aspect of genuine social change and the very phenomenon we are discussing: Collective action is essentially social behavior. In other words, once individuals have joined a group or movement, on a psychological level, something more fundamental happens: We identify with the social categories we care about. This *social identity*, the "part of an individual's self-concept which derives from his knowledge of his membership of a social group (or groups) together with the emotional significance attached to that membership" (Tajfel, 1974, p. 69), has been linked with a variety of outcomes focusing on behaviors or attitudes that can be understood as occurring out of "group interest" instead of "selfish interest." Social identification is the crucial concept we need in order to fully grasp the phenomenon of collective action in general and collective climate action in particular.

Box 8.1 Illustrating individual-level and group-level efficacy beliefs and emotions leading to environmentally friendly behavior.

	Individual-level	Group-level
Efficacy beliefs	"When I use my bike instead of my car to drive to work, I could save a lot of money"	"When our whole community cycled to work instead of driving, living quality in the neighborhood would increase dramatically"
Emotions	"My neighbor seems to use his car even for buying milk at the small shop around the corner—that's outrageous!"	"The main polluters globally also seem to be the least affected by climate change—that's outrageous!"
Behavior	Environmentally friendly behavior because of individualistic efficacy beliefs and based on individual-level emotions	Environmentally friendly engagement because of collective efficacy beliefs and based on group-level emotions

From a social identity perspective (Tajfel & Turner, 1979; Turner, Hogg, Oakes, Reicher, & Wetherell, 1987), collective action can be considered prototypical behavior as a group member, i.e., behavior as a representative of the group or behavior aimed at improving the state of the group (Wright et al., 1990). A sense of social identity has consequently been viewed as a necessary precondition for individuals to engage in collective action. In their metaanalysis, Van Zomeren et al. (2008) found an averaged random effect correlation of $r = .38$, i.e., a moderate association, between individuals' identification with the respective group and collective action participation. The more strongly we identify with a group, in other words, the more willing we are to engage in collective action such as protest on that group's behalf.

For our current objective of better understanding environmental behaviors as socially embedded behaviors, the concept of social identity can help us bridge the gap between "selfish", short-term benefits (e.g., the decision to travel by plane because it is quick and convenient) and "altruistic", long-term considerations (e.g., the decision to travel by public transportation because it will help protect the environment for future generations, even though it might be more tedious than taking the plane). Social identity can also serve as a conceptual "bridge" or link between the two seemingly unrelated rational and emotional pathways we outlined: It is linked with both collective efficacy beliefs and group-based emotions which are in turn motivators of collective action. Put differently, the rational and emotional pathways we outlined above partly mediate some of the effect social identification has on collective action participation (see Van Zomeren et al., 2008 and Fig. 8.1).

8.2.4   Collective climate action: A preliminary model

So far, we have mainly introduced concepts, synthesized theory and research from the context of social protest. We have introduced the single most influential model in the area, the SIMCA, and seen that a great deal of theory and concepts should be readily applicable to the environmental context. Before putting the pieces together into a preliminary model of collective climate action, we should revisit some loose ends from our summary above and acknowledge a few concepts that were added to the SIMCA recently—some were added to the model more generally, and some were added to address climate-related issues more specifically.

Participative efficacy beliefs. Remember the couch potato that would rather stay at home and watch television because local climate protection initiatives are already efficacious enough? In an attempt to solve the rational actor's paradox (or free rider problem, Olson, 1965) that we encountered a few pages earlier, Van Zomeren et al. (2013) introduced the concept of *participative efficacy beliefs*. These capture the belief that one's own actions will "make a difference" for the group's goal achievement. While collective efficacy beliefs and participative efficacy beliefs are obviously related, only the latter explicitly include the notion of a unique contribution of one's own involvement to the group's success. As such, Olson's (1965) rational actor may no longer consider free riding an option when they have strong participative efficacy beliefs because this would undermine the group's success. In a recent study investigating more than 600 students' willingness to engage in a climate protection initiative, participative efficacy was consequently a more powerful predictor ($\beta = .24$) of participation intention than was collective efficacy ($\beta = .12$), which was no longer relevant once the new construct was introduced in the model (Bamberg, Rees, & Seebauer, 2015).

Social norms as link between identification and behavior. Perceptions of social norms have long been established as important determinants of human behavior. In the environmental context in particular, classic social psychological studies linked norms not only with behavioral intentions but also with actual behavior (Cialdini et al., 1990; Goldstein et al., 2008). Group norms, in turn, are influenced by social identification with specific groups (Abrams & Hogg, 1990; Terry & Hogg, 1996). Put differently, we consider certain behaviors appropriate or not because we identify with certain social groups (e.g., we might consider traveling by plane the worst option because we identify as environmental psychologists), we tend to communicate these norms (e.g., we argue with our colleague who flies to a conference that she should have traveled by train), and behave according to them ourselves (e.g., avoid traveling by plane whenever possible). While this may not be specific to the environmental context, a perception of social norms has recently been found to mediate the link between a convenience sample of more than 500 participants' identification with their neighborhood and willingness to engage in a local climate protection initiative. Interestingly, social norms were also the single most influential predictor of collective climate action intention in the final model ($\beta = .70$; Rees & Bamberg, 2014).

Moral convictions. Another more recent concept to be considered is moral convictions, which can be defined as "strong and absolute stances on moral issues" (e.g., Van Zomeren et al., 2008). Such convictions may be particularly helpful to take into account in the highly moralized context of climate change. They have been linked with politicized identities and, maybe more importantly, should be linked with a host of moral emotions such as anger, outrage, guilt, or shame. In theoretical terms, moral convictions may give rise to the perception of a normative conflict—a discrepancy between the way things are and the way things should be. Such a conflict may be one of the crucial steps in becoming an activist in the first place, and we will come back to this concept below.

The role of emotions in collective climate action. Finally, because of the self-critical nature of collective climate action in comparison with collective protest, we need to refine the SIMCA's emotional pathway to apply the model to this context. As suggested above, guilt and shame should be prominent emotions when thinking about climate change. While they might not be as common as other emotions (such as worry, fear, and anger; Böhm, 2003), intriguingly they should be strongly linked with reparative behavioral intentions or even actual behavior (e.g., Allpress, Barlow, Brown, & Louis, 2010; Rees et al., 2015). Some research now suggests that anger and outrage traditionally linked with protest behavior (e.g., Iyer, Schmader, & Lickel, 2007; Tausch et al., 2011; Van Zomeren et al., 2008) do not always qualify as predictors of collective climate action intention. But such behavior, which can be viewed as a specific form of reparative behavior, may be motivated by guilt and shame. In a recent study, for example, we found that such a group-based guilty conscience was predictive of collective climate action intention ($\beta = .20$) while group-based anger was not (Rees & Bamberg, 2014).

Fig. 8.2 illustrates and summarizes our preliminary model of collective climate action. It is based mainly on the SIMCA and work by Van Zomeren et al. (2008, 2011, 2013), but it also incorporates recent work with a specific focus on collective action in the environmental domain (Bamberg et al., 2015; Rees & Bamberg, 2014). At its core lies the identification with a relevant social group— a local climate protection initiative, the neighborhood on whose behalf one engages in environmentally friendly behaviors, or an activist group such as Greenpeace. Efficacy beliefs—collective efficacy (i.e., the belief that the initiative will be effective in convincing politicians, recruiting new members, etc.) but even more importantly participative efficacy beliefs, group-based emotions (anger, outrage, guilt, shame, etc.), and also a perception of social norms—follow from this social identity. In concert, these concepts motivate collective climate action.

While such a preliminary model may be informative as a heuristic on how existing social identities can be transformed into collective climate action, the question of how sympathizers become activists—that is, develop an identification with an environmental group—in the first place should be at least as interesting.

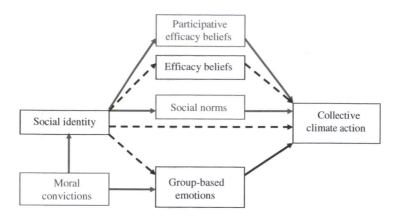

Figure 8.2 A preliminary model of collective climate action.
Note: Black elements are part of the original SIMCA, gray elements are constructs
developed more recently that could be added to the model. Dotted paths (significant in the
original SIMCA) might be rendered insignificant in such an adapted model. *SIMCA*, social
identity model of collective action.

8.3 Becoming a collective climate protection activist: From normative conflict to social validation and consensualizing

The SIMCA model assumes that people are already active and identified with a
group. This section aims to present and discuss theoretical ideas of the psychological processes how people get to that point. According to Smith, Thomas, and
McGarty (2015), the process of switching from being a sympathizer to actively participating in collective action starts when contextual triggers (e.g., media reports
about a man-made environmental catastrophe) raise a person's moral outrage and
deep concerns about the adequacy of current policymaking processes. In this case,
the person begins to critically think about the social structures and social groups
responsible for the environmental catastrophe. As a consequence, a person may
encounter a conflict between the way the world currently is (e.g., the government
allowing companies to produce in environmentally harmful ways) and the way he
or she believes the world should be (e.g., the government should enforce environmental protection). Packer (2008a) terms this kind of conflict a *normative conflict*.
In theoretical terms the discrepancy between "the way things are" and "the way
things should be" is captured by a discrepancy of the concepts of descriptive norm
(how most people behave in a given situation) and injunctive norm (how people
should behave in this situation; Cialdini et al., 1990). Experiencing such a normative conflict and trying to reduce the negative feelings caused by it may be the psychological processes underlying the impact of moral convictions on social identity
as well as group-based emotions assumed by the preliminary model of collective
climate action depicted in Fig. 8.2.

Furthermore, Smith et al. (2015) assume that people experiencing a normative conflict have a strong drive to express this conflict publicly and to talk with people holding similar opinions about their ideas on how to solve it. More precisely, people experiencing a normative conflict have the need to confirm that similar others share their beliefs of how "the world should be" (injunctive norm). Previous research has shown that such a consensus works as a source of *social validation* (Baron et al., 1996; Festinger, 1954). Social validation is defined as feedback that provides people with information about the characteristics, behaviors, or beliefs that others consider desirable.

Ashforth, Harrison, and Corley (2008) argue that need for social validation may be the underlying mechanism by which people guide each other's understanding of their preferred social reality and how to act within it (Smith & Postmes, 2011a, 2011b). There is also evidence that the social validation process can encourage the development of identification with a new group (Smith, Amiot, Callan, Terry, & Smith, 2012; Smith, Amiot, Smith, Callan, & Terry, 2013). Therefore, it seems that validation and consensual communication can both increase attachment between individuals and improve their ability to coordinate actions that they consider desirable (i.e., suitable for the shared injunctive norm). In support of this, there is evidence that when people are asked to reach consensus on a topic or idea through discussion (*consensualizing*), this process transforms their perceptions of the group norm (Smith & Postmes, 2009, 2011a, 2011b) and facilitates connection to novel group-based identities, which in turn provides the basis for their collective behavior. Discussion also increases awareness of a shared grievance, and this can also increase political action intentions (see Van Zomeren et al., 2008). This suggests that interaction can change collective behavior through increasing individuals' awareness of a shared normative conflict. For example, a person may discover that two neighboring families share his or her unease about consuming industrial livestock farming produced meat. Together they might develop the idea to establish a consumer cooperative supporting local organic farmers.

8.3.1   A more flexible basis for collective self-definition: The concept of opinion-based groups

Researchers (e.g., Smith et al., 2015) view opinion-based groups as an optimal context in which people experiencing a normative conflict can satisfy their need for social validation and consensual communication. The validation and consensualizing of ideas about effective climate protection policies during the interaction in opinion-based groups seems to be an effective strategy for developing a new collective climate action identity. Opinion-based groups are psychologically meaningful groups but are defined not by an already existing social category (e.g., being a member of Greenpeace) but by a shared opinion (e.g., shared opinion that the government should ban fossil fuel use for electricity production; Bliuc, McGarty, Reynolds, & Muntele, 2007; McGarty, Lala, & Douglas, 2011). Like other kinds of attributes, opinions are available for people to use as a basis for collective self-definition. Following the predictions of self-categorization theory (Turner et al., 1987), where people see themselves as a collective defined by a shared opinion, they would be expected to adhere to the norms of that group (e.g., expressing publicly the opinion to ban fossil fuel use, switching to a green energy provider, etc.). When opinion-based groups are defined by norms relating to climate protection, the identification with these groups is probably also a good predictor of commitment to take collective climate protection action (e.g., signing petitions requesting a new national energy policy, participating in protests in front of coal using energy producers, establishing a local solar energy cooperation; Bliuc et al., 2007).

Therefore, the processes of discussing ideas and reaching consensus in opinion-based groups can lead to the emergence of new social movements by enabling individuals involved in the discussions to validate each other's beliefs and giving them the confidence to coordinate, organize, and jointly act on them. To the extent that the new identity developed within this group context is founded upon shared injunctive norms (what we come to believe is the right thing to do), the participation in social change action (doing what we agree is right) becomes an expression of that identity (e.g., Gee & McGarty, 2013). People who identify with the emerging movement are likely to work toward shifting the undesirable descriptive norm (the status quo) to the desired injunctive norm, creating change. Thus, an injunctive norm becomes the basis of the identity of a new collective. The formation of such a new identity does not guarantee the emergence of a social movement and certainly does not ensure social change, but it contains the potential for social change action.

8.3.2   Effective group interaction through action consensus, action efficacy, and action voice

To summarize, the validation and consensualizing of ideas— perhaps particularly moral convictions—about effective climate protection policies during the interaction within opinion-based groups seems to be an effective strategy for developing a new identity organized around collectively shared injunctive norms. What is yet to be established is the specific elements that are helpful to forming this type of group interaction. According to Bongiorno, McGarty, Kurz, Haslam, & Sibley (2016; see Fig. 8.3), the following three elements are the most important ingredients of an action-oriented group interaction: (1) Supporters agree on the action that should be taken (*action consensus*); (2) They develop the belief that their actions are likely to be effective (*action efficacy*); and (3) They believe that their ideas are worthy of public expression (*action voice*). Let us consider these ingredients of an opinion-based group interaction promoting the development of a new group identity in more detail.

Action consensus: When supporters' interactions lead them to reach an agreement over how to promote their cause (e.g., by circulating a petition, organizing a strike, rally, or protest, establishing a local solar energy production cooperative, or

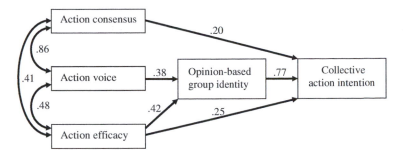

Figure 8.3 Opinion-based group formation model supported in Bongiorno et al. (2016).
Note: Only paths are displayed that were significant in the final model.

establishing a local urban gardening group), their sense of cohesion as a group is predicted to increase, along with their motivation to engage in joint collective actions.

Action efficacy: The development of a belief among supporters that the actions they agree on will produce the desired social changes is referred to as action efficacy. As discussed above, evidence shows that collective efficacy is positively related to group identification (e.g., Van Zomeren et al., 2008). It is expected that where supporters' interactions lead them to develop strategies seen as capable of producing the desired social changes, the formation of opinion-based groups will be facilitated.

Action voice: Action voice describes the process by which supporters come to believe that the ideas and strategies they agree on are worthy of public expression. Collective action can be motivated by supporters' desire to communicate valued social identities, which is separate from beliefs that taking action will produce the desired social changes. In this way, group formation may be facilitated through its ability to empower supporters to express personally important moral convictions—ideals they may not feel capable of expressing alone. Thus, where supporters establish a positive value for their ideas and strategies, such that they are seen to be worthy of public expression, their identification as opinion-based group members and intentions to take action is facilitated.

8.3.3   Getting practical: Forming groups with the opinion-based group interaction method

The theoretical mechanisms described in the last section not only help to improve our understanding of the psychological processes underlying the identification process but also provide a theoretical basis for systematically developing interventions promoting such identification processes. Based on the encapsulation model of social identity in collective action (EMSICA) described in more detail below, Thomas and McGarty (2009) develop the so-called opinion-based group interaction method. This method provides a good example of an intervention one can use to stimulate a group interaction characterized by the communication attributes described by

---

Box 8.2 The opinion-based group interaction method

On the basis of their concern about global warming and their willingness to develop locally implementable strategies to reduce its impact, Bongiorno et al. (2016) recruited 114 students who took part in 29 opinion-based group interactions, (see text) each with 3—5 participants. Fig. 8.3 presents how the three characteristics of these opinion-based group interactions (1) action consensus, (2) action efficacy, and (3) action voice were associated with the newly developed opinion-based group identity, and how strongly the newly developed opinion-based group identity was associated with collective action intentions.

Bongiorno et al. (2016): The procedure begins with all participants reading an information sheet about the respective societal problem, and the role the government or societal groups play in it. At the end of this information sheet, participants are asked to tick a box indicating whether they support an alternative policy solution for this problem. Participants are then given the task to come up with strategies to help promote sustainable solutions of the described problem and told that public institutions (e.g., the university or the researchers) are interested in these proposals and will make them public, for example, by posting them on their website. Participants then form small groups of three to five people, are provided with a sheet of paper upon which to write their recommendations, and are left to engage in the group discussion for half an hour.

Box 8.2 reports the results of a study conducted by Bongiorno et al. (2016) using the opinion-based group interaction method for creating a group interaction characterized by the three interaction characteristics and testing how the perception of these interaction characteristics was associated with the development of a new, opinion-based group identity. As predicted, perception of how strongly the group interaction was characterized by the elements action efficacy and action voice was substantially associated with the reported identification with the opinion-based group. However, the association between the third interaction element (action consensus) and identity was not confirmed. Further research is needed for clarifying the role of this interaction element. The strength of group identification itself was a substantial predictor of participants' self-reported collective action intentions.

8.3.4 The encapsulation model of social identity in collective action

The model depicted in Fig. 8.3 leaves open the question of what role the above discussed constructs "efficacy beliefs" and "group-based emotions" play in the formation of identification with an opinion-based group. Thomas, McGarty, and Mavor (2009) proposed the EMSICA as a theoretical framework explicitly

---

Box 8.3 Applying the EMSICA

Results of a multilevel structural equation model using the EMSICA for modeling
the effects of taking part in 58 opinion-based group interactions on the development of a new identity as an activist supporting governmental implementation of
antipoverty policies in Third World countries (Thomas et al., 2016).

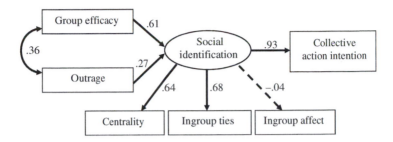

Figure 8.4 Standardized weights obtained for the EMSICA (Thomas et al., 2016). *Note:*
Solid paths were significant in the final model, the dotted path was not; error terms are
not displayed for the sake of clarity. *EMSICA*, encapsulation model of social identity in
collective action.

---

dealing with this question. Like the SIMCA, the EMSICA also recognizes the
pivotal importance of social identification processes in the identity formation.
However, the EMSICA considers a different causal order of the SIMCA constructs (see Fig. 8.4 in Box 8.3): Instead of viewing group identity as a conceptual
and psychological bridge between efficacy and affective reactions like moral outrage, the authors suggest that social identification can mediate the effects of emotions and collective efficacy on collective action intention (Thomas et al., 2009).
One way of understanding the different role the SIMCA and EMSICA ascribe to
the social identity processes is to ask whether the group membership facilitates or
gives rise to the experience of moral outrage and efficacy (as in the SIMCA); or
whether the group membership *encapsulates* it, in the sense that the experiences
of moral outrage and efficacy come to inform who "we" are (as in the EMSICA).
Further, the EMSICA suggests that the emergent group identity can come to capture (and mediate) those two reactions on intention formation, rendering the direct
paths less important in the model.

To clarify the distinct contribution of EMSICA and its potential improvement
over the SIMCA in understanding how a person becomes a collective climate protection activist, consider a situation in which an individual's attention is caught by
the normative conflict elicited by a man-made environmental catastrophe that we
briefly described above. That individual may experience strong moral outrage and
simultaneously believe that collective efforts amongst like-minded people can be

successful in overcoming the current, disastrous policy. Such reactions could plausibly precede and facilitate opinion-based group formation, and social identity is thus formed on the basis of these shared reactions. With regard to the emotion pathway, Stürmer and Simon (2009) developed arguments on the role of group-based anger in transforming identity. Consistent with EMSICA, the authors argue that anger causally precedes social identification (in this case with a social movement) and plays an important role in politicizing the identity toward social action. Similarly, Thomas and McGarty (2009) experimentally manipulated injunctive norms for outrage prior to having participants engage in an identity formation exercise (the opinion-based group interaction method) and showed that the provision of this emotion norm bolstered subsequent identification with the group. The authors argue that the provision of the outrage norm acted to qualitatively shape the emerging group identity. In line with this view then, EMSICA proposes that emotions and efficacy can themselves initiate a shared emergent understanding of "who we are" as group members. The resulting group membership is then rooted in a shared understanding of emotional reactions about the negative consequences of climate change and the belief that it can be overcome through collective efforts (see Thomas et al., 2009, for further discussion of these points).

Box 8.3 reports the results of a study conducted by Thomas, McGarty, & Mavor (2016) testing empirically the applicability of the EMSICA in the context of antipoverty policies in Third World countries. A sample of 234 students participated in 58 opinion-based group interactions discussing practical measures of how to use collective action for increasing pressure on the Australian government to support a UN led antipoverty program. The results support the EMSICA assumption: The newly formed opinion-based group identity indeed mediated the impact of moral outrage and collective efficacy on collective action intentions while all the variables increased as a result of the group discussion.

8.4   Collective climate action as a source of personality development and well-being

Now that we have discussed why social validation helps sympathizers to become activists in the first place, and individuals' psychological motivations to participate in collective action, let us take a closer look at the various outcomes of participation in collective action. What are the effects that participation in collective action may have on participants? There are some obvious disadvantages and frustrating experiences that individuals may encounter on their path to becoming activists; engagement in collective action is a time-consuming enterprise and activists' personal lives may suffer. On the other hand, there are rewarding aspects of being part of a group. Furthermore, there is growing evidence that ongoing participation in collective actions can stimulate a further development of one's personality.

8.4.1   Positive and negative outcomes of being an activist

In an extensive narrative review, Vestergren, Drury, and Chiriac (2016) summarized the *outcomes* for participants after they had taken part in protest and activism. The authors categorized the changes they found in published research articles into two domains, the behavioral or *objective* and the psychological or *subjective* changes. As already suggested, these effects point to both negative and positive personal outcomes for individuals engaging in protest and activism. On the one hand, activists reported negative objective changes, such as a higher rate of divorces, fewer children, and tension affecting personal relationships, which were not part of their activism. These effects might be related, for example, to participants' changes in attitudes toward life or a lack of time caused by the engagement in collective actions. However, on the other hand, activists also described the formation of new and strong social relationships during the collective action. They emphasized positive subjective changes of, e.g., feeling empowered by the participation, increased self-esteem and self-confidence, taking up a new job in the educational, social or creative area, gaining new organizational skills and knowledge.

Participating in collective action in general and in the context of environmental activism more specifically can be a frustrating enterprise. Especially when actions do not succeed as planned, such failures can evoke feelings of frustration and helplessness. Activists need strategies for dealing with frustration to ensure their continued participation, given that fundamental societal change usually needs a long time to unfold and that the process of change is often characterized by setbacks. One obvious psychosocial resource for coping with these negative experiences is the group itself: As part of groups, individuals experience that collective action helps them deal with what might seem like an unsolvable, overwhelming problem at first. To elaborate on this idea of the group as a psychological resource, we briefly review evidence from the London road protests including the mass occupation of a green area (Drury & Reicher, 2005). This campaign in northeast London was part of an active UK-wide antiroads movement. People living in the area were involved and hundreds of people motivated by ecological principles joined the protests. The activists mobilized for a rally at a green area, which should be removed within the construction of the road. On the day of the rally, contractors had erected a fence around the green and it was guarded by security. The rally first took place in front of the fence. After the rally had finished, participants started to climb over the fence, started to push it down, and the crowd entered the site.

8.4.2   Group identity as a resource

In their interviews with participants of the events, Drury and Reicher (2005) found that identifying with a group itself can provide an important basis for joining a risky action. In the case of the above mentioned example of the London road protests, this meant opposing together with other participants a police force that was partly considered violent. The sense of unity and sharing a common "fate" with others made people feel supported and enabled them to act with a shared understanding of practical and moral requirements. During the road protests, people demolished fences to gain access to a tree on the local green they tried to protect. This whole experience provided a form of *collective resilience* for the participants (Drury & Reicher, 2009): The group itself turned out to be a psychosocial resource. The sense of unity with other group members in extreme situations enables people to support each other and to act together where an individual would fail. Accordingly, interviewees reported that the sense of unity and mutual support to reach common goals they experienced during the road protests was meaningful to them personally.

Up to now, we gave examples of how engagement in groups can influence activists' personal lives, we summarized how being part of a larger group, i.e., identifying with a collective identity or participating in a collective action, may influence subjective well-being and the individual's abilities to deal with extreme situations. To fully appreciate the interplay of engagement, personality development, and well-being, however, we need to go one step further and include a temporal dimension into our considerations. Put differently, we should take a closer look at the influence that collective action participation can have on individuals over time. This issue might not be relevant for a singular event like the London road protests, but it is important especially in contexts of continuing protests and action, e.g., on environmental issues. The question here is what changes in people's minds when they participate repeatedly and move from a "collective-action-novice" to a "collective-action-expert." There is still a lot of work to be done before we can give a satisfying answer to this question. Nonetheless, in the following section, we collect first evidence by taking a closer look at why people continue to participate in collective action and what might motivate long-term engagement.

8.4.3   Sticking with effective groups: Empowerment as a result of successful collective action

Earlier in this chapter we argued that groups tend to be more successful in achieving change than single individuals. It makes sense that individuals like sticking with groups that are successful at achieving such change. But what exactly does successful collective action mean for the individual participant?

If a particular collective action is perceived as successful, Drury and Reicher (2005, 2009) postulate that feelings of *empowerment* can be a result. There are various ways of conceptualizing empowerment through collective action, e.g., as a set of beliefs about what we can accomplish as groups in a particular situation, similar to the collective efficacy concept we encountered earlier (e.g., Bandura, 2000), perceptions of collective agency (Simon & Klandermans, 2001) or the positive, self-changing experience of participating and understanding that a group's position of subordination is changeable (Drury, Cocking, & Reicher, 2009; Drury, Evripidou, & van Zomeren, 2015). What these conceptualizations have in common is the notion that participating in collective action leads activists to realize that they can "change the world." What distinguishes them from one another is the assumed quality of the collective experience. Bandura's definition is connected to achieving goals with the group in a particular situation, whereas Simon and Klandermans understand empowerment as the awareness for the collective reasoning and action. In contrast, Drury and Reicher (2009) include in their definition the experience of a *successful* collective action.

To understand the psychological effects of participating in successful collective action, it is worthwhile to explore the encapsulated positive "emotional experience." This emotional experience is evoked by overcoming a powerful adversary, such as the police, together with a group (Drury et al., 2015). Drury and Reicher (2005) argue that the individual's empowerment is facilitated by *collective self-objectification*, the joyful self-transforming process through which participants realize their social identity against the power of dominant outgroups. This process has four key aspects: (1) context change as self-change, (2) novelty, (3) action as realization of legitimate practice, and (4) provisionality/contingency.

First, as described earlier, identity is shaped within the social relational context (context change as self-change). In case of the London road protests, the group of protesters was acting in opposition to the security guards. During the protests, the protesters were able *to take over the power* from the guards, by demolishing the fences and imposing the behavior *they considered legitimate*. An individual's empowered self, is a function of active participation and shaping of social relations.

Second, collective actions which have never taken place before and fundamentally change the status quo of social relations empower more strongly than repeated actions (novelty). In case of the London road protests, this kind of protests had not taken place in this neighborhood before, nor had residents participated.

Third, by acting according to *their* shared understanding, formerly suppressed, or at least less powerful, participants express what they perceive as legitimate actions (action as realization of legitimate practice). In our example, the protesters "overpower" the formerly dominant forces, the security guards. Thereby they demonstrate that the group is a powerful, agentic subject. The fences symbolized the power of the authorities to prevent the protesters' ceremony and hindered the protesters enactment. By demolishing the fences, entering the green, and carrying out the ceremony in the end, the protesters enacted the behavior, which they perceived as legitimate.

Fourth, the formerly dominant group, i.e., security guards, may be able to reassert itself (provisionality/contingency). This entails another shift in power, back to the formerly dominant group, and the previously powerless group's understanding of legitimacy and their identity is suppressed again. The road protesters, for example, were evicted by the police and bailiffs after a month of occupation of the green and tree.

The theoretical work by Drury and Reicher was inspired by their participation in the described collective actions. It remains an open question whether participation in more ordinary, less confrontative forms of collective actions will have similar effects. Furthermore Drury and Reicher's work is based on qualitative ethnographic research. Currently there is little quantitative research to complement their extensive work and to help understand the potentially reciprocal relationship of collective action and empowerment: Does participation in successful collective action merely lead to empowerment? Or does a feeling of empowerment lead to long-term engagement in collective action? Or both? Christens, Peterson, and Speer (2011) conducted a study to test the reciprocal relationship between participation in community-based grassroots organizations and psychological empowerment and found evidence for a causal effect of participation on empowerment but not vice versa.

To summarize, the success or failure of collective action can only be evaluated from a particular social identity's perspective and in a particular context. Put differently, to understand whether a specific collective action is considered a success by the relevant group, it is important whether the group contributed to positive social change with their particular action.

Earlier in this chapter we showed that negative moral emotions like anger and outrage but also guilt and shame contributed significantly to explaining collective action intention. In discussing empowerment, yet another set of emotions turns out to be related to collective action: Positive emotions arise from successful engagement and can stay with the participant even long after the action. Drury and Reicher (2009) see both sets of emotions as interrelated and connected to collective action. On the one hand, the perception of a normative conflict, and the negative emotions it entails, may motivate individuals to become active in the first place (Packer, 2008b; Rees & Bamberg, 2014; Tajfel, 1978). On the other hand, once an individual has begun pursuing the pathway of an activist and been part of successful collective action, positive feelings flowing from the group experience of empowerment can motivate them to stick with the group even during difficult times and in the face of disadvantages because of their engagement (Drury & Reicher, 2009; Vestergren, Drury, & Chiriac, 2016).

8.5   Conclusion: Developing an environmental psychology approach for explaining societal transition processes

We began our chapter with the request that environmental psychology should focus more strongly on the great challenge of our century: How to transform the central sociotechnological systems of our societies toward more sustainability. The chapter's main aim was therefore to offer some first ideas on how to adjust this focus. If we as environmental psychologists really want to have an impact and contribute to understanding and managing societal change, we need to broaden the discipline's theoretical basis. More specifically, one domain environmental psychology has to engage more actively with is the transdisciplinary debate about viable societal transformation strategies.

Such a "political" debate may seem intimidating and not necessarily part of our "daily business" as researchers. As a consequence many environmental psychologists seem to have a rather simplistic understanding of how change occurs on the societal level: Most seem to assume that societal change is more or less the aggregated consequence of individual change. Such a simplistic understanding of the character of societal transition processes is problematic because it restrains environmental psychology's ability to define its place within the transformation debate and to contribute substantially to it. To do so, environmental psychology needs to be familiar with the central theoretical approaches and constructs defining this debate.

Such knowledge could then be helpful for building a bridge between the transdisciplinary transformation debate and academic environmental psychology's theories and concepts. Our own research program partly presented throughout the chapter, for example, is related to the concept of transformation niches introduced by Geels et al. (2015) within the context of his multilevel perspective framework on societal transformation processes. Geels uses the term "niche" for characterizing initiatives aiming at collectively developing and promoting new models of sustainable consumption and production styles at the local level. From the perspective of this framework, a research program on the motives behind participation in collective climate change action as well as the factors responsible for the success or failure of such initiatives would be a useful psychological contribution for further clarifying and developing the niche concept and thus to the development of a transformational strategy.

A second domain where environmental psychology may unleash more of its potential by broadening its theoretical basis relates to the metaperspectives used for studying human behavior. From our point of view, with its focus on humans as individualistic decision makers, environmental psychology is currently neglecting the aspect of human nature most essential for understanding the psychological basis of successful transformation processes: This aspect is our ability as an ultrasocial species to voluntarily cooperate with others for reaching superordinate common goals. Thus an essential and optimistic message from an environmental psychological perspective should be that *we can achieve the great transformation* because evolution has programed us as cooperative creatures. In writing this chapter, it is our conviction that for a better understanding of societal transformation processes, psychological theories about intra- and intergroup processes are of great significance. Above we demonstrated that the social identity approach already provides a sophisticated theoretical framework for analyzing how sympathizers become activists and what kind of psychological motives drive their ongoing engagement in collective climate action. As we see the role of psychology not only in analyzing the processes underlying collective action but also in promoting the successful initiation of group processes leading to collective action, we then outlined the opinion-based group interaction method as a practical intervention derived from this approach. While we focused on the social identity approach throughout the chapter, there are alternative theoretical frameworks such as identity fusion theory (Swann, Jetten, Gómez, Whitehouse, & Bastian, 2012) or a relational perspective (e.g., Van Zomeren, 2016a, 2016b) that future research may find it fruitful to focus on.

A third domain environmental psychology should focus on more is the relationship between actively participating in "changing the world," subjective well-being, and personal development. We are convinced that the necessary transformation of major sociotechnological systems will need decades and be accompanied by many backlashes and frustrations. As reviewed above, there is strong evidence that positive, supportive interaction in a group context can be an important psychosocial resource which enables the development of collective resilience and helps people resist such frustrating experiences. Apart from the frustration buffering effect of positive group interaction there is also growing evidence that participation in collective action can stimulate a general, long lasting positive psychological transformation within activists. Participation in collective action seems to strengthen identification with others and to induce collective empowerment. Feelings of social connectedness, empowerment, and efficacy emerging from the participation in collective action can feed into activists' positive, agentic self-definitions and nurture the conviction that change is possible. In times of large-scale societal transformations and in the face of seemingly overwhelming challenges for humanity as a whole, collective activism for environmental protection and for the common welfare may be a viable option for many. At the end of the day, the idea behind many grassroots movements in the field at the moment is nothing more and nothing less than a new societal idea—a new way of treating the environment, a new way of thinking about consumerism and society, a new utopia.

References

Abrahamse, W., Steg, L., Vlek, C., & Rothengatter, T. (2005). A review of intervention studies aimed at household energy conservation. *Journal of Environmental Psychology*, *25*, 273–291.

Abrams, D., & Hogg, M. A. (1990). Social identification, self categorization and social influence. *European Review of Social Psychology*, *1*, 195–228.

Ajzen, I., & Fishbein, M. (1980). *Understanding attitudes and predicting social behavior.* Englewood Cliffs, NJ: Prentice-Hall.

Allpress, J. A., Barlow, F. K., Brown, R., & Louis, W. R. (2010). Atoning for colonial injustices: Group-based shame and guilt motivate support for reparation. *International Journal of Conflict and Violence*, *4*, 75–88.

Ashforth, B. E., Harrison, S. H., & Corley, K. G. (2008). Identification in organizations: An examination of four fundamental questions. *Journal of Management*, *34*, 325–374.

Bamberg, S., & Möser, G. (2007). Twenty years after Hines, Hungerford, and Tomera: A new meta-analysis of psycho-social determinants of pro-environmental behaviour. *Journal of Environmental Psychology*, *27*, 14–25.

Bamberg, S., Rees, J. H., & Seebauer, S. (2015). Collective climate action: Determinants of participation intention in community-based pro-environmental initiatives. *Journal of Environmental Psychology*, *43*, 155–165.

Bandura, A. (1997). *Self-efficacy: The exercise of control.* New York, NY: Freeman.

Bandura, A. (2000). Exercise of human agency through collective efficacy. *Current Directions in Psychological Science*, *9*, 75–78.

Baron, R. S., Hoppe, S. I., Kao, C. F., Brunsman, B., Linneweh, B., & Rogers, D. (1996). Social corroboration and opinion extremity. *Journal of Experimental Social Psychology*, *32*, 537–560.

Barr, S., & Prillwitz, J. (2014). A smarter choice? Exploring the behaviour change agenda for environmentally sustainable mobility. *Environmental Planning*, *C 32*, 1–19.

Becker, J. C., & Wright, S. C. (2011). Yet another dark side of chivalry: Benevolent sexism undermines and hostile sexism motivates collective action for social change. *Journal of Personality and Social Psychology, 101*, 62–77.

Bliuc, A. M., McGarty, C., Reynolds, K., & Muntele, D. (2007). Opinion-based group membership as a predictor of commitment to political action. *European Journal of Social Psychology, 37*, 19–32.

Böhm, G. (2003). Emotional reactions to environmental risks: Consequentialist versus ethical evaluation. *Journal of Environmental Psychology, 23*, 199–212.

Bongiorno, R., McGarty, C., Kurz, T., Haslam, S. A., & Sibley, C. G. (2016). Mobilizing cause supporters through group-based interaction. *Journal of Applied Social Psychology, 46*, 203–215.

Borden, R. J., & Francis, J. L. (1978). Who cares about ecology? Personality and sex differences in environmental concern. *Journal of Personality, 46*, 190–203.

Christens, B. D., Peterson, N. A., & Speer, P. W. (2011). Community participation and psychological empowerment: Testing reciprocal causality using a cross-lagged panel design and latent constructs. *Health Education & Behavior, 38*, 339–347.

Cialdini, R. B., Reno, R. R., & Kallgren, C. A. (1990). A focus theory of normative conduct: Recycling the concept of norms to reduce littering in public places. *Journal of Personality and Social Psychology, 58*, 1015–1026.

Craig, M. A., & Richeson, J. A. (2012). Coalition or derogation? How perceived discrimination influences intraminority intergroup relations. *Journal of Personality and Social Psychology, 102*, 759–777.

Dixon, J., Levine, M., Reicher, S., & Durrheim, K. (2012). Beyond prejudice: Are negative evaluations the problem and is getting us to like one another more the solution? *Behavioral and Brain Sciences, 35*, 411–425.

Doosje, B., Branscombe, N., Spears, R., & Manstead, A. S. R. (1998). Guilty by association: When one's group has a negative history. *Journal of Personality and Social Psychology, 75*, 872–886.

Drury, J., & Reicher, S. (2005). Explaining enduring empowerment: A comparative study of collective action and psychological outcomes. *European Journal of Social Psychology, 35*, 35–58.

Drury, J., & Reicher, S. (2009). Collective psychological empowerment as a model of social change: Researching crowds and power. *Journal of Social Issues, 65*, 707–725.

Drury, J., Cocking, C., & Reicher, S. (2009). The nature of collective resilience: Survivor reactions to the 2005 London bombings. *International Journal of Mass Emergencies and Disasters, 27*, 66–95.

Drury, J., Evripidou, A., & van Zomeren, M. (2015). Empowerment: The intersection of identity and power in collective action. In D. Sindic, M. Barreto, & R. Costa-Lopes (Eds.), *Power and identity*. London: Psychology Press.

Drury, J., & Stott, C. (Eds.), (2012). *Crowds in the 21st century: Perspectives from contemporary social science*. London: Routledge.

Dubé-Simard, L., & Guimond, S. (1986). Relative deprivation and social protest: The personal-group issue. In J. Olson, C. Herman, & M. Zanna (Eds.), *Relative deprivation and social comparison: The Ontario symposium* (Vol. 4, pp. 201–216). Hillsdale, NJ: Erlbaum.

Dunlap, R. E. (1975). The impact of political orientation on environmental attitudes and actions. *Environment and Behavior, 7*, 428–454.

Fedrigo, D., & Hontelez, J. (2010). Sustainable consumption and production: An agenda beyond sustainable consumer procurement. *Journal of Industrial Ecology, 14*, 10–12.

Ferguson, M. A., & Branscombe, N. R. (2010). Collective guilt mediates the effect of beliefs about global warming on willingness to engage in mitigation behavior. *Journal of Environmental Psychology, 30*, 135−142.

Festinger, L. (1954). A theory of social comparison processes. *Human Relations, 7*, 117−140.

Fielding, K. S., Hornsey, M. J., & Swim, J. K. (2014). Developing a social psychology of climate change. *European Journal of Social Psychology, 44*, 413−420.

Gee, A., & McGarty, C. (2013). Aspirations for a cooperative community and support for mental health advocacy: A shared orientation through opinion-based group membership. *Journal of Applied Social Psychology, 43*(S2), E426−E441.

Geels, F. W., McMeekin, A., Mylan, J., & Southerton, D. (2015). A critical appraisal of sustainable consumption and production research: The reformist, revolutionary and reconfiguration positions. *Global Environmental Change, 34*, 1−12.

Goldstein, N. J., Cialdini, R. B., & Griskevicius, V. (2008). A room with a viewpoint: Using social norms to motivate environmental conservation in hotels. *Journal of Consumer Research, 35*, 472−482.

Harth, N. S., Leach, C. W., & Kessler, T. (2013). Are we responsible? Guilt, anger, and pride about environmental damage and protection. *Journal of Environmental Psychology, 34*, 18−26.

Iyer, A., Schmader, T., & Lickel, B. (2007). Why individuals protest the perceived transgressions of their country: The role of anger, shame and guilt. *Personality and Social Psychology Bulletin, 33*, 572−587.

Jackson, T. (2009). *Prosperity without growth? Economics for a finite planet.* New York, NY: Earthscan.

Kahan, D. (2015). Climate-science communication and the measurement problem. *Advances in Political Psychology, 36*, S1.

Klandermans, B. (1997). *The social psychology of protest.* Oxford: Blackwell.

Le Bon, G. (1895). *The crowd: A study of the popular mind.* London: Ernest Benn, trans. 1947.

McCarthy, J. D., & Zald, M. N. (1977). Resource mobilization and social movements: A partial theory. *American Journal of Sociology, 82*, 1212−1241.

McGarty, C., Bliuc, A.-M., Thomas, E. F., & Bongiorno, R. (2009). Collective action as the material expression of opinion-based group membership. *Journal of Social Issues, 65*, 839−857.

McGarty, C., Lala, G., & Douglas, K. M. (2011). Opinion-based groups: (Racist) talk and (collective) action on the internet. In Z. Birchmeier, B. Dietz-Uhler, & G. Stasser (Eds.), *Strategic uses of social technology: An interactive perspective of social psychology* (pp. 145−171). New York, USA: Cambridge University Press.

McMeekin, A., & Southerton, D. (2012). *Sustainability* transitions and final consumption: Practices and socio-technical systems. *Technology Analysis & Strategic Management, 24*, 345−361.

Mckenzie-Mohr, D. (2000). New ways to promote proenvironmental behavior: Promoting sustainable behavior: An introduction to community-based social marketing. *Journal of Social Issues, 56*(3), 543−554.

Möser, G., & Bamberg, S. (2008). The effectiveness of soft transport policy measures: A critical assessment and meta-analysis of empirical evidence. *Journal of Environmental Psychology, 28*, 10−26.

Mummendey, A., Kessler, T., Klink, A., & Mielke, R. (1999). Strategies to cope with negative social identity: Predictions by social identity theory and relative deprivation theory. *Journal of Personality and Social Psychology, 76*, 229–245.

Ojala, M. (2012). Hope and climate change: The importance of hope for pro-environmental engagement among young people. *Environmental Education Research, 18*, 625–642.

Olson, M. (1965). *The logic of collective action.* Cambridge: Harvard University Press.

Onwezen, M. C., Antonides, G., & Bartels, J. (2013). The norm activation model: An exploration of the functions of anticipated pride and guilt in pro-environmental behaviour. *Journal of Economic Psychology, 39*, 141–153.

Packer, D. J. (2008a). On being both with us and against us: A normative conflict model of dissent in social groups. *Personality and Social Psychology Review, 12*, 50–73.

Packer, D. J. (2008b). On being both with us and against us: A normative conflict model of dissent in social groups. *Personality and Social Psychology Review, 12*, 50–72.

Pfister, H.-R., & Böhm, G. (2001). Decision making in the context of environmental risks. In C. M. Allwood, & M. Selart (Eds.), *Decision making: Social and creative dimensions* (pp. 89–111). Dordrecht: Kluwer Academic Publishers.

Rees, J. H., & Bamberg, S. (2014). Climate protection needs societal change: Determinants of intention to participate in collective climate action. *European Journal of Social Psychology, 44*, 466–473.

Rees, J. H., Klug, S., & Bamberg, S. (2015). Guilty conscience: Motivating pro-environmental behavior by inducing negative moral emotions. *Climatic Change, 130*, 439–452.

Scholl, G., Rubik, F., Kalimo, H., Biedenkopf, K., & Söebech, Ó. (2010). *Policies to promote sustainable consumption: Innovative approaches in Europe, Natural resources forum* (34, pp. 39–50).

Schor, J. (2010). *Plenitude: The new economics of true wealth.* New York, NY: Penguin Press.

Simon, B., & Klandermans, B. (2001). Politicized collective identity. A social psychological analysis. *American Psychologist, 56*, 319–331.

Smith, E. R. (1993). Social identity and social emotions: Toward new conceptualizations of prejudice. In D. M. Mackie, & D. L. Hamilton (Eds.), *Affect, cognition, and stereotyping: Interactive processes in group perception* (pp. 297–315). San Diego, CA: Academic Press.

Smith, E. R., Seger, C. R., & Mackie, D. M. (2007). Can emotions be truly group level? Evidence regarding four conceptual criteria. *Journal of Personality and Social Psychology, 93*, 431–446.

Smith, L. G., Thomas, E. F., & McGarty, C. (2015). "We must be the change we want to see in the world": Integrating norms and identities through social interaction. *Political Psychology, 36*, 543–557.

Smith, L. G. E., & Postmes, T. (2009). Intra-group interaction and the development of norms which promote inter-group hostility. *European Journal of Social Psychology, 39*, 130–144.

Smith, L. G. E., & Postmes, T. (2011a). The power of talk: Developing discriminatory group norms through discussion. *British Journal of Social Psychology, 50*, 193–215.

Smith, L. G. E., & Postmes, T. (2011b). Shaping stereotypical behaviour through the discussion of social stereotypes. *British Journal of Social Psychology, 50*, 74–98.

Smith, L. G. E., Amiot, C. E., Callan, V. J., Terry, D. J., & Smith, J. R. (2012). Getting new staff to stay: The mediating role of organizational identification. *British Journal of Management, 23*, 45–64.

Smith, L. G. E., Amiot, C. E., Smith, J. R., Callan, V. J., & Terry, D. J. (2013). The social validation and coping model of organizational identity development: A longitudinal test. *Journal of Management, 39*, 1952−1978.

Stürmer, S., & Simon, B. (2004). The role of collective identification in social movement participation: A panel study in the context of the German gay movement. *Personality and Social Psychology Bulletin, 30*, 263−277.

Stürmer, S., & Simon, B. (2009). Pathways to collective protest: Calculation, identification, or emotion? A critical analysis of the role of group-based anger in social movement participation. *Journal of Social Issues, 65*, 681−705.

Swann, W. B., Jr., Jetten, J., Gómez, A., Whitehouse, H., & Bastian, B. (2012). When group membership gets personal: A theory of identity fusion. *Psychological Review, 119*(3), 441−456.

Tajfel, H. (1974). Social identity and intergroup behaviour. *Social Science Information, 13*, 65−93.

Tajfel, H. (1978). Interindividual behaviour and intergroup behaviour. In H. Tajfel (Ed.), *Differentiation between social groups: Studies in the social psychology of intergroup relations* (pp. 27−60). London: Academic Press.

Tajfel, H., & Turner, J. C. (1979). An integrative theory of inter-group conflict. In W. G. Austin, & S. Worchel (Eds.), *The social psychology of inter-group relations* (pp. 33−47). Chicago, IL: Nelson-Hall.

Tausch, N., Becker, J. C., Spears, R., Christ, O., Saab, R., Singh, P., & Siddiqui, R. N. (2011). Explaining radical group behavior: Developing emotion and efficacy routes to normative and nonnormative collective action. *Journal of Personality and Social Psychology, 101*, 129−148.

Terry, D. J., & Hogg, M. A. (1996). Group norms and the attitude-behavior relationship: A role for group identification. *Personality and Social Psychology Bulletin, 22*, 776−793.

Thaler, R. H., & Sunstein, C. R. (2008). *Nudge: Improving decisions about health, wealth, and happiness.* New Haven, CT: Yale University Press.

Thomas, E. F., & McGarty, C. A. (2009). The role of efficacy and moral outrage norms in creating the potential for international development activism through group-based interaction. *British Journal of Social Psychology, 48*, 115−134.

Thomas, E. F., McGarty, C., & Mavor, K. I. (2009). Aligning identities, emotions, and beliefs to create commitment to sustainable social and political action. *Personality and Social Psychology Review, 13*, 194−218.

Thomas, E. F., McGarty, C., & Mavor, K. (2016). Group interaction as the crucible of social identity formation: A glimpse at the foundations of social identities for collective action. *Group Processes & Intergroup Relations, 19*, 137−151.

Turner, J. C., Hogg, M. A., Oakes, P. J., Reicher, S. D., & Wetherell, M. S. (1987). *Rediscovering the social group: A self-categorization theory.* Oxford: Blackwell.

Van Zomeren, M. (2016a). *From self to social relationships: An essentially relational perspective on social motivation.* Cambridge, UK: Cambridge University Press.

Van Zomeren, M. (2016b). Synthesizing individualistic and collectivistic perspectives on environmental and collective action through a relational perspective. *Theory & Psychology, 24*, 775−794.

Van Zomeren, M., Postmes, T., & Spears, R. (2008). Toward an integrative social identity model of collective action: A quantitative research synthesis of three socio-psychological perspectives. *Psychological Bulletin, 134*, 504−535.

Van Zomeren, M., Postmes, T., Spears, R., & Bettache, K. (2011). Can moral convictions motivate the advantaged to challenge social inequality? Extending the social identity model of collective action. *Group Processes & Intergroup Relations, 14*, 735−753.

Van Zomeren, M., Saguy, T., & Schellhaas, F. M. H. (2013). Believing in "making a difference" to collective efforts: Participative efficacy as a unique predictor of collective action. *Group Processes & Intergroup Relations, 16*, 618−634.

Vestergren, S., Drury, J., & Chiriac, E. H. (2016). The biographical consequences of protest and activism: a systematic review and a new typology. *Social Movement Studies, 16*, 1−19.

Walker, I., & Smith, H. J. (2002). *).* Relative deprivation: Specification, development, and integration. Cambridge, UK: Cambridge University Press.

Wright, S. C. (2009). The next generation of collective action research. *Journal of Social Issues, 65*, 859−879.

Wright, S. C., & Baray, G. (2012). Models of social change in social psychology: Collective action or prejudice reduction, conflict or harmony. In J. Dixon, & M. Levine (Eds.), *Beyond prejudice: Extending the social psychology of conflict, inequality and social change* (pp. 225−247). Cambridge, UK: Cambridge University Press.

Wright, S. C., Taylor, D. M., & Moghaddam, F. M. (1990). Responding to membership in a disadvantaged group: From acceptance to collective protest. *Journal of Personality and Social Psychology, 58*, 994−1003.

Part III

Wellbeing and Resilience

Threats to mental health and wellbeing associated with climate change

Christie Manning[1] and Susan Clayton[2]
[1]Macalester College, Saint Paul, MN, United States, [2]The College of Wooster, Wooster, OH, United States

9.1 Introduction

Climate change is no longer a distant, unimaginable threat; it is a growing reality for communities across the globe that are already experiencing its effects. Most people are aware of the many weather-system impacts of climate change. These include an increase in average temperature; rise in sea level; changes in patterns of precipitation, including increased intensity of storms in many places; and decreased availability of fresh water in many areas of the world (for a summary of climate change impacts, see the Fifth Assessment Report of the IPCC, 2014). What is less often considered are the subsequent impacts that these climate- and weather-related changes are likely to have on the resources, systems, and services people all over the world rely upon.

Recently, attention has begun to turn to the many ways that climate change will affect human health. A comprehensive review by the US Global Change Research Program emphasizes that *all* Americans will be impacted by the widespread impacts of climate change (USGCRP, 2016), and as global temperatures rise, people worldwide will increasingly be exposed to climate-related public health threats (Watts et al., 2015; Patz, Frumkin, Holloway, Vimont, & Haines, 2014). People will not only face direct health dangers from increasingly severe weather events, heat waves, and flooding due to rising sea levels but also be confronted by less obvious, but more widespread, indirect impacts of climate change such as an increase in diseases carried by pests, lower air quality, food insecurity, and disruptions to supplies of clean water (USGCRP, 2016; Watts et al., 2015).

In addition to impacting physical health, climate change will take a serious toll on mental health and wellbeing. Both the acute impacts of a changing climate, such as extreme storms, as well as the slowly building and chronic impacts, such as increasing drought, will impose significant stress on human beings, not only through immediate threat of death and injury but also from the long-term upheaval and uncertainty they will bring. For some proportion of individuals, their ability to cope with these changes may become overwhelmed, resulting in short-term or long-term stress, anxiety, substance abuse, depression, posttraumatic stress disorder (PTSD), and, in some cases, even suicide. Other effects will be manifest at the level

Psychology and Climate Change. DOI: https://doi.org/10.1016/B978-0-12-813130-5.00009-6

of the community or the society, and may be represented not by obvious harms, but by a failure to achieve the quality of life that might have been attained in the absence of climate change.

This review describes the human health and wellbeing risks and impacts of global climate change, with a focus on mental health. We take a broad view of wellbeing, for health is more than simply the avoidance of disease and injury. Mindful of the interdependence between physical and mental health and the ways in which both can be affected by the social context, we include discussion of those indirect impacts of climate change that will affect interpersonal relationships, communities, and overall quality of life. To begin, we briefly review the physical health impacts discussed in the medical and public health literatures. We then turn attention to the mental health effects of climate change from both acute and chronic impacts and describe how certain vulnerable groups will be disproportionately affected. Finally, we discuss some of the lifestyle changes that are likely to come with a changing climate. The chapter will end with a brief discussion of the health co-benefits associated with taking action to mitigate climate change.

9.2   Physical health effects of climate change

The physical health threats of climate change will come through both direct and indirect pathways. Direct impacts are most easily identifiable in the case of extreme weather events. Extreme storms or flash floods may have high mortality rates, especially in communities that are unprepared. During extreme storms, there is an increased likelihood of acute physical trauma, such as being struck by debris or by building collapse (Alderman, Turner, & Tong, 2012), as well as an increase in traffic accidents (Leard & Roth, 2016). Drownings are likely during flash floods. The danger continues even after the flood or storm is over; acute events are generally followed by a cascade of other potentially significant impacts. For example, people may sustain nonfatal injuries such as cuts or broken bones or experience respiratory problems due to the growth of indoor mold. Floodwaters also bring the potential for indirect hazards, such as toxic materials from damaged industrial facilities or waterborne diseases (e.g., skin infections, gastrointestinal disease when hygiene resources are unavailable). In addition, disasters such as extreme storms or floods may lead to infrastructure failures, for example, power outages, breakdown in water, sewer, and other systems, or urban fires. Disruptions in emergency services or in local healthcare systems may lead minor issues to escalate into major problems. Left unaddressed, major problems may become fatal problems. Disruptions in other types of services (e.g., cell phone communication or garbage and recycling services) create difficulty during the aftermath of an acute event and may affect physical health by making it impossible to access health care (without a phone) or by potentially increasing exposure to pests or hazardous substances (e.g., when there is no garbage pickup). At least one analysis found that survivors of Hurricane Katrina faced lingering challenges such as these even a full 5 years after the disaster (Hatch, Cherry, Kytola, Lu, & Marks, 2015).

A global rise in temperatures will also have direct effects on human health and mortality. In fact, more people die due to extreme heat than due to any other type of weather event in the United States (Portier et al., 2010). A recent analysis suggests that by the end of the century, at least 48%, and perhaps as high as 74%, of the world's population will experience more than 20 days a year of "lethal" heat conditions compared to 30% today (Mora et al., 2017). Prolonged heat exposure is particularly hard on people with preexisting health problems as it can worsen cardiovascular, respiratory, and cerebrovascular diseases like diabetes and asthma (Portier et al. 2010).

Increased temperatures also contribute to some of the most profound *indirect* impacts on human health, such as respiratory troubles from exposure to increased ground-level ozone; asthma from rising pollen levels and higher particulate air pollution; and increased water-related illnesses caused by algal blooms, bacteria, or contaminated water, all predicted to increase due to climate change (USGCRP, 2016). Allergy season is likely to be more severe in many places due to a higher pollen count (Seeley, 2012), and climate change is also expected to increase the spread and toxicity of poison ivy (Mohan et al., 2006). Higher temperatures allow pathogen-carrying pests such as ticks, mosquitoes, and fleas—including the ticks carrying Lyme disease or the mosquitos carrying the West Nile virus—to expand their traditional range, exposing more people to the disease (USGCRP, 2016).

9.3 Mental health impacts from acute climate-related events

Physical and mental health are interdependent. Not only do extreme storms and other sudden weather events have a high potential to harm physical health, they may also cause immediate and severe psychological trauma. Trauma can stem from personal injury, injury or death of a loved one, damage to or loss of personal property (e.g., home) and pets, and disruption in work or livelihood (Neria & Schultz, 2012; Simpson, Weissbecker, & Sephton, 2011; Terpstra, 2011). The initial response to a disaster is usually characterized by emotions such as terror, anger, and shock (Raphael, 2007). In one study of people who had experienced a significant flood, people used words such as "horrifying," "panic stricken," and "petrified" to describe what it was like to live through the flood (Carroll, Morbey, Balogh, and Araoz, 2009 pg. 542; see also Tapsell & Tunstall, 2008).

According to a much-cited metaanalysis, some form of psychopathology was observed in between 7% and 40% of people who had experienced natural disasters (Rubonis & Bickman, 1991). Though general anxiety was most common, many other mental health problems were observed; phobic responses, somatic responses, substance abuse, and depression were all higher among disaster survivors compared to people in the general population, and rates were highest when measured directly after the disaster (Rubonis & Bickman, 1991). More recent studies and reviews find that acute traumatic stress, which is similar to PTSD but with shorter duration, is the most prevalent mental health problem immediately after a disaster, though anxiety, depression, and drug and alcohol abuse are also common (Fritze, Blashki, Burke, & Wiseman, 2008). Furthermore, in the aftermath of disasters, people are more prone to many behaviors that have a negative impact on their overall health and wellbeing such as smoking, risk-taking, and unhealthy eating habits (e.g., Beaudoin, 2011; Bryant et al., 2014; Flory, Hankin, Kloos, Cheely, & Turecki, 2009).

For most people, trauma symptoms decrease significantly after calm has been restored. However, many continue to experience some form of psychological difficulty for a significant time period after the acute event. A sense of troubling uncertainty can linger well after the initial disaster, and this adds an additional emotional stress burden (Lyon, Nezat, Cherry, & Marks, 2015). More significantly, PTSD, depression, general anxiety, and suicide can persist at higher levels even many months or years after a disaster. For example, within 5−7 months after Hurricane Katrina, approximately 15% of those directly impacted by the hurricane developed PTSD, and 49% of people living in affected areas developed an anxiety or mood disorder such as depression, even if they themselves had not been directly impacted (Galea et al., 2007; Kessler et al., 2008). According to Kessler et al., this compares to an expected PTSD prevalence of 1.4% among people with no hurricane-related stress. (Overall, approximately 27% of Americans suffer from an anxiety or mood disorder in a given year, and 3.5% suffer from PTSD, according to the National Institutes of Mental Health; this includes people who are experiencing other sources of stress. https://www.nimh.nih.gov/health/statistics/prevalence/index.shtml.) A year after the hurricane, anxiety disorders had not decreased, and PTSD and suicidal thoughts actually increased (Kessler et al, 2008). Similar mental health outcomes were found in communities that experienced Hurricane Sandy: 14.5% showed symptoms of PTSD 6 months later (Boscarino, Hoffman, Adams, Figley, & Solhkhah, 2014). A metaanalysis of studies examining the impacts of floods also found a clear increase in PTSD in flood-affected areas. Across the studies examined, higher reported levels of PTSD were linked to greater flood exposure (Fernandez, et al., 2015). Forest fires and bush fires, which are projected to rise due to the increase in dry conditions associated with climate change, have also been found to carry long-term psychological impacts. In one study of bushfire-impacted areas, 15.6% of a particularly hard-hit community showed symptoms of PTSD as many as several years after extreme bush fires (Bryant et al., 2014). As if the burden of PTSD were not enough, the disorder has been found to increase the likelihood of substance abuse, depression and anxiety, violence and aggression, interpersonal difficulties, and job-related difficulties (Simpson et al., 2011).

Many factors influence the likelihood that an individual exposed to trauma will later develop PTSD, such as that individual's trauma history and the type of disaster they have experienced. As the studies described above indicate, PTSD is more prevalent in areas hardest hit by acute events. PTSD is also more likely among individuals who have experienced the kinds of losses that can never be recovered, such as the loss of close family members or significant property loss (Gerhart, Canetti, & Hobfoll, 2015; Wasini, West, Mills, & Usher, 2014). Furthermore, those who experience multiple acute events—for example, more than one disaster, or multiple years of drought—tend to show greater levels of psychological trauma and appear to be even more susceptible to PTSD (e.g., Edwards & Wiseman, 2011; Hobfoll, 2007). The impact of multiple acute events is particularly problematic if the disasters occur rapidly enough that there is little time to recover between. One study of refugees exposed to multiple acute events (e.g., more than one natural disaster, along with loss of loved one or other personal trauma) showed an increase in both immediate and long-term PTSD and lower probability of remission than refugees who had experienced few traumatic events (Kolassa et al., 2010). Suicide, which is often linked to PTSD, has also been found to be a greater risk for those who have experienced multiple severe disasters (Norris, Friedman, & Watson, 2002).

Individual circumstances also influence long-term rates of distress and anxiety. Many, perhaps even most, disaster survivors experience worry about future disasters, feelings of vulnerability, helplessness, mourning, grief, and despair (Neria & Schultz, 2012). For some, these concerns may be heightened by economic losses from missed workdays, use of medical services, recovery from injury, or other disaster-related exposure. Individuals who have greater resources to draw upon generally fare better in the long-term than those with less (Hobfoll, Stevens, & Zalta, 2015) In addition, personal emotional response can amplify stress. A study of Australian residents impacted by bush fires suggests that feelings of anger, directed both at the unfairness of the disaster itself as well as at authorities responsible for inadequate recovery programs, increased negative mental health outcomes, particularly for men (Forbes et al., 2015). Finally, it appears to be those most rooted in their communities who experience more pronounced psychological distress as a result of disaster-related changes to the landscape and community (Lyon et al., 2015; also see Lee and Blanchard, 2012). Specifically, strong attachments to, and identification with, one's home and community increases the pain of seeing them irrevocably changed. Both during and after a natural disaster, the local environment can change abruptly. This, as found in a study of tornado survivors, may lead to high levels of emotional pain and disorientation, even for those who have not experienced other personal loss from the disaster (Silver & Grek-Martin, 2015). Furthermore, the sense of one's home as a safe and secure environment may be devastated by an acute event (Tapsell & Tunstall, 2008), increasing the long-term emotional stress burden.

9.4 Mental health impacts from chronic climate changes

Most accounts of climate change focus upon the tangible and acute events associated with it—heat waves, coastal flooding, extreme storms, or the sudden collapse of an ice shelf—and often overlook its chronic, slowly building impacts. Although it is critical to understand the dangers of clear and identifiable acute events, an exclusive focus on them occludes the more gradual and less dramatic impacts of climate change that ultimately will affect a much larger number of people on a daily basis. The chronic effects of a changing climate not only tend to be slow-growing and often diffuse but also widespread and persistent. For example, plants and animals are gradually disappearing from areas they have inhabited for thousands of years, and the timing of events such as animal migrations and plant flowerings are shifting (Root et al., 2003). The destruction caused by chronic climate change impacts may initially seem insignificant, but, as time passes, the cumulative effects have the potential to be destructive to both ecological systems and human communities.

Some of the specific threats posed by gradual changes in climate are increased temperatures, drought, migration, and more abstract changes associated with loss and worry. Climate change is likely to bring other changes as well, such as repeated minor ("nuisance") flooding or changing patterns of recreation, whose impacts on wellbeing are mostly still unknown (e.g., Dahl, Fitzpatrick, & Spanger-Siegried, 2017; Upton, 2017).

9.4.1 High temperatures

One of the major long-term, chronic impacts of climate change is increased temperatures. It has been estimated that the average American citizen will experience between 4 and 8 times as many days above 95°F each year as they do now by the end of the century (Houser, Hsiang, Kopp, & Larsen, 2015). Higher temperatures have been shown to increase levels of suicide, a form of violence against the self (Preti, Lentini, & Maugeri, 2007; Williams, Hill, and Spicer, 2016). Ranson (2012) calculates that between 2010 and 2099, climate change will cause an estimated additional 30,000 murders, 200,000 cases of rape, and 3.2 million burglaries in large part due to increased average temperatures.

Higher temperatures have many other, less visible impacts. For example, they may lead to a decrease in school performance among children and teens (Bartlett, 2008; Park, 2017). Furthermore, some evidence shows that increases in mean temperature are associated with greater use of emergency mental health services. For example, one study, conducted in Australia, found a 7% increase in psychiatric hospital admissions during a heat wave (Hansen et al., 2008).

These effects are found not only in hot countries like Israel, Australia, and parts of the United States but also in relatively cooler countries such as France and Canada (Basu, Gavin, Pearson, Ebisu, & Malig, 2017; Vida, Durocher, Ouarda, & Gosselin, 2012). Higher temperatures appear to put an additional source of stress on people that can overwhelm their coping ability, particularly for those who are already psychologically fragile. This may be worsened if people reduce some stress-relieving activities, such as outdoor recreation or exercise, in extremely hot weather (Böcker, Dijst, & Prillwitz, 2013), which in turn may undermine physical health.

9.4.2 Drought

The changing patterns of precipitation due to climate change mean longer periods of drought. Unlike the acute disasters of climate change, drought occurs slowly and over time. It can last weeks, months, or even multiple years. Drought is a contributing factor to global food insecurity and hunger, and this link is strongest in areas already vulnerable to food shortages and volatile prices. In some parts of the world, the combination of higher temperatures and changing rainfall patterns will cause an increase in food production; however, overall the impact of climate change on food security is projected to be negative. A recent analysis found a direct and consistent relationship between food insecurity and mental health: As access to food decreased, mental health difficulties increased (Jones, 2017). A 2°C increase in temperature would place millions of people at risk of hunger (Friel, Butler, & McMichael, 2011; McMichael, 2013; Whiting, 2016), impacting not only their physical heath but their mental and emotional wellbeing as well.

Several studies have confirmed that even without the threat of food insecurity, the experience of drought creates a significant stress burden through, for example, financial loss or having to watch people, plants, and animals suffer (O'Brien, Berry, Coleman, & Hanigan, 2014; Stanke, Kerac, Prudhomme, Medlock, & Murray, 2013). One outcome of exposure to drought lasting many years is emotional distress, which one study found was worse in rural areas where people's livelihoods were connected to the land (O'Brien, et al., 2014). During prolonged drought, suicide rates among farmers has been shown to increase (Hanigan, Butler, Kokicc, & Hutchinson, 2012). In addition, the chronic distress experienced by those living through long-term drought results in a lowered immune system response and leaves people more vulnerable to many physical ailments (Alderman et al., 2012; Simpson et al., 2011).

A study conducted in Australia after 7 years of drought (called "the big dry") found that the distress of drought was worsened by interactions with other drought-related stressors, such as difficult economic circumstances, and lower availability and higher prices of healthy foods. Distress was highest among those who had been forced to miss meals, but others, most notably rural residents, felt added distress because drought and economic circumstances led them to eat cheaper but lower quality foods (Friel, Berry, Dinh, O'Brien, & Walls, 2014).

9.4.3 Migration

One of the most significant ways in which climate change is anticipated to affect human wellbeing is by increasing migration. People are more likely to be displaced by natural disasters than by conflict, and displacement due to environmental conditions is on the rise (Wolsko & Marino, 2016). When people lose their home to rising sea levels, or when drought or increased heat make an area unable to support food crops or unsuitable for human habitation, the inhabitants are forced to find a new place to live. Scholars refer to environmentally driven displacements as "eco-migration" and those who migrate as "environmental refugees" (e.g., Myers, 1993;

Reuveny, 2008). While it may be difficult to identify climate change as the causal factor in a complex sequence of events affecting ecomigration, it has been estimated that climate change will lead to the displacement of as many as 200 million people (approximately the population of Brazil) by 2050 (Fritze et al., 2008). One recent analysis suggests that a projected sea-level rise of 1.8 m (by year 2100) means that 56% of US counties will be in some way impacted by ecomigration: Coastal areas will see movement of residents inland as homes are abandoned in inundated coastal areas, and inland counties will see an influx of migrants escaping sea-level rise (Hauer, 2017), straining resources and social relationships.

The act of migration creates enormous health and wellbeing risks for the individuals involved. In the first place, having to migrate is a stressful event. It is generally not a positive choice but a decision made under duress and due to intolerable living conditions (Ingleby, 2004). Second, during the process of relocation, migrants frequently bear a multitude of discomforts, both physical (e.g., lack of regular meals or a bed to sleep in) and emotional (e.g., uncertainty, lack of power, fear) as well as real physical dangers. The status of being an immigrant imposes an additional stress burden; immigrants are generally at high risk of developing mental health problems (Pumariega, Rothe, & Pumariega, 2005). A 2016 report from Germany suggested that up to 50% of arriving migrants were suffering from PTSD, and about the same number experienced severe depression (Bailey, 2016). While it is important to note that these rates may be unusually high because of the complex geopolitical dimensions of the 2016 refugee crisis, they suggest the level of psychological impact that is possible for many migrants. A rare but dramatic illustration of the mental health problems associated with migration can be seen in the case of Swedish victims of what has been called "resignation syndrome" (Sallin et al., 2016). Sufferers of this not yet clinically confirmed syndrome, all children and adolescent refugees, stop responding to external stimuli and must be fed through a tube. Remission appears to be linked to obtaining a permanent residency permit, though obtaining the permit is neither always necessary nor always sufficient (Sallin et al., 2016).

Even under more positive circumstances, immigrants are more likely than non-immigrants to develop mental health problems. This is attributable not only to the accumulated stressors associated with their move to a new and unknown country and culture but also to the condition of being in "exile" (Hauff & Vaglum, 1995; Miller, Worthington, Muzurovic, Tipping, & Goldman, 2002). Acclimating to a new place, learning a new language, rebuilding a social community, and redefining one's identity are all emotionally difficult and stressful. Migration also breaks apart people's social networks, as communities disperse in different directions. Because social networks provide important practical and emotional resources and are strongly associated with health and wellbeing, the loss of such networks places migrants at greater risk for mental health impacts. In addition, migrants most often live in or near poverty level, at least initially, a condition which strongly and negatively influences wellbeing (Fox & Chancey, 1998).

Those who must migrate face one further mental health vulnerability: a disruption in their attachment to place. It is common for people to form a strong attachment to their homes and the local area around them; this connection provides a sense of stability, security, and self-definition, and people with a strong place attachment report greater happiness, life satisfaction, and optimism (Brehm, Eisenhauer, & Krannich, 2004). Place attachment also plays an important role in personal identity (e.g., Scannell & Gifford, 2016). Because of these important psychological benefits of place attachment, migration and other forms of displacement may leave people literally alienated, with a diminished sense of self and increased vulnerability to stress. Although empirical research on the psychological impacts of migration is rare, based on studies from multiple countries, Adger, Barnett, Brown, Marshall, and O'Brien (2013) conclude that being forced to leave one's home territory can threaten both a sense of continuity as well as a sense of belonging. Tschakert, Tutu, and Alcaro (2013) studied the emotional experience among residents of Ghana who were forced to move from the northern part of the country to the capital, Accra, because local conditions no longer supported their farming practices. All interviewees expressed some nostalgia and sadness for the home left behind. Respondents also frequently described the deforestation of their communities as sad and scary and said the changes to their environments had made them feel helpless. Based on studies from multiple countries, Adger et al. (2013) conclude that being forced to leave one's home territory can threaten both a sense of continuity as well as a sense of belonging.

9.4.4 Loss

The chronic impacts of climate change include some that are less tangible, yet still significant to people's overall wellbeing. Many of these intangible impacts can be characterized by the word "loss." For example, climate change is irrevocably changing the landscapes where people live, and large numbers are likely to experience a feeling that they are losing a place that is important to them. People may notice, and be concerned by, unusually early spring weather, for example, bringing animals out of hibernation early and causing plants to bloom before local pollinators have arrived. They may sense that things in the natural world around them have shifted and become uneasy. Albrecht (2011) calls these feelings and concerns "solastalgia": "the lived experience of negatively perceived change to a home environment" (pg. 50). This psychological phenomenon is often characterized by feelings of loss similar to those experienced by people who have been forced to leave their home environment. In the case of climate change, solastalgia may be gradual as the changes are still slowly accumulating; however, some disruption in people's place attachment is likely to be felt as the landscape changes, which may negatively affect work performance, interpersonal relationships, and physical health (Fullilove, 2013).

An individual's personal identity, the way one sees and understands oneself, is also often tightly connected to place-based occupations like farming and fishing (Devine-Wright, 2013), and thus, when these occupations are threatened due to climatic changes, it may create a crisis of identity. Loss of identity has already been observed in farmers in Australia suffering from drought (Ellis & Albrecht, 2017;

Stain et al., 2008). This kind of loss of occupation has been associated with increased risk of depression following natural disasters (Wasini et al., 2014). Personal identity may also be affected by the loss of treasured objects because of migration or other climate change impacts. Possessions provide a continuing sense of self-definition, especially those objects that represent important moments in life (e.g., journals), relationships (e.g., gifts or photographs), or personal/family history (e.g., family heirlooms) (Dittmar, 2011).

These losses, of place, identity, and of a way of life, are examples of ambiguous loss. Ambiguous loss may not be evident to an outsider and is more difficult for the person experiencing it to explain or understand compared to concrete and easily identifiable losses (Boss, 2016). Ambiguous loss is often accompanied by feelings of helplessness and hopelessness, as well as anxiety and immobilization (Boss, 2016).

9.4.5 Worry and loss of control

As climate change becomes an increasingly pervasive theme in local and world news, qualitative research suggests that people experience feelings of frustration, powerlessness, fear, anger, and exhaustion (Moser, 2007, 2013). Albrecht (2011) has termed worries such as these "ecoanxiety" and contends that they are on the rise worldwide. Due to a lack of agreement on clinical definition and measurement, it is difficult to assess how prevalent ecoanxiety may be, who is affected by it, and whether it is indeed increasing. A recent representative survey in four European countries (France, Germany, Norway, and the United Kingdom; Steentjes et al., 2017) found between 20% (United Kingdom) and 41% (France) of respondents describing themselves as "very or extremely worried about climate change." In a nonrandom sample of 132 online participants in the United States and Europe, most of whom were university students, over 90% said they had some worries about the environment, and 15% said they worried "all the time." Importantly, level of worry was not correlated with a general tendency toward dysfunctional worry; in other words, habitual worry about the environment did not reflect individual pathology (Verplanken & Roy, 2013). Worries about the future, and concern for the destructive impacts of climate change on today's children and future generations, are certainly a source of stress (Searle & Gow, 2010), and while these feelings may be tolerable by someone with many sources of support, they may also be a tipping point for those who have fewer resources or who are already experiencing other stressors. For example, one study of obsessive—compulsive disorder (OCD) sufferers (with the OCD checking subtype) found that 28% of the sampled patient population reported climate change concerns as a motivation for their compulsions (Jones, Wootton, Vaccaro, & Menzies, 2012).

The chronic impacts of climate change will bring about noticeable changes in the environments where people live, work, and recreate, through, for example, altered weather patterns and changes in the plant and animal species that thrive in a particular location. Exposure to unwanted change in one's environment such as these likely reduces an individual's sense of control over his or her life

(Fresque-Baxter & Armitage, 2012; Silver & Grek-Martin, 2015). This in turn has other psychosocial effects such as increases in substance abuse, anxiety disorders, and rates of depression; climate change appears to be an emerging contributor to stress-related problems such as these (Neria & Schultz, 2012).

9.5 Impacts of climate change on social relationships

The possible impacts of both acute and chronic aspects of climate change on social relationships are underresearched and not well understood, but likely to be significant. Natural disasters, for example, have the potential to impair critical connections to family members. When homes are severely damaged or destroyed by a flood, storm, or wildfire, families often need to be relocated, sometimes multiple times, before being reunited and settling permanently. The stress experienced through relocation is immense (Ursano, McCaughey, & Fullerton, 1995), and, because a person's home provides an important context for social relationships (Carroll et al., 2009), the loss of a home may have significant negative influence on a family's social dynamics. Indeed, researchers have documented higher rates of domestic abuse, including child abuse, among families who have experienced disasters (Fritze et al., 2008; Harville, Taylor, Tesfai, Xiong, & Buekens, 2011; Keenan, Marshall, Nocera, & Runyan, 2004; Yun, Lurie, & Hyde, 2010).

Postdisaster stressors appear to have a negative impact on less intimate social relationships and interactions as well (friends, coworkers, etc.; e.g., Palinkas, Downs, Petterson, & Russell, 1993; Simpson et al., 2011), perhaps in part because heightened anxiety and uncertainty about one's own future can reduce the ability to focus on others. In addition, extreme weather events, which tend to hit an entire community, weaken the very social support networks that normally provide help to people when they are most in need (Aldrich & Meyer, 2014). For example, after Hurricane Katrina, the areas hardest hit were also the most likely to have lost the physical gathering place of the community, such as a community church, which had served as the center of social networking and support (Cherry, Marks, Adamek, & Lyon, 2015). This made it more difficult for the community to come to each other's aid during the difficult disaster aftermath.

With respect to the chronic impacts of climate change, one of the social consequences most frequently mentioned is the potential for increased violence. The psychological impacts of warmer weather are fairly well understood based on decades of research on this topic. One paper synthesized the results of 60 quantitative studies examining the link between climate conditions and various types of violence, for example, domestic crime, murder, rape. This metaanalysis included both lab-based experiments and quasiexperiments in the field and found a causal relationship between heat and aggression: As the temperature goes up, so does interpersonal aggression (Hsiang, Burke, & Miguel, 2013) This has led researchers to predict that the increased average temperatures associated with climate change will cause a significant uptick in violence (Anderson, 2012), including violent crime, rape, and intergroup conflict (Carleton & Hsiang, 2016; Hsiang et al., 2013). In several recent analyses, Carleton and Hsiang (2016) and Hsiang et al. (2013) also found evidence that rising temperatures increased the frequency of interpersonal violence. Other researchers have presented both correlational and experimental data demonstrating that increased heat leads to a decrease in helping behavior (Belkin & Kouchaki, 2017).

Several other mechanisms in addition to heat and extreme rainfall contribute to a predicted rise in interpersonal conflict. First, violence and aggression may increase when competition for scarce natural resources increases, or when ecomigration brings formerly separate communities into contact and compete for resources like jobs and land. Second, as communities disperse and their social networks become disrupted, the restraints on crime that exist in dense and well-established social networks are no longer present, leading to higher probability of criminal behavior. This is worsened when government resources are diverted away from criminal justice systems, mental health agencies, and educational institutions, all of which tend to help mitigate crime (Agnew, 2012). Finally, climate change appears likely to increase economic pressures and uncertainty through, for example, labor productivity losses from heat stress; high demand for electricity that strains the electrical grid, particularly on hot days; lower agricultural yields from both high temperatures and extreme rainfall events; and fluctuations in local economic activity and demand as climate conditions change (Carleton & Hsiang, 2016). These unpredictable economic effects will likely raise the general level of frustration in society and consequently aggravate interpersonal aggression.

Recent research suggests that climate change not only leads to greater interpersonal conflict but it also exacerbates the potential for larger scale intergroup violence (e.g., Carleton & Hsiang, 2016; Hsiang et al., 2013), through, for example, economic hardship or intergroup competition for scarce resources. Indeed, the Department of Defense and the UN Security Council, among others, have recognized climate change as a "threat multiplier," increasing the likelihood of intergroup conflict and for that reason threatening our national security. In addition to showing a link between climate changes such as rising temperatures and extreme rainfall, on the one hand, and interpersonal violence on the other, Hsiang et al. (2013) also found an association with intergroup conflict such as minority expulsion, civil conflict, political unrest, and social collapse. Climate change is likely to exacerbate many of the factors that inhibit community members from working together across social group boundaries, such as decreased social cohesion and connectedness and lack of trust between community members and for institutions (Norris, Stevens, Pfefferbaum, Wyche, & Pfefferbaum, 2008). For example, one study found that people who were thinking about climate change became more hostile to individuals outside of their social group (Fritsche, Cohrs, Kessler, & Bauer, 2012), which can be a precipitating factor for larger scale conflict.

9.6   Vulnerable populations

As Gifford and Gifford (2016) and others have stated, climate change is an issue of social justice. Although everyone will be affected by climate change, and the effects on everyone are of concern, it is important to recognize the disparities in the ways that effects are experienced. These disparities will tend to increase the overall level of inequity in society, increasing intergroup tensions and resentment. At greatest risk are those who have fewer economic or social resources to support them—individuals from poor and minority communities; those whose exposure is greater, such as first responders; and those who are for one reason or another are more susceptible. The elderly, for example, are often at greater threat from the physical effects of climate change, such as heat; research also suggests that they are more likely to develop mental health problems following natural disasters (Parker et al., 2016). People who are already suffering from mental illness are also more susceptible, due to the possibility that their treatment will be disrupted as well as to the fact that some psychoactive medicines induce a stronger physiological response to heat (Page, Hajat, Kovats, & Howard, 2012). Some communities will be more strongly affected by climate change by virtue of their geographical location. A thorough review of demographic differences in vulnerability to climate change can be found in Dodgen, Donato, and Kelly (2016).

At the community level, demographic factors linked to high sensitivity to climate impacts include high levels of poverty, lower education levels, and large populations of elderly, children and infants, disabled people, and recently arrived immigrants, migrants, or refugees, all of whom tend to require greater access to services that climate change impacts can put at risk (Weissbecker & Czinez, 2011). People in these groups tend to have fewer physical and emotional resources, and this in turn weakens the community's ability to respond to all its members' needs. Areas with high number of residents lacking access to health care or health insurance, or already experiencing poor health (Edwards & Wiseman, 2011), are especially likely to be negatively affected by climate change. Communities in which people's livelihoods are directly tied to the natural environment, through agriculture, fishing, or tourism, are also at greater risk, and there are detailed reports of farmers in Australia who have been negatively affected by prolonged periods of drought (e.g., Alston, 2012; Hanigan, et al., 2012).

Some groups of particular concern because of their higher vulnerability to the many negative effects of climate change include women, children, low-income and racial minority groups, and indigenous communities.

9.6.1 Women

On average, women are likely to be more affected by climate change compared to men. A 2009 United Nations report (United Nations Population Fund, 2009) cites them as particularly vulnerable for several reasons. In developing countries women are often overrepresented among agricultural workers, leading to more direct exposure to the climate. Because of their caregiver role, women may also be more affected in general by the stress and trauma of natural disasters, particularly when pregnant or postpartum, due to the physiological and psychological stress of physically supporting a child (e.g., during pregnancy, or while nursing) as well as the responsibility to look after it. Even apparently unrelated aspects of gender roles, such as the clothing they are expected to wear and restrictions on their public role, can lead women to be more strongly affected by natural disasters (Trumbo, Lueck, Marlatt, & Peek, 2011; Wasini et al., 2014; World Health Organization, 2014).

Their lack of social and economic power means that women tend to have fewer economic resources than men on average, making it harder to cope with negative changes and events. In countries with pronounced gender disparities, girls may receive a smaller share of compensatory aid following disasters than boys do, leading to lasting impacts on their developmental trajectory. Datar, Liu, Linnemayr, and Stecher (2013) reviewed data on over 80,000 children and concluded that natural disasters had a greater stunting effect on the growth of girls than on boys in rural India. Other research has shown that women are more likely than men to die after natural disasters in countries with high levels of gender inequality, but not in societies with greater gender equality (Neumayer & Plümper, 2007).

9.6.2   Children

The impact of climate change on children is of particular concern. One reason is that children are more vulnerable to many of the effects due to their small size, developing organs and nervous systems, and rapid metabolisms (Bartlett, 2008). Children are more sensitive to temperature, both because their physiological regulatory systems may be less effective (e.g., they sweat less) and because they are more likely to depend on others to help them regulate their behavior (Zivin & Shrader, 2016). Their small size makes very young children more susceptible to dehydration, and children under 5 represent 80% of victims of sanitation-related illnesses and diarrheal disease (Bartlett, 2008).

The impacts on children are also of significant concern because of the potential for long-term and even irreversible effects, changing the developmental potential and trajectory of the child. Currie and Almond (2011) review evidence that even minor disturbances during childhood may have effects on health and earning potential that last into adulthood. Fetuses are vulnerable to heat waves. Research in the United States showed that exposure to heat waves, especially during the second and third trimesters of pregnancy, leads to a lower average birth weight and possible a greater incidence of preterm birth (Kousky, 2016). Studies have shown that children who experience a flood or a drought during key developmental periods are shorter, on average, as adults (Bartlett, 2008). Malnourishment or severe threat to health during the early years is associated with fewer years of schooling and reduced economic activity as adults, as well as with behavioral and motor problems and reduced IQ (Kousky, 2016).

There are multiple pathways for climate change's impact on children's mental health. Like adults, children can experience PTSD and depression following traumatic or stressful experiences; in fact, some evidence suggests that they are more strongly affected (Fritze et al., 2008). A study of youth who lived through both Hurricane Katrina and Hurricane Gustav found that higher storm trauma exposure was linked to worse long-term outcomes, such as PTSD and depression, even 3 years later (Weems & Banks; 2015).

Children's mental health can also be affected not only just by their experiences of stressors such as natural disasters, extreme weather, and ecomigration but also by the mental health of their caregivers (Simpson et al., 2011) or by disruptions in family life or school (Weems & Banks, 2015). Secondary stressors, such as family illness or financial stress, also appear to be more problematic for youth and may exacerbate risk of poorer mental health outcomes (Weems & Banks, 2015). They also have the potential to be emotionally affected if they become separated from their primary caregivers. And like physical experiences, traumatic mental experiences can have lifelong effects. Of course, early childhood is critical for brain development. Studies have documented that high levels of stress during childhood can affect the development of neural pathways in ways that impair memory, executive function, and decision-making in later life (e.g., Shonkoff et al., 2012). There is a growing body of research emphasizing the potential for impacts of traumatic childhood experiences to persist into adulthood, leading to a persistent increase in vulnerability to psychopathology that may be related to increased emotional reactivity to stress (e.g., McLaughlin et al., 2010).

Children are also at risk from disruptions to the educational system (Kousky, 2016). Natural disasters, in particular, can damage or destroy schools or make them inaccessible to teachers and students. After Hurricane Katrina, for example, 196,000 public school students had to change schools, and many of them missed a month or more of schooling. In this case, because the hardest hit school districts were also some of the worst performing ones, in many cases because they were located in poorer, underresourced communities, some students benefitted by transferring to better schools. Overall, however, the effects on school achievement were negative (Kousky, 2016). Research in Ethiopia has shown that children tend to receive less schooling as temperatures increase, suggesting that climate change may hinder progress toward education and other important human development goals, such as progress toward education, which influence a number of factors linked to quality of life such as family size, employability, and income (Randell & Gray, 2016).

9.6.3 Low-income and minority communities

Low income and ethnic minority communities are disproportionately vulnerable to the effects of climate change due to their lower status and power in society, demonstrating the importance of social and economic resources in fostering resilience. Many analyses show that poorer communities are more likely to be located in physically vulnerable locations (e.g., urban heat islands, coastal flood plains, near industrial facilities, in neighborhoods with older infrastructure) and experience impacts more strongly. Poor communities are more likely to have outdated infrastructure, such as a lack of extreme weather warning systems, inadequate storm surge preparedness, and clogged or inadequate storm sewer systems, which places them at greater risk from the physical impacts of climate change. Poor communities also tend to feel a lower sense of efficacy to create change and have higher preexisting needs for services, such as health-care or mental health services. When disaster strikes these communities, it likely causes greater damage, the damage meets deeper susceptibility, and the communities have fewer resources to heal (e.g., Upton, 2017).

In addition to physical vulnerabilities, communities are less resilient when they are weakened by social stressors resulting from racism, economic inequality, and environmental injustices. Many of the communities in New Orleans that were affected by Hurricane Katrina possessed all of these characteristics. As discussed in Chapter 5, A diversity science approach to climate change, minority groups in the United States have historically borne a disproportionate share of negative environmental impacts, and climate change is likely to continue this trajectory.

9.6.4 Indigenous communities

There is increasing awareness of the potential for climate change to have particularly significant impacts on indigenous communities, whose inhabitants often depend on natural resources for their livelihoods, and which are often located in geographically vulnerable regions (e.g., Maldonado, Pandya, & Colombi, 2014). Such impacts are found around the world, including the United States. In Alaska, for example, some native Alaskans have seen their villages literally vanish due to the thawing permafrost, and others are facing a similar outcome in the near future. Some communities in coastal Louisiana are also losing their land to erosion (Davenport & Robertson, 2016), with one such community being the first in the United States to receive federal funds for being environmental refugees (Davenport & Robertson, 2016). For indigenous communities, climate change may threaten not only their physical home but also their lifestyle, including access to traditional food and culturally meaningful practices (Rigby, Rosen, Berry, & Hart, 2011). One result may be decreased resilience to mental health threats. In fact, Cunsolo Willox et al. (2013) reported an increase in substance abuse and use of mental health services in response to climate impacts in a small Inuit community.

Looking at community impacts more broadly, Cunsolo Willox et al. (2013) report that members of the community, all of whom described a strong attachment to the land, said they had noticed changes in the local climate and that these changes were having negative effects. In addition to citing increased food insecurity, sadness, anger, and increased family stress, members of the community also said their sense of self-worth and community cohesion had decreased as a result of the fact that their traditional interactions with the natural environment had changed.

Ford, Pearce, Duerden, Furgal, and Smit (2010) review case studies of several Inuit communities and report weakening social networks, increased levels of conflict, and significant stress associated with relocation or even thinking about relocation. Willette, Norgaard, and Reed (2016) note that environmentally induced declines in the availability of wild food can lead to reduced family interaction time; they document the reduced transmission of cultural values and knowledge that result for a native Karuk tribe in Southern Oregon. The personal and cultural identity for indigenous communities, directly tied to the land through history as well as lived experience, may be at risk (Cochran et al., 2013; Durkalec, Furgal, Skinner, & Sheldon, 2015; Voggesser, Lynn, Daigle, Lake, & Ranco, 2013). As Chief Albert Naquin of a

Louisiana tribal community threatened by climate change mourned, "We're going to lose all our heritage, all our culture" (quoted in Davenport & Robertson, 2016).

9.7   Toward resilience

"Resilience" is the ability of a system to function in the face of adversity, to survive, and, perhaps, even to thrive (Hobfoll et al., 2015). The "system" could be an individual person, or a household, or even a community—resilience can be seen at many scales (Abramson et al., 2015; see Chapter 11: Psychological perspectives on community resilience and climate change: Insights, examples, and directions for future research). At the level of the individual person, resilience is the norm. People face many forms of adversity, and most come through it with positive adjustment and without psychopathology (Bonanno, 2008; Hanbury & Indart, 2013). Even so, much can be done to increase the resilience capacity of individuals and communities, particularly in response to climate change.

As stated earlier, health is more than the absence of disease or injury. Addressing climate change could improve health in ways beyond the mere avoidance of disaster. For example, many of the arguments for moving to clean energy emphasize the health improvements associated with a reduction in air pollution (e.g., Perera, 2017). Encouraging people to walk or ride their bikes rather than relying on automobiles for transportation will improve physical fitness and reduce obesity (Bain et al., 2016). Reducing the consumption of red meat could have a significant impact on both carbon emissions and cardiovascular health (Westhoek et al., 2014).

Protecting green spaces will not only provide ecosystem benefits through trees' role in carbon capture but green spaces also provide access to the range of benefits that bring about human wellbeing. This is documented by a rapidly growing body of research (e.g., Bowler, Buyung-Ali, Knight, & Pullin, 2010; Carrus et al., 2015). Increasing evidence suggests that not only individual wellbeing but also community relationships may be positively affected by access to green space: natural spaces encourage social interactions and more positive attitudes toward others (e.g., Kuo & Sullivan, 2001; Weinstein et al., 2015). Weinstein et al. found that both objective amount of nature in a neighborhood and the amount of reported contact with nature were positively associated with social cohesion and negatively associated with crime, even after controlling for socioeconomic factors.

Following natural disasters, social capital may be one of the factors most strongly associated with resilience (Mathbor, 2007). Resilience research suggests the value of strong social networks in overcoming adversity, because connected communities possess the trust, cooperation, and communication that undergird any type of group effort (Aldrich & Meyer, 2014; Aldrich, 2012). Community social capital and trust has been linked to lower rates of crime and violence as well as higher participation in civic activities that benefit the entire community (Hirschfield & Bowers, 1997). Social cohesion also benefits individuals. Personal mental health is better in communities with stronger social fabric (Friedli, 2009); when social networks are dense and inclusive, they offer residents a wider array of meaningful social interactions. Social interactions are particularly important during difficult times (e.g., Terpstra, 2011), and people experience an extra boost in their own wellbeing through opportunities to help others in need.

As stated by Wolsko and Marino (2016), helping people to adapt to climate change requires attending to more than material needs. Enabling cultural continuity and the ability to connect to the natural world are also important. As emphasized by Doherty (this volume) and others (e.g., Clayton, Manning, & Hodge, 2014; Clayton, Manning, & Krygsman, 2017), greater resilience is also achieved through improved social equity. Reducing poverty, for example, reduces the number of individuals and communities that lack the resources they need to cope with climate change. Greater equity also contributes to stronger social cohesion within a community, which in turn expands the social networks that provide individuals with essential support during difficult times.

9.8 Conclusion

This chapter has described the many serious risks that climate change poses for human wellbeing. A substantial body of research has documented the impacts of natural disasters, which are projected to increase due to climate change, on mental health and community relations. The psychological impacts of more gradual changes in the climate have received less research attention, but as the studies reviewed here suggest, there is substantial reason for concern. Chronic climate impacts, such as drought, rising temperatures, and other slowly unfolding changes to the landscape, are a source of stress and are likely to increase individual distress as well as overall aggression and intergroup conflict. Climate change will also require changes in the ways in which people think about themselves, their culture, and their relationship to place, changes which will impact mental health in ways that are not fully clear.

Importantly, these impacts will be unevenly distributed. Physical, social, and/or geographic sources of vulnerability combine to determine different levels of risk. Children and the elderly are most physiologically susceptible. Women, indigenous groups, minority groups, and the poor are vulnerable due in part to their social positions and lack of access to power. People who live in geographically vulnerable areas, such as coastal areas, the Arctic, or areas subject to desertification, will see more dramatic impacts of climate change, but those with the economic resources will be able to protect themselves to some extent. The resulting inequities will likely contribute to social conflict.

Climate change is more than a series of negative consequences to be avoided. It is a challenge to our current way of life. As such, it is also an opportunity to reevaluate and recalibrate dysfunctional aspects of our society. The threat of climate change may be able to motivate changes in physical and social infrastructure that can provide cobenefits for physical and psychological health.

The impacts on individual and collective wellbeing make this a crucial area for psychological research. We highlight a few important research questions:

1. There has been speculation, and a small amount of evidence, about the existence of generalized anxiety about threats to the environment due to climate change. We need to know more about the nature and extent of "ecoanxiety." How prevalent is it? Does it include an element of guilt? Is place attachment a buffer, or does it exacerbate the threat?

2. Some evidence indicates that the attributions people make for a disaster—reasons or explanations for why it happened—affect the psychological consequences of that disaster (e.g., Lack & Sullivan, 2008; Zinzow & Jackson, 2009). One study found that blaming someone or something else for a disaster was correlated with higher postdisaster distress (Lack & Sullivan, 2008). As disasters are more frequently linked to climate change, how might this affect the attributions people make? In addition, do people's attributions vary with the extent they believe climate change is caused by human activity, particularly given the continued political (though not scientific) controversy about this? What is the relevance of the cause of a disaster, both real and perceived, to the impacts on wellbeing?

3. Perhaps more importantly, what are the most promising ways to promote resilience among individuals, communities, and societies? As several of the chapters in this volume attest, researchers are moving beyond a focus on mitigation of climate change to consider ways to promote adaptation. The goal of a more sustainable society must include consideration of mental health and wellbeing, and there is a growing trend of programs that focus on helping people cope with their emotional response to climate change (Doppelt, 2016; Preston, 2017). Researchers should take a critical look at the impact of emotional coping strategies to see whether they have a positive or perhaps a negative impact on problem-focused coping and behavioral adaptation. Perhaps coming to terms with thinking about climate change will even facilitate the necessary behavioral changes.

References

Abramson, D., Grattan, L., Mayer, B., Colten, C., Arosemena, F., Bedimo-Rung, A., & Lichtveld, M. (2015). The resilience activation framework: A conceptual model of how access to social resources promotes adaptation and rapid recovery in post-disaster settings. *Journal of Behavioral Health Services & Research*, *42*(1), 42−57. Available from https://doi.org/10.1007/s11414-014-9410-2.

Adger, W. N., Barnett, J., Brown, K., Marshall, N., & O'Brien, K. (2013). Cultural dimensions of climate change impacts and adaptation. *Nature Climate Change*, *3*, 112−117.

Agnew, R. (2012). Dire forecast: A theoretical model of the impact of climate change on crime. *Theoretical Criminology*, *23*(3), 209−221.

Albrecht, G. (2011). Chronic environmental change: Emerging 'psychoterratic' syndromes. In I. Weissbecker (Ed.), *Climate change and human well-being: Global challenges and opportunities* (pp. 43−56). New York, NY: Springer.

Alderman, K., Turner, L. R., & Tong, S. L. (2012). Floods and human health: A systematic review. *Environment International*, *47*, 37−47. Available from https://doi.org/10.1016/j.envint.2012.06.003.

Aldrich, D. P. (2012). *Building resilience: Social capital in post-disaster recovery*. Chicago, IL: University of Chicago Press.

Aldrich, D. P., & Meyer, M. A. (2014). Social capital and community resilience. *American Behavioral Scientist*, *59*(2), 254−269. Available from https://doi.org/10.1177/0002764214550299.

Alston, M. (2012). Rural male suicide in Australia. *Social Science & Medicine*, *74*, 515−522. Available from https://doi.org/10.1016/j.socscimed.2010.04.036.

Anderson, C. A. (2012). Climate change and violence. In D. Christie (Ed.), *The encyclopedia of peace psychology*. Hoboken, NJ: Wiley-Blackwell, 10.1002/9780470672532.wbepp032.

Bailey, C. (2016). Experts sound alarm over mental health toll borne by migrants and refugees*The Guardian*, Retrieved from . Available from https://www.theguardian.com/global-development/2016/jun/08/experts-sound-alarm-mental-health-toll-migrants-refugees-depression-anxiety-psychosis.

Bain, P. G., Milfont, T. L., Kashima, Y., Bilewicz, M., Doron, G., Garðarsdóttir, R. B., ... Corral-Verdugo, V. (2016). Co-benefits of addressing climate change can motivate action around the world. *Nature Climate Change*, *6*(2), 154−157.

Bartlett, S. (2008). Climate change and urban children: Impacts and implications for adaptation in low- and middle-income countries. *Environment and Urbanization*, *20*, 501−519.

Basu, R., Gavin, L., Pearson, D., Ebisu, K., & Malig, B. (2017). Examining the association between temperature and emergency room visits from mental health-related outcomes in California. *American Journal of Epidemiology*. Available from https://doi.org/10.1093/aje/kwx295.

Beaudoin, C. (2011). Hurricane Katrina: Addictive behavior trends and predictors. *Public Health Reports*, *126*, 400−409.

Belkin, L. Y., & Kouchaki, M. (2017). Exploring the impact of ambient temperature on helping. *European Journal of Social Psychology*. Available from https://doi.org/10.1002/ejsp.2242.

Böcker, L., Dijst, M., & Prillwitz, J. (2013). Impact of everyday weather on individual daily travel behaviours in perspective: A literature review. *Transport Reviews*, *33*(1), 71−91.

Bonanno, G. A. (2008). Loss, trauma, and human resilience. Have we underestimated the human capacity to thrive after extremely aversive events? *American Psychologist*, *59*(1), 20−28.

Boscarino, J., Hoffman, S., Adams, R., Figley, C., & Solhkhah, R. (2014). Mental health outcomes among vulnerable residents after Hurricane Sandy. *American Journal of Disaster Medicine*, *9*, 107−120.

Boss, P. (2016). The context and process of theory development: The story of ambiguous loss. *Journal of Family Theory and Review*, *8*(3), 269−286.

Bowler, D. E., Buyung-Ali, L. M., Knight, T. M., & Pullin, A. S. (2010). A systematic review of evidence for the added benefits to health of exposure to natural environments. *BMC Public Health*, *10*, 456.

Brehm, J. M., Eisenhauer, B. W., & Krannich, R. S. (2004). Dimensions of community attachment and their relationship to well-being in the amenity-rich rural west. *Rural Sociology*, *69*(3), 405−429. Available from https://doi.org/10.1526/0036011041730545.

Bryant, R., Waters, E., Gibbs, L., Gallagher, H. C., Pattison, P., Lusher, D., ... Forbes, D. (2014). Psychological outcomes following the Victorian Black Saturday bushfires. *Australian and New Zealand Journal of Psychiatry*, *48*, 634−643.

Carleton, T. A., & Hsiang, S. D. (2016). Social and economic impacts of climate. *Science*, *353*(6304), 1−15.

Carroll, B., Morbey, H., Balogh, R., & Araoz, G. (2009). Flooded homes, broken bonds, the meaning of home, psychological processes and their impact on psychological health in a disaster. *Health and Place*, *15*(2), 540−547.

Carrus, G., Scopelliti, M., Lafortezza, R., Colangelo, G., Ferrini, F., Salbitano, F., ... Sanesi, G. (2015). Go greener, feel better? The positive effects of biodiversity on the well-being of individuals visiting urban and peri-urban green areas. *Landscape and Urban Planning*, *134*, 221−228.

Chapman D.A., Trott C.D., Silka L., Lickel B., Clayton C., Psychological perspectives on community resilience and climate change: Insights, examples, and directions for future research. Psychology and Climate Change, Elsevier, Amsterdam (this volume).

Cherry, K. E., Marks, L. D., Adamek, R., & Lyon, B. A. (2015). Younger and older coastal fishers face catastrophic loss after Hurricane Katrina. In K. Cherry (Ed.), *Traumatic stress and long-term recovery: Coping with disasters and other negative life events* (pp. 327−348). Cham: Springer. Available from https://doi.org/10.1007/978-3-319-18866-9.

Clayton, S., Manning, C. M., & Hodge, C. (2014). *Beyond storms & droughts: The psychological impacts of climate change*. Washington, DC: American Psychological Association and ecoAmerica.

Clayton, S., Manning, C. M., & Krygsman, K. (2017). *Mental health and our changing climate: Impacts, implications, and guidance*. Washington, DC: American Psychological Association, and ecoAmerica.

Cochran, P., Huntington, O., Pungowiyi, C., Stanley, T., Chapin, F. S., Huntington, H., ... Trainor, S. (2013). Indigenous frameworks for observing and responding to climate change in Alaska. *Climatic Change*, *120*, 557−567.

Cunsolo Willox, A., Harper, S., Ford, J. D., Edge, V., Landman, K., Houle, K., ... Wolfrey, C. (2013). Climate change and mental health: An exploratory case study from Rigolet, Nunatsiavut, Labrador. *Climatic Change*, *121*, 255−270. Available from https://doi.org/10.1007/s10584-013-0875-4.

Currie, J., & Almond, D. (2011). Human capital development before age five. In D. Card, & O. Ashenfelter (Eds.), *Handbook of labor economics* (4B, pp. 1315−1486). Amsterdam: North Holland Press.

Dahl, K. A., Fitzpatrick, M. F., & Spanger-Siegfried, E. (2017). Sea level rise drives increased tidal flooding frequency at tide gauges along the U.S. East and Gulf Coasts: Projections for 2030 and 2045. *PLoS ONE*, *12*(2), e0170949. Available from https://doi.org/10.1371/journal.pone.0170949.

Datar, A., Liu, J., Linnemayr, S., & Stecher, C. (2013). The impact of natural disasters on child health and investments in rural India. *Social Science & Medicine*, *76*, 83−91.

Davenport, C., & Robertson, C. (2016). Resettling the first American 'climate refugees' *New York Times*, Retrieved from . Available from https://www.nytimes.com/2016/05/03/us/resettling-the-first-american-climate-refugees.html?_r = 0.

Devine-Wright, P. (2013). Think global, act local? The relevance of place attachments and place identities in a climate changed world. *Global Environmental Change*, *23*, 61−69.

Dittmar, H. (2011). Material and consumer identities. In S. J. Schwartz, K. Luyckx, & V. L. Vignoles (Eds.), *Handbook of identity theory and research* (Volume 2, pp. 745−769). New York, NY: Springer.

Dodgen, D., Donato, D., Kelly, N., et al. (2016). *Ch. 8: Mental health and well-being. The impacts of Climate Change on Human Health in the United States 2016: A scientific assessment* (pp. 217−246). Washington, DC: U.S. Global Change Research Program. Available from http://dx.doi.org/10.7930/J0TX3C9H.

Doherty, T. J., & Clayton, S. C. (2011). The psychological impacts of global climate change. *American Psychologist*, *66*(4), 265−276.

Doppelt, B. (2016). *Transformational resilience: How building human resilience to climate disruption can safeguard society and increase wellbeing.* Sheffield, UK: Greenleaf Publishing.

Durkalec, A., Furgal, C., Skinner, M., & Sheldon, T. (2015). Climate change influences on environment as a determinant of Indigenous health: Relationships to place, sea ice, and health in an Inuit community. *Social Science and Medicine, 136-137*, 17−26.

Edwards, T., & Wiseman, J. (2011). Climate change, resilience, and transformation: Challenges and opportunities for local communities. In I. Weissbecker (Ed.), *Climate change and human well-being: Global challenges and opportunities* (pp. 185−209). New York, NY: Springer.

Ellis, N. R., & Albrecht, G. A. (2017). Climate change threats to family farmers' sense of place and mental wellbeing: A case study from the Western Australian Wheatbelt. *Social Science & Medicine, 175*, 161−168. Available from https://doi.org/10.1016/j. socscimed.2017.01.009.

Fernandez, A., Black, J., Jones, M., Wilson, L., Salvador-Carulla, L., Astell-Burt, T., & Black, D. (2015). Flooding and mental health: A systematic mapping review. *PLoS ONE., 10*(4), e0119929.

Flory, K., Hankin, B., Kloos, C., Cheely, C., & Turecki, G. (2009). Alcohol and cigarette use and misuse among Hurricane Katrina survivors: Psychosocial risk and protective factors. *Substance Use and Misuse, 44*, 1711−1724.

Forbes, D., Alkemade, N., Waters, E., Gibbs, L., Gallagher, C., Pattison, P., . . . Bryant, R. A. (2015). The role of anger and ongoing stressors in mental health following a natural disaster. *Australian & New Zealand Journal of Psychiatry, 49*(8), 706−713. Available from https://doi.org/10.1177/0004867414565478.

Ford, J., Pearce, T., Duerden, F., Furgal, C., & Smit, B. (2010). Climate change policy responses for Canada's Inuit population: The importance of and opportunities for adaptation. *Global Environmental Change, 20*, 177−191.

Fox, G. L., & Chancey, D. (1998). Sources of economic distress: Individual and family outcomes. *Journal of Family Issues, 19*(6), 725−749. Available from https://doi.org/10.1177/019251398019006004.

Fresque-Baxter, J., & Armitage, D. (2012). Place identity and climate change adaptation: A synthesis and framework for understanding. *WIREs Climate Change, 3*, 251−266. Available from https://doi.org/10.1002/wcc.164.

Friedli, L. (2009). *Mental health, resilience, and inequalities.* Copenhagen: World Health Organization.

Friel, S., Butler, C., & McMichael, A. (2011). Climate change and health: Risks and inequities. In S. Benatar, & G. Brock (Eds.), *Global health and global health ethics* (pp. 198−209). Cambridge, UK: Cambridge University Press.

Friel, S., Berry, H., Dinh, H., O'Brien, L., & Walls, H. L. (2014). The impact of drought on the association between food security and mental health in a nationally representative Australian sample. *BMC Public Health, 14*(1), 1102. Available from https://doi.org/10.1186/1471-2458-14-1102.

Fritsche, I., Cohrs, J., Kessler, T., & Bauer, J. (2012). Global warming is breeding social conflict: The subtle impact of climate change threat on authoritarian tendencies. *Journal of Environmental Psychology, 32*(1), 1−10.

Fritze, J., Blashki, G. A., Burke, S., & Wiseman, J. (2008). Hope, despair and transformation: Climate change and the promotion of mental health and wellbeing. *International Journal of Mental Health Systems, 2*, 13.

Fullilove, M. T. (2013). 'The Frayed Knot': What happens to place attachment in the context of serial forced displacement? In L. Manzo, & P. Devine-Wright (Eds.), *Place attachment: Advances in theory, method and applications* (pp. 141–153). Abingdon, UK: Routledge.

Galea, S., Brewin, C. R., Jones, R. T., King, D. W., King, L. A., McNally, L. A., . . . Kessler, R. C. (2007). Exposure to hurricane-related stressors and mental illness after Hurricane Katrina. *Archives of General Psychiatry, 64*(12), 1427–1434.

Gerhart, J. I., Canetti, D., & Hobfoll, S. E. (2015). Traumatic stress in overview: Definition, context, scope, and long-term outcomes. In K. Cherry (Ed.), *Traumatic stress and long-term recovery: Coping with disasters and other negative life events* (pp. 3–24). Cham: Springer. Available from https://doi.org/10.1007/978-3-319-18866-9.

Gifford, E., & Gifford, R. (2016). The largely unacknowledged impact of climate change on mental health. *Bulletin of the Atomic Scientists, 72*(5), 292–297.

Hanbury R. F. & Indart M. J., Resilience revisited: Toward an expanding understanding of post-disaster adaptation. In S. Prince-Embury (Ed.), Resilience in children, adolescents, and adults, 2013, (pp. 213–225). https://doi.org/10.1007/978-1-4614-4939-3.

Hanigan, I. C., Butler, C. D., Kokicc, C. N., & Hutchinson, M. F. (2012). Suicide and drought in New South Wales, Australia, 1970–2007. *Proceedings of the National Academy of Sciences of the United States of America, 109*(35), 13950–13955.

Hansen, A., Bi, P., Nitschke, M., Ryan, P., Pisaniello, D., & Tucker, G. (2008). The effect of heat waves on mental health in a temperate Australian city. *Environmental Health Perspectives, 116*(10), 1369.

Harville, E., Taylor, C., Tesfai, H., Xiong, X., & Buekens, P. (2011). Experience of Hurricane Katrina and reported intimate partner violence. *Journal of Interpersonal Violence, 26*, 833–845.

Hatch, T. G., Cherry, K. E., Kytola, K. L., Lu, Y., & Marks, L. D. (2015). Loss, chaos, survival, and despair: The storm after the storms. In K. Cherry (Ed.), *Traumatic stress and long-term recovery: Coping with disasters and other negative life events* (pp. 231–246). Cham: Springer. Available from https://doi.org/10.1007/978-3-319-18866-9.

Hauer, M. (2017). Migration induced by sea-level rise could reshape the US population landscape. *Nature Climate Change, 7*(5), 321–325. Available from https://doi.org/10.1038/nclimate3271.

Hauff, E., & Vaglum, P. (1995). Organised violence and the stress of exile. Predictors of mental health in a community cohort of Vietnamese refugees three years after resettlement. *The British Journal of Psychiatry, 166*(3), 360–367.

Hirschfield, A., & Bowers, K. (1997). The effect of social cohesion on levels of recorded crime in disadvantaged areas. *Urban Studies, 34*(8), 1275–1295.

Hobfoll, S. E. (2007). Five essential elements of immediate and mid–term mass trauma intervention: Empirical evidence. *Psychiatry, 70*(4), 283–315.

Hobfoll, S. E., Stevens, N. R., & Zalta, A. K. (2015). Expanding the science of resilience: Conserving resources in the aid of adaptation. *Psychological Inquiry, 26*(2), 174–180. Available from https://doi.org/10.1080/1047840X.2015.1002377.

Houser, T., Hsiang, S., Kopp, R., & Larsen, K. (2015). *Economic risks of climate change: An American prospectus.* New York, NY: Columbia University Press.

Hsiang, S., Burke, M., & Miguel, E. (2013). *Science, 341*, 1235367. Available from https://doi.org/10.1126/science.1235367.

Ingleby, D. (Ed.), (2004). *Forced migration and mental health: Rethinking the care of refugees and displaced persons.* New York, NY: Springer Science & Business Media.

IPCC. (2014). In R. K. Pachauri, & L. A. Meyer (Eds.), *Climate change 2014: synthesis report. Contribution of working groups i, ii and iii to the fifth assessment report of the intergovernmental panel on climate change* (p. 151). Geneva, Switzerland: IPCC, Core Writing Team.

Jones, A. D. (2017). Food insecurity and mental health status: A global analysis of 149 countries. *American Journal of Preventive Medicine, 53*(2), 264−273.

Jones, M. K., Wootton, B. M., Vaccaro, L. D., & Menzies, R. G. (2012). The impact of climate change on obsessive compulsive checking concerns. *Australian & New Zealand Journal of Psychiatry, 46*(3), 265−270. Available from https://doi.org/10.1177/0004867411433951.

Keenan, H., Marshall, S., Nocera, M. A., & Runyan, D. (2004). Increased incidence of inflicted traumatic brain injury in children after a natural disaster. *American Journal of Preventive Medicine, 26,* 189−193.

Kessler, R., Galea, S., Gruber, M., Sampson, N., Ursano, R., & Wessely, S. (2008). Trends in mental illness and suicidality after Hurricane Katrina. *Molecular Psychiatry, 13,* 374−384.

Kolassa, I. T., Ertl, V., Eckart, C., Kolassa, S., Onyut, L. P., & Elbert, T. (2010). Spontaneous remission from PTSD depends on the number of traumatic event types experienced. *Psychological Trauma: Theory, Research, Practice and Policy, 2*(3), 169−174.

Kousky, C. (2016). Impacts of natural disasters on children. *The Future of Children, 26,* 73−92.

Kuo, F. E., & Sullivan, W. C. (2001). Environment and crime in the inner city: Does vegetation reduce crime? *Environment and Behavior, 33*(3), 343−367.

Lack, C. W., & Sullivan, M. A. (2008). Attributions, coping, and exposure as predictors of long-term posttraumatic distress in tornado-exposed children. *Journal of Loss and Trauma, 13*(1), 72−84. Available from https://doi.org/10.1080/15325020701741906.

Leard, B., & Roth, K. (2016). How climate change affects traffic accidents. *Resources, 191,* 22−25.

Lee, M., & Blanchard, T. (2012). Community attachment and negative affective states in the context of the BP Deepwater Horizon disaster. *American Behavioral Scientist, 56*(1), 24−57.

Lyon, B. A., Nezat, P. F., Cherry, K. E., & Marks, L. D. (2015). When multiple disasters strike: Louisiana fishers in the aftermath of hurricanes and the British petroleum Deepwater Horizon oil spill. In K. E. Cherry (Ed.), *Traumatic stress and long-term recovery: Coping with disasters and other negative life events.* (pp. 57−70). New York, NY: Springer.

Maldonado, J. K., Pandya, R., & Colombi, B. (Eds.), (2014). Climate change and indigenous peoples in the united states: Impacts, experiences and actions. *Climatic Change, 120*(3).

Mathbor, G. M. (2007). Enhancement of community preparedness for natural disasters: The role of social work in building social capital for sustainable disaster relief and management. *International Social Work, 50,* 357−369.

McLaughlin, K. A., Kubzansky, L. D., Dunn, E. C., Waldinger, R., Vaillant, G., & Koenen, K. C. (2010). Childhood social environment, emotional reactivity to stress, and mood and anxiety disorders across the life course. *Depression and Anxiety, 27*(12), 1087−1094.

McMichael, A. J. (2013). Globalization, climate change, and human health. *The New England Journal of Medicine, 368*(14), 1335−1343.

Miller, K. E., Worthington, G. J., Muzurovic, J., Tipping, S., & Goldman, A. (2002). Bosnian refugees and the stressors of exile: A narrative study. *American Journal of Orthopsychiatry*, *72*(3), 341.

Mohan, J. E., Ziska, L. H., Schlesinger, W. H., Thomas, R. B., Sicher, R. C., George, K., & Clar, J. S. (2006). Biomass and toxicity responses of poison ivy (*Toxicodendron radicans*) to elevated atmospheric CO_2. *Proceedings of the National Academy of Sciences of the United States of America*, *103*(24), 9086−9089. Available from www.pnas.org/cgi/doi/10.1073/pnas.0602392103.

Mora, C., Dousset, B., Caldwell, I. R., Powell, F. E., Geronimo, R. C., Bielecki, C. R., ... Trauernicht, C. (2017). *Nature Climate Change*, *7*, 501−506. Available from https://doi.org/10.1038/nclimate3322.

Moser, S. C. (2007). More bad news: The risk of neglecting emotional responses to climate change information. In S. C. Moser, & L. Dilling (Eds.), *Creating a climate for change: Communicating climate change and facilitating social change* (1st ed., pp. 64−80). Cambridge: Cambridge University Press. Cambridge Books Online.

Moser, S. C. (2013). Navigating the political and emotional terrain of adaptation: Community engagement when climate change comes home. In S. C. Moser, & M. T. Boykoff (Eds.), *Successful adaptation to climate change: Linking science and policy in a rapidly changing world* (pp. 289−305). New York, NY: Routledge.

Myers, N. (1993). Environmental refugees in a globally warmed world. *Bioscience*, *43*(11), 752−761.

Neria, P., & Schultz, J. M. (2012). Mental health effects of hurricane Sandy characteristics, potential aftermath, and response. *The Journal of the American Medical Association*, *308*(24), 2571−2572.

Neumayer, E., & Plümper, T. (2007). The gendered nature of natural disasters: The impact of catastrophic events on the gender gap in life expectancy, 1981−2002. *Annals of the Association of American Geographers*, *97*(3), 551−566.

Norris, F. H., Friedman, M. J., & Watson, P. J. (2002). 60,000 disaster victims speak: Part II. Summary and implications of the disaster mental health research. *Psychiatry*, *65*(3), 240−260.

Norris, F. H., Stevens, S. P., Pfefferbaum, B., Wyche, K. R., & Pfefferbaum, R. L. (2008). Community resilience as a metaphor, theory, set of capacities, and strategy for disaster readiness. *American Journal of Community Psychology*, *41*, 127−150. Available from https://doi.org/10.1007/s10464-007-9156-6.

O'Brien, L. V., Berry, H. L., Coleman, C., & Hanigan, I. C. (2014). Drought as a mental health exposure. *Environmental Research*, *131*, 181−187. ISSN 0013-9351, https://doi.org/10.1016/j.envres.2014.03.014.

Page, L., Hajat, S., Kovats, R. S., & Howard, L. (2012). Temperature-related deaths in people with psychosis, dementia, and substance misuse. *British Journal of Psychiatry*, *200*, 485−490.

Palinkas, L., Downs, M., Petterson, J., & Russell, J. (1993). Social, cultural, and psychological impacts of the Exxon Valdez oil spill. *Human Organization*, *52*, 1−13.

Park, J. (2017). Hot temperature, human capital, and adaptation to climate change. Unpublished manuscript. Available at https://scholar.harvard.edu/jisungpark/publications.

Parker, G., Lie, D., Siskind, D. J., Martin-Khan, M., Raphael, B., Crompton, D., & Kisely, S. (2016). Mental health implications for older adults after natural disasters—A systematic review and meta-analysis. *International Psychogeriatrics*, *28*(01), 11−20.

Patz, J. A., Frumkin, H., Holloway, T., Vimont, D. J., & Haines, A. (2014). Climate change challenges and opportunities for global health. *The Journal of the American Medical Association*, *312*(15), 1565−1580. Available from https://doi.org/10.1001/jama.2014.13186.

Perera, F. P. (2017). Multiple threats to child health from fossil fuel combustion: Impacts of air pollution and climate change. *Environmental Health Perspectives*, *125*(2), 141.

Portier, C. J., Thigpen., Tart, K., Carter, S. R., Dilworth, C. H., Grambsch, A. E., ... Whung, P.-Y. (2010). *A human health perspective on climate change: A report outlining the research needs on the human health effects of climate change*. Research Triangle Park, NC: Environmental Health Perspectives/National Institute of Environmental Health Sciences. Available from http://dx.doi.org/10.1289/ehp.1002272. Available: www.niehs.nih.gov/climatereport.

Preston, C. (2017). Depressed about climate change? There's a 9-step program for that. *Grist.* <http://grist.org/article/depressed-about-climate-change-theres-a-9-step-program-for-that/>.

Preti, A., Lentini, G., & Maugeri, M. (2007). Global warming possibly linked to an enhanced risk of suicide: Data from Italy, 1974−2003. *Journal of Affective Disorders*, *102*(1-3), 19−25. Available from https://doi.org/10.1016/j.jad.2006.12.003.

Pumariega, A. J., Rothe, E., & Pumariega, J. B. (2005). Mental health of immigrants and refugees. *Community Mental Health Journal*, *41*(5), 581−597. Available from https://doi.org/10.1007/s10597-005-6363-1.

Randell, H., & Gray, C. (2016). Climate variability and educational attainment: Evidence from rural Ethiopia. *Global Environmental Change*, *41*, 111−123.

Ranson, M. (2012). Crime, weather, and climate change. Harvard Kennedy School M-RCBG associate working paper series no. 8. Available at SSRN: http://ssrn.com/abstract = 2111377 or https://doi.org/10.2139/ssrn.2111377.

Raphael, B. (2007). The human touch and mass catastrophe. *Psychiatry*, *70*(4), 329−336.

Reuveny, R. (2008). Ecomigration and violent conflict: Case studies and public policy implications. *Human Ecology*, *36*(1), 1−13.

Rigby, C., Rosen, A., Berry, H., & Hart, C. (2011). If the land's sick, we're sick: The impact of prolonged drought on the social and emotional wellbeing of Aboriginal communities in rural New South Wales. *Australian Journal of Rural Health*, *19*, 249−254.

Root, T. L., Price, J. T., Hall, K. R., Schneider, S. H., Rosenzweig, C., & Pounds. (2003). Fingerprints of global warming on wild animals and plants. *Nature*, *421*(6918), 57−60.

Rubonis, A. V., & Bickman, L. (1991). Psychological impairment in the wake of disaster: The disaster-psychopathology relationship. *Psychological Bulletin*, *109*(3), 384−399.

Sallin, K., Lagercrantz, H., Evers, K., Engström, I., Hjern, A., & Petrovic, P. (2016). Resignation Syndrome: Catatonia? Culture-Bound? *Frontiers in Behavioral Neuroscience*, *10*, 7. Available from https://doi.org/10.3389/fnbeh.2016.00007.

Scannell, L., & Gifford, R. (2016). Place attachment enhances psychological need satisfaction. *Environment and Behavior*, *1*(31). Available from https://doi.org/10.1177/0013916516637648.

Searle, K., & Gow, K. (2010). Do concerns about climate change lead to distress? *International Journal of Climate Change Strategies and Management*, *2*(4), 362−379.

Seeley, M. (2012). *Climate trends and climate change in Minnesota: A review*. Minnesota State Climatology Office Available at . Available from http://climate.umn.edu/seeley/.

Shonkoff, J., Garner, A., Siegel, B., Dobbins, M., Earls, M., Garner, A., & Wood, D. (2012). The committee on psychosocial aspects of child and family health, committee on early childhood, adoption, and dependent care, and section on developmental and behavioral paediatrics – The lifelong effects of early childhood adversity and toxic stress. *American Academy of Pediatrics*, *129*, e232–2246. Available from https://doi.org/10.1542/peds.2011-2663.

Silver, A., & Grek-Martin, J. (2015). "Now we understand what community really means:" Reconceptualizing the role of sense of place in the disaster recovery process. *Journal of Environmental Psychology*, *42*, 35–41.

Simpson, D. M., Weissbecker, I., & Sephton, S. E. (2011). Extreme weather-related events: Implications for mental health and well-being. In I. Weissbecker (Ed.), *Climate change and human well-being: Global challenges and opportunities* (pp. 57–78). New York, NY: Springer.

Stain, H. J., Kelly, B., Lewin, T. J., et al. (2008). *Social Psychiatry and Psychiatric Epidemiology*, *43*, 843. Available from https://doi-org.ezproxy.macalester.edu/10.1007/s00127-008-0374-5.

Stanke, C., Kerac, M., Prudhomme, C., Medlock, J., & Murray, V. (2013). Health effects of drought: A systematic review of the evidence, 1st ed *PLoS Currents Disasters*. Available from https://doi.org/10.1371/currents.dis.7a2cee9e980f91ad7697b570bcc4b004.

Steentjes, K., Pidgeon, N., Poortinga, W., Corner, A., Arnold, A., Böhm, G., ... Tvinnereim, E. (2017). *European perceptions of climate change: Topline findings of a survey conducted in four European countries in 2016*. Cardiff: Cardiff University.

Tapsell, S. M., & Tunstall, S. M. (2008). "'I wish I'd never heard of Banbury": The relationship between 'place' and the health impacts of flooding. *Health & Place*, *14*(2), 133–154.

Terpstra, T. (2011). Emotions, trust, and perceived risk: Affective and cognitive routes to flood preparedness behavior. *Risk Analysis*, *31*(10), 1658–1675. Available from https://doi.org/10.1111/j.1539-6924.2011.01616.x.

Trumbo, C., Lueck, M., Marlatt, H., & Peek, L. (2011). The effect of proximity to hurricanes Katrina and Rita on subsequent hurricane outlook and optimistic bias. *Risk Analysis*, *31* (12), 1907–1918. Available from https://doi.org/10.1111/j.1539-6924.2011.01633.x.

Tschakert, P., Tutu, R., & Alcaro, A. (2013). Embodied experiences of landscape and climatic changes in landscapes of everyday life in Ghana. *Emotion, Space, and Society*, *7*, 13–25.

United Nations Population Fund. (2009). *Facing a changing world: Women, population, and climate*. New York, NY: UNFPA. Available from https://www.unfpa.org/sites/default/files/pub-pdf/state_of_world_population_2009.pdf.

Upton, J. (2017, May 10). The injustice of Atlantic City's floods. Climate Central, http://reports.climatecentral.org/atlantic-city/sea-level-rise/.

USGCRP. (2016). In A. Crimmins, J. Balbus, J. L. Gamble, C. B. Beard, J. E. Bell, D. Dodgen, R. J. Eisen, N. Fann, M. D. Hawkins, S. C. Herring, L. Jantarasami, D. M. Mills, S. Saha, M. C. Sarofim, J. Trtanj, & L. Ziska (Eds.), *The impacts of climate change on human health in the United States: A scientific assessment* (p. 312). Washington, DC: U.S. Global Change Research Program. Available from http://dx.doi.org/10.7930/J0R49NQX.

Ursano, R. J., McCaughey, B., & Fullerton, C. S. (Eds.), (1995). *Individual and community responses to trauma and disaster: The structure of human chaos*. London, UK: Cambridge University Press.

Verplanken, B., & Roy, D. (2013). "My worries are rational, climate change is not": Habitual ecological worrying is an adaptive response. *PLoS ONE*, *8*(9), e74708.

Vida, S., Durocher, M., Ouarda, T., & Gosselin, P. (2012). Relationship between ambient temperature and humidity and visits to mental health emergency departments in Quebec. *Psychiatric Services, 63*(11), 1150–1153.

Voggesser, G., Lynn, K., Daigle, J., Lake, F., & Ranco, D. (2013). Cultural impacts to tribes from climate change influences on forests. *Climatic Change, 120,* 615–626.

Wasini, S., West, C., Mills, J., & Usher, K. (2014). The psychosocial impact of natural disasters among adult survivors: An integrative review. *Issues in Mental Health Nursing, 35,* 420–436.

Watts, N., Adger, W. N., Agnolucci, P., Blackstock, J., Byass, P., Cai, W., ... Costello, A. (2015). Health and climate change: Policy responses to protect public health. *Lancet, 386,* 1861–1914. Available from https://doi.org/10.1016/S0140-6736(15)60854-6.

Weems, C. F., & Banks, D. M. (2015). Severe stress and anxiety disorders in adolescence: The long-term effects of disasters. In K. Cherry (Ed.), *Traumatic stress and long-term recovery: Coping with disasters and other negative life events* (pp. 177–194). Cham: Springer. Available from https://dx.org/10.1007/978-3-319-18866-9.

Weinstein, N., Balmford, A., DeHaan, C. R., Gladwell, V., Bradbury, R. B., & Amano, T. (2015). Seeing community for the trees: The links among contact with natural environments, community cohesion, and crime. *BioScience, 65*(12), 1141–1153.

Weissbecker, I., & Czinez, J. (2011). Humanitarian crises: The need for cultural competence and local capacity building. In I. Weissbecker (Ed.), *Climate change and human well-being: Global challenges and opportunities.* (pp. 79–96). New York, NY: Springer.

Westhoek, H., Lesschen, J. P., Rood, T., Wagner, S., De Marco, A., Murphy-Bokern, D., ... Oenema, O. (2014). Food choices, health and environment: Effects of cutting Europe's meat and dairy intake. *Global Environmental Change, 26,* 196–205.

Whiting, A. (2016). Without urgent action, climate change will push millions into hunger: U.N. *Reuters.* Available from http://www.reuters.com/article/us-farming-climatechange-hunger/without-urgent-action-climate-change-will-push-millions-into-hunger-u-n-idUSKBN12H121.

Willette, M., Norgaard, K., & Reed, R. (2016). You got to have fish: Families, environmental decline and cultural reproduction. *Families, Relationships, and Societies, 5,* 375–392.

Williams, M. N., Hill, S. R., & Spicer, J. (2016). Do hotter temperatures increase the incidence of self-harm hospitalisations?. *Psychology, Health & Medicine, 21*(2), 226–235. Available from https://doi.org/10.1080/13548506.2015.1028945.

Wolsko, C., & Marino, E. (2016). Disasters, migrations, and the unintended consequences of urbanization: What's the harm in getting out of harm's way? *Population and Environment, 37*(4), 411–428.

World Health Organization. (2014). *Gender, climate change, and health.* Geneva: WHO. Available from http://www.who.int/globalchange/publications/reports/gender_climate_change/en/.

Yun, K., Lurie, N., & Hyde, P. S. (2010). Moving mental health into the disaster-preparedness spotlight. *The New England Journal of Medicine, 363*(13), 1193–1194. Available from https://doi.org/10.1056/NEJMp1008304.

Zinzow, H. M., & Jackson, J. L. (2009). *Attributions for different types of traumatic events and post-traumatic stress among women. *Journal of Aggression, Maltreatment & Trauma, 18*(5), 499–515.

Zivin, J., & Shrader, J. (2016). Temperature extremes, health, and human capital. *The Future of Children, 26,* 31–50.

Individual impacts and resilience

10

Thomas J. Doherty
Sustainable Self, LLC, Portland, OR, United States

Among the greatest challenges of the unfolding problem of global climate change is marshalling the best of our intellectual and creative resources to engage with the enormity of the issues involved while also being conscious and expressive of our emotional reactions. Nowhere is the tension between the intellectual and the emotional aspects of climate change, between head and heart, more salient than at the individual level of human functioning: How people make sense of climate change on a personal level and how they deal with the psychological effects of climate change.

The scope of this chapter includes an overview of individual psychological impacts of climate change in their direct, indirect, and vicarious forms. The chapter highlights the importance of cultural values and ideals of social and environment justice; these provide the lenses through which many people around the world understand how and why climate change issues affect them. When envisioning psychological impacts of climate change, a conceptual distinction is made between adverse effects on *mental health*, such as the trauma or psychiatric symptoms in the wake of disasters, and adverse effects on *flourishing* as the burden of climate change jeopardizes people's ability to enjoy positive emotions and to trust in the future. This distinction is important as climate change affects both facets of human psychological functioning.

Moving beyond an understanding of psychological impacts to identify the most effective long-term strategies and techniques for coping with climate change is important task for future research and practice. The chapter describes how healthy coping responses to climate change range along a spectrum from the bare survival of individuals and communities to thriving and optimum health in the context of one's culture and values. Under the broad umbrella of psychological coping, there are potentials for resiliency, healing, and posttraumatic growth among individuals affected by climate change. The chapter proposes using a systems perspective as a framework that allows for understanding both (1) the ways that global scale climate issues affect individual people at the local level and (2) how to rationalize the benefits of individuals taking personal actions to positively address climate issues at larger scales. Adjusting to climate change with integrity and resilience will require a combination of realistic goal setting, building one's capacity for engagement though positive imagery and self-restoration, and commitment to long-term actions and goals including continuing education about climate change, making responsible lifestyle choices, and promoting political and structural changes in society.

Psychology and Climate Change. DOI: https://doi.org/10.1016/B978-0-12-813130-5.00010-2

There are several takeaways from this chapter:

- It is a difficult to thoroughly describe the mental health impacts of climate change as they occur at multiple scales of place and time, and are viewed through diverse cultural lens. Some psychological effects, such as anxiety or despair about the traumas, injustices, and extinctions associated with climate change, are experienced at a distance from disaster events.
- There is an urgent need to address the impacts of climate change disaster events on mental health. But, it is also important not to be limited by a disaster framework. The psychological impacts of climate change can also be chronic and gradual, driven by changes in economic well-being and losses to quality of life. Also, individuals buffered from the effects of disasters due to their region or relative wealth can still experience mental health impacts.
- The mental health impacts of climate change, even in the same geographic location, will differ between privileged and nonprivileged individuals, among genders, and between those of different cultures and values. Intersectionality and environmental justice frameworks can illuminate the unique impacts experienced by individuals across the sociocultural spectrum.
- The mental health impacts of climate change are influenced both by a person's psychological vulnerabilities and by the severity of the climate change impact they endure. For example, individuals with psychiatric issues (e.g., tendency toward anxiety, substance abuse or major mental illness) will be at higher risk for trauma associated with climate change. However, even among the most healthy and resilient individuals, severe disruptions due to climate change can cause mental health problems.
- The presence of pro-environmental values and environmental connectedness have both positive and negative influences on climate change impacts and coping. Individuals with strong environmental or social ethics, or a personal sense of connectedness to nature and other species, are at more risk for distress associated with climate change. However, environmental values and connections also promote action regarding climate change and a tendency toward health restoring and stress reducing nature-based recreation activities that buffer impacts.
- There is no one way to cope with climate change. When taking the perspectives of individuals around the globe, coping can range from basic survival, to maintaining a culturally intact community and way of life, to fostering one's personal growth and flourishing given the reality of climate change and its moral and practical dilemmas.
- An upside to the systemic nature of climate is that there are many ways to engage with the problems associated with climate change, and it is possible to intervene at multiple scales (i.e., at personal, community, or international levels) depending on one's goals and resources. Making progress on any subset of issues, such as alleviating poverty or disparities in one area, can contribute to system-wide improvements.
- Activities that address climate change and reducing one's carbon footprint (e.g., active commuting; practicing nonmaterialistic lifestyles, and creating urban greenspaces) also promote good health. Overall, addressing climate change is good for people's mental health.

10.1   How climate change impacts mental health: Three pathways

How can a planet-wide process like anthropogenic climate change influence people's mental health and well-being at the individual level? Simply put, climate change combines with other issues to create an ongoing, global health crisis. For example, changes in climate and local weather have synergistic interactions with poverty, discrimination, population pressures, competition for resources, and environmental problems. This makes impacts quite severe for some individuals, to the point of complete disruption of their lives and communities. Conversely, those who are geographically protected from negative effects, have resources to adapt to climate-related issues, or who have a sense of control over climate-related actions or policies are likely to experience fewer stressors, and, at least in the short term, may have their lives be largely unaffected.

While the potential for individual mental health impacts of climate change is highly varied, it is possible to identify general principles that predict psychological impacts and buffers. We can generalize that, at the individual level, climate change will affect mental health through:

1. Direct impacts related to disasters and acute environmental disruptions
2. Indirect impacts as climate-related issues ripple through societies and cultures, and
3. Vicarious impacts as those distant or buffered from direct impacts experience psychological distress or vicarious trauma.

There is also the potential for mental health impacts to be mixed (e.g., a person or community experiencing acute issues and chronic climate stressors). And, it is also helpful to characterize impacts as simple or complex in terms of their severity and the presence of compounding problems. For example, a resilient individual or community may cope with a single, discrete stressor such as the need for relocation due to erosion or rising sea levels. Alternatively, an individual or community may be hampered by a complex burden of pre-existing mental health issues, chronic environmental stressors, and limited resources from which to draw from.

Direct impacts: The causal pathways of the direct mental health impacts of climate change are relatively clear. Geophysical effects of climate change include flooding in coastal cities and inland cities near large rivers, hotter and drier weather associated with heat waves, increased wildfire, and stresses to fresh water supplies, and in northern regions, recession of sea ice causing increased erosion and threatening communities with relocation. Issues like severe weather events, poorer air quality, degraded food and water systems, and climate-related illnesses all impact individual health and increase the prevalence and severity of mental disorders (USGCRP, 2016). These issues also place increased demand on mental healthcare services in affected communities. In impoverished or marginalized communities, this added stress can overwhelm already compromised healthcare infrastructure (see review in Dodgen, et al., 2016, and discussion in Doherty, 2015a).

Some mental health injuries from natural and technological disasters associated with climate change are immediate. Climate disasters have a high potential for psychological trauma from personal injury, injury or death of loved ones and pets, damage or loss of home and possessions, and disruption or loss of community systems and livelihood. In disaster situations, pre-existing issues such as depression, family problems, psychiatric disorders, and alcohol and substance abuse can also be made more serious (see WHO: Impact of emergencies http://www.who.int/media-centre/factsheets/fs383/en/). Other disaster effects unfold more gradually because of changing temperatures, rising sea levels, and impacts on social infrastructure and food systems. (For reviews of direct psychological impacts see Chapter 9: Threats to mental health and wellbeing associated with climate change; Berry, Bowen & Kjellstrom, 2010; Clayton, Manning, Krygsman & Speiser, 2017; Doherty, 2015b; Gifford & Gifford, 2016; Satcher, Friel & Bell, 2007) (Fig. 10.1).

Indirect impacts: Climate disasters and acute environmental disruptions cause indirect impacts as these long-term and chronic disruptions manifest on the level of economics and societal infrastructures. For example, lingering droughts can impact people's livelihood, create food insecurity, exacerbate community divisions, and lead to forced relocation, refugee status and land-use conflicts (Hatfield, et al., 2014; Devine-Wright, 2013; Hsiang, Burke & Miguel, 2013; Fritze et al., 2008). All these issues impact mental health.

Social issues that arise or become more severe after disasters include economic problems, crime, and discrimination against marginalized groups. There can also be problems or side-effects created by humanitarian responses to disasters including overcrowding and lack of privacy in refugee camps, loss of community agency and traditional supports, and anxiety due to a lack of information about food distribution or how to obtain other basic services.

In many cases, acute disaster level impacts of climate change cascade into cultural level upheavals that promote a sense of dislocation, meaninglessness, or despair among affected individuals and their social groups (Silver & Grek-Martin, 2015; Adger, Barnett, Brown, Marshall & O'Brien, 2013). For example, the origins of the civil war in Syria and its resulting European refugee crisis are seen as being exacerbated by climate issues including a several year drought that contributed to

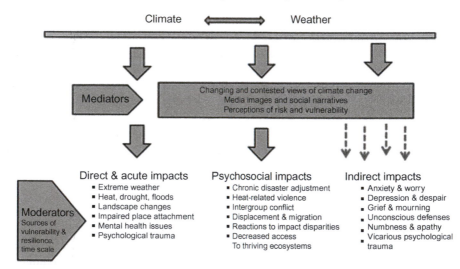

Figure 10.1 Mental health impacts—direct and indirect pathways from Doherty & Clayton, 2011

crop failures, hunger, and social conflicts (Kelley, Mohtadi, Cane, Seager & Kushnir, 2015). Cultural level impacts of climate change may be most salient in indigenous, land-based cultures of the far North (Cunsolo Willox et al., 2012; Durkalec, Furgal, Skinner & Sheldon, 2015). However, cultural impacts can also occur among individuals in developed nations who are experiencing chronic climate-related issues such as droughts, wildfires, or flooding (e.g., Morrissey & Reser, 2007; Tapsell & Tunstall, 2008).

Vicarious impacts: The most widespread and difficult to measure mental health effects of climate change are those that occur outside of a short-term or localized disaster frame. Vicarious mental health impacts occur as those distant or buffered from direct and indirect climate stressors experience psychological distress or trauma. Even in the absence of disaster impacts, people may still experience distress about climate change including worry, anxiety, and despair (Moser, 2013; Searle & Gow, 2010; Verplanken, & Roy 2013). In the United States, approximately half of people surveyed have reported feeling disgusted, helpless, or sad about climate change. About 35% report feeling angry or afraid, and 25% report feeling depressed or guilty. Americans characterized as Alarmed (16%) or Concerned (27%) are much more likely to report being convinced of the danger of climate change and to feel sad, disgusted, angry, or afraid (Leiserowitz, et al., 2014). Some individuals equate their climate concerns with other experiences of trauma or victimization (Simmons, 2016). Distress about climate issues can also manifest as a subtle sense of disconnection from local places or from a sense of ecological or planetary wholeness (Albrecht, 2011).

There are several mechanisms for vicarious mental health impacts. Rapid changes in technology, population, global conflicts, and environmental problems can create a sense of crisis among individuals, particularly given instantaneous news and information technologies (Stokols, Misra, Runnerstrom & Hipp, 2009). Vicarious traumatization regarding climate issues is more likely in those who are personally exposed to climate change stressors (e.g., disaster professionals, healthcare providers, and journalists) (Palm, Polusny & Follette, 2004). The potential for vicarious posttraumatic stress disorders is reflected in current psychiatric literature (Jones & Cureton, 2014). In general, traumatic stress is amplified by rapid, enhanced and visceral media experiences of disasters, and terror events (e.g., Ahern, Galea & Resnick, 2002; Schuster, Stein, Jaycox, Collins, Marshall, Elliott, et al., 2001). From a sociological perspective, impacts from climate change and global issues such as famine, war, or species extinction can be perceived as "distant suffering" (see Boltanski, 2009). The process of bearing witness to these issues from a place of safety or privilege can prompt moral and ethical dilemmas in some individuals.

10.2 Cultural diversity, intersectionality and climate justice

From a global, multicultural perceptive, there are multiple truths about the impacts of climate change. When individuals around the world talk about "impacts" they refer to many separate, interrelated issues. Climate change can be understood from the perspective of physics and geophysical changes in the land and seas; from the perspective of changing regional weather and temperatures; from the perspective of human or environmental disasters related to abrupt climactic changes; and from a social and political perspective on contentious and often stalemated responses to climate change among nations. These perspectives become frames through which the people understand what affects themselves and their families and communities, and in turn through which we can understand people's responses to these impacts. For example, climate change takes on certain meanings when considered from the perspective of a citizen of the "Global South" (e.g., Ghosh, 2017) who might view climate change effects in their region (e.g., on the Indian subcontinent) through a broader cultural and political context that includes a history of European colonialism and more recent effects of globalization and uneven economic and technological progress.

The feminist social science perspective of intersectionality (see Rosenthal, 2016) is helpful in identifying individual climate change impacts, because it highlights the relationship between structural and societal-level oppression and discrimination against individuals based on attributes such as gender and race. In this frame, mental health impacts of climate change are seen to intersect with individuals' identity and power, as well as the inequities and stigmas they face. For examples, consider climate impacts experienced globally by low income women of color such as increased burdens of obtaining fresh drinking water in chronic drought conditions (see Terry, 2009) and by workers and laborers in areas prone to excessive heat such as Southeast Asia and the Indian subcontinent (see Berry et al., 2010).

Closely related to an intersectionality frame, an environmental justice or "Just Sustainability" perspective highlights the increased vulnerability of socially marginalized groups to environmental stressors such as those caused by climate change (Agyeman, Bullard & Evans, 2003). Notions of justice and fairness are present across the spectrum of climate change issues, for example, how communities safeguard the elderly or infirm during heat waves, how regional authorities adequately disperse water and aid supplies in drought affected areas, or how government funds are used for disaster response and rebuilding efforts. An environmental justice perspective involves individuals' access to legal frameworks and tools to seek redress or compensation for environmental harms, fairness in distribution of resources, or benefits, participation in decision-making, and ethical protections for those least vulnerable. When these conditions are threatened or absent, individuals and communities will experience a lack of climate justice (see Hurlbert, 2015).

10.3 Climate change: Vulnerability and risk factors for mental health impacts

Understanding how an individual will respond to climate change is contingent on the severity of the climate impact or stressor they experience and its time frame (i.e., sudden or chronic) and on personal and contextual factors such their age, wealth and pre-existing physical and mental health; individual and cultural differences; as well as their understanding of climate change, environmental values, social influences, and community resources (Doherty, 2015a). For example, buffers to climate disaster impacts include a privileged social position, ability to travel or relocate, and access to educational and economic opportunities. Individuals with psychiatric issues (e.g., tendency toward anxiety, substance abuse, or major mental illness) will be at higher risk for trauma associated with climate change. The most vulnerable populations include people living in disaster-prone areas, indigenous communities, some communities of color, occupational groups with direct climate change, or disaster exposure (e.g., field workers, emergency first responders), those with existing disabilities or chronic illness, and older adults, women, and children (Gamble, et al., 2016). From an environmental justice perspective, people of color are often more vulnerable to the health-related impacts of climate change given their geographic placement and socioeconomic and demographic inequalities, such as income and education level (Grineski, et al., 2012; Parks & Roberts, 2006). Individuals from indigenous cultures are at risk for health impacts as well as additional impacts as climate changes disrupt traditional place-based lifeways (Durkalec et al., 2015; Maldonado, Colombi & Pandya, 2013).

Psychiatric risk factors: Even the most healthy and resilient persons may develop fatigue, strain, anxiety, and mood or behavioral problems when subjected to extreme stressors such as those associated with climate-related disasters. In disasters, mental reactions may also be superimposed upon pre-existing anxiety, mood, or psychotic disorders or upon brain or other physical injuries. Trauma-related psychological disorders are associated with risk and protective factors. For example, pre-trauma risk factors include prior mental disorders, environmental or socioeconomic stressors, and younger age at the time of exposure, while pre-trauma protective factors include social support and optimistic coping strategies. Risk factors *during* a disaster include personal injury or experiencing the death or injury of a loved one. Post-disaster risk factors include negative thoughts, unhealthy coping strategies, exposure to upsetting reminders, subsequent adverse life events, and financial or other trauma-related losses (Haskett, Scott, Nears, & Grimmett, 2008; Neria & Shultz, 2012).

Children: For children, direct and indirect disaster impacts can cause changes in behavior, development, memory, executive function, decision-making, and scholastic achievement (Somasundaram & van de Put, 2006). Direct experience of natural disasters can cause anxiety, nightmares, phobic behavior, and obsessive-compulsive symptoms, with the potential for physical-focused symptoms such as stomachaches among younger children (see Haase, 2017; Somasundaram & van de Put, 2006). In terms of the vicarious impacts of living in a climate-changed world, for both children and adolescents, problem-focused coping is associated with more worry more about climate change, while meaning-focused coping is positively related to well-being and optimism (Ojala, 2012, 2013).

Risks among educated and environmentally aware individuals: The presence of pro-environmental values and environmental connectedness have both positive and negative influences on climate change impacts and coping. Among many cultures, there are individuals or groups who see their identity as connected to nature, other species and natural processes (see Clayton, 2003). For those who consider the rights and well-being of other peoples, the natural world and other species to be in their scope of concern and ethical responsibility, climate change is a threat to identity and moral values. Education and awareness alone can increase the risk of distress regarding global climate change. Studies of environmental activists show that there is often a multidirectional relationship between one's accumulated knowledge, their empowerment to act, and their ability to notice and experience environmental problems (Kempton & Holland, 2003). Some individuals learn about climate change in an abstract way and then become more sensitive and aware of local climate impacts. Alternatively, individuals may be thrust into action due to experience of local climate impacts which then leads them to further understand the nature and scope of climate change worldwide.

10.4   Mental health disorders associated with global climate change

In terms of psychiatric diagnosis, the mental health impacts of climate change will manifest as (1) trauma or stressor-related disorders, (2) anxiety and depression, (3) substance use disorders, (4) increased severity or complications of existing disorders or mental health issues, (5) short-term or chronic adjustment disorders, and (6) psychosocial problems such as family or occupational issues (see discussion in Doherty, 2015b). An early meta-analysis of studies on the relationship between disasters and mental health impacts found that between 7% and 40% of all subjects in 36 studies showed some form of psychopathology. General anxiety was the type of psychopathology with the highest prevalence rate, followed by phobic, somatic, and alcohol impairment, and then depression and drug impairment, which were all elevated relative to prevalence in the general population (Rubonis & Bickman, 1991).

Given the variety and multiple scales of climate change impacts, and the possibility of vicarious stress or traumatization, the potential for diagnosable climate change-related mental health disorders is high. In many cases, issues like disasters or significant environmental stressors will be the proximal cause of the disorder. In the case of individuals who are buffered from direct impacts but experiencing vicarious stress and trauma, diagnosis will likely also be associated with more compounding psychological stressors such as occupational or relationship issues. In all cases, accurate psychiatric diagnosis requires clinical judgment based on a person's history and their cultural norms for expression of distress in the context of loss.

Trauma disorders: Consequences of climate-related disasters can include short-term acute stress disorder (lasting 3 days to 1 month) as well as posttraumatic stress disorder, characterized by significant impairment, intrusive memories, negative mood, dissociation, avoidance, and heightened arousal (manifested as sleep disturbance, irritable behavior, and/or hypervigilance). Based on current guidelines, formal diagnosis requires that a person has experienced a traumatic event, has witnessed it occurring to family members or friends, or has had repeated or extreme exposure to aversive details of events (American Psychiatric Association, 2013). Traumatic exposure via electronic media is considered a diagnostic criterion if the exposure occurred in a work setting, such as among hospital or emergency services professionals. Notably, vicarious posttraumatic symptoms have also been observed in the public among those exposed to repeated media images of traumatic events (e.g., Schuster et al., 2001).

Anxiety disorders: It is difficult to differentiate between normal and pathological anxiety and worry about environmental threats, such as climate change. Ecological worrying is a normal and expectable behavior that has been correlated with pro-environmental attitudes and behaviors and with positive personality traits, such as openness and agreeableness (Verplanken & Roy, 2013). This normal worry is often portrayed as "eco-anxiety" in popular media. An anxiety disorder may be diagnosed in the case of obsessive and disabling worry about climate change risks or with evidence of extreme physiological arousal or panic symptoms. It is important to note that psychological stress responses, including those regarding environmental issues, can manifest in a variety of physical symptoms.

Depressive disorders: Responses to natural disasters can be associated with depressive symptoms, including intense sadness, rumination, insomnia, poor appetite, and weight loss. Those experiencing a major impairment lasting 2 weeks or more may meet criteria for a major depressive episode. In issues of disasters or losses, it is important to delineate normal sadness and bereavement from clinical depression, those these may co-exist in the case of highly vulnerable individuals or in those with more severe symptoms or impairments.

Adjustment disorders: In the case of an identifiable stressor associated with marked emotional or behavioral symptoms and significant impairment relative to the community context and cultural norms, a diagnosis of adjustment disorder may be made. Notably, stressors associated with an adjustment disorder may affect a large group or, in the case of a natural disaster, a community. Adjustment disorders are typically self-limiting, but some may be considered chronic in the case of ongoing or unresolved stressors.

10.5   How climate change threatens psychological flourishing

To fully appreciate the impacts of global climate change on mental health, we must look beyond the prevalence and severity of mental illness and malaise to individuals' potential for well-being and flourishing. This is particularly important if one uses the perspective of health as a state of complete physical, mental, and social well-being and not merely the absence of disease or infirmity (i.e., WHO, n.d.). To assess the full range of climate change's psychological impacts across all regions and peoples, including among individuals and communities buffered from acute disaster events, it is necessary to view mental illness and mental health and well-ness as two distinct continua. Beyond the absence of illness or impairment, mental health and wellness includes the degree to which one feels positive and enthusiastic about their life, can thrive in the face of stress, and can realize their potential to work productively and contribute to her or his community (see Manderscheid et al., 2010).

From a positive psychology perspective (see Keyes, 2007), mental health and wellness includes the potential for *flourishing*. Climate change inhibits flourishing by impacting peoples' ability to experience:

- Positive emotions and avowed quality of life
- Positive psychological functioning (i.e., self-acceptance, mastery, meaning, and purpose)
- Positive social functioning (i.e., positive attitudes toward human differences and belief in societal potential).

It is in the diminishment of mental well-being and flourishing that the more far-ranging and chronic ripple effects of climate change disasters on individual's mental life become apparent.

Even among globally privileged individuals for whom climate change may be a relatively abstract or distant phenomenon, unfolding climate events and impacts can threaten or delegitimize one's sense of flourishing, their sense of meaning, and their trust in government and societal potential. This is particularly true when witnessing the frank inequalities among those affected by climate change and the muddled and conflicting societal responses to these issues Fig. 10.2.

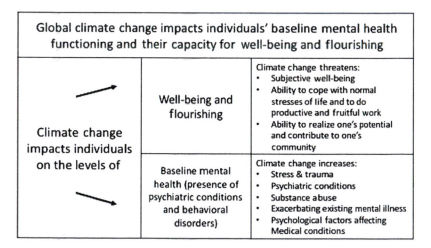

Figure 10.2 Climate change threatens individuals' mental health and capacity for flourishing.

10.6   Barriers to psychological coping with climate change: Complexity, disinformation, and powerlessness

In the popular mind, climate change presents a challenging psychological task: Rapid adjustment to changed ecosystems worldwide and an acceptance of human causation and responsibility for environmental losses and extinctions (Kolbert, 2014). Climate change also creates an over-arching narrative that connects and frames disparate global events (e.g., storms and weather events, natural and technological disasters, political and economic issues) with the potential to trouble people's daily lives and diminish their expectations for the future (Reser & Swim, 2011). Indeed, some theorists contend that perceived public apathy about climate change is more accurately considered paralysis at the size of the problem (see Weintrobe, 2013).

Even in optimum circumstances, the multiple scales inherent in climate change and the conflicted meanings attributed to climate phenomena makes the issue complex and confusing. In real-word settings, individuals must chart a course through the emotions and values of their families and social groups, and the often-abstract scientific nature of climate change discourse (Rudiak-Gould, 2013). Open dialog about climate issues is suppressed due to political polarization, censorship of climate change findings, and active antiscience disinformation and propaganda campaigns (Dunlap, McCright & Yarosh, 2016; Oreskes and Conway, 2010)—and pluralistic ignorance of shared climate concern of one's fellow citizens (see Chapter 4: Social construction of scientifically grounded climate change discussions). Problems with emotional expression are further enabled by coping styles that can promote various forms of minimization or denial at the individual and social group level (McDonald, Chai & Newell, 2015; Shepherd & Kay, 2012).

Coping with climate change is a global burden that eventually falls on individuals, and is most acutely felt by those who become sensitized to the issue due to their education, values, or direct experiences and vulnerability. There is support for legislation to confront climate action in every county of the United States (Marlon, Fine & Leiserowitz, 2017). However, a fairly small group of powerful corporate actors and elected officials have stymied concerted action (see Dunlap et al., 2016; Oreskes and Conway, 2010). Citizens confronted with urgent calls for action to prevent climactic tipping points are, in effect, "climate hostages" trapped by global political and economic dynamics beyond their control. This is particularly true of groups with limited political or economic power who must cope with local climate impacts created by distant processes (see discussion in Clayton et al., 2017).

10.7   Steps toward coping with global climate change as an individual

Moving beyond an understanding of mental health impacts of climate change to identify effective long-term strategies and techniques for psychological coping and flourishing is important task for the future research and practice. Across societies, successful coping can come in many forms, including preventive public health measures that promote resiliency and adaptation to environmental changes, therapeutic interventions in response to climate impacts, healing and posttraumatic growth following climate-related trauma. Psychological flourishing in the context of climate change transcends mental health to include positive emotions, self-acceptance, a sense of meaning, and a belief in society. As an initial direction, a systems perspective is one framework that allows for understanding (1) the ways that global scale climate issues affect individual people at local levels and (2) how to rationalize the benefits of individual actions on climate issues at larger scales. Ultimately, adjusting to climate change with integrity and resilience will require a combination of realistic personal goal setting, building one's capacity for engagement though hopeful imagery and self-restoration, and commitment to long-term actions and goals (including continuing education about climate change, making responsible lifestyle choices, and promoting structural changes in society by engaging in the politic process and undertaking nonviolent activism). As discussed below, resources from disaster mental health, and psychotherapy and counseling can augment individuals' self-help activities.

Using a systems perspective to give meaning to personal actions: When coping with climate change, it is very important to hold a systems perspective in mind. That is, the phenomenon / problem of climate change is an (1) interconnected set of (2) varied elements (i.e., human and natural systems) that (3) serve varied functions and purposes (i.e., the earth's climate and weather systems have synergistic interactions with human societies and technological infrastructure) (see Meadows, 2008 for a systems primer). A systems perspective allows us to see how changes in the natural environment (e.g., long-term droughts) can have ripple effects in human systems that in turn affect individual's personal health and well-being. Systems thinking also opens the possibility that many actions, even small ones, can positively contribute to the situation. For example, if an individual or group can help to ameliorate poverty, improve community healthcare or disaster response capabilities, promote regional cooperation, or create innovative ways to scale up sustainable energy sources, they will be making an important contribution to "solving" the problem of climate change. Further, systems concepts like resilience—*the ability of a system to maintain its functions after experiencing a disturbance*—guide collective actions that aid in human adaptation to climate change. For example, resilience thinking provides a rationale to protect the biological integrity of sensitive natural areas that in turn buffer communities from weather disasters and promote their long-term functioning (see National Oceanic and Atmospheric Administration (n.d.); Pelling, 2011; Tompkins & Adger, 2004). Concepts like resilience also provide inspiring images and metaphors that can aid in psychological coping (see Doppelt, 2016).

Finding validation and hope. At the outset, it is important to recognize that just as the mental health impacts of climate change are varied and diverse, so are potential ways to cope and to seek optimum health. In terms of long-term coping outside of disaster situations, there are several potential steps individuals can take. These include adopting positive attitudes and habits and mind, as well as making structural and behavioral changes to one's life †hat promote a sense of wellness and sustainability. At the level of thought and emotions, honest and reality-based psychological coping requires a balance of acceptance and validation of the troubling and despair-inducing nature of climate issues, including lack of control and sense of being a hostage to larger forces, with an equivalent commitment to hope, creativity, and personal renewal. In the context of long-term climate advocacy, hope can be considered one's highest vision of the possible, or the ecological world toward which the person strives for through their actions (see Roy & Roy, 2011). Hope constitutes a deep-seated guiding focus that is contrasted with the fluctuating emotions of optimism or pessimism prompted by short-term political and environment events. To support hope and a guiding vision, it is also important to continue to develop, reconnect with, and celebrate one's environmental values, the core values that prompt concerns with climate change and its negative effects.

Supporting environmental identity and restoration in nature: To the extent, one can articulate their sense of environmental identify (i.e., their personal identity and life history in relation to nature) their potential for integrity regarding their climate-related values and actions is increased. Engagement with climate change can be a way of practicing one's core values, using one's personal or professional gifts, expressing meaning and spirituality, and giving back in an altruistic way for the benefits one has received from nature. Climate arts and literature can be an inspiration in this regard. There are increasing number of climate change-related initiatives in the arts, including climate fiction and graphic novels (Milkoreit, Martinez & Eschrich, 2016; Squarzoni, 2014) as well as theater, photography and visual arts (e.g., see Bilodeau, 2016; Cape Farewell Project, n. d.). These works illustrate the individual journeys of the creators and provide examples of how people engage with the complex emotions and ethical dilemmas they experience regarding climate change. Memories of past growth-enhancing and restorative experiences in the outdoors and with other species provide examples for nature-based activities that individuals can practice for restoring their health, well-being and positive emotions. As the author has counseled individuals suffering from environmental grief: "Despair is fatigue in disguise." Restoration in nature through active adventures and recreation, or through esthetic or relaxing activities can re-inspire motivation and creativity.

Linking climate adaptation and mitigation with mental health: It is helpful for mental health professionals seeking to address climate change impacts to be familiar with the scientific literature on climate change, in particular, concepts of climate change mitigation and adaptation (see Chapter 1: Introduction: Psychology and climate change). Most therapeutic activities associated with climate change can be considered efforts to adapt to changes and mental health impacts. Further, the idea of going a step farther and seeking to *prevent* mental health impacts by addressing their causes move into the realm of climate change mitigation. In practice, efforts toward mental health, adaptation, and mitigation are entwined. For examples, for individuals who are experiencing climate impacts—and who also have resources and empowerment—strong feelings, personal responsibility and an impulse to take corrective action are an expected psychological response (see Reser & Swim, 2011). These feelings and motivations can in turn mediate those individuals' engagement in environmentally significant behaviors, such as seeking to limit their greenhouse gas emissions (Milfont, 2012). Promoting people's confidence in their ability to adapt to climate impacts can also increase their confidence to act to address the primary drivers of climate change—a so-called "adaptation-mitigation cascade" (see Doherty, 2015a, p. 208). In this regard, it is very important to promote the coping of privileged people who are minimally affected by climate change directly but are experiencing vicarious stressors and traumas. Their adaptation to vicarious impacts can encompass mitigation behaviors on their part, for example, when people in industrialized nations address their climate concerns by adopting a lifestyle with a smaller carbon footprint.

A focus on the co-benefits of climate action is also important to note. Echoing systems insights, a "personal sustainability" perspective (Doherty, 2015b) reminds us that humans are an integral part of nature. Actions that improve a person's individual health such as pursuing rest, exercise, nurturing social interactions, and engaging in restorative nature activities can be seen as ecological acts. This is not simply a matter of philosophy. As Clayton et al., (2017) note, behavioral options to address climate change are available now, are widespread, and these also tend to support individuals' psychological health. For example, increased adoption of active commuting, public transportation, green spaces, and clean energy are solutions that people can support and integrate into their daily lives, and help to curb stress, anxiety, and other mental problems incurred from the decline of economies, infrastructure, and social identity that comes from damage to the global climate.

Directly addressing climate justice issues: For marginalized individuals facing impacts and suffering from limited survival options, coping with climate change will begin with petitioning for social and environmental justice and "speaking truth to power." When addressing climate impacts with individuals in marginalized communities, there are several strategies useful to foster individuals' empowerment. These are drawn from an intersectionality framework (Rosenthal, 2016). It is important to recognize and collaborate with community members as social actors with *agency*, who are *responding to* and not simply experiencing global climate change and its impacts. It is appropriate to call out and critique unjust social structures and to build coalitions of individuals experiencing similar stressors. In the context of unjust or oppressive systems, it is necessary to recognize the value to individuals of *resistance* as well as resilience. To promote engagement, it is often necessary to begin with consciousness raising about climate issues and to support education and fact finding on the part of community members so they can tell their story. Local public health departments and grassroots environmental justice organizations are important resources for individuals seeking to become involved. Initial consciousness raising can in turn prompt education, increased awareness of issues and strategies, and more potential for people to see themselves as empowered agents of change. From a legal perspective, those seeking redress for environmental justice cases often use a pragmatic "whatever works" approach that includes knowledge of governance, legal statutes and scientific information, and also community

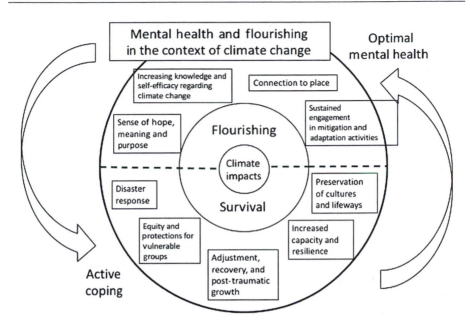

Figure 10.3 Mental health and flourishing in the context of climate change.

organizing, media messaging, lobbying efforts, negotiations, and other tactics (Zachek, Rubin & Scammell, 2015) Fig. 10.3.

The potential for optimal mental health and flourishing (e.g., hope, efficacy, connection to place, and engagement in mitigation activities) is built on a foundation of coping responses and outcomes predicated by individuals' survival needs (e.g., disaster response, adjustment and recovery, resilience, and cultural preservation).

10.8   Therapeutic responses to climate change impacts

Beyond self-help coping attempts, there is a spectrum of therapeutic practices with the potential to help individuals experiencing mental health impacts of climate change. These range from public health measures, to disaster response, and to counseling and psychotherapy. Ensuring mental health in a climate change context includes both alleviating symptoms and problems as well as promoting strengths and supporting personal expression and empowerment. Indeed, an important and under-recognized task of mental health professionals is helping individuals imagine a life of flourishing and meaning while maintaining a full consciousness of climate change and its complexity. Improving mental health at the individual level also includes empowering individuals to identify their resources for engaging with the climate issues that affect them. For example, mental health professionals can help people to identify information needed to educate themselves about how climate change affects their region or community, and to envision what climate-related actions they might take in their own lives, given their other life priorities, their social milieu, and the resources or skills they can offer.

Disaster mental health interventions: In the aftermath of disasters, early interventions to assist with basic needs and functional recovery have profound benefits; the most effective measures at the personal level are attentive to family context and emotional factors (Norris, Friedman & Watson, 2002). Effective disaster response can create the conditions for recovery and resiliency among affected individuals. For example, evidence and experience show that people who feel safe, connected, calm, and hopeful; have access to social, physical, and emotional support; and find ways to help themselves after a disaster will be better able to recover long-term from mental health effects (see http://www.who.int/mediacentre/factsheets/fs383/en/). Thus, early to mid-stage intervention and prevention measures should promote a sense of safety, self-efficacy, connectedness, and hope (e.g., by helping individuals to reconnect with family and friends and begin to imagine their recovery plans, see Hobfoll, Watson & Carl, 2007). Post-disaster efforts can also support people's sense of place and connections to their home region, through recognizing and honoring people's personal environmental identity and local cultural traditions and values. (Re)connection to place may entail either rebuilding a home or finding a new home in the case of relocation or refugee status.

Mental health providers serving disaster victims should remain aware of the potential for resilience and posttraumatic growth. After disasters, resilient individuals will continue to have positive emotions and show only minor and transient disruptions in their ability to function. This resiliency is a trajectory distinct from an injury-recovery process (Bonanno, 2004). Further, as examples of posttraumatic growth, some individuals come through a significant disruption with the feeling of having gained something positive, such as stronger social relationships, specific skills, or insights about their lives and home regions (Lowe, Manove & Rhodes, 2013; Ramsay & Manderson, 2011). Therapeutic activities can deepen individual's sense of healing and posttraumatic growth following disasters and, in turn, build future resilience.

Addressing climate change in psychotherapy and counseling: Short-term cognitive behavioral therapies can be useful to help those recovering from disasters to transition from high stress and life disruptions, to set goals, and to assess barriers to rebuilding their lives. For individuals experiencing indirect or vicarious impacts, cognitive behavioral therapies can help individuals to assess environmental threats, to base these on realistic appraisals of their life situations, and to commit to concrete actions that address their concerns and are within their scope of influence. Existential-humanistic or mindfulness-based therapies can help individuals to build their capacity to be present with the gravity and complexity of climate change while also creating a holding space for their emotional responses. Nature-based counseling and ecotherapy may be a particularly good fit for individuals with strong environmental values and connection with place (see Doherty, 2016). Any approach that encourages people to spend time doing safe, nature-based, activities, such as outdoor walking, gardening, or recreational activities can be helpful to reduce physiological stress, take a break from social or news media, and promote perspective-taking and creativity. For many individuals, nature is also a space to reconnect with their deeper spiritual or religious values.

Climate-specific psychotherapies: In addition to standard psychotherapeutic approaches, mental health theorists and clinicians have begun to create more specific guidance regarding climate change and other environmental issues. Writings in the *ecopsychology* tradition have long considered the interplay between personal mental health, connection to nature and the experience of environmental losses (e.g., Nicholsen, 2001; Macy & Young-Brown, 1998; Roszak, Gomes & Kanner, 1995). Weintrobe (2013) and Kiehl (2016) have approached climate change from the perspective of psychoanalytic and Jungian psychotherapy, while Davenport (2017) has created a clinician's guide to resiliency in an era of climate change. Randall (2009) has developed a group therapy for individuals coping with climate change and other environmental concerns. More recently, grassroots initiatives based on a 12-step Recovery approach have addressed people's grief about climate change (see Simmons, 2016). What these approaches have in common is a validation of the emotional aspects of climate change and engagement of the affected individuals' values and hopes. By creating connections among like-minded individuals and a space to share stories and receive social support, these interventions create an opportunity for distressed individuals to move from isolation and despair to a sense of community and empowerment. To the extent that individuals can create or recover a sense of ecological connectedness to their home places, and see their local climate actions as important, they are less likely to fall prey to a disempowering focus on distant global problems beyond their control.

10.9 A positive message: Thriving in the era of global climate change

When reflecting on the mental health impacts of global climate change, one is confronted by two truths: We are all living as a "Climate Hostages" on a warming planet, and all humans have the potential for flourishing in adverse conditions. From a positive perspective, climate change is an invitation to reframe global consciousness from that of a collection of over-arching "wicked problems" to a wealth of possibilities for humanitarian and ecological actions. No one person or group can possibly address all the systemic issues related to global climate change. This realization is sobering. But, it also contains seeds of possibility for coping and response. The systemic nature of global climate change allows for many ways to engage. To positively address the problem of climate change, each person or group must engage with and help solve the problems within their scope of influence. Making progress on any one set of issues can contribute to both local and widespread solutions. As noted, if an individual or group can help to ameliorate poverty, improve regional cooperation, create innovative ways to scale up sustainable energy sources, or improve community healthcare or disaster response capabilities, they will be making an important contribution to "solving" the problem of climate change.

This chapter addressed the challenge of framing the mental health impacts of climate change broadly, by examining a spectrum of issues from direct and acute disaster impacts, to chronic social and economic stresses, to despair at witnessing climate problems at a distance. The mental health functioning of individuals was distinguished from their positive opportunities for flourishing, as these are both negatively affected by climate change. Groups vulnerable to climate change impacts and common barriers to coping were highlighted, as well as strategies for engagement and personal and therapeutic responses. To foster psychological flourishing in the context of climate change requires protecting and bolstering mental health in the wake of disasters as well as promoting positive emotions, a sense of meaning, and belief in society. To this end, psychologists and other mental health professionals have a role to play as researchers, disaster first responders, and as confidants in intimate therapeutic settings. To the extent that individuals (and psychologists and other mental health professionals) can manifest their potential for flourishing, and to use their capabilities to address the societal impacts of climate change within their scope of influence, it is possible to imagine thriving in an era of global climate change.

References

Adger, W. N., Barnett, J., Brown, K., Marshall, N., & O'Brien, K. (2013). Cultural dimensions of climate change impacts and adaptation. *Nature Climate Change*, *3*, 112–117. Available from https://doi.org/10.1038/nclimate1666.

Agyeman, J., Bullard, R. D., & Evans, B. (2003). *Just sustainabilities*. Cambridge, MA: MIT Press.

Ahern, J., Galea, S., Resnick, H., Kilpatrick, D., Bucuvalas, M., Gold, J., et al. (2002). Television images and psychological symptoms after the September 11 terrorist attacks. *Psychiatry: Interpersonal & Biological Processes*, *65(4)*, 289–300.

Albrecht, G. (2011). Chronic environmental change: emerging "psychoterratic" syndromes. In I. Weissbecker (Ed.), *Climate change and human well-being: Global challenges and opportunities* (pp. 43–56). New York, NY: Springer.

American Psychiatric Association. (2013). *Diagnostic and statistical manual of mental disorders: DSM-5*. Washington, DC: American Psychiatric Association.

Berry, H. L., Bowen, K., & Kjellstrom, T. (2010). Climate change and mental health: a causal pathways framework. *International Journal of Public Health*, *55(2)*, 123–132. Available from https://doi.org/10.1007/s00038-009-0112-0.

Bilodeau, C. (2016). *As the climate change threat grows, so does a theatrical response.* American Theater. Retrieved from: http://www.americantheatre.org/2016/03/30/as-the-climate-change-threat-grows-so-does-a-theatrical-response/.

Boltanski, L. (2009). Distant suffering: Morality, media and politics (G. Burchell, Trans.) London: Cambridge University Press.

Bonanno, G. A. (2004). Loss, trauma, and human resilience: have we underestimated the human capacity to thrive after extremely aversive events? *American Psychologist*, *59(1)*, 20–28. Available from https://doi.org/10.1037/0003-066X.59.1.20.

Cape Farewell Project (n.d.). Retrieved from: http://www.capefarewell.com/

Clayton, S. (2003). *Environmental identity: A conceptual and operational definition in Clayton & Opotow Eds. Identity and the natural environment.* Cambridge, MA: MIT Press.

Clayton, S., Manning, C. M., Krygsman, K., & Speiser, M. (2017). *Mental health and our changing climate: Impacts, implications, and guidance.* Washington, DC: American Psychological Association, and ecoAmerica.

Cunsolo Willox, A., Harper, S., Ford, J., Landman, K., Houle, K., & Edge, V. (2012). From this place and of this place: Climate change, health, and place in Rigolet, Nunatsiavut, Canada, & the Rigolet Inuit Community Government *Social Sciences and Medicine, 75* (3), 538–547.

Davenport, L. (2017). *Emotional resiliency in the era of climate change.* London: Jessica Kingsley Publishers.

Dodgen, D., Donato, D., Kelly, N., La Greca, A., Morganstein, J., Reser, J., et al. (2016). Ch. 8: Mental health and well-being. In A. Crimmins, J. Balbus, J. L. Gamble, C. B. Beard, J. E. Bell, D. Dodgen, et al. (Eds.), *The impacts of climate change on human health in the United States: A scientific assessment* (pp. 217–246). Washington, DC: U.S. Global Change Research Program. Available from https://doi.org/10.7930/J0TX3C9H.

Doherty, T. J. (2015a). Mental health impacts. In J. Patz, & B. S. Levy (Eds.), *Climate change and public health.* New York: Oxford University Press.

Doherty, T. J. (2015b). *Invited address. Supporting sustainable self: reflections of an ecopsychologist. Presented at the cultivating the globally sustainable self research-to-practice summit.* Harrisonburg, VA:: George Mason University.

Doherty, T. J. (2016). Theoretical and empirical foundations for ecotherapy. In M. Jordan, & J. Hinds (Eds.), Ecotherapy: Theory, research & practice (pp. 12–26)). London: Palgrave.

Doppelt, B. (2016). *Transformational resilience.* Oxford, UK: Greenleaf Publishing.

Dunlap, R. E., McCright, A. M., & Yarosh, J. H. (2016). The political divide on climate change: Partisan polarization widens in the U.S. *Environment: Science and Policy for Sustainable Development, 58*(5), 4–23. Available from https://doi.org/10.1080/00139157.2016.1208995.

Durkalec, A., Furgal, C., Skinner, M., & Sheldon, T. (2015). Climate change influences on environment as a determinant of indigenous health: Relationships to place, sea ice, and health in an Inuit community. *Social Science and Medicine, 136–137,* 17–26.

Gamble, J. L., Balbus, J., Berger, M., Bouye, K., Campbell, V., Chief, K., et al. (2016). *Populations of concern. The impacts of climate change on human health in the United States: A scientific assessment* (pp. 247–286). Washington, DC: U.S. Global ChangeResearch Program. Available from https://doi.org/10.7930/J0Q81B0T.

Ghosh, A. (2017). *The great derangement: Climate change and the unthinkable.* Chicago, US: University of Chicago Press.

Gifford, E., & Gifford, R. (2016). The largely unacknowledged impact of climate change on mental health. *Bulletin of the Atomic Scientists, 72*(5), 292–297. Available from https://doi.org/10.1080/00963402.2016.1216505.

Grineski, S. E., Collins, T. W., Ford, P., Fitzgerald, R., Aldouri, R., Velázquez-Angulo., et al. (2012). Climate change and environmental injustice in a bi-national context. *Applied Geography, 33,* 25–35.

Haase, E. (2017). A closer look: children's emotional responses to climate change. In S. Clayton, C. M. Manning, K. Krygsman, & M. Speiser (Eds.), *Mental health and our changing climate: Impacts, implications, and guidance.* Washington, DC: American Psychological Association, and ecoAmerica.

Haskett, M. E., Scott, S. S., Nears, K., & Grimmett, M. A. (2008). Lessons from Katrina: Disaster mental health service in the Gulf Coast region. *Professional Psychology: Research and Practice, 39*, 93−99.

Hatfield, J., Takle, G., Grotjahn, R., Holden, P., Izaurralde, R. C., Mader, T., et al. (2014). Agriculture. In J. M. Melillo, T. C. Richmond, & G. W. Yohe (Eds.), *Climate change impacts in the United States: The thirdnational climate assessment* (pp. 150−174). Washington, DC: U.S. Global Change Research Program. Available from https://doi.org/10.7930/.

Hobfoll, S. E., Watson, P. B., Carl, C., Bryant, R. A., Brymer, M. J., Friedman, M. J., et al. (2007). Five essential elements of immediate and mid-term mass trauma intervention: Empirical evidence. *Psychiatry: Interpersonal and Biological Processes, 70*(4), 283−315.

Hurlbert, M. (2015). Climate justice: A call for leadership. *Environmental Justice, 8*(2), 51−55. Available from https://doi.org/10.1089/env.2014.0035.

Jones, L. K., & Cureton, J. L. (2014). Trauma redefined in the DSM-5: Rationale and implications for counseling practice. *The Professional Counselor, 4*, 257−271. Retrieved from: http://tpcjournal.nbcc.org/trauma-redefined-in-the-dsm-5-rationale-and-implications-for-counseling-practice/.

Kelley, C. P., Mohtadi, S., Cane, M. A., Seager, R., & Kushnir, Y. (2015). Climate change in the Fertile Crescent and implications of the recent Syrian drought. *Proceedings of the National Academy of Sciences, 112*(11), 3241−3246.

Kempton, & Holland. (2003). Identity and sustained environmental practice. In S. Clayton, & S. Opotow (Eds.), *Identity and the natural environment* (pp. 317−342)). Cambridge, MA: MIT Press.

Keyes, C. L. (2007). Promoting and protecting mental health as flourishing. *American Psychologist, 62*(2), 95−108.

Kolbert, E. (2014). *The sixth extinction.* New York: Henry Holt and Co.

Leiserowitz, A., Maibach, E., Roser-Renouf, C., Feinberg, G., Rosenthal, S., & Marlon, J. (2014). *Climate change in the American mind: Americans' global warming beliefs and attitudes in November, 2013.* New Haven, CT: Yale University and George Mason University, Yale Project on Climate Change Communication.

Lowe, S. R., Manove, E. E., & Rhodes, J. E. (2013). Posttraumatic stress and posttraumatic growth among low-income mothers who survived Hurricane Katrina. *Journal of Consulting and Clinical Psychology, 81*(5), 877−889. Available from https://doi.org/10.1037/a0033252.

Maldonado, J., Colombi, B., & Pandya, R. (2013). Climate change and indigenous peoples in the United States (Special Issue). *Climatic Change, 120*(3), 509−682.

Macy, J., & Young Brown, M. (1998). *Coming back to life: Practices to reconnect our lives, our world.* Gabriola Island, BC: New Society Publishers.

Manderscheid, R. W., Ryff, C. D., Freeman, E. J., McKnight-Eily, L. R., Dhingra, S., & Strine, T. (2010). Evolving definitions of mental illness and wellness. *Preventing Chronic Disease, 7*. Available from http://www.cdc.gov/pcd/issues/2010/jan/09_0124.htm, Accessed 20.02.18.

Marlon, J. R., Fine, E., & Leiserowitz, A. (2017). *A majority of Americans in every state say the U.S. should participate in the Paris Climate Agreement.* New Haven, CT: Yale University, Yale Program on Climate Change Communication.

McDonald, R., Chai, H., & Newell, B. (2015). Personal experience and the 'psychological distance' of climate change: An integrative review. *Journal of Environmental Psychology, 44*, 109−118.

Meadows, D. H. (2008). *Thinking in systems*. White River Junction, VT: Chelsea Green Publishing.

Milfont, T. L. (2012). The interplay between knowledge, perceived efficacy and concern about global warming and climate change: a one-year longitudinal study. *Risk Analysis, 32(6)*, 1003–1020.

Milkoreit, M., Martinez, M., & Eschrich, J. (Eds.), (2016). *Everything change*. Tempe, AZ: Arizona State University. Retrieved from: https://climateimagination.asu.edu/everything-change/.

Morrissey, S. A., & Reser, J. P. (2007). Natural disasters, climate change and mental health considerations for rural Australia. *Australian Journal of Rural Health, 15(2)*, 120–125.

Moser, S. C. (2013). Navigating the political and emotional terrain of adaptation: Community engagement when climate change comes home. In S. C. Moser, & M. T. Boykoff (Eds.), *Successful adaptation to climate change: Linking science and policy in a rapidly changing world* (pp. 289–305). New York, NY: Routledge.

National Oceanic and Atmospheric Administration (n.d.). US Climate Resilience Toolkit. Retrieved from: https://toolkit.climate.gov/

Neria, Y., & Shultz, J. M. (2012). Mental health effects of Hurricane Sandy: Characteristics, potential aftermath, and response. *JAMA, 308(24)*, 2571–2572.

Nicholsen, S. W. (2001). *The love of nature at the end of the world*. Cambridge, MA: MIT Press 978-0-262640-51-0.

Norris, F. H., Friedman, M. J., & Watson, P. J. (2002). 60,000 disaster victims speak: part II. summary and implications of the disaster mental health research. *Psychiatry: Interpersonal and Biological Processes, 65(3)*, 240–260.

Ojala, M. (2012). How do children cope with global climate change? Coping strategies, engagement, and well-being. *Journal of Environmental Psychology, 32*, 225–233. Available from https://doi.org/10.1016/j.jenvp.2012.02.004.

Ojala, M. (2013). Coping with climate change among adolescents: implications for subjective well-being and environmental engagement. *Sustainability, 5*, 2191–2209. Available from https://doi.org/10.3390/su5052191.

Oreskes, N., & Conway, E. M. (2010). Defeating the merchants of doubt. *Nature., 465*, 686–687. Available from https://doi.org/10.1038/465686a.

Palm, K. M., Polusny, M. A., & Follette, V. M. (2004). Vicarious traumatization: potential hazards and interventions for disaster and trauma workers. *Prehospital and Disaster Medicine, 19(1)*, 73–78.

Parks, B. C., & Roberts, J. T. (2006). Globalization, vulnerability to climate change, and perceived injustice. *Society and Natural Resources, 19(4)*, 337–355.

Pelling, M. (2011). *Adaptation to climate change: From resilience to transformation*. New York: Routledge.

Ramsay, T., & Manderson, L. (2011). Resilience, spirituality and posttraumatic growth: Reshaping the effects. In I. Weissbecker (Ed.), *Climate change and human well-being: Global challenges and opportunities* (pp. 165–184). London: Springer.

Reser, J. P., & Swim, J. K. (2011). Adapting to and coping with the threat and impacts of climate change. *American Psychologist, 66(4)*, 277–289. Available from https://doi.org/10.1037/a0023412.

Rosenthal, L. (2016). Incorporating intersectionality into psychology: an opportunity to promote social justice and equity. *American Psychologist, 71(6)*, 474–485.

Roszak, T., Gomes, M. E., & Kanner, A. D. (Eds.), (1995). *Ecopsychology: Restoring the earth, healing the mind*. San Francisco: Sierra Club books.

Roy, D. & Roy, J. (2011). *The Practice of Hope*. Presented at TEDxConcordiaUPortland. Retrieved from: https://www.youtube.com/watch?v = jJcV2v_M6t4.

Rubonis, A. V., & Bickman, L. (1991). Psychological impairment in the wake of disaster: The disaster—psychopathology relationship. *Psychological Bulletin, 109*(3), 384—399.

Rudiak-Gould, P. (2013). We have seen it with our own eyes: Why we disagree about climate change visibility. *Weather, Climate, and Society, 5*(2), 120—132. Available from https://doi.org/10.1175/WCAS-D-12-00034.1.

Satcher, D., Friel, S., & Bell, R. (2007). Natural and manmade disasters and mental health. *JAMA, 298*(21), 2540—2542. Available from https://doi.org/10.1001/jama.298.21.2540.

Schuster, M., Stein, B., Jaycox, L., Collins, R., Marshall, G., Elliott, M., . . . Berry, S. (2001). A national survey of stress reactions after the September 11, 2001, terrorist attacks. *New England Journal of Medicine, 345*(20), 1507—1512. Available from https://doi.org/10.1056/NEJM200111153452024.

Searle, K., & Gow, K. (2010). Do concerns about climate change lead to distress? *International Journal of Climate Change Strategies and Management, 2*(4), 362—379.

Shepherd, S., & Kay, A. (2012). On the perpetuation of ignorance: System dependence, system justification, and the motivated avoidance of sociopolitical information. *Journal of Personality and Social Psychology, 102*(2), 264—280.

Silver, A., & Grek-Martin, J. (2015). Now we understand what community really means: reconceptualizing the role of sense of place in the disaster recovery process. *Journal of Environmental Psychology, 42*, 32—41. Available from http://dx.doi.org/10.1016/j.jenvp.2015.01.004.

Simmons, D. (2016). *Sad about climate change? There's a support group for that*. Yale Climate Connections. Retrieved from: https://www.yaleclimateconnections.org/2016/11/climate-change-support-group-launches/.

Somasundaram, D. J., & van de Put, W. A. C. M. (2006). Management of trauma in special populations after a disaster. *The Journal of Clinical Psychiatry, 67*(2), 64—73.

Stokols, D., Misra, S., Runnerstrom, M. G., & Hipp, J. A. (2009). Psychology in an age of ecological crisis: From personal angst to collective action. *American Psychologist, 64*(3), 181—193.

Tapsell, S. M., & Tunstall, S. M. (2008). I wish I'd never heard of Banbury": the relationship between "place" and the health impacts of flooding. *Health & Place, 14*(2), 133—154.

Terry, G. (2009). *Climate change and gender justice*. Bourton on Dunmore, UK: Practical Action Publishing/Oxfam GB.

Tompkins, E. L., & Adger, W. N. (2004). Does adaptive management of natural resources enhance resilience to climate change? *Ecology and Society, 9*(2), 10. Retrieved from http://www.ecologyandsociety.org/vol9/iss2/art10/.

United States Global Change Research Program. (2016). The *impacts* of *climate change* on *human health* in the United States: A *scientific assessment*. Washington, DC: Author. Available from https://doi.org/10.7930/J0R49NQX.

Verplanken, B., & Roy, D. (2013). My worries are rational, climate change is not: Habitual ecological worrying is an adaptive response. *PLoS ONE, 8*(9), e74708. Available from https://doi.org/10.1371/journal.pone.0074708.

Weintrobe, S. (2013). *Engaging with climate change*. London: Routledge.

World Health Organization. (n.d.). Frequently asked questions. Retrieved from: http://www.who.int/suggestions/faq/en/

Zachek, C. M., Rubin, S. M., & Scammell, M. K. (2015). Whatever works: Legal tactics and scientific evidence in environmental justice cases. *Environmental Justice, 8*(1), 20—25. Available from https://doi.org/10.1089/env.2014.0024.

Psychological perspectives on community resilience and climate change: Insights, examples, and directions for future research

Daniel A. Chapman[1], Carlie D. Trott[2], Linda Silka[3], Brian Lickel[1] and Susan Clayton[4]
[1]University of Massachusetts Amherst, Amherst, MA, United States, [2]Colorado State University, Fort Collins, CO, United States, [3]University of Maine, Orono, ME, United States, [4]The College of Wooster, Wooster, OH, United States

Research investigating the psychological dynamics involved in climate change decision-making and policy support has grown exponentially in recent years, as evidenced by the multiplicity and depth of topics reviewed in this volume. The accumulated research has significantly expanded our understanding of the variety of beliefs and values individuals hold regarding climate change-related issues, how these appraisals as well as direct experiences with climate change influence perceptions and behaviors, and the promise of utilizing evidence-based communication strategies to more effectively promote pro-environmental, climate change-directed action. In spite of the many strengths of this work, several gaps require additional attention from psychological researchers. This chapter addresses the under-studied topic of climate change community resilience: The study of how neighborhoods, local communities, and regional actors can prepare and effectively "bounce back" following impacts of climate change. We argue that this is an important area in which increased involvement from the psychological research community can yield important theoretical insights while simultaneously increasing the applied value of psychological research on climate change.

Investigating psychological issues at the community level opens new perspectives and avenues for understanding individuals and their relationship to public issues such as sustainability (Geigis, Hamin, & Silka, 2007; Portes & Rumbaut, 2006; Riemer & Reich, 2011). Many kinds of social entities fall under the scope of being a "community," ranging from neighborhoods within cities to largely rural regions incorporating smaller cities and towns. Communities are in some sense the "glue" of individuals' lives, where dense networks of social bonds are established and where individuals have concrete opportunities for enacting social and political change. Many of people's daily activities take place in their local communities and have a direct impact on shaping those communities. Communities are where

Psychology and Climate Change. DOI: https://doi.org/10.1016/B978-0-12-813130-5.00011-4

children are educated, families seek their health care, and police and law enforcement operate; the housing, parks, and neighborhoods where people carry out their daily activities are all in the community, as is the public transportation people take and often the jobs that they hold (Santiago, Jennings & Carrion, 2005; Silka, 2007). These systems are the locations where changes are profoundly felt and where those working in these systems are confronted—often on a daily basis—with the limits of approaches they found useful in the past (Turcotte & Silka, 2007). It is within these systems that people are pressed to find solutions to problems such as how to provide local services in the face of climate change.

Communities are also where pressing disparities are most evident (both within and between communities), including novel or exacerbated problems due to climate change. Fundamental resources for promoting well-being, cohesion, and resilience (e.g., parks, schools, libraries, and emergency centers) are less available in some areas than others. Infrastructure vulnerability and adaptive capacity are variable and unequal across communities, and different geographic regions are more or less vulnerable to different types of climate change impacts. Amidst the wide range of experiences of climate change, psychological research can contribute to understanding of how to promote community resilience and well-being.

In this chapter, we begin by describing perspectives on community resilience and offer insights into what constitutes a "resilient community." This is followed by a discussion of benefits to psychological researchers from focusing on climate change resilience at the community level, and a review of the characteristics that research suggests are important to creating resilient communities. The chapter concludes with practical recommendations for fostering community resilience and recommendations for future research.

11.1 What is community resilience?

Climate change will bring challenges to many communities. Their relative success at facing these challenges will have significant consequences for the individual members of the community, as well as for the larger polities within which those communities exist. Scholarship on environmental (as well as economic) challenges to local communities has developed a set of conceptual frameworks to understand the adaptive response of communities to challenges. Chief among these concepts is *community resilience*. The idea of community resilience (and the idea of resilience more broadly) has roots in multiple areas of research, including trauma and human development, ecological systems thinking, engineering, disaster preparedness, and developmental economics (e.g., Brown & Kulig, 1996/1997; Buikstra et al., 2010; Cox & Perry, 2011; Murphy, 2007). These different research areas bring unique methods and topical expertise to what is an inherently broad and complex topic. However, this breadth also poses challenges for the knowledge integration, clarity, and focus required for productive and useful interdisciplinary research.

11.1.1 Community resilience has diverse origins and multiple definitions

In everyday language, resilience has two meanings: Elasticity, and being able to spring back into shape after deformation; and a more subjective meaning of the capacity to recover quickly from difficulties and having "toughness" (Resilience, 2017). The idea of community resilience can be linked historically to at least two other streams of research using the idea of resilience as a metaphor for complex processes that reflect these everyday meanings. The first, and probably the most influential, was work in the early 1970s characterizing how ecosystems responded to stress and change (Holling, 1973). Over time, this work, with its beginnings in the study of ecological systems, has grown to recognize the interplay of human and natural systems, and efforts increasingly focus on investigating the ways in which social and ecological resilience are both similar and are contextually connected (e.g., Adger, 2000; Berkes, Colding & Folke, 2008; Magis, 2010; Ostrom, 2009; Walker, Holling, Carpenter & Kinzig, 2004).

In contrast to how resilience is often viewed in ecosystems, researchers in the social sciences studying human development tend to examine resilience in terms of individual responses to adversity, coping behaviors, and preparedness for future hardships. This work grows out of research on protective factors that attenuate the impact of risks associated with childhood development under adversity (e.g., work on poverty; Garmezy, 1991). This work has also undergone development over time, with researchers arguing for a study of social and developmental processes rather than cataloging static factors (Egeland, Carlson & Sroufe, 1993; Rutter, 1987). Outside of the childhood development literature, researchers studying people's responses to trauma (including large scale disasters) began to recognize that traumatic experiences do not always result in uniformly negative outcomes. Instead, some people show significant resilience and even post-traumatic growth in the context of challenging events (Bonanno, 2004). To date, however, merging the different conceptions of resilience together or developing frameworks capable of incorporating both resilience perspectives simultaneously has proven difficult. Furthermore, in comparison with infrastructure and ecosystems resilience, the study on individual and community resilience is considerably less well-developed.

11.1.2 Defining and studying resilience in the context of communities and climate change

Work on community resilience is rooted strongly in research and policy work on disaster response and disaster risk reduction. As discussed by Cutter et al. (2008), US federal government analysis of the human and financial consequences of disaster risks motivated the development of programs for disaster-resistant communities which included not only disaster resilient infrastructure, but also social coordination, communication, and planning processes. This work was important in prompting the development of community resilience as an organizing principle in policy analysis and scholarship. Three concepts closely related to community resilience are *vulnerability, adaptive capacity,* and *agency.* Although vulnerability and resilience can be seen as two sides of the same coin, they are also defined separately in some analyses. For example, Cutter et al. (2008) define vulnerabilities as the inherent pre-event characteristics that create the potential for harm, but resilience as not only static buffering characteristics but also the abilities of the community to respond flexibly and productively when confronted with a challenge.

This definition of community resilience has close connection to the idea of adaptive capacity (Brown & Westaway, 2011; Cutter et al., 2008). Brown and Westaway (2011) define adaptive capacity as the "set of latent characteristics, or the potential, needed to adapt to climate change and the ability to be actively involved in the process of change" (p. 324). Agency is also an important element of their analysis of resilience. Drawing from McLaughlin and Dietz (2008), Brown and Westaway define agency as the ability of individuals and groups to make choices and have a causal role in their own history. In contrast to more static conceptions of resilience, the agency perspective highlights that individuals and communities are not passive spectators whose vulnerability or resilience is a product of factors exogenous to their actions. We agree with this perspective, conceptualizing community resilience as *both the static resources and characteristics that buffer a community's vulnerabilities, and also the agentic qualities of community members and the community as a whole that allow it to adaptively prepare, respond, and grow in response to environmental challenges or harmful events.*

Several important prior reviews provide frameworks for community resilience that are in many respects consistent with our perspective, and may be usefully applied to psychological research. Cutter et al.'s (2008) disaster resilience of place (DROP) model presents both a temporal framework for understanding how community resilience operates in response to natural disasters and also a set of categories for measuring what they call "inherent resilience." These categories include ecological, social, economic, institutional, infrastructure, and "community competence" variables. As Cutter et al. note, in most instances, these categories of resilience have not been extensively operationalized or studied at the local level.

Norris, Stevens, Pfefferbaum, Wyche, and Pfefferbaum (2008) provide a comprehensive review and framework for community resilience that is rooted in both the disaster-risk and community psychology literatures. They argue that community resilience should be conceptualized as both an embedded set of community *capacities* that aid in successfully responding to challenges and also as a *strategy* for promoting effective readiness and responses to challenges. Their framework identifies four categories of capacities underlying resilience (economic development, information and communication, social capital, and community competence), each with multiple components. Importantly, they argue against viewing these aspects as a set of static indicators, and stress the importance of understanding them as networked and causally dynamic properties. From their perspective, strategies that promote community resilience will focus not only on building static buffering capacities, but also on increasing the dynamic properties of community resilience by understanding their operation and interconnections. Norris et al. (2008) category of *community competence* (including components of community action, collective efficacy, community flexibility, and reflective and problem-solving skills), in particular, represents aspects of resilience that require a psychological process perspective to both measure and facilitate. The roles of these different community characteristics in promoting resilience are discussed at length in subsequent sections.

11.2 Why are community resilience perspectives important for advancing climate change psychology?

Given current climate change projections and geo-political dynamics, a focus on localized, community-based resilience in particular may be vital for our understanding of the psychology of climate change and how to promote optimally adaptive responses. We describe four important reasons.

11.2.1 Climate change is globally pressing, but locally experienced

While climate change is a complex and geographically diffuse phenomenon, many of the most immediate impacts of climate change (e.g., extreme weather hazards) are localized, being experienced in individual communities at different times and on different scales (IPCC, 2014). In many cases, these communities are vulnerable to vastly different types of projected climate change impacts. Communities also have different political, cultural, socio-economic, and environmental histories, which raise important questions about how to most effectively manage climate change through policy support and behavioral changes in these different contexts (Adger, Barnett, Brown, Marshall & O'Brien, 2013). The processes at play in how a community manages climate change in Miami Beach as compared to a town in the rural mountain West of the United States may involve different forms of engagement, steps for preparedness (due to different potential impacts), and resilience efforts. For example, Miami Beach faces threats from salt water intrusion and increasing sunny day flooding, as well as ever-increasing threats from the consequences of tropical storms. Thus, community engagement in this area must focus both on increasing local investment in infrastructure changes to cope with the creeping sea-level rise and on building community disaster resilience to cope in the aftermath of future storms (e.g., fostering stronger social ties among community members to promote cohesive disaster responses). In contrast, the Western town faces the threat of wildfire as well as water insecurity due to drought risks, which demand different forms of resilience planning and community preparedness. Thus, in the Western United States, local communities face different challenges in building engagement for local neighborhood action (e.g., brush cutting), as well as individual and community-level action for water conservation. Community-level perspectives are vital in order to account for these different adaptive challenges.

Aside from the need for community-level perspectives to account for reactions to community-level issues, the decisions that individuals make to deal with climate change are influenced (or constrained) by their context (c.f. Baum & Gross, 2017). In the case of adaptation behaviors, the opportunities available to individuals may be especially constrained by their community capabilities (e.g., the capacity for migration, the availability of emergency response infrastructure and resources; Black, Bennett, Thomas & Beddington, 2011; Evans et al., 2016). While there are undoubtedly some psychological processes that influence climate change attitude formation and decision-making across all contexts, the role of any particular psychological factor depends upon the affordances and constraints that come into play based on the characteristics of a community and the particular challenges that it faces. For example, a person whose household is in an area with high risk of wildfire may make individual decisions about fire hardening/protecting based not just on a calculus of individual risk but also about community risk and action. Being in a community where there is a grassroots effort to work together to "protect the town" may evoke psychological processes of community loyalty, identity, and responsibility for homeowners, in addition to the individual "rational" calculus about protecting one's own personal structures from risk.

11.2.2   Community-level research can inform and transcend multiple levels of analysis

The majority of research on the psychology of climate change has focused on individuals as the unit of analysis and agent of change (although several of the chapters in the present volume represent exceptions): How individuals' worldviews shape their perceptions of climate change, determinants of individuals' sustainable behavior changes, and factors that increase or decrease individual support for national-level policy changes have all been studied in considerable depth. Fewer studies in the climate change psychology literature have adopted an explicit focus on local communities and regional actors as units of analysis in their investigations. This *community-centered* approach to climate change psychology raises questions such as how the interaction of individual and intergroup dynamics influence community climate change decision-making, whether factors that influence individuals' support for national-level climate change policy similarly motivate engaged action in local community initiatives, and more broadly how the perspectives from the extant literature on individual climate change decision-making apply in the context of local community actions and politics.

At the micro-level, individuals' thoughts, feelings, and behaviors, embedded within social settings, are the primary focus of scholarship. For example, researchers may investigate whether a person chooses to bike to work instead of driving a car, depending on their attitudes toward the environment or the social norms of their personal networks (Heinen, van Wee & Maat, 2010). A limitation of this research is that individual behavior changes vary widely, both in terms of their potential impact and in the extent to which people can "choose" to engage in them (see Chapter 6: Contributions of psychology to limiting climate change: Opportunities through consumer behavior). For example, the choice to rely on public transportation is not available to many citizens. And, in an area with narrow roads or no bike lanes, it may simply be too dangerous for individuals to commute by bicycle as opposed to car (Heinen et al., 2010; Stern, 2000). The environmental impact of bicycling versus driving will also depend on the type and distance of commute required in that particular community.

A community resilience approach to addressing climate change requires a shift in focus towards the center space between the micro-level (i.e., individuals) and the macro-level (e.g., entire populations), referred to as the meso-level of analysis (Bergström & Dekker, 2014). This middle ground allows researchers to look at groups of people in context—such as neighborhoods, organizations, or cities—as the primary focus. Strengthening community resilience to climate change requires attending to specific features of local environments, and building on local strengths and vulnerabilities. Due to their wide variability, these features are often treated as contextual "noise" in psychological research, with rigorous efforts undertaken to control their influence on variables of interest. However, this individualist approach attempts to extract individuals from their environment in ways that lead to a narrow interpretation of resilience and may threaten ecological validity (Parker, 2015). In contrast, distinctive features of local communities become the foreground of community-based research, as they are understood to envelop and shape community responses to climate change (Okvat & Zautra, 2011; Trickett, 2009). Moreover, attending to groups of people embedded in places can shed light on individual decision-making or underscore a need for higher-level policy change, thus bridging micro- and macro-level understandings through community-level analyses (Bergström & Dekker, 2014; Ross & Berkes, 2014). Revisiting the earlier example, understanding distinctive features of communities can help to identify micro-level barriers to individuals' use of existing bicycle-friendly infrastructure (e.g., feeling unsafe), or macro-level factors underlying a lack of political momentum to invest in local public transportation (e.g., absence of federal incentives).

By explicitly attending to contextual features of local environments, community resilience research offers unique avenues through which to examine and promote the health and well-being of individuals and communities in the context of climate change. This presents an exciting opportunity for psychological theorizing and research; a better understanding of the psychological processes involved in climate change decision-making and resilience at the community level could aid in the production of psychosocial assessments to complement and contextualize the geophysical assessments that currently comprise most region-specific adaptation plans.

11.2.3 Climate change necessitates a psychology of community adaptation and resilience

The growing consensus that some impacts of climate change are already underway, and others are unlikely to be prevented regardless of current efforts (IPCC, 2014), makes the study of community resilience vital. The rapid progression of climatic changes and their implications for extreme weather and agricultural disruption (e.g., Fischer & Knutti, 2015; Trenberth, Fasullo & Shepherd, 2015) have substantially increased attention to the need for adaptation to climate change, in contrast with the historically predominant focus on mitigation/prevention (Moser & Boykoff, 2013; Moser & Ekstrom, 2010; Moser, 2010). The realization of the need for adaptation, and its implications for well-being and resilience, has resulted in a substantial interest in the influence of characteristics such as values and culture on local adaptive capacity and decision-making (Barnett, Tschakert, Head & Adger, 2016), with some scholars specifically pointing to the need to understand communities as key actors in promoting healthy adaptation to climate change and resilience to disaster impacts (Adger et al., 2009; Adger et al., 2013).

In response to calls for more research on adaptation in communities, psychological and public health researchers are beginning to contribute to initiatives aimed at climate change adaptation and resilience by applying, for example, principles from the literature on depression, stress, and coping processes to better understand individual-level resilience in the wake of climate change (e.g., Berry, Bowen & Kjellstrom, 2010; Clayton et al., 2015; Keim, 2008; Nurse, Basher, Bone & Bird, 2010; Reser & Swim, 2011). This work discusses how climate change impacts (e.g., weather disasters) may increase mental health problems often already associated with the loss of one's property and destruction of cherished places, loss of life, and enhanced financial strain from disaster preparedness and response. Thus, greater attention to the individual mental health needs of community members may be necessary and require additional resources. Aside from this interest in mental health, the body of literature discussing psychological dimensions of resilience and adaptation to climate change, especially those encompassing the interaction of individual and collective psychological processes, is very limited (Riemer & Reich, 2011; Riemer, 2010).

In addition to the individual-centered study of resilience, psychological research on community resilience can help respond to the crucial need for interdisciplinary adaptation scholarship (Clayton et al., 2015, 2016). This is because, at its core, community resilience research aims to enhance adaptive capacity (Folke, Hahn, Olsson & Norberg, 2005). Strengthening community resilience involves supporting community members' knowledge, capacities, and skills. This includes their awareness of the problem (e.g., via risk perceptions; vulnerability assessments), knowledge of potential solutions (e.g., via social learning; self-organization), and ability to enact solutions through policies and programs to further build adaptive capacity (e.g., via social mobilization; community-based planning and organization), all of which are well within the domain of psychology. Understanding and strengthening these processes are essential to protecting safety and well-being of individuals and communities. As such, community resilience research can both expand psychology's role in adaptation scholarship and respond to an increasingly urgent need. The study of adaptive capacity and resilience in particular necessitates context and place-specific research programs due to the fact that the climatic processes at play and the specific behaviors to be targeted by researchers are going to vary considerably from region to region (Adger et al., 2013; Barnett et al., 2014; Barnett & Waters, 2016).

11.2.4   Community-focused initiatives provide psychologists with an opportunity to inform and influence policy-making

An enhanced emphasis on place-based, community-focused research initiatives has the potential to provide scholars with a direct route to apply their research to the policy and planning process. One of the major obstacles to concerted climate change action has been the persistent political gridlock in high-emissions countries such as the United States (Dunlap, McCright & Yarosh, 2016). While gridlock may also exist in local politics, a focus on climate change in a way that is locally relevant and intended to practically benefit communities could reduce the psychological distance of climate change (McDonald, Chai & Newell, 2015), shifting the focus of action away from reinforcing political identities (Kahan, 2012; Kahan, Jenkins-Smith & Braman, 2011) and toward enacting solutions, and thus enabling concerted efforts in spite of national and/or international legislative impasse. The capacity for community-focused initiatives to attenuate the negative influence of political gridlock on climate change action warrants investigation (e.g., the Southeast Florida Evidence-based Science Communication Initiative; Cultural Cognition Project, 2017). Furthermore, given the complexity of national and international policy, it can be difficult even in favorable political conditions for social scientists to directly apply research findings to influence the decision-making process at this macro-level scale. Influencing public perceptions and decision processes in local or regional politics and community deliberations may thus be a (relatively) direct, and more accessible, route for psychologists to engage with citizens and apply their research.

A focus on local issues and community-based group processes when studying climate change psychology offers researchers the opportunity to move "out of the lab" and to test findings in applied settings, a theme which has been discussed by a number of scholars recently in the context of climate change psychology and communications (Kahan & Carpenter, 2017; Kahan, 2014; Levine & Kline, 2017). As an example of organizational response, the Society for the Psychological Study of Social Issues has recognized the promise of place-based, localized approaches through new funding initiatives for psychologists working to improve state and local policy decision-making. University-community partnerships may be a promising vehicle for enabling psychologists to apply their research to community resilience needs (e.g., Cooperative Extension System; www.extension.org). Community-focused initiatives could also be a natural locus for spurring interdisciplinary scholarship, another emerging and pressing theme highlighted by climate change psychologists in recent years (Clayton et al., 2016). Studying and enhancing community resilience to climate change necessitates a focus on the psychological, sociological, and political environments as well as the potential geophysical stressors and infrastructure strengths and weaknesses.

Therefore, there is a compelling rationale for psychologists to work to produce and apply insights on how to best promote community resilience to climate change. However, as Riemer and Reich (2011) note (in their introduction to a special section of the *American Journal of Community Psychology* on community psychology and climate change), the literature to date focusing explicitly on climate change and community psychology is very limited, especially in comparison to other issues such as social justice and race relations. Furthermore, this research area has not witnessed much growth in the years since Riemer and Reich's (2011) paper. Nevertheless, the emerging contributions from psychology, coupled with the aforementioned interdisciplinary research literatures on resilience climate change adaptation, have the potential to bolster our understanding of community resilience.

11.3   Research on community resilience

Researchers in community psychology have begun investigating the relationship between resilience concepts (e.g., community competence, efficacy, and place attachment) and other core community psychology principles. For example, Quimby and Angelique (2011) provide an initial exploration of potential barriers and opportunities for community climate change engagement, focusing on 84 participants in the Harrisburg, Pennsylvania area who were involved/interested in environmental activism and groups. Their exploratory survey asked questions about knowledge, efficacy, and perceived barriers (e.g., time, cost, and poor community infrastructure), along with a series of open-ended questions to better unpack the themes present in participants' perceptions of barriers to climate change action. Their analysis suggests that the tragedy of the commons (i.e., inaction of individuals to manage collective problems) and the free-rider problem (i.e., individuals who do not take action/incur costs yet still obtain benefits when others act) are key obstacles to extending and promoting broader community action on climate change. Low perceived efficacy, poor community infrastructure, and lack of social support were also salient barriers identified by community members, which largely aligns with findings from the broader resilience work. In this study, participants felt that shifting broader community social norms, such as norms which led to the free-rider problem, would be a key step in overcoming these barriers and promoting effective community actions. Through in-depth research in Tuvalu, Corlew (2012) characterized the role of culture (history, social norms, ways of life) and attachment to place in guiding how local citizens are adapting to climate change and extreme weather. Corlew (2012) described how social norms of interconnectedness and making sacrifices for other community members can help lead to more cohesive post-disaster and climate change-related responses in the region. Also described are the efforts taken by community members (e.g., youth groups) in the face of disasters and loss of locally cherished places to help assist with rebuilding of homes and public gathering places such as churches.

Putting research into action, Dittmer and Riemer (2012) implemented a community-based education project with youth on environmental issues such as climate change, followed by a study to evaluate key takeaways by participants. The project involved a series of workshops to educate youth on climate change and its relevance to their lives. Results of post-workshop interviews suggest that these intensive workshops enhanced critical thinking, understanding of complex environmental issues, (i.e., enhanced systems thinking) and motivation to take actions to mitigate environmental problems. Thus, this research suggests that locally organized education initiatives may be a promising tool for increasing dimensions of resilience. While the study of community resilience in psychology is still limited to a small number of studies incorporating different methodologies and theoretical focuses, the research that does exist suggests that consideration of core community psychology principles in conjunction with the broader literature on resilience may help inform more effective approaches to promoting community resilience in the midst of the barriers that can impede community action.

Considering the findings from community psychology and the broader interdisciplinary resilience literature, several insights emerge with regards to what a resilient community might look like in the context of the coming challenges of climate change. In particular, leaving aside those relatively static factors that endow some communities with inherent resilience in the face of climate change (such as being surrounded by fertile and ecologically stable agricultural lands, or a diverse and vibrant economic base) how can a community with significant climate-change related vulnerabilities develop greater community resilience? While empirical research is limited, the aforementioned perspectives on community resilience suggests some answers. At the broadest level, resilient communities take a perspective of increasing their *collective agency* to respond to challenges. This agency perspective focuses attention on capabilities that the community can work together to develop further. Resilient communities also focus on the *networked capacities for resilience* rather than viewing resilience as a set of disconnected factors.

11.3.1 Applying the findings: characteristics of resilient communities

With these insights in mind, we can sketch more specifically what a climate-change resilient community looks like. Perhaps most importantly, such communities will have developed what Norris and colleagues refer to as *community competence* with the capacity for collective action and a sense of collective empowerment to creatively and flexibly respond to challenges. This community competence would be reflected in problem solving abilities embedded in political structures but also at grass-roots level organizing. However, such community competence is likely to be developed and built over time by the development of the *social capital* of the community (Norris et al., 2008; Robin & Elah, 2011). The people in resilient communities have a deep attachment to place and community (Cutter et al., 2008), with strong bonds between community members and active participation in community life through diverse and impactful community organizations.

Communities striving to develop greater resilience may best consider the development of community competence and social capital as these can progressively scaffold and build one another (Aldrich & Meyer, 2015; Poortinga, 2012). Indeed, outside of crisis periods, development of community social capital and competence should probably be the major implicit goal of most community organizations. For example, imagine a community in which people have developed a community organization whose explicit goal is *intergenerational community service and learning*, in which projects are oriented around bringing together and doing service by and for people across generations. As one project, high school and college students might be paired with retired contractors to build community housing modeled after the approach of Habitat for Humanity. In another project, the local historical society could partner with local schools to train students to gather oral histories from the oldest community members about their life and community history. These projects would both build social capital and, because of the organizing required for action, also build community competence. This increased community agency and embedded knowledge and training may then be called upon and come to the fore when the community is developing climate change risk preparedness plans or when it faces an acute crisis of some kind.

Once communities have developed strong social capital and community competence, other aspects of climate change resilience may thus be more easily and effectively developed. A resilient community needs a strong base of *economic development* that is fair and equitable and which does not place vulnerable community members at disproportionate risk to climate change induced hazards. It also needs effective *communication and information* methods, some of which may be specialized for disaster preparedness and response, but which are also grounded less formally in the social networks and organizations that are developed through community competence and social capital.

Lastly, climate-change resilient communities should have planning, development, and infrastructure that help the community adapt to climate change risks (Cutter et al., 2008). These include planning and zoning to protect communities from developing in areas that face long terms risks (such as due to flooding), as well as infrastructure specifically to protect the community such as seawalls. Importantly, as noted by Cutter et al. (2008), community resilience also rests in part in the ecological resilience of the natural community in which people reside. Rather than being only a passive resource, the local ecology is something that can be made less resilient through poor use or potentially made more resilient with judicious human involvement (e.g., agricultural set-asides as a native species seed bank or for storm run-off buffering).

11.4   Practical recommendations to foster resilience

While macro-level policy and economic considerations are beyond the scope of this chapter, there are a variety of ways in which applied researchers and community members may begin to help foster resilience through the incorporation of psychological insights. Resilient communities possess key characteristics such as attachment to place and familiarity with the local problems, social capital and interconnectivity among community members, and programs and grassroots organizing that can facilitate community competence and efficacy to deal with local issues. Thus, activities, programs, and communication strategies that seek to foster/emphasize these aspects are key for enhancing resilience. Planners, policy makers, engaged scholars, and community members might begin fostering resilience by coordinating workshops, education, and outreach programs to better inform and equip local community members with the knowledge and tools necessary to act appropriately. Indeed, preliminary evidence from Dittmer and Riemer (2012) suggests that educational workshops with youth may be one strategy in increasing engagement with climate change issues in local communities.

Fostering community participation through the development of local climate change action plans may also be a beneficial approach in increasing community competence, efficacy, and participation. For example, Iowa City in recent years has suffered from large scale floods. Nearly a decade ago the historic Iowa River flood swamped this small city and left behind an estimated $1 billion in damages. Part of the response in Iowa City has been for local policymakers and community members to begin to work together to look at what they can do as a community about climate change. Community members are developing a climate action plan proposing such actions as "Bringing Climate Action to the Public Commons," "Climate Action Partnerships," "Incubating Green Jobs and Green Business," and "Local Food: 40% by 2020" (Biggers, 2016). While no research to our knowledge has examined the effects of community involvement in climate action plans such as this, we might expect that this involvement would increase awareness, knowledge, social capital, and efficacy, all of which are vital for promoting resilience.

Given that there is considerable variation from community to community, those interested in fostering resilience might consider approaches they can take to identify and harness the specific community strengths already present. For example, in Corlew's (2012) work in Tuvalu, it is clear that a strong sense of shared place attachment and community interdependence was already part of local social norms. Thus, a region such as this may be able to tap into and promote adaptive resilience strategies by appealing to shared values and the priority of taking care of one another in promoting resilience strategies in local planning. Where such norms are not already present, practitioners might consider methods of community engagement (e.g., cohesiveness-building exercises) while also focusing on shared values and the co-benefits of resilience strategies. Some resilience strategies, such as improving local infrastructure, could yield benefits both for climate change responses as well as more general community stability and growth into the future. Additionally, fostering stronger community ties and social capital is likely to also benefit the community in other decision-making process for important local issues (e.g., poverty reduction).

There is also a growing number of freely available resources for interested parties to consult which may be of relevance to practitioners interested in promoting resilience. The *Community Tool Box* (ctb.ku.edu), for example, is a vetted online resource including detailed information about recent research from community psychology along with how the research might be put into action. This resource, while not about climate change community resilience per se, may be an informative tool for practitioners by opening up access to both scholarly knowledge and the experiences of other communities seeking to work on similar issues. Furthermore, Clayton, Silka, Trott, Chapman, and Mancoll (2016) provide a brief overview of climate change-related issues for communities, a summary of approaches to engaging with communities described in this chapter, and strategies for effective communication, along with links to additional useful resources (e.g., climate change communications guides, suggestions for the use of visual imagery, and narrative storytelling). Finally, many insights from previous chapters in this volume, such as the extensive work on climate change communication, behavior change programs, and collective action, could help organizers develop methods to increase local community members' interest in climate change and resilience processes.

11.5   Future directions for research

Based on the research reviewed above, the potential theoretical and practical contributions, and instructive examples from the community psychology literature, there is ample justification for an expanded psychological study of community resilience. We identify several broad areas where future research directions may be particularly beneficial for both theory and practice. We focus on novel research directions as well as avenues to integrate and mobilize this research for optimal community engagement and application.

11.5.1   Identify and investigate structural and psychological barriers as well as opportunities for community resilience

Given the inherent difficulties in investigating complex, multifaceted topics such as resilience, identifying, developing, and empirically investigating community-level engagement may help inform novel theoretical frameworks of how individual and collective psychological processes interact, while also shedding light on vital practical considerations for promoting community resilience. This may involve considering the barriers to entry into community-engaged research (e.g., access to local planners, developing the trust of community members, availability of resources, and practicalities of the research), means of overcoming those barriers (e.g., psychologically informed community-level interventions of communications strategies), as well as identifying novel opportunities to study psychological processes underlying resilience-related behaviors. Modifying existing influential frameworks, such as Cutter et al. (2008) and Norris et al. (2008), to include perspectives more extensively informed by the psychological research may be a valuable first step. These existing frameworks, for example, identify topics such as collective action, place attachment, and efficacy as important elements of resilience, but leave room for substantial expansion and incorporation of knowledge from the psychological literature on how to best conceptualize and measure these constructs. Thus, integrating the valuable work from community, social, environmental, and political psychology literatures discussed throughout this volume in order to expand current frameworks of resilience could be a compelling first step toward a more integrated, psychologically informed framework.

11.5.2 Expand the investigation of collective climate change psychology

Collaborative, collective action initiatives for community resilience, which are adaptive in nature, are understudied as a form of collective action (See Chapter 8: Environmental protection through societal change: What psychologyknows about collective climate action—and what it needs to find out). Existing theories and frameworks of individual climate change psychology should therefore be examined in the context of collective processes, group dynamics, and community decision-making. This involves more than just testing micro- and macro- level concepts in the meso-level context, implying the development of a theoretically informed but practically applicable collective climate change psychology at the meso-level. Psychology's role in social movements scholarship, within and beyond environmental action, has largely focused on a "politics of demand" (e.g., public protest), rather than on a "politics of the act," such as collaborative projects for community resilience (Trott, 2016). Whereas demands-based forms of collective action consist primarily of identity- or issue-based groups demanding rights, recognition, or policy reform, action-based groups pursue alternative routes to social change by "locating power and possibility in the local and the everyday" within self-organized communities (Trott, 2016, p. 269). Through a collective action lens, the creative and prosocial resilience-building efforts taking place in community settings come into focus as processes of collective self-intervention and collaborative experimentation to support individual and community well-being. These more unconventional, process-oriented approaches to collective action have received relatively little attention by psychologists when compared to more visible, events-based activism such as marches and rallies (Haiven & Khasnabish, 2014). Therefore, this is a particularly promising domain for psychologists to contribute and would complement the ongoing research on other forms of climate change collective action (Adger, 2003; Bamberg, Rees & Seebauer, 2015; Louis, 2009; van Zomeren, Spears & Leach, 2010).

There is also a growing recognition of the need to test the applicability of these more individualized psychological theories in the context of real-world collective decision-making (e.g., Kahan & Carpenter, 2017). Community psychology is in harmony with this view; with its experience in the study of local empowerment, it can help to inform such investigations and offer a unique context in which to study collective climate change psychology. Researchers should therefore continue to examine the extent to which psychological theories of climate change beliefs and action apply and inform engagement and policy in regions experiencing different potential climate change impacts. This contextualization and expansion of the psychology literature may help psychologists maximize their influence on decision processes.

11.5.3   Contextualize resilience research to address region-specific adaptation problems

Because different regions have different cultural, economic, political, and geophysical processes, understandings of community resilience must be contextualized in place-based approaches to meet region-specific problems. Thus, rather than adopting a generic idea of community resilience as a factor that may facilitate successful adaptation to climate change, researchers must develop context-specific ideas about the facets of community resilience that are important in the locality where they are conducting research. From a psychologist's point of view, this opens up a series of exciting research directions. How do different types of community dynamics and histories influence receptivity to different types of resilience policies? Does community resilience to climate change involve different psychological principles and processes in rural versus urban areas, or in areas prone to drought versus flooding? Do different climate change communication strategies work more or less effectively depending on the dynamics of a community? These examples touch only the surface of the many questions and avenues of research open to psychologists through the examination of community resilience, especially as it pertains to adaptation. Making strides in this direction, community psychologists are developing resources like the Community Toolbox, which includes a system by which people from anywhere around the globe are encouraged to submit questions about how research findings might be applied to their own setting; community psychologists are available to respond with suggestions of how to use the research. In the sustainability realm, Silka, McGreavy and Hart (in press) have advanced an analysis of generalizable strategies for learning across these different contexts. Scholars from other areas of psychology studying climate change might also consider becoming involved in such initiatives, and future research in this domain might consider using this as a case study to develop full-fledged frameworks and region-specific application of resilience principles.

11.5.4   Foster interdisciplinary collaboration across natural and social sciences

To understand and promote community resilience in the face of climate change, interdisciplinary collaboration across the natural and social sciences is essential. However, given competing priorities and incentives, the implementation of such programs of research can be complicated. Connecting on issues of direct applied importance, such as focusing on specific local outcomes (e.g., applying strategies to increase voter turnout for newly developed local adaptation policies) could be a fruitful avenue for fostering effective inter- and trans-disciplinary work centered around goals of mutual interest in responding to climate change. Therefore, we encourage psychologists to bring their research into conversation with other disciplines and approaches to studying climate change and resilience. For example, the integration of psychological perspectives on collective action and efficacy with existing frameworks such as the socio-ecological resilience framework (e.g., Adger, Hughes, Folke, Carpenter & Rockström, 2005; Berkes et al. 2008) would be a welcomed advance.

This focus on context-specific outcomes to guide interdisciplinary investigations involving psychologists could also be a prime opportunity for contributing to the growing interest in the study of coupled human and natural systems (Liu et al., 2007). Collaboration between natural and social scientists, as well as collaboration with local citizens (Ballard & Belsky, 2010; Jordan, Ballard & Phillips, 2012) may also advance the capacity to develop and implement effective regional climate change adaptation plans that involve both geophysical and psychosocial perspectives.

11.5.5   Explore community-university partnerships and other engagement opportunities

It is vital that psychologists explore new avenues of engagement with the populations and communities they are seeking to benefit. As with interdisciplinary research, these approaches can be difficult to achieve. Nevertheless, to advance a nuanced yet applicable scholarship of community resilience, partnerships with stakeholders can be immensely useful and generative. These partnerships may take a variety of different forms. For example, community-university partnerships, such as the cooperative extension programs carried out by land-grant universities in the United States are an opportunity for scholars to work with members of their communities on developing programs and interventions. Programs aimed at developing community resilience profiles in different states, or collaborating on the development of regional climate change adaptation plans, are just two examples of ways in which these community-university partnerships could be beneficial. Psychologists might also consider other engagement opportunities for disseminating knowledge to inform public policy and to generate local interest in new projects, such as through contributing op-eds to local newspapers, or serving on local scientific advisory panels. In addition to scholarly outreach, such engagement could also generate future community collaborations and inform the development of novel research questions. Community engagement and outreach would thus both advance the applicability of psychology for community resilience to climate change as well as uncover new directions for scholarly pursuit.

11.5.6   Scale up community resilience research

While there is much to be gained by adding a focus on the community to that on the individual, much remains outside community control. Some of the "levers" producing climate change are well beyond the borders of a community, and climate change is unlikely to be eradicated through the actions of a single community. As such, researchers should consider the ways in which their findings could be applicable both within and across contexts to the greatest degree possible. For example, researchers should consider approaches for studying communities that can contribute to the understanding of issues in larger geographical contexts—such as watersheds, large water bodies, and oceans—where social capital opportunities may be different and where contact between people may take forms other than face-to-face interactions. Future research and practice needs to bring together studies of the individual and the community, and develop means of both integrating and scaling up psychological research.

11.6 Conclusion

Community resilience scholarship is inherently interdisciplinary. Like climate change research more broadly, both its progress and practical application are invigorated by diverse perspectives. While nascent, this interdisciplinary literature highlights the importance of considering community-level factors in order to help individuals engage with local climate change problems, foster community competence and efficacy (e.g., through developing collaborative workshops and education programs), and build partnerships among academics, scholars, and citizens to promote optimally useful and adaptive resilience efforts that have community support. This research also suggests that developing greater community social capital, which can be a byproduct of these other forms of engagement, is a vital building block for resilience.

As a critical research area, community resilience represents a promising space for cross-disciplinary convergence and exchange, wherein psychologists may benefit academic and collaborative community initiatives, while simultaneously benefitting from scholarly plurality and applied engagement. The distinctive dimensions and unique contributions of community resilience research arise in part due its interdisciplinary complexity and appeal, which together provide a bridge along which psychologists may traverse disciplinary boundaries, and engage multiple levels of analysis, adaptation processes, and under-examined topics of resilience to address the threats of climate change.

References

Adger, W. N. (2000). Social and ecological resilience: are they related? *Progress in Human Geography*, 24(3), 347–364.

Adger, W. N. (2003). Social capital, collective action, and adaptation to climate change. *Economic Geography*, 79(4), 387–404. Available from https://doi.org/10.1007/978-3-531-92258-4_19.

Adger, W. N., Barnett, J., Brown, K., Marshall, N., & O'Brien, K. (2013). Cultural dimensions of climate change impacts and adaptation. *Nature Climate Change*, 3(2), 112–117.

Adger, W. N., Dessai, S., Goulden, M., Hulme, M., Lorenzoni, I., & Nelson, D. R. , et al (2009). Are there social limits to adaptation to climate change? *Climatic Change*, 93(3), 335–354.

Adger, W. N., Hughes, T. P., Folke, C., Carpenter, S. R., & Rockström, J. (2005). Social-ecological resilience to coastal disasters. *Science*, 309(5737), 1036–1039.

Aldrich, D. P., & Meyer, M. A. (2015). Social capital and community resilience. *American Behavioral Scientist*, 59(2), 254–269.

Ballard, H. L., & Belsky, J. M. (2010). Participatory action research and environmental learning: implications for resilient forests and communities. *Environmental Education Research, 16*(5/6), 611−627.

Bamberg, S., Rees, J., & Seebauer, S. (2015). Collective climate action: determinants of participation intention in community-based pro-environmental initiatives. *Journal of Environmental Psychology, 43*, 155−165. Available from https://doi.org/10.1016/j.jenvp.2015.06.006.

Barnett, J., Graham, C., Mortreux, S., Fincher, R., Waters, E., & Hurlimann, A. (2014). A local coastal adaptation pathway. *Nature Climate Change, 4*(12), 1103−1108.

Barnett, J., Tschakert, P., Head, L., & Adger, W. N. (2016). A science of loss. *Nature Climate Change, 6(11)*, 976−978.

Barnett, J., & Waters, E. (2016). Rethinking the vulnerability of small island states: climate change and development in the Pacific Islands. In J. Grugel, & D. Hammett (Eds.), *The Palgrave handbook of international development* (pp. 731−748). Basingstoke, UK: Palgrave Macmillan.

Baum, C. M., & Gross, C. (2017). Sustainability policy as if people mattered: developing a framework for environmentally significant behavioral change. *Journal of Bioeconomics, 19*(1), 53−95.

Bergström, J., & Dekker, S. (2014). Bridging the macro and the micro by considering the meso: reflections on the fractal nature of resilience. *Ecology and Society, 19*(4), 22. Available from https://doi.org/10.5751/ES-06956-190422.

Berkes, F., Colding, J., & Folke, C. (Eds.), (2008). *Navigating social-ecological systems: Building resilience for complexity and change.* Cambridge, UK: Cambridge University Press.

Berry, H. L., Bowen, K., & Kjellstrom, T. (2010). Climate change and mental health: a causal pathways framework. *International Journal of Public Health, 55*(2), 123−132.

Biggers, J. (2016). Iowa city climate action plan: creating a regenerative city in the heartland. *The Huffington Post*. Retrieved from: http://www.huffingtonpost.com

Black, R., Bennett, S. R. G., Thomas, S. M., & Beddington, J. R. (2011). Climate change: migration as adaptation. *Nature, 478*(7370), 447−449.

Bonanno, G. A. (2004). Loss, trauma, and human resilience: have we underestimated the human capacity to thrive after extremely aversive events? *American Psychologist, 59*(1), 20.

Brown, D., & Kulig, J. C. (1996/1997). The concept of resilience: theoretical lessons from community research. *Health and Canadian Society, 4*(1), 29−52.

Brown, K., & Westaway, E. (2011). Agency, capacity, and resilience to environmental change: lessons from human development, well-being, and disasters. *Annual Review of Environment and Resources, 36(1)*, 321−342.

Buikstra, E., Ross, H., King, C. A., Baker, P. G., Hegney, D., McLachlan, K., et al. (2010). The components of resilience—perceptions of an Australian rural community. *Journal of Community Psychology, 38*(8), 975−991. Available from https://doi.org/10.1002/jcop.20409.

Clayton, S., Devine-Wright, P., Stern, P. C., Whitmarsh, L., Carrico, A., Steg, L.... (2015). Psychological research and global climate change. *Nature Climate Change, 5*(7), 640−646. Available from https://doi.org/10.1038/NCLIMATE2622.

Clayton, S., Devine-Wright, P., Swim, J., Bonnes, M., Steg, L., Whitmarsh, L., et al. (2016). Expanding the role for psychology in addressing environmental problems. *American Psychologist, 71*(3), 199−215.

Clayton, S., Silka, L., Trott, C.D., Chapman, D.A., & Mancoll, S. (2016). *Building Resilient Communities in the Face of Climate Change: A Resource for Local*

Communities. Report commissioned by the Society for the Psychological Study of Social Issues. Available at: http://www.spssi.org/index.cfm?fuseaction = page. viewPage&pageID = 2098&nodeID = 1

Corlew, L.K. (2012). *The cultural impacts of climate change: Sense of place and sense of community in Tuvalu, a country threatened by sea level rise.* (Doctoral Dissertation). Retrieved from ProQest Dissertations & Theses. (UMI Number 3520677).

Cox, R. S., & Perry, K. M. E. (2011). Like a fish out of water: reconsidering disaster recovery and the role of place and social capital in community disaster resilience. *American Journal of Community Psychology, 48*(3−4), 395−411.

Cultural Cognition Project (2017). The southeast Florida evidence-based science communication initiative. Retrieved from http://www.culturalcognition.net/southeast-florida-ebsci/

Cutter, S. L., Barnes, L., Berry, M., Burton, C., Evans, E., Tate, E., et al. (2008). A place-based model for understanding community resilience to natural disasters. *Global Environmental Change, 18*(4), 598−606.

Dittmer, L. D., & Riemer, M. (2012). Fostering critical thinking about climate change: applying community psychology to an environmental education project with youth. *Global Journal of Community Psychology, 3,* 1−9.

Dunlap, R., McCright, A. M., & Yarosh, J. H. (2016). The political divide on climate change: partisan polarization widens in the US. *Environment: Science and Policy for Sustainable Development, 58*(5), 4−23.

Egeland, B., Carlson, E., & Sroufe, L. A. (1993). Resilience as process. *Development and Psychopathology, 5*(04), 517−528.

Evans, L. S., Hicks, C. C., Adger, W. N., Barnett, J., Perry, A. L., Fidelman, P., et al. (2016). Structural and psycho-social limits to climate change adaptation in the great barrier reef region. *PLOS One, 11*(3), e0150575.

Fischer, E. M., & Knutti, R. (2015). Anthropogenic contribution to global occurrence of heavy precipitation and high-temperature extremes. *Nature Climate Change, 5*(6), 560−564.

Folke, C., Hahn, T., Olsson, P., & Norberg, J. (2005). Adaptive governance of social-ecological systems. *Annual Review of Environment and Resources, 30,* 441−472.

Garmezy, N. (1991). Resiliency and vulnerability to adverse developmental outcomes associated with poverty. *American Behavioral Scientist, 34*(4), 416−430.

Geigis, P., Hamin, E., & Silka, L. (Eds.), (2007). *Preserving and enhancing communities: A guide for citizens, planners and policymakers.* Amherst: University of Massachusetts Press.

Haiven, M., & Khasnabish, A. (2014). *The radical imagination: Social movement research in the age of austerity.* London, United Kingdom: Zed Books.

Heinen, E., van Wee, B., & Maat, K. (2010). Commuting by bicycle: an overview of the literature. *Transport Reviews, 30*(1), 59−96. Available from https://doi.org/10.1080/01441640903187001.

Holling, C. S. (1973). Resilience and stability of ecological systems. *Annual Review of Ecology and Systematics, 4*(1), 1−23.

Intergovernmental Panel on Climate Change. (2014). *Climate change 2014: Impacts, adaptation, and vulnerability.* New York, NY: Cambridge University Press. Retrieved from https://ipcc-wg2.gov/AR5/images/uploads/WGIIAR5-PartA_FINAL.pdf.

Jordan, R. C., Ballard, H. L., & Phillips, T. B. (2012). Key issues and new approaches for evaluating citizen-science learning outcomes. *Frontiers in Ecology and Environment, 10* (6), 307−309.

Kahan, D., Jenkins-Smith, H., & Braman, D. (2011). Cultural cognition of scientific consensus. *Journal of Risk Research, 14*(2), 147−174.

Kahan, D. M. (2012). Why we are poles apart on climate change. *Nature, 488*(7411), 255.

Kahan, D. M. (2014). Making climate-science communication evidence-based—all the way down. In D. Crow, & M. Boykoff (Eds.), *Culture, politics and climate change: How information shapes our common future* (pp. 203–220). New York: Routledge.

Kahan, D. M., & Carpenter, K. (2017). Out of the lab and into the field. *Nature Climate Change, 7*(5), 309–311.

Keim, M. E. (2008). Building human resilience: the role of public heath preparedness and response as an adaptation to climate change. *American Journal of Preventative Medicine, 35*(5), 508–516.

Levine, A. S., & Kline, R. (2017). A new approach for evaluating climate change communication. *Climatic Change, 142*(1), 301–309.

Liu, J., Dietz, T., Carpenter, S. R., Folke, C., Alberti, M., Redman, C. L.... (2007). Coupled human and natural systems. *AMBIO: A Journal of the Human Environment, 36*(8), 639–649.

Louis, W. R. (2009). Collective action—and then what? *Journal of Social Issues, 65*(4), 727–748. Available from https://doi.org/10.1111/j.1540-4560.2009.01623.x.

Magis, K. (2010). Community resilience: an indicator of social sustainability. *Society and Natural Resources, 23*(5), 401–416.

McDonald, R. I., Chai, H. Y., & Newell, B. R. (2015). Personal experience and the "psychological distance" of climate change: an integrative review. *Journal of Environmental Psychology, 44*, 109–118.

McLaughlin, P., & Dietz, T. (2008). Structure, agency and environment: toward an integrated perspective on vulnerability. *Global Environmental Change, 18*, 99–111.

Moser, S. C. (2010). Now more than ever: the need for more societally-relevant research on vulnerability and adaptation to climate change. *Applied Geography, 30*(4), 464–474.

Moser, S. C., & Ekstrom, J. A. (2010). A framework to diagnose barriers to climate change adaptation. *Proceedings of the National Academies of Science, 107*(51), 22026–22031.

Moser, S. C., & Boykoff, M. T. (2013). Climate change and successful adaptation: the scope of the challenge. In S. C. Moser, & M. T. Boykoff (Eds.), *Successful adaptation to climate change: Linking science and practice in a rapidly changing world* (pp. 1–33)). London:: Routledge.

Murphy, B. L. (2007). Locating social capital in resilient community-level emergency management. *Natural Hazards, 41*(2), 297–315.

Norris, F. H., Stevens, S. P., Pfefferbaum, B., Wyche, K. F., & Pfefferbaum, R. L. (2008). Community resilience as a metaphor, theory, set of capacities, and strategy for disaster readiness. *American Journal of Community Psychology, 41*(1–2), 127–150.

Nurse, J., Basher, D., Bone, A., & Bird, W. (2010). An ecological approach to promoting population mental health and well-being—a response to the challenge of climate change. *Perspectives in Public Health, 130*, 27–33.

Okvat, H. A., & Zautra, A. J. (2011). Community gardening: a parsimonious path to individual, community, and environmental resilience. *American Journal of Community Psychology, 47*(3–4), 374–387. Available from https://doi.org/10.1007/s10464-010-9404-z.

Ostrom, E. (2009). A general framework for analyzing sustainability of social-ecological systems. *Science, 325*(5939), 419–422.

Parker, I. (2015). Global change: micro-climates of social development, adaption and behavior. In I. Parker (Ed.), *Psychology after the crisis: Scientific paradigms and political debate* (pp. 79–93). New York, NY: Routledge.

Poortinga, W. (2012). Community resilience and health: the role of bonding, bridging, and linking aspects of social capital. *Health & Place, 18*(2), 286–295.

Portes, A., & Rumbaut, R. G. (2006). *Immigrant America: A portrait*. University of California Press.

Quimby, C. C., & Angelique, H. (2011). Identifying barriers and catalysts to fostering pro-environmental behavior: opportunities and challenges for community psychology. *American Journal of Community Psychology*, 47, 388–396.

Reser, J. P., & Swim, J. K. (2011). Adapting to and coping with the threat and impacts of climate change. *American Psychologist*, 66(4), 277–289.

Resilience [Def. 1, 2]. (2017). In *Oxford Dictionary*, Retrieved September 11, 2017, from https://en.oxforddictionaries.com/definition/resilience

Riemer, M. (2010). Community psychology, the natural environment, and global climate change. In G. Nelson, & I. Prilleltensky (Eds.), *Community psychology: In pursuit of liberation and well-being* (pp. 498–516). New York, NY: Palgrave.

Riemer, M., & Reich, S. M. (2011). Community psychology and global climate change: introduction to the special section. *American Journal of Community Psychology*, 47, 349–353.

Robin, C., & Elah, P. K.-M. (2011). Like a fish out of water: reconsidering disaster recovery and the role of place and social capital in community disaster resilience. *American Journal of Community Psychology*, 48(3–4).

Ross, H., & Berkes, F. (2014). Research approaches for understanding, enhancing, and monitoring community resilience. *Society & Natural Resources*, 27(8), 787–804. Available from https://doi.org/10.1080/08941920.2014.905668.

Rutter, M. (1987). Psychosocial resilience and protective mechanisms. *American Journal of Orthopsychiatry*, 57(3), 316.

Santiago, J., Jennings, J., & Carrion, L. (2005). *Immigrant homebuyers in Lawrence and Lowell Massachusetts: Keys to the revitalization of cities*. Malden, MA: Immigrant Learning Center. Available at http://www.tufts.edu/~jjenni02/pdf/homebuyers-lawrence-lowell.pdf. Accessed August 12, 2007.

Silka, L. (2007). Immigrants in the community: new opportunities, new struggles. *Analyses of Social Issues and Public Policy*, 7(1), 75–91.

Silka, L., McGreavy, B., Hart, D. (in press). Health, the environment, and sustainability: Emergent communication lessons across highly diverse public participation activities. Lead chapter to appear in Hunt, K. P., Walker, G., & Depoe, S. *Expanding the boundaries of communication and public participation in environmental decision-making*.

Stern, P. C. (2000). New environmental theories: toward a coherent theory of environmentally significant behavior. *Journal of Social Issues*, 56(3), 407–424.

Trenberth, K. E., Fasullo, J. T., & Shepherd, T. G. (2015). Attribution of climate extreme events. *Nature Climate Change*, 5(8), 725–730.

Trickett, E. (2009). Community psychology: individuals and interventions in community context. *Annual Review of Psychology*, 60, 395–419.

Trott, C. D. (2016). Constructing alternatives: envisioning a critical psychology of prefigurative politics. *Journal of Social and Political Psychology*, 4(1), 266–285.

Turcotte, D. A., & Silka, L. (2007). Reflections on the concept of social capital: complex partnerships in refugee and immigrant communities. In J. Jennings (Ed.), *Race, neighborhoods, and misuse of social capital* (pp. 109–132). New York: Palgrave Macmillan.

van Zomeren, M., Spears, R., & Leach, C. W. (2010). Experimental evidence for a dual pathway model analysis of coping with the climate crisis. *Journal of Environmental Psychology*, 30(4), 339–346. Available from https://doi.org/10.1016/j.jenvp.2010.02.006.

Walker, B., Holling, C. S., Carpenter, S., & Kinzig, A. (2004). Resilience, adaptability and transformability in social–ecological systems. *Ecology and Society*, 9(2), 5.

Index